Ethnographies of the State in Central Asia

ETHNOGRAPHIES OF THE STATE IN CENTRAL ASIA Performing Politics

Edited by Madeleine Reeves, Johan Rasanayagam, and Judith Beyer

INDIANA UNIVERSITY PRESS
Bloomington and Indianapolis

Indiana University Press
Office of Scholarly Publishing
Herman B Wells Library 350
1320 East 10th Street
Bloomington, Indiana 47405 USA

iupress.indiana.edu

Telephone 800-842-6796
Fax 812-855-7931

⊜ The paper used in this publication meets the minimum requirements of the American National Standard for Information Sciences—Permanence of Paper for Printed Library Materials, ANSI Z39.48–1992.

Manufactured in the United States of America

Cataloging information is available from the Library of Congress.

ISBN 978-0-253-01140-4 (cloth)
ISBN 978-0-253-01141-1 (paperback)
ISBN 978-0-253-01147-3 (ebook)

1 2 3 4 5 19 18 17 16 15 14

Contents

Note on Transliteration

Sources in several languages appear in this book. In choosing a system of transliteration we have aimed for consistency across chapters with regard to the names of people and places for ease of cross-referencing, while also remaining faithful to the language in which a comment was originally spoken in cases of direct quotation. For languages written in the Cyrillic or Arabic scripts (Russian, Uyghur, Kyrgyz, Kazakh, and Tajik), we have used a modified version of the U.S. Library of Congress system of transliteration, except in those cases where alternative spellings have become more familiar to North American readers (for instance, Nazarbayev rather than Nazarbaev; Uyghur rather than Uighur). For quotations from Uzbek, we used the official Latin script.

Acknowledgments

This volume emerges from an ongoing conversation among a group of anthropologists and political scientists interested in exploring the everyday, localized practice of politics in Central Asia, drawing on long-term fieldwork in local languages. This conversation developed over e-mail, in reading groups, and at the corners of conferences for several years. In 2009, a grant from the Wenner Gren Foundation for Anthropological Research enabled us to meet for a dedicated three-day workshop in Buxton, England, entitled "Rethinking the Political in Central Asia: Perspectives from the Anthropology of the State." This workshop afforded the luxury of close, unhurried discussion of pre-circulated papers in conversation with senior scholars, and it provided a space for reflecting on how we might develop those papers in dialogue with one another for eventual co-publication.

In addition to the Wenner Gren Foundation, which generously funded a group of relatively junior scholars, post-docs, and PhD students in financially straitened times, we would like to thank the organizations and institutions that co-sponsored that 2009 meeting, including the University of Manchester, the ESRC Centre for Research on Socio-Cultural Change, the Centre for East European Language Based Area Studies (CEELBAS), and the Centre for Russian, Central and East European Studies (CRCEES). The papers that emerged from that workshop benefited from the careful, insightful, and spirited readings of our co-presenters, discussants, and chairs. We would particularly like to thank Felix Girke, Penny Harvey, Deniz Kandiyoti, David Montgomery, Michelle Obeid, Stefanie Ortmann, Atreyee Sen, Katie Swancutt, and Chad Thompson for their insightful and generous comments. Josine Opmeer's wonderful administrative support ensured the workshop ran smoothly. As editors we discovered the work of Jonathan Spencer, professor of anthropology at the University of Edinburgh, at a critical moment in the development of our ideas. We are indebted to him for the intellectual inspiration of his work and his support for this project, both moral and practical.

As editors we have each had an active role in working with the contributing authors and crafting the volume as a whole. We are grateful to Rebecca Tolen, sponsoring editor, and to Sarah Jacobi and Angela Burton at Indiana University

Press for supporting the project through to publication. We are indebted to two anonymous reviewers for their careful reading of the manuscript and helpful suggestions, to Sarah Brown for her careful copyediting, and to Dr. Monica Sandor, Jonas Katzmann, and Judith Marie Eggers at the Max Planck Institute for Social Anthropology in Halle for their help with the index. We would like to thank our contributors for their patience, generosity, and responsiveness as we have developed this project from workshop to book. Above all, we would like to thank the many friends and acquaintances in our respective fieldsites who have shared their welcome, their time, and their insight. We hope we have done justice to their words and experiences in the chapters that follow.

Ethnographies of the State in Central Asia

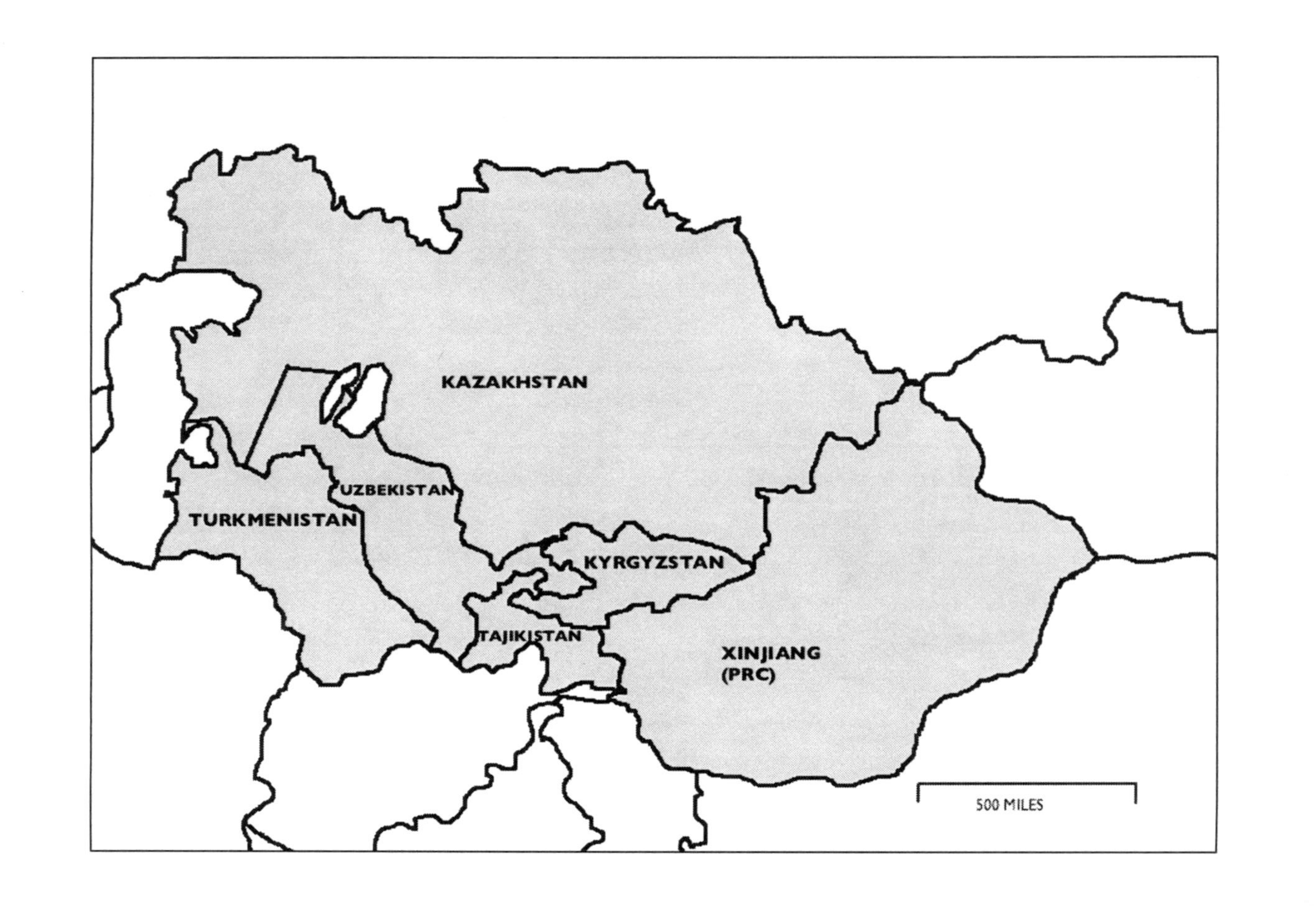
KAZAKHSTAN
UZBEKISTAN
TURKMENISTAN
KYRGYZSTAN
TAJIKISTAN
XINJIANG
(PRC)
500 MILES

Introduction

Performances, Possibilities, and Practices of the Political in Central Asia

Johan Rasanayagam, Judith Beyer, and Madeleine Reeves

What does politics look like in Central Asia? How is politics performed, and what is at stake? How should we, in fact, understand "the political" as a sphere of activity and what sort of object is "the state," in Central Asia or elsewhere? Central Asia, in this collection, refers to the five former Soviet republics of Kazakhstan, Kyrgyzstan, Tajikistan, Turkmenistan, and Uzbekistan, as well as the Xinjiang Uyghur Autonomous Region of the People's Republic of China. The post-Soviet Central Asian republics are relatively recent creations. Their territorial boundaries were established under Bolshevik rule in the 1920s, carved out of the former Tsarist administrative entity of Turkestan and the protectorates of Bukhara and Khiva. Soviet nationalities policy classified Central Asian populations into ethno-national groups, each associated with a distinct linguistic, cultural, and historical lineage and a defined territory. While not entirely arbitrary, Soviet policy and practice reified previously fluid registers of identification and belonging, and in some cases created entirely new nationality categories.[1] Those ethno-national groups that were regarded as most advanced along a supposed evolutionary trajectory toward nationhood—the Uzbeks, Kazakhs, Kyrgyz, Tajiks, and Turkmens—were constituted as national republics within the framework of the Soviet Union.

When the Soviet Union disintegrated in 1991, its Central Asian republics were abruptly cut loose from the economic and political infrastructure that had sustained them. The ideological frame that had located individual citizens within an encompassing polity was lost along with it. The national leaderships were forced to reinvent their republics as independent nation-states. They have sought to fashion new state ideologies and narratives of nationhood. Central Asian populations have had to cope with the collapse of previous certainties; the abrupt withdrawal of the state provision of employment, housing, and social welfare; and the ensuing material hardship (Kandiyoti and Mandel 1998). They have had to negotiate within new modes and practices of governance. This dynamic moment of invention and creative negotiation makes Central Asia a particularly productive site for comparative study of the political and the state.

The inclusion of China's Xinjiang Uyghur Autonomous Region in this volume provides an important comparative perspective. The region is territorially contiguous with the former Soviet republics, the populations have much in common, linguistically and culturally, and there are Uyghur populations in many of the former Soviet states, particularly in Kazakhstan. The continuing experience of the Chinese version of socialism, moreover, provides an illuminating point of comparison with the post-Soviet situation, as Ildikó Bellér-Hann's contribution to this volume makes clear.[2]

The five post-Soviet Central Asian states share a common historical legacy of seven decades of Soviet communism, but they have experienced the two post-Soviet decades in their own, distinct ways. Tajikistan's experience has been most traumatic. There, civil war broke out shortly after independence in 1992 and lasted through much of that decade. John Heathershaw, one of the contributors to this volume, identifies four broad explanations for conflict, although none of these are sufficient explanations in themselves: those that emphasize competition among ethno-regional solidarity groups (with an Uzbek-dominated western region and Tajik south and north); as a battle of ideologies between Communist Party conservatives, reformers, and nationalist and Islamist groups; as a struggle over recourses; and as a competition among elites, each with their patronage networks (Heathershaw 2009). A peace agreement was signed in 1997, but renegade commanders continued to be active until the early 2000s. Since 1992, Tajikistan has been under the authoritarian leadership of Emomali Rahmon, a former head of a state farm, initially as chairman of the Supreme Soviet of Tajikistan and later as president. As Heathershaw shows in his contribution to this volume, for all that Tajikistan has been celebrated as an example of successful post-conflict transition, the practical politics of peace-building over the last decade and a half has in many respects served to entrench and legitimize an authoritarian politics.

None of the former Soviet Central Asian republics can be described as liberal democracies that guarantee individual freedoms and support vibrant civil societies. Uzbekistan and Turkmenistan are the most authoritarian regimes, while Kyrgyzstan was, in the early years of independence, sometimes referred to by outside observers as an "island of democracy" in the region. The Soviet-era Communist Party leaderships of these republics continued as presidents of their independent states. President Islam Karimov of Uzbekistan and Nursultan Nazarbayev of Kazakhstan still remain in power, while the first president of independent Turkmenistan, Saparmurat Niyazov, died in office in 2006, succeeded by Gurbanguly Berdymukhamedov.

It is perhaps worth noting at this point the "absent presence" of Turkmenistan in this volume: it is the only Central Asian state on which we do not include a chapter. This absence is striking in view of the considerable interest of Turkmenistan to a comparative anthropology of the state in Central Asia and, in a context where popular paeans to the president are screened on prime-time television, for thinking about the diversity of ways in which politics is performed in the region. The lack of a chapter on Turkmenistan reflects less a deliberate editorial exclusion than the current realities of academic production on the region. Anthropologically informed articles and doctoral dissertations based on research in other Central Asian states, while hardly numerous when compared with the scale of scholarly output on other global regions, have nonetheless grown in number and scope over the previous decade (a decade, characteristic of this young field, in which eleven of the fourteen contributors to this volume received their doctorate). The same growth in scholarly production cannot be said of Turkmenistan. Writing in 2004, historian Adrienne Edgar noted the difficulties of conducting historical research in independent Turkmenistan, with the Turkmen State Archive remaining firmly off-limits to foreign researchers (Edgar 2004, xii). Nearly a decade later, the kind of sustained participant observation on which ethnographic research depends remains nearly impossible in Turkmenistan, and this is particularly true for any research that might address issues of everyday politics in a critical or questioning voice.

At the same time, scholarly production within Turkmenistan itself is highly circumscribed, with state-funded historical and archaeological research often deliberately conceived to give legitimacy to narratives of state continuity and national specificity that have already been articulated in presidential writings. The "state," while a pervasive referent of official Turkmen discourse (along with the nation and the president), forms part of the "hegemony of form" (Yurchak 2006) in Turkmenistan that remains beyond sustained critical analysis. In September 2011, for instance, the Institute of History of the Academy of Sciences of Turkmenistan was instructed, by presidential decree, to conduct an international scientific conference on the "Revival of the Great Silk Road in the Prosperous Epoch of the Powerful State: Deep Roots and Modern Opportunities." Such events, lavishly funded, internationally attended, and extensively rebroadcast, can themselves be considered an important mode of performing politics in Turkmenistan. They have yet, however, to receive the critical scholarly analysis they deserve.

If the political field in Turkmenistan has been characterized to a considerable degree by personalized rule, limited international collaboration, and relative political stability, Kyrgyzstan's first two decades of independence are radically different. The country's first post-independence president, Askar Akaev, was ousted in 2005 following mass protests sparked by the conduct of parliamentary elections. Kurmanbek Bakiev won the subsequent presidential elections, although he too was forced to resign after protests against his rule spread throughout Kyrgyzstan's northern regions in the first half of 2010. Political upheaval was followed by violent conflict in June 2010, leaving many ordinary Kyrgyzstanis looking to Russia not just as a source of livelihood but as a model of a (presumed) stable, benign, and paternalist leadership.

In a comparative study of three of the Central Asian states, Uzbekistan, Kazakhstan, and Kyrgyzstan, the political scientist Eric McGlinchey has sought to account for the differing paths of autocratic governance (McGlinchey 2011). He employs the usefully evocative labels "Kyrgyz chaos," "Uzbek violence," and "Kazakh dynasty" as shorthand descriptors for the variations in what he terms the "patronage politics" of these states. McGlinchey traces the different autocracies to three variables: the involvement of central Soviet authorities in mediating the leaderships of these republics in the Gorbachev era, the level of endowment of natural resources available to the Central Asian leaderships, and differing degrees of Islamist revivalism. Gorbachev managed change in the republican leaderships in Uzbekistan and Kazakhstan in the late 1980s, which meant that Karimov and Nazarbayev had a firm control on power at independence. By contrast, Gorbachev's decision to stay aloof from the leadership contest in Kyrgyzstan in 1990 meant that no candidate emerged unchallenged, resulting in the unstable political situation. In addition, Nazarbayev and his family control Kazakhstan's abundant oil wealth. It finances the president's patronage networks and at the same time allows the regime to maintain relatively comfortable living standards for the population. Uzbekistan, on the other hand, has significantly smaller reserves of oil and gas, and coercive patronage politics is the rule. State repression and violence in Uzbekistan is further exacerbated, McGlinchey argues, by the threat the Karimov regime perceives in the emergence of Islamic networks and charities, which provide support and welfare in the absence of the state.

We have used the term "authoritarian" here as shorthand to describe Central Asian regimes. But power is not simply a capacity held by certain individuals to be exercised over others. The state is not an institution that exists in and of itself, separate from populations. And democracy is not simply a formal arrangement of legal frameworks, governing institutions, and procedures. The state constantly has to be performed into being—it takes shape through a host of actions, mundane and spectacular, in which ordinary people are enlisted as both audience and actor. Moments of profound political transformation do not simply undermine the coherence of the state. Rather, as Carol Greenhouse (2002) has argued, they expose with particular clarity the creative energy of ordinary people in "maintaining the illusion of states' concreteness" (2002, 1). The contributors to this volume shed light on this work of constituting the state in the realm of the everyday. All of the contributors have engaged in many years of field research in Central Asia. Their essays are intimate explorations of how the state is experienced and produced in everyday encounters, of the capillary workings of politics, and they provide insights into the nature of contemporary authoritarianism. They suggest that what we call "politics" is *performed*. It is performed in, for example, the local conduct of elections (see Aksana Ismailbekova's contribution), or poetry competitions (Eva-Marie Dubuisson's chapter). The state itself is not an object or fact but materializes in the grand project of constructing a new capital in Kazakhstan (Mateusz Laszczkowski). It takes on particular qualities and shapes in the local operation of courts of elders in Kyrgyzstan (Judith Beyer) or in the attempts to relocate a cross-border market onto more obviously "national" territory by villagers who live along the newly relevant borders of independent nation-states (Madeleine Reeves).

The contributions to this volume speak from an anthropological perspective. This perspective is rooted in Central Asian lifeworlds but goes beyond simple ethnographic description. An anthropological perspective opens out to located experiences and practices of the political, to alternative ways of being and doing, and so encourages us to rethink our seemingly universal, taken-for-granted categories and assumptions. Our starting point is a broad conception of the political, as relations and interventions, often agonistic, that are enacted with a "public" dimension; they are performed in an arena, refer to discourses, or articulate with relations of power, which transcend the personal location of the actors involved. We do not conceive of the political with reference to pregiven categories, or assumed entities and actors, such as state and society, elites and the populace, political parties and interest groups, with competition over power and resources assumed to take place by and through them. Instead, we seek to explore how the political comes to be constituted, and the categories themselves, like "the state" and "the people," come to be imagined, experienced, invoked, and performed.

The Problem of Rationality

Many analyses of politics and the state in Central Asia, emerging in particular from the disciplines of political science and international relations, have set out precisely to question established analytical frames. Anna Grzymala-Busse and Pauline Jones Luong have critiqued conceptions of the state assumed in political science literature on post-communist "transitions" (Grzymala-Busse and Jones Luong 2002). They question conceptions of the state as a clearly identifiable set of institutions and actors exerting legitimate authority over a given territory, operating collectively as a unitary political agent, with clear boundaries between state and society. These conceptions, they argue, arise from a Western European experience. Instead, through an analysis of the Central Asian situation, they present a processual approach that takes into account the dramatic changes following the break-up of the Soviet Union. They present an analysis that seeks to bring people back into the state and that acknowledges multiple, competing actors, both local elites and international governments and organizations. These various individual and corporate actors compete to create policy and fashion policy-making institutions. They describe the blurring of boundaries between state and society, a boundary that was consciously transgressed in Soviet ideology and practices of governance, and one that they argue to be transgressed in the post-communist era in the form of patronage networks and regional political identities (Jones Luong 2002). Post-communist states are a "bricolage," built on existing formal structures inherited from the Soviet past but also informal ones, which are Soviet legacies of a different kind.

Kathleen Collins, also from the disciplinary perspective of political science, has similarly questioned conceptions of state and society that posit these as being essentially distinct, separate entities, and she attempts to show how in Central Asia they are mutually entwined (Collins 2004). She does this by introducing culture into the analysis. Taking inspiration from anthropological literature on kinship, Collins argues that Central Asian politics is characterized by the persistence of clans, which she understands as informal identity networks based on kin or fictive kin bonds. These are primarily "affective," offering psychological support, but they also include "rational" elements; elites or clan leaders need a network of support to maintain status and political influence, while non-elites need clan leaders as patrons to secure access to jobs, trading opportunities in the bazaar, and education, as well as to obtain goods in an economy of shortage. She criticizes the transitions literature for too great a focus on formal institutions and elites and for assuming that "traditional" social institutions are incompatible with modern political formations.

"Traditionalism" is something that Olivier Roy also emphasizes in his analysis of Central Asian politics. He argues that the Soviet apparatus was "re-inhabited" by traditional patterns of political life (Roy 2000). For example, the pre-Soviet category of "rural notable" continued in the position of chairman of the collective farm, mediating relations of its members with the state, with the collective farm itself becoming a new "tribe." Far from eliminating pre-existing traditional forms of social and political organization, Soviet rule institutionalized them within a state regulatory framework, giving them an economic and administrative reality. It was not so much the case that pre-Soviet traditional structures continued in their objective forms, but what he calls a "habitus" of traditional patterns of clientelism and patronage was reproduced within Soviet institutional hierarchies of governance and allocation of resources. Moreover, the national ideologies and narratives that form the core of the new state-building efforts are deeply rooted in Soviet nationalities policy. The post-Soviet political field, therefore, should be understood not so much as a replica of some pre-Soviet pattern but rather as a neo-traditional hybrid.

Approaches such as these that are founded on a concept of traditionalism might be criticized for presenting, albeit unintentionally, conceptions of Central Asian society as a traditional Other, opposed to a progressive, modern Western model grounded in a scientific rationality and founded upon individual, rather than collective, subjectivities (Dave 2007, 11). Such approaches can be seen to perpetuate a conception of traditionalism developed through the practical application of Soviet ideology, which placed "traditional" practices such as clan organization alongside what it saw as other pre-modern "survivals" such as the veneration of the shrines of "saints" or healing rituals (Poliakov 1992). These survivals were in turn viewed as obstacles to the development of a rational, scientific, socialist consciousness and therefore needed to be expunged (see Hirsch 2005, 215–221; Kandiyoti 2007 for an analysis). Both Collins and Roy, however, explicitly locate the development of "neo-traditionalism" in Soviet structures themselves, so they do not imagine a pristine or authentic tradition that reasserts itself in a modern setting. Both authors are attempting to deal with the important question of how the political is shaped by specific histories and relations of power that are expressed through institutional structures and what we might think of as "culture." Jones Luong frames her answer to this question in terms of "regionalism" rather than clan or kinship. These are networks of patronage grounded in the hierarchies of Soviet government administration and the Communist Party, as they operated at the republican level and below, as well as in Soviet policies of *korenizatsiia,* the promotion of native cadres in their titular republics (Jones Luong 2002). Although they adopt different analytical frames, all these authors point to the postcolonial condition of the contemporary Central Asian polities by showing how the political is shaped by Soviet heritage.

Valuable and insightful though these analyses are, they privilege a certain kind of instrumental rationality. This is explicit in Jones Luong's work, where she presents an analysis of elite competition as a bargaining game, in which rational actors make choices depending on their perceptions of gains and losses, constrained by available resources and existing institutional structures. It is also at least implicit in the analyses of Roy and Collins. Culture, clan, and tradition in their presentations of the political serve as a "black box" containing all the "non-rational" motivations and incentives, which ultimately boil down, in all these works, to patron-client relations and calculations of costs and benefits.

The concepts of clan politics and traditionalism, described in an associated language of "solidarity," "kinship norms," or psychological affective relations, enfold and ultimately occlude the complex questions of why people do the things they do, when these actions are not clearly motivated by a calculation of individual interests, in terms that are understandable to the outside (Western academic) observer.

With the terms "regionalism," "clan," and "traditionalism," these authors are attempting to account for the connection between elites and wider society. But the picture they present is of corporate groups competing to promote corporate interests (Gullette 2007, 2010). This simply transposes the rational actor model from an individual onto a corporate actor. Scott Radnitz addresses the political mobilization of local populations differently, through his investigation of the protests in southern Kyrgyzstan in 2002, which followed the arrest of a local member of parliament who had been critical of President Akaev (Radnitz 2005, 2010). Radnitz describes the vertical organization of committees to defend the MP, organized by his closest associates, which connected activists in the national capital Bishkek to village-level subcommittees in the MP's home region. These village-level committees incorporated *Juz-Boshi,* informal community activists who were accustomed to taking a leadership role in mobilizing their neighbors in projects of communal benefit. In this way, the central committee leadership was able to initiate and plan protests and work through local authority structures and networks of sociality and obligation to mobilize protestors. Radnitz goes on to examine the motivation for individual village members to take part in the protests, which he identifies as norms of solidarity, reputation, and the threat of sanction. In the MP's home village, participation in the protests was seen as supporting "one's own," but once the protests expanded to surrounding villages, Radnitz argues that the community exercised a "tyranny of the majority." In order to maintain a good reputation and so remain included within neighborhood and village networks of material support on which many depended in this poor region of Kyrgyzstan, even reluctant or indifferent villagers were forced to participate out of fear (see Ismailbekova's contribution to this volume for a comparable account of local performances of democracy).

Of all the authors discussed so far, Radnitz provides the most fine-grained account of the practical operation of networks through which national politicians can mobilize support at the local level, and his account is a valuable insight into this process. At the same time, like those previously discussed, his approach is limited by its language of community norms and solidarity. Motivation is once more a matter of rational choice and material interest, or undefined cultural factors. What is left unexamined is the contingent, located nature of authority. Authority is not best conceived in the static terms of traditional norms or local structures but as situationally performed and constituted in specific interactions (Rasanayagam 2006; Reeves 2008; Beyer 2010).

What we need, then, and what this collection aims to provide, is an approach to the political in Central Asia that extends beyond a limited understanding of rationality as an instrumental calculation of costs and benefits. We seek to explore how the scope for the political, the categories through which political action proceeds, the possibilities for how the political is constituted, are located within Central Asian lifeworlds. In short, we seek a cultural account of the political, but one where the culture concept opens out to alternative possibilities of action and experience.

The anthropologist Jonathan Spencer has advocated an approach to the political that is culturally inflected, recognizing that politics and culture are not two discrete things but that that the political emerges in located social practices and imaginative possibilities that decenter teleological conceptions of modernity and, we might add, rationality (Spencer 2007). He calls for recognition of the dynamic and creative potential of political institutions. His discussion of elections, political action, and violence in South Asia is informative. He argues firstly that politics is an expression of everyday agonistic relations; that interpersonal disputes that, for example, were fought out through courts and claims over land in the colonial period, because this was the avenue available at that time, in the postcolonial period are carried out through electoral politics. He argues further that the institutions and infrastructure of the multi-party electoral political system are themselves creative. Thus, for instance, communal violence in Sri Lanka is not just an expression of locally rooted agonistic relations but is enabled and produced by the political system itself, but in ways that are not intended by political parties or governments (compare Ismailbekova, this volume).

Spencer notes how anthropologists have, for the past two or three decades, become suspicious of framing their work explicitly as "political anthropology." This disciplinary subfield had its heyday between the 1940s and 1960s and was characterized by a positivist stance that tended to exclude culture (Spencer 1995). In the British tradition of this period, the tone was set in large part by the project to establish anthropology as a natural science of society by figures such as Alfred Reginald Radcliffe Brown, a key member of what became known as the structural functional school (Radcliffe Brown 1952). Others, like Edmund Leach, Fredrik Barth, and F. G. Bailey, reacted against what they saw as an overemphasis on social structure and focused instead on the individual pursuit of interest within locally established rules of the game (Barth 1959; Leach 1961; Bailey 1969). Since the 1970s anthropologists have recognized that what we might think of as politics cannot be abstracted from social, cultural, or institutional settings. More fundamentally, following the post-structuralist turn influenced by Michel Foucault and others, the question of power has come to displace politics as the key analytic. For Foucault, power is not an object or quality to be held by individuals or located in institutions such as the state. It is a relation and an effect of the distribution of bodies, the division and ordering of space, the disciplinary techniques of surveillance, supervision, and hierarchical ranking that take place in modern institutions such as army barracks, hospitals, schools, and factories. By acting on the individual body in this way, controlling and shaping movements, gestures, and attitudes, it is productive of subjectivities. The interests that individuals pursue, the means and institutions through which they do so, their subjectivities, desires, and imaginative possibilities, need to be recognized as themselves produced within relations of power.

For the past two decades Foucault has heavily influenced anthropological thinking on the state. His analytics of power have led to a critique of the assumption, implicit in much social scientific writing, that the state is an object somehow "above" society and distinct from it. Timothy Mitchell draws on Foucault to emphasize the activity and techniques involved in producing "two-dimensional effects"; that is, the practices that "contribute to constructing a world that appears to consist not of a complex of social practices but of a binary order: on the one hand individuals and their activities, on the other an inert 'structure' that somehow stands apart from individuals, precedes them and contains them and gives a framework to their lives" (Mitchell 1999, 89). James Ferguson and Akhil Gupta (2002) have extended this critique to draw attention to the implicit spatial narratives that produce hierarchies of encompassment, where locality is encompassed by region, and region by nation-state. Penny Harvey has used an ethnography of road building in rural Peru to critique implicit assumptions about scale in studies of the state. She takes the state to be an effect, one that can productively be approached tangentially through its material manifestations. According to Harvey, such "a tangential approach may well be the only option [for getting at the state] given the way in which the state is entangled in mundane sociality" (Harvey 2005, 138). A concern for materiality at once locates the state in particular, located lives and reveals the constructed and fragile nature of the state effect of ordering and encompassment. While we attend to the way in which the state materializes in certain institutions, persons, and objects, we also pay attention in this volume to the ways in which such material worlds exceed the visions that are invested in them: the capacity of things, flexible or inflexible, sturdy or crumbly, to undermine official visions of the state or modernist projects of reform. We are thus interested in the structural and material traces of the state in terms of how and when they are experienced as enabling or constraining and in the dialectical processes involved.

As Harvey and others have pointed out (see also Abu-Lughod 1991), an ethnography of the particular does not simply produce a "grassroots" perspective, a view from below. Rather, the ethnographic method sidesteps spatial oppositions altogether by locating the "global" in particular lives, bodies, and materialities. The anthropological perspective, then, displaces the state as an external, encompassing object. It tends toward an "unmasking" of its imagined and constructed nature and emphasizes the process, practices, and performances that produce the mask or effect. It also points to the ambiguous, contingent nature of this constructed object. The state can be experienced as hierarchical and oppressive (Bellér-Hann, this volume), or subjects of regulation might sometimes be able to make deals and negotiate and manipulate the rules in pursuit of their own separate objectives (see the chapters by Cynthia Werner and Kathleen Purvis-Roberts and by Tommaso Trevisani). The state can be invoked as absent or deficient, just as it can be imagined in idealized ways (Beyer, this volume), or implicitly invoked as a solid, benevolent, and powerful structure (Morgan Liu, Reeves, and Laszczkowski, this volume).

Performing Politics

We seek to provide a culturally inflected account of the political in Central Asia, which looks at how the political is performed into being and how it is locally situated. A shift to a performance approach is a shift from asking "what?"—a question that presumes a unified form—to asking "how?" This approach allows for a multiplicity of action and interpretation, as it takes seriously the capacities for reflection of our informants. Thus, the perspective that we seek in this collection is one that emphasizes contingency, ambiguity, and indeterminacy. While a lot of attention has been given to the question "What does the state do?" or "How does it see?" (e.g., Scott 1998), our main interest lies in the question "How is the state being done?" This perspective allows us to also address questions such as "In what ways does the performance of politics reproduce, enable, challenge, or naturalize ideologies about the state?" "What are the specific techniques of governance that Central Asian actors employ in this regard?" "How and where do these performances occur?" and "In what ways do they help produce or hinder alternative visions of moral community and personhood?"

We interpret the term "performance" in a broad way as a mode of communication that includes but is not restricted to ritualized and public speech practice. Performances can be a means of ordinary peoples' resistance (Bruner and Kirshenblatt-Gimblett 1994) as much as an instrument of the ruling elite (Adams 2010). In the Central Asian context, performances have mostly been analyzed in terms of the symbolic power of the state (Cummings 2010). However, as a performance always inheres in the "doing" of things, we shift our attention to the causes and procedures of symbolism and less to its effects. Thus, we do not accept the power of "symbols" uncritically, or assume that their meanings are given, as this often precludes an analysis of how symbolism and meaning are generated in the first place (Strecker 1998). A performance approach draws from a social linguistics literature that insists that all language is social action (Austin 1962) and that meaning is generated in the moment when words are put to use (Wittgenstein 1979). Categories of politics, economics, and religion; notions of private, domestic, and public, are not fixed and objective. Such categories, as thinkers like Talal Asad and Foucault have argued, are the product of historically developed discursive moves to classify and control social space, to fashion particular subjectivities, and the boundaries between them are the contested products of the regimes of power (Asad 1993, 2003; Foucault 1991, 1994). Governing elites in Central Asia attempt to fix these categories and their boundaries through ideologies and narratives of nationhood, but as the contributions to this volume show, these moral and empirical claims only come to life in their performance. Thus, performances of the political are not simply the locus of instrumental rationality; they are also sites of material and moral investments, of hopeful expectation and of disillusionment (Navaro-Yashin 2002, 2003; Aretxaga 2005; Spencer 2007; Reeves 2011; Beyer forthcoming). Thinking performatively about the state in Central Asia allows for a more nuanced analysis of different aspects of the political, revealing how "the state" is the result of creative, multi-vocal interactions in ways that go beyond a simple opposition of resistance and oppression.

The following three sections introduce the individual chapters of this volume and highlight the ways in which the performance of politics in Central Asia results in a particular kind of state-making that is distinctive for this region.

Staging the Political

What unites the four chapters in the first section of the book is that they all deal with performances of a more theatrical kind; that is, performances on stage, in front of an audience and involving public dialogue. By systematically drawing on these theatrical metaphors the authors in this section have found a useful way to address the otherwise abstract concepts of "the political" and "the state." Moreover, they also acknowledge that when politics are performed in Central Asia, people often use theatrical techniques, which are distinguishable from everyday behavior. While Goffman (1990) has argued that any occasion of face-to-face interaction can be interpreted as a theatrical performance, there are some performances that are clearly more political and public than others.

To concentrate on these kinds of performances in this section is not to embrace a narrow understanding of performance as a particular sphere, a separate and separable realm, rather than an aspect of all behavior but to show particularly vivid cases of when and how the state is being done in Central Asia. We thus do not hold that a performance is only "a certain type of activity, set apart from other activities by space, time, attitude, or all three, that can be spoken of and analyzed as performance" (Carlson 2004, 13), but we acknowledge that people themselves choose to mark certain patterns of their behavior when staging the political.

All four chapters emphasize the importance of an audience in front of whom a performance takes place. Goffman's definition of performance centered on this very element. He defined performance as "all the activity of an individual which occurs during a period marked by his continuous presence before a particular set of observers and which has some influence on the observers" (Goffman 1990, 22). In the cases presented here, the observers actively contribute to the content of the performance, so that one can speak of dialogic performances. While there is little to no balance of power between the different participants involved in the particular performances, which is often regarded as characteristic of the concept of dialogue (Conquergood 1985; Girke and Meyer 2011), what is dialogic about the performances discussed in this section is that a multitude of voices can be heard, talking about "the state." However, these dialogues all serve to objectify the state as a singular political entity. There is, in other words, a dialogue of form only and not a dialectic of argument when it comes to performing "the state" in the public realm. These performances cut across all social groups, lining up the actions of government officials and citizens alike. The dialogical moment in these performances creates legitimacy as it happens in front of and in relation to other people.

The stage Heathershaw investigates in his chapter on Tajikistan is that of roundtables and discussion clubs that have initially been set up by international actors, such as non-governmental organizations (NGOs), with the intention of stimulating a plurality of opinion and strengthening democratic participation in public decision-making processes. Heathershaw shows how on this stage, the idea of the state as representing the general will of the people is pursued by all participants. In the roundtables and discussion clubs we mostly find government elites speaking to an audience of carefully selected civil servants. Even if participants formally represent a plurality of actors such as political parties, local NGOs, or informal authority figures, Heathershaw claims that these citizens are also often state officials in disguise. He continues to observe this tendency to speak with two voices and one mind also on other stages such as public ceremonies at border posts. The chapter investigates the means by which signs of the state are articulated and circulated, combining post-structuralist analysis, ethnographic approaches to the state, and Heathershaw's own empirical material from Tajikistan.

In the second chapter, Dubuisson explores a living poetic tradition among Kazakhs in Kazakhstan, a verbal duel called *aitys,* which presents a positive and inclusive model of cultural belonging. These duels are performed on stage between two *akhyn,* or poets, who claim to voice "the truth of the Kazakh people." The verbal duels take place in front of an audience and in the presence of the two poets' respective sponsors. Dubuisson describes *aitys* (from the verb *aitysu,* to talk to each other) as an alternate form of dialogic leadership in an otherwise authoritarian environment. She argues that the *aitys* tradition evokes an idealized "khan-like" form of Central Asian leadership, where a strong ruler makes himself available and accountable to the people he governs. That model of rule is embodied in two ways in *aitys:* in the dialogic relation of poets to contemporary leaders, and in the activity of the tradition's wealthy sponsors. In the end, poets draw from sponsors' economic and political capital in order to stage their performances, while sponsors draw from the poets' cultural and historical legitimacy.

In the chapter by Ismailbekova, we encounter Kyrgyz citizens who quite contradictorily perform politics during election day in 2007 in Kyrgyzstan by ensuring that the rules of the new electoral system are adhered to, even as they circumvent or even violate legally defined procedural norms. This serves to support the village's own candidate, who also happens to be the main village patron. Electoral personnel manipulate and redefine the rules and conditions of the election in the interests of the witnessing and voting community, helping to "elect" their patron into parliament. This chapter shows that it is precisely such public political events that foster a local sense of democratic participation in state processes. Ismailbekova exemplifies how practices of patronage, discourses of corruption, and the creative appeal to principles of democracy are verbalized in local terms of fairness and respect.

In the final chapter of this section, Beyer investigates the enactment of "the state" in the neo-traditional courts of elders in Kyrgyzstan. The first president of the country, Askar Akaev, initially set up this institution in the early 1990s as an arena in which customary law (*salt*) was supposed to become officialized as part of state law. Drawing on ethnographic fieldwork in northern Talas province between 2005 and 2010, the chapter addresses the question of how it was that precisely in this institution not *salt* but imagined state law (Benda-Beckmann 2005) has acquired an important position. During public court sessions, actors situationally invoke the state as part of their concrete interactions by appropriating the language, rituals, and symbols that they associate with it. Beyer explores how this embodiment of the state and its law, coupled with a feeling of "abandonment" by the state, has led to a process she refers to as "customization." Focusing on dialogues from inside and outside the courtroom, it becomes clear that an image of the state as "above" and "beyond" is constantly being (re-)created by all parties involved in the dispute.

The four chapters exemplify how a focus on stage, audience, and dialogue helps us perceive a public realm in which a particular kind of politics is performed that is characteristic for the Central Asian context. The authors in this section are interested in how public and dialogic performances, during which actors stage their very own interpretation of proper political action, can lead us to understand how democracy, corruption, law, and the state are perceived and acted out in contemporary Central Asia. As it turns out, the discrepancies between what is performed on-stage and what off-stage diminish when it comes to imagining the state: everyone involved in the action happens to participate in what we have called a dialogue of form. This form, while constituted by a plurality of voices, does not lead to a plurality of opinion but rather seems to (re-)create "the state" as a unified, solitary, and personified object. This proves to be a major difference from Soviet times where the authoritative discourse and the power of the party forced people to "render many of their activities invisible to, or misrecognized by, the state" by means of what Alexei Yurchak has called a "performative shift" (Yurchak 2006, 298). What we see in these chapters is the manifestation and (re-)creation of political action through dialogic performances on stages that are no longer dominated by one powerful actor alone. Moreover, state narratives are often positioned against the Soviet past even though they are in fact mostly rooted in this legacy. Likewise, a powerful image of the "khan" as the personification of political leadership dominates in most Central Asian societies (see Liu 2012). These narratives derive their force from the fact that they are shared by and circulate among elites and ordinary citizens.

Political Materials, Political Fantasies

If the first group of papers is concerned with the public staging of politics and performative enactments of the state, the second group draws attention to the fact that the state is also encountered, invoked, imagined, or desired in and through its material and infrastructural forms: in buildings and roads; in documents and checkpoints; in the planning, projecting, construction, and creative destruction of urban space. The ethnographic sites for these explorations are diverse: from Kazakhstan's glittering new capital, Astana, to the radically remade urban Uyghur space of Qumul, Xinjiang, to a mountainous rural border between Kyrgyzstan and Uzbekistan where state territoriality is being enacted in new and sometimes violently performative ways. These sites provide diverse explorations of what Harvey (2005) has called the "materiality of state effects":

that is, the material forms through which the state comes to appear naturally "above" society and encompassing of it, having determinate spatial contours and territorial limits.

Such an approach opens up new avenues for interrogating the state ethnographically. Projects of construction, destruction, and territorial demarcation provide an insight into the workings of power and the material forms that ideological projects take. State effects result not just from discursive enactments but are consolidated in "visible everyday forms, such as the language of legal practice, the architecture of public buildings, the wearing of military uniforms, or the marking and policing of frontiers" (Mitchell 1999, 81). Such a focus highlights the role of material infrastructures in the organization of state power (Bennett and Joyce 2010), revealing the particular dynamics this has taken in the shift from socialist to capitalist modes of economic accumulation.

But this is not all. On the one hand, such projects also remind us that state sovereignty is a work-in-progress, requiring compromise, improvisation, and co-optation to translate ideological visions into concrete (or plate glass) structures. A focus on materiality highlights the way in which projects of reform can be forestalled or deflected by "intransigent infrastructure" (Collier 2004; Humphrey 2005; Reeves 2009). On the other hand, a focus on built forms also reveals the way in which the state becomes the site of affective investment on the part of its citizens and thus can afford a more dynamic account of the workings of state power. As Harvey notes, state infrastructural projects "*do* render people more legible, they *can* be monitored and controlled more easily." But this does not exhaust their effects. "Demonstrable connection to external sources of power affords recognition and meets certain desires for legitimation. In this framework the state appears in yet another guise, as object of desire and fantasy and people's fears are as likely to focus on abandonment as on control" (Harvey 2005, 135).

As a self-consciously new and aspiringly "global" capital city, the material face of which is transforming at breakneck speed, Astana provides a generative site for engaging such questions. Drawing on ethnography in the heart of the offices of the Astana General Plan, Alima Bissenova focuses on the elaboration and implementation of a master plan for Kazakhstan's new capital in a context of radical economic change. How to create a city that is at once national, Eurasian, and global? How to make of it a place where capital "sticks"? How to transform economic capital in the form of petro-dollars into the cultural capital needed to become a "global city"? And how to unite the post-modern vision of the plan's chief architect with the decidedly modernist desire for an ordered, rational urban space—and with the pragmatics of practical urban planning?

Bissenova highlights the compromises and reworkings to the ambitious *Gen-Plan* for Astana as urban planners sought to reconcile the post-modern architectural vision of Kisho Kurokawa with the pragmatics of rapid urban growth and the modernist desire to foster a "civilized" urban habitus amongst its residents. Just a few years after it was approved, the original Master Plan was "corrected" into an altogether new document, one that in turn signaled a radically different vision of urban growth from the Japanese-authored original. Astana has been dramatically transformed—and the stress on international architectural expertise has indeed had traction in generating capital, even as the original vision has been reworked and corrected in subsequent years. And yet, as Bissenova notes, the result is ambiguous. For in pinning political legitimacy to architectural "vision," the risk is that a charge of aesthetic "tastelessness" can easily morph into a claim of political inefficacy.

It is this affective quality of built forms that is the focus of Laszczkowski's chapter. Taking us from the offices of Astana GenPlan to the homes of Astana residents, both old-time residents of Soviet Tselinograd and new migrants, Laszczkowski asks how it is that the materiality of built forms provides such a powerful idiom for articulating the state, both affirmatively and critically. Laszczkowski's ethnography reveals how spectacular processes of urban construction—processes that are endlessly dramatized and televised as metaphors for the building of the state—provide an ordering frame, quite literally locating citizens within a shared endeavor of nation-building and producing a subjective attitude of *grazhdansvennost'* or civic virtue: an active and engaged commitment to the nation. At the same time, the "wobbly" nature of many of the new buildings, their cheap materials and hasty construction, their cracked and peeling surfaces, and in some cases their temporary character, elicit ironic commentary about the state. Such material instability also indexes the dissonance between public presentations and experienced reality, the corruption and immorality of those in positions of political power and the fragility of Astana's utopia. Here, as elsewhere in the volume, Laszczkowski's account contests a simple opposition between compliance and resistance; unambiguous identification and searing critique. Both are simultaneously encompassed within the ironic attitude and the materiality of the buildings themselves. Indeed, it is precisely through this multi-vocality of material forms that the inherent ambiguity of the state can be apprehended: simultaneously "magnificent and unstable, the locus of awe, hope, desire, disillusionment, and trickery."

Bellér-Hann's chapter is an important contribution, not least because it extends the scope of this volume to include the Xinjiang Uyghur Autonomous Region of the People's Republic of China, which is too often treated separately from the post-Soviet republics. This region is of course not "post," whether colonial or communist, but its history of top-down socialist modernization and incorporation within the Chinese version of ethno-nationalities policy has much to say to its post-Soviet neighbors. Bellér-Hann's chapter resonates with Laszczkowski's in that it, too, concerns the materiality of state effects and deals with the enactment of a state modernization project of construction. The Chinese project, though, is one of "creative destruction," in which historical old towns are replaced with modern apartment buildings, and in which palaces and shrines are demolished or replaced with Han Chinese interpretations of folklorized Uyghur materiality. Bellér-Hann uses the term "bulldozer state" to capture the relationship between state, space, and power, and the way the state is materialized in the reordering of space and the built environment. State-organized creative destruction produces the category of modern urban space, dominated by Han Chinese, in opposition to traditional, less developed Uyghur village space. In this region of China there is much less scope for the alternative, ironic expression that Laszczkowski describes in Kazakhstan, and the freedom of the researcher to investigate it is severely constrained by the restrictions imposed by the Chinese government. But even here Bellér-Hann describes temporary inversions of categories as a museumized palace and mausoleum complex once more becomes Uyghur sacred space for a few hours during the major Islamic festivals, and official ticket collectors, who are themselves local people, surreptitiously allow neighbors to enter freely to pray at the tombs of their ancestors.

The final chapter in this section focuses on the contested work of materializing state space in a region of rural borderland between Kyrgyzstan and Uzbekistan in the Fergana Valley. Reeves takes as her ethnographic focus a moment of intensified village-level contestation over the allocation of irrigation water between upstream and downstream villages that are located on either side of this new international border. This incident, which occurred in a context of polarizing possibilities for the articulation of political demands in Kyrgyzstan and Uzbekistan, came to crystallize local debates over the material and institutional correlates of sovereign statehood in a rural setting where roads, markets, and waterways transect new international borders. The incident highlights the fractious work of producing "territorial integrity" in a context where Soviet-era infrastructure continues to bind border villages in relations of material interdependence, and where multiple informal authorities are competing to "perform the state." By situating this moment of cross-border conflict in the context of wider uncertainty about political authority in Uzbekistan and Kyrgyzstan, the chapter stresses the significance of plural local authorities and questions the narrative of ongoing interethnic conflict into which the incident was inserted by news reports at the time.

Moral Positionings

The themes developed in the third and final section revolve around questions of morality, authority, and legitimacy. The question of legitimacy has been a recurring theme in studies of the political in Central Asia, exploring, for instance, how national leaderships engage with populations; why such a great effort is devoted to developing official state ideologies and narratives of nationhood; and how we should understand the operation of such narratives (see, e.g., Adams 2010). The "newness" of the post-Soviet Central Asian states, both in relation to their delineation under Soviet rule in the early twentieth century and also the manner in which they were thrust into independence following the disintegration of the Soviet Union, has pushed the post-independence leaderships into a self-conscious work of nation-building. In all the republics there has been a dedicated effort at constructing distinct national ideologies and narratives of nationhood, to replace the Soviet-era socialist narrative, to naturalize the nation as a cultural and historically developed ethno-territorial entity, and to legitimize current regimes. The condition of nationhood-in-the-making foregrounds questions of representation and legitimacy and what might be called Central Asian political imaginaries (see Liu's chapter).

Central Asian political leaderships are typically described as "authoritarian," and the relation between rulers and population is often characterized as one of coercion or consent, patron-client or Mafia-victim. Anna Matveeva has argued that the durability of authoritarian regimes in Central Asia is secured by a mixture of coercion and repression on the one hand, and the different symbolic means these regimes have employed to project an image of the inevitability of their rule, on the other (Matveeva 2009). She identifies the difficulty of assessing the subjective beliefs of populations living under authoritarian political orders and of ascertaining the extent to which people are actually convinced by state narratives and ideologies or merely simulate compliance. She argues that Central Asian regimes are characterized by what she calls "weak legitimacy"; rulers secure the active support of elites but only ensure a more passive compliance of the general population through a mixture of asserting a monopoly over symbolic production, coercion, networks of patronage, and providing, or at least claiming to provide, a minimum level of security and social welfare.

Subjective belief, when viewed as the internal orientation of an individual, would indeed pose a problem for social scientific analysis. This is perhaps why many previous studies that address questions of political legitimacy in Central Asia have avoided belief altogether and concentrated instead on the strategies of elites themselves and their textually available ideological productions (Jones Luong 2002; March 2003; Cummings 2006). However, the problem of belief arises from the manner in which the question of legitimacy is framed. The implicit assumption is often that a largely faceless population is managed and manipulated by elites who control institutions of the state. The engagement of the individual within a polity or moral community is reduced to "common sense" or rational motivations, seemingly immediately evident material calculations (patron-client relations), or bald coercion.

The contributions to this volume suggest more productive approaches to the question of legitimacy and notions of representation that go beyond textual production and that open out to the creativity, complexity, and contradictory nature of experience. If the chapters in the first section of this volume emphasize how symbolic words and narratives are not merely presented to passive populations but actively engaged with in performative and dialogical productions, the contributions to this third section on "Moral Positionings" explore how conceptions of legitimate representation emerge from political imaginaries and how they are performed and contested within locally rooted moral worlds and dynamics of social interaction. Questions of legitimacy concern not simply the production of state narratives by elites and their reception by passive populations. Narratives take form within shared imaginaries of the political, which circulate beyond elite groups. Moreover, symbolic productions are not inert or merely textual but are performed into existence, and it is in their performance that the multi-vocality of symbols becomes evident: their potential to be creatively interpreted in multiple and contradictory ways within individual lives often subverting the attempts of elites to fix their meaning.

Contested moralities are at the heart of Sarah Kendzior's contribution to this volume. Her chapter describes how political opposition figures outside Uzbekistan directly challenge the present regime's construction of *ma'naviyat*, or morality, and the cultural authenticity at the heart of the government of Uzbekistan's Idea of National Independence. The new national ideology constructs the notion of culture as an essential quality of the Central Asian person. Ma'naviyat, as developed in state discourse, is a broad concept that encompasses individual behavior, the form of the ideal moral community, what constitutes correct Islam, the nature of political leadership, and the duties of rulers and governed. The post-independence ideological vision sees culture as an inherent quality of the Central Asian person developed though history, a natural quality of a particular ethno-territorial group, so that political opposition is equated with a betrayal of a person's very being as an Uzbek. Political opposition in this context takes the form of a struggle to define an authentic morality, as political opposition figures outside Uzbekistan directly contest the present regime's construction of ma'naviyat and cultural authenticity. This counter-discourse points to the hypocrisy of the ruling regime, which it characterizes as morally corrupt and corrupting of society, and presents an alternative moral ideal informed to a significant degree by Islamic notions of virtue. The opposition here, by directly challenging the regime's conceptions of morality and authenticity, is putting forward a very different ideal of moral personhood and citizenship.

If Kendzior's informants in exile sought actively to carve out an authentic morality of cultivated opposition to the regime, Trevisani's chapter, which also deals with Uzbekistan, suggests a picture of active, albeit ambivalent, consent on the part of citizens, not wholly produced by fear and coercion. His contribution deals with the emergence of what he calls the "new Uzbeks" in the city of Namangan in Uzbekistan's Fergana Valley. New Uzbeks, for Trevisani, constitute a middle stratum between the elites and the poor. They might be mid-level state employees, militiamen, traders and entrepreneurs, university lecturers and journalists; people who are able to work the economic possibilities of the new post-independent environment with some degree of success, but who, importantly, remain politically acquiescent. He describes the changing situation of the city of Namangan, once regarded as a center of Islamist opposition to the regime but in the second decade of independence the beneficiary of a large state-led reconstruction and modernization project. This has resulted in a new urbanism where low-rise European-styled housing has replaced traditional residential quarters, once said to host "Wahhabis," and where a former "Wahhabist" mosque has been reconstructed as a regional center for Islamic higher education. This new urbanism, Trevisani argues, is accompanied by a new type of citizen with more "modern" sensibilities, preferring fewer children, aspiring to luxury courtyard houses (*hovli*) in the city suburbs, apolitical, and consumerist. Things are never so clear-cut, however, and Trevisani also describes the ambivalent attitudes toward the state. Resentment at the forced demolition of shops and other buildings to make way for the new construction, anger at the corruption and extortion of state officials who act like a Mafia, coexist with confidence in a better future and a feeling that opportunities for individual prosperity are greater today than in the Soviet period.

The theme of socio-political imaginaries and moral reasoning is developed in Liu's chapter. The focus on Uzbekistan continues but shifts to a perspective from the Kyrgyz side of the border. His ethnographic location is the Uzbek population in the city of Osh in Kyrgyzstan, and he follows the debates and deliberations over the nature of legitimate governance following the massacre of demonstrators in 2005 in the nearby city of Andijan in Uzbekistan's portion of the Fergana Valley. The chapter charts a range of responses, from those that broadly support the Uzbekistan government's assertion that they were forced to act to counter the threat of armed Islamist extremists and that no "innocents" were killed, to those who characterized the government's actions as a bloody massacre of unarmed civilians. Liu places these narratives in the context of moral reasoning over notions of the "common good." The socio-political imaginaries that inform this reasoning include universalistic calls for fairness and equal treatment and opportunities for all ethnic groups in Kyrgyzstan (the Uzbeks constitute a minority in the republic), Soviet ideals of "friendship of peoples," Islamic notions of virtue and public piety, and also the khan imagery that is referred to in Dubuisson's chapter. In addition, ideals of nation and governance are informed by an ethic and practice of localism and patronage. Local "big men," successful entrepreneurs, have invested in local commercial and community enterprises, including universities and cultural centers. They provide much of the livelihood and social support, which the post-Soviet state is no longer able or willing to provide.

From Uzbekistan, we move to Kazakhstan with the chapter by Werner and Purvis-Roberts, which explores how individuals engage with the political through a bodily experience of disorder and victimhood. They deal with the subject of nuclear testing in Soviet Kazakhstan, which took place between 1949 and 1989, and the legacy of radiation poisoning suffered by local residents of the test site who were not properly informed about the dangers, nor protected from them. Since independence, the issue of testing has been an important part of the government's national narrative, which portrays Kazakhstan as the victim of the overbearing Soviet state: victim not only of the testing but also of the forced collectivization of agriculture, which is blamed for famine on a massive scale. The issue is used in state narratives to establish a break from the Soviet past and the emergence of a new Kazakhstan, to contrast the immorality of past, illegitimate Soviet domination with the morally enlightened post-independence leadership. Werner and Purvis-Roberts frame their discussion in terms of memory and narrative. Memory is not simply a recollection of past events but is a moral commentary on the present that needs to be understood in narrative terms, as defining legitimate ends and means and establishing winners, losers, and entitlements. They locate their analysis in the narratives and memories of residents of the test site who are officially classified as suffering various degrees of poisoning. They show how individuals situate themselves and their claims to entitlement within the frame of the national story, legitimating the discursive production of national elites but at the same time making their own claims as victims of the uncaring exercise of state power in relation to the post-independence state. Once more, the multi-vocality of symbols is evident, as legitimation and critique are simultaneously produced. But this chapter also demonstrates how a subjective, bodily engagement with a national polity is shaped within the narrative of nationhood produced by elites for their own ends.

The chapters in this section provide insights into how conceptions of legitimacy and representation take particular form within shared imaginaries. They take ideology beyond textual productions and representation beyond symbolic productions. They point to the essential moral nature of the political: moral because it addresses questions of the nature of the person and the location of the person within a shared community, history, and ideals of the good.

The contributions to this volume share the aspiration of earlier analyses of politics and the state in Central Asia to understand the dynamic moment of creativity that followed the demise of the Soviet Union.[3] They investigate how the political is shaped by this Soviet heritage but how it is also an ongoing re-invention; and they develop new conceptual tools to capture these processes. They provide what Spencer has called a culturally inflected account of the Central Asian political, which opens out to multiple imaginaries, to the contingency, multi-vocality, and creativity of symbols, located within Central Asian lifeworlds. They provide insights into how we might understand the discursive production of national elites, the relation of elites and citizens, and the nature of authority and legitimacy. They also highlight what is distinctive about the political in Central Asia, which might facilitate comparison with other regions that inhabit their own particular colonial and postcolonial histories.

Notes

1. For an account of Soviet nationalities policy in Central Asia and more generally in the Soviet Union, see Roy (2000), Hirsch (2005), and Abashin (2007).

2. For a valuable collection of essays on the Xinjiang Uyghur Autonomous Region, see Bellér-Hann et al. (2007).

3. For an important recent contribution to this literature, see Sengupta and Chatterjee (2013).

References

Abashin, Sergei. 2007. *Natsionalizmy v Srednei Azii: v poiskakh identichnosti.* St. Petersburg: Ateleia.

Abu-Lughod, Lila. 1991. "Writing Against Culture." In *Recapturing Anthropology: Working in the Present,* edited by Richard Gabriel Fox, 137–162. Santa Fe, N.M.: School of American Research Press.

Adams, Laura. 2010. *The Spectacular State: Culture and National Identity in Uzbekistan.* Durham, N.C.: Duke University Press.

Aretxaga, Begoña. 2005. "Maddening States." In *In States of Terror: Begoña Aretxaga's Essays,* edited by Joseba Zulaika, 255–268. Reno, Nev.: Centre for Basque Studies.

Asad, Talal. 1993. *Genealogies of Religion: Discipline and Reasons of Power in Christianity and Islam.* Baltimore: John Hopkins University Press.

———. 2003. *Formations of the Secular: Christianity, Islam, Modernity.* Stanford, Calif.: Stanford University Press.

Austin, John Langshaw. 1962. *How to Do Things with Words: The William James Lectures Delivered at Harvard University in 1955.* Oxford: Oxford University Press.

Bailey, Frederick George. 1969. *Stratagems and Spoils: A Social Anthropology of Politics.* Oxford: Blackwell.

Barth, Frederik. 1959. "Segmentary Opposition and the Theory of Games: A Study of Pathan Organization." *Journal of the Royal Anthropological Institute of Great Britain and Ireland* 89, no. 1: 5–21.

Bellér-Hann, Ildikó, M. Christina Cesàro, Rachel Harris, and Joanne Smith Finley, eds. 2007. *Situating the Uyghurs between China and Central Asia.* Aldershot, UK: Ashgate.

Benda-Beckmann, Frantz von. 2005. "Pak Dusa's Law: Thoughts on Law, Legal Knowledge and Power." *Journal of Transdisciplinary Environmental Studies* 4: 1–12.
Bennett, Tony, and Patrick Joyce, eds. 2010. *Material Powers: Cultural Studies, History and the Material Turn*. Abingdon, UK: Routledge.
Beyer, Judith. 2010. "Authority as Accomplishment: Intergenerational Dynamics in Talas, Northern Kyrgyzstan." In *Eurasian Perspectives: In Search of Alternatives*, edited by A. Sengupta and S. Chatterjee, 87–92. New Delhi: Shipra.
———. 2013 "Constitutional Faith: Law and Hope in Revolutionary Kyrgyzstan." *Ethnos: Journal of Anthropology*. iFirst doi: 10.1080/00141844.2013.841270.
Bruner, Edward, and Barbara Kirshenblatt-Gimblett. 1994. "Maasai on the Lawn. Tourist Realism in East Africa." *Cultural Anthropology* 9, no. 4: 435–470
Carlson, Marvin. 2004. *Performance: A Critical Introduction*. London: Routledge.
Collier, Stephen. 2004. "Pipes." In *Patterned Ground: Entanglements of Nature and Culture*, edited by Stephen Harrison, Steve Pile, and Nigel Thrift, 50–52. London: Reaktion Books.
Collins, Kathleen. 2004. "The Logic of Clan Politics: Evidence from Central Asian Trajectories." *World Politics* 56, no. 2: 224–261.
Conquergood, Dwight. 1985. "Performing as a Moral Act: Ethical Dimensions of the Ethnography of Performance." *Literature in Performance* 5: 1–13.
Cummings, Sally. 2006. "Legitimation and Identification in Kazakhstan." *Nationalism and Ethnic Politics* 12, no. 2: 177–204.
———, ed. 2010. *Symbolism and Power in Central Asia: Politics of the Spectacular*. Abingdon, UK: Routledge.
Dave, Bhavna. 2007. *Kazakhstan: Ethnicity, Language and Power*. London: Routledge.
Edgar, Adrienne. 2004. *Tribal Nation: The Making of Soviet Turkmenistan*. Princeton, N.J.: Princeton University Press.
Ferguson, James, and Akhil Gupta. 2002. "Spatializing States: Towards an Ethnography of Neoliberal Governmentality." *American Ethnologist* 29, no. 4: 981–1002.
Foucault, Michel. 1991. "Governmentality." In *The Foucault Effect: Studies in Governmentality*, edited by Graham Burchell, Colin Gordon, and Peter Miller, 87–104. Chicago: University of Chicago Press.
———. 1994. "The Subject and Power." In *The Essential Foucault: Selections from Essential Works of Foucault, 1954–1984*, edited by P. Rabinow and N. Rose, 126–144. New York: New Press.
Girke, Felix, and Christian Meyer. 2011. "Introduction." In *The Rhetorical Emergence of Culture*, edited by Christian Meyer and Felix Girke, 1–32. Oxford: Berghahn.
Goffman, Erving. 1990. *The Presentation of Self in Everyday Life*. London: Penguin.
Greenhouse, Carol. 2002. "Introduction: Altered States, Altered Lives." In *Ethnography in Unstable Places: Everyday Lives in Contexts of Dramatic Political Change*, 1–34. Durham, N.C.: Duke University Press.
Grzymala-Busse, Anna, and Pauline Jones Luong. 2002. "Reconceptualizing the State: Lessons from Post-Communism." *Politics and Society* 30, no. 4: 529–554.
Gullette, David. 2007. "Theories of Central Asian Factionalism: The Debate in Political Science and Its Wider Implications." *Central Asian Survey* 26, no. 3: 373–387.

———. 2010. *The Genealogical Construction of the Kyrgyz Republic: Kinship, State and Tribalism*. Folkestone, UK: Global Oriental.

Harvey, Penny. 2005. "The Materiality of State-Effects: An Ethnography of a Road in the Peruvian Andes." In *State Formation: Anthropological Perspectives,* edited by Christian Krohn-Hansen and Knut Nustad, 123–141. London: Pluto Press.

Heathershaw, John. 2009. *Post-Conflict Tajikistan: The Politics of Peacebuilding and the Emergence of Legitimate Order.* London: Routledge.

Hirsch, Francine. 2005. *Empire of Nations: Ethnographic Knowledge and the Making of the Soviet Union.* Ithaca, N.Y.: Cornell University Press.

Humphrey, Caroline. 2005. "Ideology in Infrastructure: Architecture and the Soviet Imagination." *Journal of the Royal Anthropological Institute* 11: 39–58.

Jones Luong, Pauline. 2002. *Institutional Change and Political Continuity in Post-Soviet Central Asia: Power, Perceptions, and Pacts.* Cambridge: Cambridge University Press.

Kandiyoti, Deniz. 2007. "The Politics of Gender and the Soviet Paradox: Neither Colonized nor Modern?" *Central Asian Survey* 26, no. 4: 601–623.

Kandiyoti, Deniz, and Ruth Mandel, eds. 1998. "Market Reforms, Social Dislocations and Survival in Post-Soviet Central Asia." Special issue, *Central Asian Survey* 17, no. 4.

Leach, Edward. 1961. *Pul Eliya, a Village in Ceylon: A Study of Land Tenure and Kinship.* Cambridge: Cambridge University Press.

Liu, Morgan. 2012. *Under Solomon's Throne: Uzbek Visions of Renewal in Osh.* Pittsburgh: University of Pittsburgh Press.

March, Andrew. 2003. "State Ideology and the Legitimation of Authoritarianism. The Case of Post-Soviet Uzbekistan." *Journal of Political Ideologies* 8, no. 2: 209–232.

Matveeva, Anna. 2009. "Legitimising Central Asian Authoritarianism: Political Manipulation and Symbolic Power." *Europe-Asia Studies* 61, no. 7: 1095–1121.

McGlinchey, Eric. 2011. *Chaos, Violence, Dynasty: Politics and Islam in Central Asia.* Pittsburgh: University of Pittsburgh Press.

Mitchell, Timothy 1999. "Society, Economy and the State Effect." In *State/Culture: State-Formation after the Cultural Turn,* edited by George Steinmetz, 76–97. Ithaca, N.Y.: Cornell University Press.

Navaro-Yashin, Yael. 2002. *Faces of the State: Secularism and Public Life in Turkey.* Princeton, N.J.: Princeton University Press.

———. 2003. "'Life Is Dead Here': Sensing the Political in 'No Man's Land.'" *Anthropological Theory* 3, no. 1: 107–125.

Poliakov, Sergei. 1992. *Everyday Islam: Religion and Tradition in Rural Central Asia.* New York: M. E. Sharpe.

Radcliffe-Brown, Alfred Reginald. 1952. *Structure and Function in Primitive Society.* London: Cohen and West.

Radnitz, Scott. 2005. "Networks, Localism and Mobilization in Aksy, Kyrgyzstan." *Central Asian Survey* 24, no. 4: 405–424.

———. 2010. *Weapons of the Wealthy: Predatory Regimes and Elite-Led Protests in Central Asia.* Ithaca, N.Y.: Cornell University Press.

Rasanayagam, Johan. 2006. "I'm Not a Wahhabi! State Power and Muslim Orthodoxy in Uzbekistan." In *The Postsocialist Religious Question,* edited by C. Hann, 99–124. Munich: LIT.

Reeves, Madeleine. 2008. "Border Work: An Ethnography of the State at Its Limits in the Ferghana Valley." PhD diss., University of Cambridge.

———. 2009. "Materializing State Space: 'Creeping Migration' and Territorial Integrity in Southern Kyrgyzstan." *Europe-Asia Studies* 62, no. 7: 1277–1313.

———. 2011. "Fixing the Border: On the Affective Life of the State in Southern Kyrgyzstan." *Environment and Planning D: Society and Space* 29, no. 4: 905–923.

Roy, Olivier. 2000. *The New Central Asia: The Creation of Nations.* London: I. B. Tauris.

Scott, James. 1998. *Seeing Like a State: How Certain Schemes to Improve the Human Condition Have Failed.* New Haven, Conn.: Yale University Press.

Sengupta, Anita and Suchandana Chatterjee, eds. 2013. *The State in Eurasia: Local and Global Arenas.* New Delhi: Kalpana Shukla Publishers.

Spencer, Jonathan. 1995. "Post-Colonialism and the Political Imagination." *Journal of the Royal Anthropological Institute* (N.S.) 3, no. 1: 1–19.

———. 2007. *Anthropology, Politics and the State: Democracy and Violence in South Asia.* Cambridge: Cambridge University Press.

Strecker, Ivo. 1998. *The Social Practice of Symbolization: An Anthropological Analysis.* London: Athlone Press.

Wittgenstein, Ludwig. 1979. *Wittgenstein's Lectures, Cambridge 1932–1935,* edited by Alice Ambrose. Totowa, N.J.: Rowman and Littlefield.

Yurchak, Alexei. 2006. *Everything Was Forever, Until It Was No More: The Last Soviet Generation.* Princeton, N.J.: Princeton University Press.

Part 1
Staging the Political

1. The Global Performance State

A Reconsideration of the Central Asian "Weak State"

John Heathershaw

Strolling through Tajikistan's capital city of Dushanbe in April 2010, almost twenty years after its declaration of independence from the Soviet Union, one is bombarded with images of the state, the president who represents it, and his appearances on the global stage. The state and its personal embodiment are apparently everywhere—monopolizing legitimate violence and defining legitimate public space in Tajikistan. Its citizens walk and chat in safety along a thoroughfare, which not fifteen years before saw violent demonstrations, sniper attacks, and guerilla warfare during the brutal civil war over control of the state. Just ten years earlier they would have rushed home to be indoors for the regular curfew. Across the street, the last wedding of the day spills joyfully out from the state registrar's office, yet the cost of festivities has been reduced due to the 2007 state law that limited expenditures on traditional celebrations. As the wedding party departs, its vehicles pass under banners that are hung above the road and draped over state buildings, envisioning the construction of the Roghun Dam, a state project of Soviet origin and gigantic scale. Images of President Emomoli Rahmon, the safety helmet–wearing engineer-in-chief, adorn these banners.

Moreover, these are no Potemkin villages.[1] Behind these signs of the state we find institutional, material, and coercive power attached to these state forms. Numerous side roads are closed to traffic to facilitate the reconstruction of the city according to the high-modernist plans of its mayor. Police gather ready to clear the streets for the presidential motorcade travelling between the presidential administration building and official residence little over a kilometer along the road. Whistles are blown, illuminous sticks are waved, police officers glare. In a jail just off Rudaki Avenue, and unbeknownst to most Tajiks, enemies of the state that have been captured by the security services and convicted of terrorist offenses in the courts are confined to a high-security state prison. The state has, by a mixture of coercion and persuasion, collected in excess of US$160 million in local currency from its citizens in the form of shares in the ongoing Roghun project. Officials of the Tajikistani state have considerable declaratory and commissary powers that have changed the political environment from one of armed conflict, little more than ten years ago, to hegemonic and relatively stable authoritarian governance today.

However, another story can be told. Apparent state strength seems to conceal another reality of systemic state weakness. In August 2010, the forty-nine prisoners of the high-security prison, including the aforementioned "terrorists" escaped. The police, loathed by many of those excluded from the patronage networks that distribute posts, stop drivers, and take payments. The funds collected for the Roghun project may not be convertible on foreign markets without driving down the value of the somoni. Their most significant effect has been to increase poverty. While most Tajiks deem the Roghun project essential for national development, they are often skeptical in private about whether it is realistic. Many of the citizens who walk the streets rely on remittances from relatives working in Russia, but few have confidence to save their extra monies in banks or have the connections to set up and grow a business free from state intimidation.[2] They still look to the state for pensions, healthcare, and education but are growing increasingly cynical about its corruption and ineffectiveness.

We are thus faced with a contradictory picture regarding the sovereign state that was brought forth unexpectedly after the unraveling of the Soviet Union in 1991. The state seems at once omnipresent and perennially absent, both omniscient and powerless, both omnific and wholly lacking in productive capacity. What is the significance of these gigantic flagpoles and the proliferation of images of statehood across the capitals and countrysides of Central Asian states? Are they merely a symbolic gloss deployed to conceal institutional failure and the lack of the basic materials of statehood (armed forces, balanced budgets, and so forth)? Or do they point to a deeper reality of the conditions of statehood in an era of "reputation management" and increasing global connectedness of new media and vastly increased rates of overseas development assistance? This chapter seeks to address, conceptually and empirically, this tension found in political science studies of Central Asian and other postcolonial states.

This polyvalent picture and these outstanding questions are reflected in a literature which has barely begun to grasp these apparent contradictions and oftentimes favors premature declarations of the weakness or collapse of a given state. It is increasingly said that the Central Asian state is dysfunctional and, in Tajikistan's case, "on the road to failure" (ICG 2009). Political scientists of Central Asia have sought to understand the dysfunctionalities in terms of hybrid forms of statehood and political life, such as "strong-weak states" (Migdal 1994; McMann 2004), the "state against itself" or the "dispersed" state (Jones-Luong 2004), and "modern clan politics" (Schatz 2004). Many of these analyses are informed by the conceptual precepts of neo-institutionalism. In the same vein, Mark Beissinger and Crawford Young (2002) compared post-Soviet Eurasian states to those of postcolonial Africa and argued that such state-societal intertwining is a sign not of strength but of weakness (Beissinger and Young 2002). On the other hand, the Central Asian state is also denoted as "spectacular" (Adams 2010), having a hyper-real quality that sustains it despite its supposed weakness. One promising intellectual response to these developments has been to chart what Andrew Wilson labels the "virtual politics" of the post-Soviet state—how authoritarian regimes directly and strategically fake democracy in its absence through political technologies, staged elections, and faux opposition parties. This approach is increasingly applied or adapted to the Central Asian region (Allison 2008; Heathershaw 2009b; Lewis 2008a).

However, there is little attempt to theorize the "virtual state" in this work, and overall there remains a distinct lack of clarity on the nature of symbolic, spectacular, or virtual politics in the region. Although virtual politics is said to be "radically top-down" (Wilson 2005, 48), such conclusions dodge the question of the "hegemony of form" (Yurchak 2006) raised in cultural studies—that is, in Adams's terms, "the meaning being made within the models" (2008, 617). While empirical accounts of virtual politics in political science are useful supplements to materialist and behavioralist analyses, they are often conceptually and theoretically limited. Many of these authors assume a clear distinction between constructed fakes (virtual politics) and real practices ("inner politics" [Wilson 2005, 47]). Here "the state" is pared down to "the regime," which maintains a bare semblance of order under conditions of weak statehood or state failure. The problem with such an approach is that it concentrates on the instrumentality of virtual politics while failing to recognize its constitutive functions—semiological and sociological.

In particular, two conditions or dimensions of Central Asian states are often overlooked by political scientists who dismiss them as weak, postcolonial forms. Firstly, limited by the dichotomy of state-idea and state-system, they disregard the performative dimension of its signs and their enactments. Signs of the state don't float freely but are performed by state representatives and their interlocutors. Such signs are not merely representative of abstract ideas or ideology but they themselves may legitimize the authority of the state within its societal context. Secondly, hamstrung by the Weberian conception of the territoriality of the state, they disregard the global dimension of the society of the state.[3] The social constitution of Central Asian states that have been born in an era of global governmentality is not limited to the activities of the national territorial unit. Moreover, such states neither monopolize their own territories nor are they confined to them. Their representatives launch off-shore yet fully state-owned companies just as they allow international organizations to set up project teams inside their own ministries or create new executive agencies at the behest of donors. The contention of this chapter is that these two aspects of performance and globality should be considered as intertwined dimensions of what can be defined as "the global performance state." Such statehood is not fake—not a facade that conceals an underlying reality. However, it is not discernible if one insists on imposing dichotomies of state versus society, idea versus system, or inside versus outside. This performative and global statehood is perhaps particularly acute amongst postcolonial states that have only recently gained independence.

The argument is elaborated across three sections. Each draws on theoretical literature and empirical examples taken from my work on Tajikistan and research on other Central Asian states, to propose a new concept of the global performance state in the study of Central Asia. The three sections each begin by critically engaging one of three false dichotomies of the state that are foundational to the state weakness literature. Section one considers the state/society dichotomy itself and examines how the state is viewed in political science, particularly in terms of virtual politics (Wilson 2005). As is shown with reference to my research on post-conflict peace-building in Tajikistan, those that occupy places in the state are able to deploy fakes and simulate real politics (Heathershaw 2009a). However, acts of virtual politics such as donor-sponsored dialogue exercises must be considered not as purely epiphenomenal but as constituting and constituted by a symbolic order where the state is pre-eminent. The following sections consider the two conditions that sustain such "virtual states": performance and globality. Section two interrogates the idea/system dichotomy and considers research in Soviet and post-Soviet studies on the performative nature of statehood and politics more broadly, especially the work of Alexei Yurchak (2006). In the example of the handover of the Tajikistan-Afghanistan border from Russian to national control we find state performance in the process by which state sovereignty is simulated and dissimulated by national and international actors. Finally, in section three, the global aspect of the Central Asian state is foregrounded as the chapter interrogates the inside/outside dichotomy of the state. The chapter considers the adoption of the Law on Self-Governance by Tajikistan in 2009, a process directed by the United States Agency for International Development, in light of the arguments of this chapter and the literature on "global assemblages" and the denationalization of the state (Sassen 2006).

State/Society: Virtual States?

The state is commonly defined in political science as "a distinct set of political institutions whose specific concern is with the organization of domination, in the name of the common interest, within a delimited territory" (Burnham 2005, 512).[4] The use of the term "distinct" in this definition is illuminating, as it reflects the intellectual preference to conceptualize the state as an autonomous institution while recognizing that it is "in society" (Migdal 1994). However, for other state theorists this search for distinctness is a blind alley. Timothy Mitchell notes that "the elusiveness of the state-society boundary needs to be taken seriously, not as a problem of conceptual precision but as a clue to the nature of the phenomenon" (Mitchell 1999, 78). Moreover, "the appearance that state and society are separate things is part of the way a given financial and economic order is maintained" (ibid., 90). Contra Mitchell, most state theorists have nevertheless dealt with the elusiveness of the state-society boundary as a matter of degree that is subject to measurement and/or categorization. For Migdal (1994) and those that seek to measure amount of state on a strength-weakness scale, stateness is a quantifiable condition, from state failure on the one end of the spectrum to the complete objectification of the state at the other. This is in keeping with a literature on state weakness and collapse largely begun in African studies (Zartman 1995), which diagnoses that "the real business of politics is taking place where analysts are often not looking" (Chabal and Daloz 1999, 1). Political scientists of Central Asia, following the lead of these and similar scholars, have explained the state's weakness in terms of its capture by regional factions (Jones-Luong 2002), clans (Schatz 2004; Collins 2006), warlords and criminal networks (Nourzhanov 2005; Marat 2006), or coalitions of disaffected elites (Radnitz 2010). Taken to the extreme, such analysis suggests that institutions of the state then become mere tools of a regime that has captured the state for its own ends.

The Virtual State

Wilson's (2005) analysis of virtual politics is in keeping with such accounts, as he considers how regimes fake democratic elections and signs of state strength for both domestic and international audiences. Wilson's study constitutes an exceptional attempt to get a handle on the difference between apparent form and actual practice of the state that remains characteristic of post-Soviet politics. Politics is thus represented in narrative and theatrical form (*dramaturgiia*) where opponents are discredited and supporters finally emerge vindicated. In that Wilson's argument pertains to the instruments and institutions of the state—

elections, political parties, fights for control of state agencies and utilities—it can be considered a conceptualization of "the virtual state." Such a state is "purely epiphenomenal or instrumental," a vehicle for keeping hold of power or brokering international agreements. Beyond this virtual state lies an "inner" or "real" state-system found in the informal institutions, networks, and material instantiations of power of ruling regimes (Wilson 2005, 47). In other words, the state is wholly subservient to a given societal faction—the regime. While the regime is resilient, the state is weak.

It is hardly surprising that this account of virtual politics has been a popular intellectual direction for political scientists studying Central Asia. This is an analytical path trodden by David Lewis (Lewis 2008b), who identifies a "virtual Kyrgyzstan" (2008a, 124) during the later years of President Askar Akaev (1990–2005)—the more-or-less democratizing state that was manufactured by the international community in connivance with certain cooperative actors in the state. However, as a fake, this Kyrgyzstan succumbed to "virtual state collapse" (ibid.,148)—that is, the collapse of the virtual state that was no longer able to maintain the pretense of sovereignty and legitimacy. As Lewis argues,

> in many cases, the international community was dealing with a virtual state, centred around "Project Implementation Units" within the government, more enlightened officials from the ministry of foreign affairs, and a small but sometimes vocal NGO community. (Lewis 2008a, 235)

According to this powerful analysis, international organizations are complicit with, if not acquiescent to, the virtual state. As such, they fail to grasp the inner reality that is the real stuff of politics. These virtual states remain epiphenomenal of regimes with the litmus test of their strength or weakness being regime change. In Kyrgyzstan and unspecified other cases, Lewis argues, "when [Central Asian leaders] left power, much of the state disappeared too" (2008a, 158–159).

Roy Allison extends the gaze of virtual politics to regional international relations in his account of "virtual regionalism" (Allison 2008). Virtual regionalism here is defined by the hollow agreements and ultimately inconsequential summits that are found throughout Central Asian regional cooperation. Kazakhstan, Kyrgyzstan, and Tajikistan, in particular, have proven willing to engage in almost any regional forum on offer. Allison argues that such a superficial and promiscuous approach to regional cooperation "offers the benefits of political solidarity and a vicarious legitimacy to Central Asian political leaders who find difficulty in establishing this on the wider international stage" (2008, 198). Thus the ostensible objective of these agreements is in practice supplanted by a greater goal: recognition of sovereign statehood and the accompanying payoff of this recognition for regime security. Indeed, for Allison, the sovereignty prerogative explains both the rush to sign agreements and the absence of any practical consequences of them (ibid., 186). Recalling Wilson's and Lewis's arguments, Allison sees "a possible relationship between the virtual quality of regionalism and the political fabric of Central Asia—the flows of power and the ways in which leaders seek effective control over the distribution of material and political resources" (ibid., 188). In this shared claim all these authors are surely correct, but it may be that this relationship between virtuality and statehood goes far deeper than the instrumental feigning of cooperation. Moreover, if state sovereignty is the virtual form according to which politics takes place, then it is no mere instrument of individuals and networks. Rather, it is a discourse of global politics—a "dialogue of form" in the words of the introduction to this volume—with its own Central Asian varieties.

Tajikistan's Virtual Peace-Building

In sum, there are three dimensions of virtual politics as an instrument of personalized regimes: national (Wilson), regional-international (Allison), and global-international (Lewis). Thus, by these accounts the virtual state is epiphenomenal and appears in different guises to national elites, regional neighbors and the Western-dominated international community. According to these authors, behind these guises or masks we can find an inner reality—where power really lies. This account seems to fit the messy empirical "reality" very well. After all, political technologists are no more omnipotent than any other political actor. However, as an instrumentalist account of the virtual—where symbols are deployed and controlled by agents as masks for their inner beliefs and actual behavior—it is inadequately theorized. It neither provides a convincing semiological nor sociological account of the virtual state. A better-developed concept of virtual politics might help us reinterpret the Soviet as well as the post-Soviet state (see below). It may also help us understand how instrumental acts of virtual politics described by Wilson are only possible given a wider discursive environment where form has triumphed over content.

The case of international peace-building in Tajikistan suggests that virtual politics has wider implications than admitted by Wilson. In the discourses of international peace-building and democratic transition, events such as "election observation" or "dialogue exercises" and "study tours" for state and civil society representatives are deemed to create space for political participation where it would not otherwise exist. Such projects have been lauded by one practitioner as "substitutes [for] the lack of open political discussion in the parliament" (Malekzade 2005, 1). This substitution function is a useful one to dwell on in terms of virtual politics. According to international peace-builders, such substitutions are, at best, constructive of new political space or, at worst, neutral in their impact on democratization. However, it is by no means certain that substitutions or simulations of state-societal interaction serve as prototypes of "real" engagement; they may indeed have quite different effects. Time and again officials in Tajikistan took the opportunity to assert the authority of the state over political parties and independent groups. However, the liberal-institutionalist narrative of peace-building made its purveyors blind to the possibility that these symbolic acts might be self-defeating; that they might function to facilitate the resurgence of an authoritarian state rather than democratic opening.

Even in cases where it was obvious that such initiatives have been met with elite incomprehension or open hostility, and led to a closure of political space, it was assumed that they were part of a process of opening up the state to society. The hostility of government officials toward "political" actions by non-governmental organizations (NGOs), according to one program coordinator, demands that they follow the maxim: "get government permission in advance, always invite the *hukumat* [local state administration]."[5] When the *hukumat* is unwilling to give permission, even for very small events, it is often necessary to involve the presidential administration. Working from day to day in such an environment, the activities of international organizations, which must be authorized by state officials, serve to objectify the state as a singular political form. One program officer noted:

> We organized a workshop with 70 participants and asked the local government to participate in order to work with them—you know the idea was to increase the role of citizens in talking about issues in their area, to have roundtables on priority issues to feed into local government who normally don't listen at all. In actuality the *hukumat* had the say in who is invited and who speaks, but I think you can say that it was a step in the right direction—to get anyone to participate is a positive thing. (Interview with Stephanie Wheeler, February 23, 2005)

A "step in the right direction" is all that remains of international peace-building in this case. However, it is an important remainder; it reaffirms the authority of the state to act as gatekeeper to external actors and supreme political authority in the territory.

In addition to this function of exclusion, such international peace-building and democratization events also allow the regime to publicly include its loyalists in orchestrated expressions of support for the state. For example, in Khujond in 2004 a meeting of the UN-sponsored Political Discussion Club was dominated by governmental elites who used it as an opportunity to perform their loyalty to the state. The meeting was held in government buildings while initially opposition representatives were shut outside as the head of UN Tajikistan Office of Peace-building (UNTOP) and senior officials of the Organization for Security and Cooperation in Europe (OSCE) sat inside. A series of governmental speakers praised the regime in front of an audience of hundreds of state officials (*gos-chinovniki*) who applauded every speech. When the opposition parties were allowed in they were required to stand along the sidelines. After they were eventually given a few minutes to speak they were met with silence.[6] Such events are in keeping with the vision of state-societal relations propounded by mayor of Dushanbe, Mahmadsaid Ubaidulloyev, who in a speech to an OSCE dialogue exercise noted,

> I at once want to note that it must not weaken the ability of all branches of the state (*vlast'*) to command and regulate the situation as it takes shape, and it must not set one group or party against another, and in such a way as to divert it from the fundamental work of supplying rapid economic growth and the reduction of poverty. (Ubaidulloyev 2003, 62)

This representation of "fundamental work" places the government and the state (*vlast'*) at the symbolic head of this societal enterprise.

These examples indicate that there is both more and less to the state than suggested by the concept of virtual politics. Firstly, the state cannot be dismissed as merely captured by the regime as it is objectified, in Migdal's terms, by many of its citizens and visiting international organizations. These subjects of the state do not necessarily draw a distinction between regime (real) and state (virtual). Citizens often fear the state and speak of it as a powerful actor and gatekeeper in their lives. International organizations and foreign governments are bound by international norms to recognize the authority of the state and refrain from significant criticism in what are considered domestic matters. Secondly, as an object the state does not take a pre-existing and universal form and content but is constituted in these performances. The actual boundary between state and society and thus the distinctiveness of the state is difficult to determine and is subject to constant renegotiation. Participants in dialogue exercises often formally represent political parties and NGOs while also being state officials. Elsewhere in my research it was clear that local informal authority figures, mullahs, elders (*aksakals*), ex-commanders from the civil war, and heads of internationally sponsored community-based organizations often also represented the state either in an official role or, at least, as an informant (Heathershaw 2009b). In short, we are faced with the paradox that it seems to be the very lack of boundary between society and state that gives the state its presence in society and its distinctive claim to represent the general will. The remaining two parts of this chapter explore how this apparent logical contradiction can be resolved via the concept of the global performance state.

Idea/System: The Performance of the State

The above examples of virtual peace-building suggest that virtual politics is not merely epiphenomenal but indirectly helps constitute political order. In keeping with an emerging literature on the anthropology of the state (Mitchell 1999; Chalfin 2001; Hansen and Stepputat 2001; Navaro-Yashin 2002), the introduction to this volume suggests that the state can be looked at in terms of the ways it emerges as the outcome of "creative, multi-vocal interactions." Engaging with performance requires that we think through the relationship between the state as an idea and as a system that remains fundamental to the way social scientists view the state. Weak state analysis rests on the existence of an external normative and empirical standard of the state against which actually existing states can be judged. But this is to view idea and system in dichotomous terms. The historical sociologist Philip Abrams famously declared in a much-cited paper that,

> The state is not the reality which stands behind the mask of political practice. It is itself the mask which prevents our seeing political practice as it is. There is a state-system: a palpable nexus of practice and institutional structure centred in government and more or less extensive, unified and dominant in any given society. There is, too, a state-idea, projected, purveyed and variously believed in different societies at different times. We are only making difficulties for ourselves in supposing that we have also to study the state—an entity, agent, function or relation over and above the *state-system* and the *state-idea*. (1988, 82)

The reification of the state-idea is the work of "illusion," according to Abrams, but his notion of illusion is quite different to that offered in the virtual politics literature, as it is an illusion that actually constitutes the state as res publica (ibid.).

The Variously Performed State

The road to this better concept of the Central Asian state is sketched in Yurchak's (2006) analysis of the end of the Soviet Union. He shows how the collapse was a surprise for which Soviet citizens were nonetheless well prepared; why the USSR as a state was a site of both hope and disaffection. Since the late-1960s, Yurchak argues, "it became less important to read ideological representations for 'literal' (referential) meanings than to reproduce their precise structural forms" (2006, 14). Thus he finds in this era a hegemony of form over content in political practice and a popular response that he labels the cynical reason of late socialism. The value of Yurchak's work for this study is in the conceptual resources he offers us to understand Soviet and, potentially, post-Soviet state performance. Yurchak seeks to move beyond explanations that dismiss such political practice as a masquerade: where individuals act subjunctively as if something were true when in fact knowing this performance is a lie (Scott 1990; Žižek 1991; Sloterdijk 1993), akin to Wilson's (2005) virtual politics. He makes an alternative distinction between two functions of discourse: constative and performative. Drawing on J. L. Austin's speech act theory, Yurchak summarizes that "constative utterances convey meaning and can be true or false; performative utterances deliver force and cannot be true or false—instead they can be felicitous or infelicitous" (2006, 19).

Thus while public transcripts, official practices, and indeed state institutions may be constatively false they may also be performatively felicitous, that is, they reconstitute the discursive and institutional environment of which they are part. National citizens and international officials may not believe in the image of the state proffered by the government but may accept that the state exists apart from and above society.

This turn to questions of the performative is a vital one that has proved beneficial in international relations (IR) and security studies over the last two decades. It has made seminal contributions to IR in its Austinian guise as in Ole Waever and Barry Buzan's use of speech act theory in the concept of securitization (the process by which something becomes a security issue; Waever 1995; Buzan, Waever, and De Wilde 1998). James Der Derian (2001) argues that such "speech acts" should be considered simulations of reality (Baudrillard 1983; Der Derian 1994). However, they are productive in a performative sense: they "produce real symptoms, hyper-real effects" (Der Derian 1994, 214). It is this "order of simulation" that "marks the legitimate range of [the state's] legitimate powers and competencies" (Weber 1995, 129). However, in the study of Central Asia the concept of performance has only recently been deployed (Adams 2008, 2010; Reeves 2008; Beyer 2009; Ismailbekova 2011). Yurchak's work suggests that the way forward for (post-)Soviet studies is in the study of the performative production of reality, both institutional and semiotic. Pierre Bourdieu's work demonstrates that the power of performance lies in "the delegated power of external social contexts and institutions" (Yurchak 2006, 20). Equally, it is semiologically constituted ambiguity that provides "the possibility for change in discourse that institutions cannot determine or anticipate in advance" (Yurchak 2006, 20, 21). Both institutions and semiotics should be attended to in an empirical analysis of state performance. It is the institution of formal state sovereignty that enables, for example, a ragtag and disunited bunch of oppositionists to claim authority to rule just a day or two after the collapse of the Akaev regime in Kyrgyzstan on March 23, 2005. Equally, their assertions of a new Kyrgyzstan were subject to the semiotic power of discourse to produce unintended meanings for audiences of poor Kyrgyz who in the immediate aftermath saw the revolution as a justification to grab land from ethnic minorities.

Central Asian states appear to be constituted in post-Soviet performance activities. Adams (2010) argues, following Yurchak (2006), that Uzbekistan's authoritarian state was partly constructed by the making of new meanings in Soviet-era state holiday displays and celebrations. Others have explored how state sovereignty is constituted in terms of the performance of Uzbekistan's ideology of independence (Megoran 2008) and its violent impersonation by state actors in everyday life (Reeves 2008). Andrew March (2003) finds that such authority is derived not from any substantive basis but from a scientific and teleological political ideology. Chad Thompson (2008) comes to similar conclusions in exploring how Western and modernist concepts were attributed with new meanings in Uzbekistani elite discourse:

> Membership within the world community was predicated on a mimetic reproduction of the institutional forms of the West, while preserving a system which bears little relationship to a democratic imaginary. Such a contention is inherent within the epistemological premises which continue to govern the post-Soviet world, but which are surprisingly compatible with the formal institutions of liberal democratic societies. (Thompson 2008, 4–5)

These epistemological premises favor "the displacement of debate by expertise," a tendency found to a greater or lesser extent across the modern world, which was particularly acute in the Soviet Union and which has become the mantra of governance in contemporary Uzbekistan (Thompson 2008, 18). Thus, in language similar to that of Wilson but with much more profound implications, Thompson contends that "politics become form, while the substance moves elsewhere" (2008, 68).

The Performance of Central Asian Borders and Sovereignties

My own work on Tajikistan has sought to draw out how dominant Western conceptions of state sovereignty make their way into the political performances of Central Asian states. In Tajikistan, and I think across Central Asia, state sovereignty, and the security the state claims to ensure, seem at once both ever present (in that they are constantly and successfully asserted by officials) and yet strangely absent (amidst massive levels of external interference, the rent-seeking actions of "state" actors, and the insecurities of daily life). Tajikistan's southern border with Afghanistan was officially guarded by Russia until 2005, after which it formally passed to national control. Since then the Tajikistan-

Afghanistan border has been subject to massive international assistance with border-guarding infrastructure built with European and American money, the establishment and rearrangement of government agencies at the request of donors, and regular meetings with foreign ambassadors regarding border management. This puzzle of concomitant sovereignty and intervention can only be resolved analytically through the acceptance of contradiction that it is both present (as a formal principle attested to by both insiders and outsiders) and absent (in that there is no single sovereign actor but a multiplicity of authorities and security actors at play).

Firstly, state sovereignty is performed by national actors with some receptiveness on the part of a national audience. The handing over of the border to formal Tajik control, while making little immediate difference in practice (the border had previously been guarded by Tajik contract troops under Russian officers while after the handover these officers became "advisors"), was absolutely essential to the Tajik government's claim to nation statehood (*davlatdori melli*). The period of the transition, from 2004 to 2006, was marked by multiple performances of state sovereignty, such as the declaration that "we are able to defend our border" (*mo sorhadoti hudro hifz karda metavonem*) on official border guards days.[7] The government passed a law on border military forces of Tajikistan and made great spectacle of the various stages of handover in public ceremonies at border posts, each reported in the press. These acts of state, both legislative and ceremonial, were performative of the national, unified, and personified state. It was emphasized moreover that the president has authority over the border and "personally checks on the status of achievements" (UNDP 2005, no pagination). Moreover, declarations of *davlatdori melli* were routinely accompanied by warnings of the external threats of Afghanistan, terrorism, and drugs (Heathershaw 2009a, 130–133).

Secondly, Tajikistan's state sovereignty was also performed by Western states who emphasized their role in funding state border management. The European Union emphasized "multilateral cooperation," "integrated border management," and "legal and institutional reforms" (European Commission 2005). The role of Russia, the ex-colonial power, was more complex but is also indicative of the triumph of form over content. While Russia agreed to the handover as part of a larger agreement between Presidents Putin and Rahmon in 2004, it continued to assert the authority of Russian advisors at the border that Yeltsin had described as "in effect, Russia's" in 1993 (cited in Rubin 1998, 155). Many Russian security officials seemingly continue to regard Tajikistan's sovereignty over the border as conditional on this cooperation with Russia. As late as August 2011, Boris Gryzlov, the speaker of the lower house of the Russian parliament, suggested that Russian forces could retake control of the border from Tajikistan, leading to a rapid response from Tajikistani officials (Sodiqov 2011).

Such calls invite claims and counter-claims regarding the effectiveness or otherwise of Tajikistani state border guards. Yet such discussions are mere code for the real question of sovereignty and statehood. Guarding the southern border with Afghanistan may be a profitable pursuit for some Tajikistani officers, but the symbolic power that control of the border accrues for the state is all the more significant.

This simulation of sovereignty and the performance of the state may be most pronounced in Central Asia's newly independent states but is produced by global discursive practices that have become universal via the dispersion of the state form through decolonization. Weber (1995) argues that it is no longer possible to fix sovereignty according to a single representation of the nation-state. Sovereignty and intervention, she argues, are frequently invoked in the same sentence. Weber contends,

> If in the same discursive locale where one finds a "legitimate" claim to sovereignty, one finds a "legitimate" example of intervention, sovereignty and intervention cannot be opposed to one another. Rather they can be substituted for one another. Sovereignty is intervention, and intervention is sovereignty. (1995, 121)

This interpretation—of how formal sovereignty is built by acts of intervention that directly negate that sovereignty—is consistent with the reading of performance in the wider post-structuralist and feminist literature, where oppositional or adversarial acts are, if they are productive at all, reliant on the very order they seek to challenge (Butler 1997; Disch 1999). It is in this performative analysis that the wider significance of the virtual state of Wilson becomes apparent. Often agents are able to avoid the functional fulfillment of agreements but simultaneously adhere to contrasting "codes" of sovereignty and intervention. Tajik elites are well practiced in this, having signed dozens of international agreements that remain unfulfilled (Lavrakas 2004). State actors will increasingly attempt to gain control of these representations of sovereign authority. They adopt the registers of discourse of the "international community" and "regional cooperation"—attending meetings, making cosmetic concessions, and accepting massive external assistance and interference—while simultaneously asserting national sovereignty. However, in seeking to manage the effects of these performances on their national and international audiences they can never be completely successful, as they are not able to control the making of meanings.

These studies of Tajikistan and Uzbekistan suggest that a dichotomy between state-idea and state-system is misleading in the case of the Central Asian performance state. The confusing assemblages of power that are often denoted as the state-system would lose their authority, legitimacy, and ultimately effectiveness without performances by individuals and groups under the mantra of "the state." Mitchell (1999) has conceptualized the outcome of such statist performances as a "state effect" where highly fractured and personalized regimes are treated by their citizens and interlocutors as unified states even as they confront their inconsistency, heterogeneity, and even "corruption" in practice (see also Beyer, this volume; Bichsel 2009; Reeves 2008). As Madeleine Reeves has noted, "these paradoxes and puzzles [of state weakness] arise from an initial assumption that the state 'ought,' in both a normative and descriptive sense, to be a singular rather than multiple entity" (2006, 11). This leaves us with a rearticulation of the dichotomy of state-idea and state-system into a more intellectually promising puzzle. Idea and system are neither completely consistent nor wholly contradictory but constitute one another in complex ways. It is because of the salience of the idea of the state as a single sovereign entity that the Central Asian state is a multiplicitous and dispersed system: performed or "impersonated" in diverse ways by informal actors who are networked to the regime (Reeves 2008). By paying attention to the importance of performance we can begin to grasp how different types of state performance constitute different types of state. To speculate, if state performances are dominant and exclusive, as in Uzbekistan and Turkmenistan, then we can expect state practice to live up to this image with state violence and repression. If state performances are diverse and widely disregarded (the state effect doesn't take hold), then we may expect to see the kind of fracturing of political order that we saw in Tajikistan in the early 1990s and have seen in Kyrgyzstan since the early 2000s and, perhaps, in Xinjiang in recent years (see Béller-Hann, this volume). Such propositions suggest directions in the study of Central Asian states that are arguably much more promising than analyses of state weakness that predict state failure or demand generic paths of state-building.

Inside/Outside: The Globality of the State

This conception of the state as constituted not by its form but by its performance leads to an important question of definition: where do the boundaries of the state lie? To accept that all that lies within official national boundaries is under the state while all that lies beyond is not is to fall victim to "methodological nationalism" (Wimmer and Glick Schiller 2002). Such a misstep constitutes what we might call the dichotomy of territoriality, where all space can be divided into that which is inside or outside the state. This is the foundational myth of international relations—the so-called "myth of 1648" (Teschke 2003)—as the national/international became the inside/outside of politics (Walker 1993). The Peace of Westphalia (of 1648), which concluded the Thirty Years War, is often attributed as the genesis of this crucial division that not only determines inside and outside but hierarchy and anarchy, peace and war. This is a powerful myth that both helps constitute the state in practice and hinders our study of its emergence, formation, and mutability. "Failed states"—states that fail to maintain an inside/outside boundary—are often dismissed as anarchical and war-torn spaces where external actors compete for influence in order to maximize their own security. However, states that are neither fully sovereign (Northern Cyprus, Transdniestr, Kosovo), nor hierarchically organized (Switzerland, Bosnia, Central African Republic), nor practically peaceful (Mexico, Colombia, Russia) are very much a part of global politics and seem to avoid the failure that is often forecast. In fact, it is the very universality of the state form in global politics that has spawned academic concepts of "quasi-states" (Jackson 1990), "phantom states" (ICG 2007), "informal states" (Isachenko 2010), and "denationalized states" (Sassen 2006). It has also produced the inexorable emergence of state forms, despite significant opposition to formal recognition of statehood, in the polities (unrecognized states) of Kosovo, Palestine, Somaliland, and Transdniestr Moldovan Republic to name but a few (Isachenko 2010). It is the contention of this final section of the paper that such states survive, in part, because they are, legally or illegally, politically and economically, networked into global politics as a consequence of their late decolonization (Dannreuther 2007). It is these networks that allow the performance of statehood and the provision of resources to fulfill the functions of government. In short, we must consider the globality of the state.

The Globally Assembled State

Much literature on global governance and globalization has framed its questions in terms of the emergence of trans- or supranational institutions that are authoritative over the state.[8] This literature is hamstrung by a spatio-hierarchical conception of the global as being trans- or supranational, that is, above the state.[9] The concept of "global assemblages" (Ong and Collier 2005; Sassen 2006) offers a way forward to assess this relationship. These assemblages are global forms where new territorializations, authorities, and rights emerge from "new material, collective and discursive relationships" (Ong and Collier 2005, 4) that "begin to escape the grip of national institutional frames" (Sassen 2008, 61).[10] Thus we have the co-existence, imbrication, and even integration of new and old types of ordering—global networks that incorporate the national state actors and patterns of interstate relations that emerged and evolved in Europe and were spread across the world through decolonization. George Lawson, paraphrasing Saskia Sassen, argues, "globalization, even as it adds to the sense of decreasing state capacity, must still be shaped, channeled and enabled by institutions and networks which are rooted in the nation state" (2008, 68).

By this account, globalization is not a teleological process toward some kind of supranational system of world government or, at least, global governance. Rather it is an open-ended process that has shifted the character of statehood to such an extent that "we can no longer speak of 'the' state, and hence of 'the' national state versus 'the' global order" (Sassen 2008, 72). Importantly, in terms of thinking about statehood, "global forms are limited or delimited by specific technical infrastructures, administrative apparatuses, or value regimes, not by the vagaries of the social and cultural field" (Sassen 2006, 11). For example, technical infrastructures include complex tolling arrangements and financial audits. Administrative apparatuses include the procedural systems of the high court in London. Value regimes include the legal norms of international arbitration (Heathershaw 2011). As global forms are assembled and reassembled so too is the nature of statehood shaped and reshaped as the state-system partially works through these technologies, apparatuses, and regimes.

Sassen (2006, 2) characterizes this process as "denationalization." This term should neither be equated with privatization nor the subjugation of the state by regional or global organizations. Although both private and global actors play a greater role, the state remains a powerful medium of global politics and economics. It is not eroded but transformed via its increased adoption of private and global technologies, policies, and ethics. Sassen notes that global assemblages are "instantiations of the global, which are in good part structured inside the national"; they emerge as "state institutions reorient their particular policy work or, more broadly, state agendas toward the requirements of the global economy" (2006, 2, 22). In short, they "denationalize what has been constructed as national but do not necessarily make this evident" (2006, 2). Both Tajikistan's acceptance of an Ernst & Young audit of its National Bank (in 2008) and the jurisdiction of the London Court of International Arbitration over its state-owned aluminum company TALCO (2006–2008; see Heathershaw 2011) are examples of the state's increasingly global orientation after a Soviet era in which it was explicitly cut off from the global market. I will argue below that the position of Tajikistan amidst these global assemblages is fundamentally different to the core-periphery relations of Soviet times. These assemblages are not the relatively stable and hierarchical relationships of a command economy but are the product of networks that are very much subject to the uncertainty and innovations of the market (Heathershaw 2011).

Globalizing Local Government Law in Tajikistan

Another example of global performance is Tajikistan's 2009 Law on Self-Governance in a Town or Township (*Konuni Jumhurii Tojikiston "Dar Borai Makomoti Khudidorakunii Shahrak va Dehot"* [USAID 2009]). The Law on Self-

Governance was planned by international donors in Tajikistan for many years after they began work on decentralization in the early 2000s following the civil war of the 1990s. The U.S. Agency for International Development's (USAID) Tajikistan Local Government Initiative (LGI) subcontracted American NGO partners to work on legal reform. In March 2003, the Urban Institute, under LGI Phase II, published an analysis of Tajikistan's local governance in terms of European Charter of Local Self-Government standards and with comparisons to other "transitional states"—Albania, Slovakia, and Kyrgyzstan (Urban Institute 2003). A draft of a new law was reached in 2004 under the auspices of USAID.[11] Since that time, donors and their international NGO partners continued to press the government for the adoption of a new law consistent with the European Charter. USAID launched the Local Governance and Citizen Participation (LGCP) Project in 2006 as a successor to LGI. One staff member noted that "one of the milestones under the LGCP Project [was] the number of EU Charter articles adopted [in the final law]." The overall aim of this process was to strengthen the Jamoat as a fiscally and politically decentralized organ of local government. Despite tens of millions of dollars spent on self-governance and decentralization programs in Tajikistan (see Heathershaw 2009a, 147–148), a much-lauded Public Administration Reform Strategy (of March 2006), and numerous waves of advocacy in the form of USAID-supported study tours to Hungary, Poland, Slovakia, Albania, Croatia, and Latvia, by 2009 a USAID-funded study admitted that little had changed in the legal and practical form of local government in Tajikistan since 2003 (Conway 2009, 1).

However, just a few months later, a new law was finally in place. The Law on Self-Governance that was passed on June 23, 2009 is composed of forty-seven articles and provides permanent legal status to the Jamoat councils and for the election of Jamoat Chairs (article 19). It also stipulates and defines the financial autonomy of Jamoats (article 45). Under the previous law, Jamoat heads (*raisi Jamoat*) were appointed by regional officials who were themselves appointed by the president. Moreover, all local taxation was transferred upward while budgets were decided in regional centers. Although the new law does not inaugurate a complete system of fiscal decentralization, it does enable various local sources of income and legalize local budgetary management (article 26). Any reasonable legal analysis would conclude that the new law represents a dramatic shift toward a formally more open and accountable local government. However, political analysis does not address merely this formal outcome but the conditions and processes that brought about this sea change. A study of the legal documents, donor reports, and interviews with three employees of the USAID's LGCP Project provides some rough answers to these questions.

In late 2008 progress on the new law began to gain some momentum. Central to the process was the Presidential Working Group (PWG) on local self-government. An international Donor Coordination Group (DCG), chaired by USAID, followed the progress of the PWG and made specific proposals for changes to the law. The PWG, which had been established in 2003–2004, became more active and responsive to donor initiatives again in 2008–2009, indicating a willingness in the presidential administration to move on the issue. Members of the PWG gathered with experts from former Soviet states and USAID-financed consultants to redraft the law on a two-day legislative retreat in February 2009. According to an LGCP staff member, while a few parliamentarians and members of Jamoat councils were present, the most important actors in this redrafting were "participants of Presidential Working Group, project lawyers and consultants," specifically Dustmurod Murodov, head of the legal department of the presidential administration; Liliya Leskova, an expert from Kazakhstan; and Richard Winnie, an American consultant. Another LGCP staff member confirms that Winnie "flew in for the two-day working conference and quietly reshuffled some of the articles." This reordering of the articles was based on a law that Winnie had helped draft in Armenia and was retained in the final version. While the roles of the presidential administration and donor organizations were primary, parliament was, at best, a secondary actor, and civil society and interest groups were absent. The role of parliament is summarized in the following exchange with the same LGCP staff member.

> Heathershaw: How much, if any, of the formulation and negotiation of the new law took place within parliament?
>
> LGCP staff member: The chairman of the parliamentary committee on state structure and local self-governance participated at the retreat and mostly he was the person at the parliament who defended the law and explained the novelties included to the law. Regarding the negotiation of the law, if the political will exists the most and significant part of the law will be approved. (Interview with LGCP staff member, September 28, 2010)

Another LGCP staff member confirmed that the role of parliament was that of approval, noting that parliament "did not get to the point" where it drafted or reviewed the legislation. In keeping with political practice in Tajikistan, this approval is typically automatic, as parliament is entirely subservient to the president.

The passing of the Law on Self-Governance indicates neither a shift to liberal reform in Tajikistan nor the complete subservience of Tajikistan to international donors. This is because, on the one hand, the law has not coincided with other advances in liberal reform and because, on the other hand, the law was passed through Tajikistani state institutions and its implementation is the sole responsibility of the government of Tajikistan. "In practice," one interviewee noted, "these [self-government] bodies are not independent from the government; they have no financial capacity to be independent." Two of the three interviewees noted that a likely explanation for the government's agreement to the demands of donors to pass the law was a response to the financial scandals involving the misappropriation of international donor assistance, which came to light in 2008. "I think the outcomes of the global financial crisis gave the government of Tajikistan an incentive to move forward with the law and get assistance from IMF and the World Bank institutions," one LGCP staff member noted. "Among all changes they had to make, they found that [the Law on Self-Governance] is the less threatening change." The law's passage constitutes the establishment of a new political form (the Law on Self-Governance) through a global process that privileges executive power (in marked contrast to the ostensible meaning of "self-governance"). In short, we have the triumph of performance over content.

This triumph of performance (an ostensibly national legislative process) over content of local government (actual decentralization) indicates the globality of the Tajikistani state. In the success story that was written to publicize the donor's achievement it is claimed that the initiative for the law came from Tajikistan's government and that the assistance provided was technical rather than political. "The leadership [of Tajikistan]," notes USAID (2009), "recognized that political restructuring adhering to the transparent, accountable democratic process and the rule of law is essential if local governments are to have the political and financial powers required to respond well to the needs of citizens." This portrayal contains two grains of truth. Firstly, it is correct that the president could have refused to cooperate and vetoed the law. Secondly, it is also correct that the form of government envisioned in the law would provide for far greater transparency and accountability if it were adopted in a political context where such discourses and practices were already widespread. That the content of politics is not of that kind in Tajikistan is the crucial matter that is completely overlooked by the USAID success story but readily acknowledged by those working for the project itself in the private interviews cited above. The Law on Self-Governance, which was adopted, came about through a globalized and denationalized process. However, this process went through the state, particularly the presidential administration, and is quite consistent with how laws are made and the country is governed. Globalized assemblages, including audit procedures, project implementation units, PWGs, and DCGs, are intrinsic to law making in contemporary Central Asian and other postcolonial states. One outcome of globalization, when understood in these terms, is the empowerment of the state's executive apparatus, which works behind closed doors with international donor organizations and to the detriment of the public sphere.

The Local Government Law and TALCO examples are by no means exceptional. Other examples of such global political-economic and technical assemblages are found in border management, dialogue exercises (see above), and elections (Heathershaw 2009b; Ismailbekova, this volume). Indeed, few areas of government in Tajikistan and similarly open Central Asian states (Afghanistan, Kazakhstan, and Kyrgyzstan)[12] are not subject to specialized technical assemblages that emerge from regional or global spaces. One analysis by two Tajikistani legal scholars found that all Tajikistani laws adopted between 1991 and 2010 were modeled on laws drafted in Russia or another Central Asian state and/or drafted by consultants employed by international organizations with the exception of a single statute: the law on traditions and festivities. As state law is a republican political form that is deemed central to the idealized modern social contract between a state and its citizens, it is instructive to consider the shallow national roots and considerable transnational entwinements of many of the state laws adopted in Central Asian states since 1991. Moreover, while local or national government formally enacts laws, it is a marker of processes of colonization and decolonization that few if any of the laws on the statute books in Central Asian states are the product of a national bargaining process between executives, parliaments, and interest groups.

Dismissing Central Asian states as quantitatively weak is to disregard the performative processes by which they are qualitatively transformed to become globalized polities with relatively strong executives. Equally, to consider these states as captured by clans, regional factions, or other nationally confined networks misses the importance of the state form as the medium for global, national, and local relations. This is a complex political reality. The porosity of the boundaries between state and society, idea and system, and inside and outside are indeed clues to the nature of the phenomenon in question. Central Asian states, as the editors of the volume argue, are political forms constituted through performances, which have various dimensions. Ethno-national artistic forms, raw violence, or rather more banal distributions of basic public goods may be part of the local and national dimensions of state performance. But it is via international and transnational performances that states become institutional structures through which global economic and political networks flow. It is through these technocratic, neo-liberal performances that state actors maintain commissary powers to enable and disable such flows. In this sense, international donors, foreign governments, and multi-national businesses are complicit in sustaining Central Asia's "weak states."

There is analytical value in adopting the conceptual resources of performance and globalization to study the Central Asian state. Global performance states also have local and national lives. Such states enable their official representatives to act instrumentally for their particular interests but in the name of the state. In terms of the concept of the global performance state, the virtual "dialogue exercises" of peace-building, border management, or law making are not just epiphenomenal but constitute the state. In this sense it is in conflicts over these performances that state politics takes place. There is a research agenda here to explore the multiple scales of Central Asian state performance: local, national, *and* global.

Notes

1. See Beyer, this volume.

2. According to World Bank data, Tajikistan is officially the world's most remittance-dependent country. In 2009, 35% of GDP was composed of remittances (World Bank 2011, 14).

3. The moniker "global" here is used not to indicate that Central Asian states are linked to all corners of the globe but to suggest that their connections include both international and transnational relations and are not limited to the Central Asian or post-Soviet regions.

4. Parts of this section are developed from Heathershaw (2009b).

5. Interview, Stephanie Wheeler, IREX, Dushanbe, February 23, 2005.

6. Accounts of OSCE, UNTOP, and party representatives, June 2005.

7. *Jumhuriyat*, no. 59, May 28, 2005.

8. Parts of this section are developed from Heathershaw (2011).

9. For the debate between globalists and skeptics, see Held and McGrew (2003); for critiques of the spatio-hierarchical premises of the globalization debate, see Brenner (1999); Ferguson and Gupta (2002).

10. Sassen uses "Territory, Authority, Rights" (TAR) as the criteria of assessment while Ong and Collier speak of territorialization. I prefer the process noun ("territorialization") over the object noun ("territory") because it allows us to consider incomplete processes of making and remaking territories as much as the emergence of new territories themselves (see Sassen 2006; Ong and Collier 2006). Sassen speaks of the global city and Special Economic Zones as examples of new territories made under globalization as well as "emergent institutionalizations of territory that unsettle the national encasement of territory" (see Sassen 2008, 64). In the case of Tajikistan we see new territorializations and spatializations occurring under the dynamics of land reform and seasonal labor migration networks. See also Heathershaw (2009a). For a study of the early Soviet territorialization of Tajikistan, see Kassymbekova (2011).

11. The following analysis is supported by data and quotes from interviews with several employees at the LGCP conducted by phone and e-mail between August and September 2010.

12. Turkmenistan and Uzbekistan would seem to be less appropriate as examples of global performance states than Kazakhstan (high levels of global economic relations), Kyrgyzstan (high levels of international political and technical assistance), Tajikistan

(high levels of international intervention and subsequently assistance), and Afghanistan (very high levels of international intervention).

References

Abrams, Philip 1988. "Notes on the Difficulty of Studying the State." *Journal of Historical Sociology* 1: 58–89.

Adams, Laura. 2008. "Globalization, Universalism and Cultural Form." *Comparative Studies in Society and History* 50, no. 3: 614–640.

———. 2010. *The Spectacular State: Culture and Identity in Uzbekistan*. Durham, N.C.: Duke University Press.

Allison, Roy. 2008. "Virtual Regionalism, Regional Structures and Regime Security in Central Asia." *Central Asian Survey* 27, no. 2: 185–202.

Baudrillard, Jean. 1983. *Simulations*. New York: Semiotext[e].

Beissinger, Mark R., and Crawford Young, eds. 2002. *Beyond State Crisis: Post-Colonial Africa and Post-Soviet Eurasia in Comparative Perspective*. Baltimore: John Hopkins University Press.

Beyer, Judith. 2009. "According to *Salt*: An Ethnography of Customary Law in Talas, Kyrgyzstan." PhD diss., Martin-Luther-University, Halle/Wittenberg.

Bichsel, Christine. 2009. *Conflict Transformation in Central Asia: Irrigation Disputes in the Ferghana Valley*. London: Routledge.

Brenner, Neil. 1999. "Beyond State-Centrism? Space, Territoriality, and Geographical Scale in Globalization Studies." *Theory and Society* 28: 39–78

Burnham, Peter. 2005. "The State." In *The Oxford Concise Dictionary of Politics*, edited by Ian McLean and Alistair McMillan, 512. Oxford: Oxford University Press.

Butler, Judith. 1997. *Excitable Speech: A Politics of the Performative*. London: Routledge.

Buzan, Barry, Ole Waever, and Jaap De Wilde, eds. 1998. *Security: A New Framework for Analysis*. Boulder, Colo.: Lynne Rienner.

Chabal, Patrick, and Daloz, Jean-Pascal. 1999. *Africa Works: Disorder as Political Instrument*. Bloomington: Indiana University Press.

Chalfin, Brenda. 2001. "Working the Border: Constructing Sovereignty in the Context of Liberalism." *Political and Legal Anthropology Review* 24, no. 1: 197–224.

Collins, Kathleen. 2006. *Clan Politics and Regime Transition in Central Asia: Its Impact in Regime Transformation*. Cambridge: Cambridge University Press.

Conway, Francis. 2009. "Local Governance and Citizen Participation Program in Tajikistan: Sub-National Government Assessment—2009." Dushanbe, Tajikistan: USAID.

Dannreuther, Roland. 2007. "War and Insecurity: Legacies of Northern and Southern State Formation." *Review of International Studies* 33: 307–326.

Der Derian, James. 1994. "Simulation: The Highest Stage of Capitalism?" In *Baudrillard: A Critical Reader*, edited by Douglas Kellner, 189–207. Oxford: Blackwell.

———. 2001. *Virtuous War: Mapping the Military-Industrial-Media-Entertainment Network*. Boulder, Colo.: Westview.

Disch, Lisa. 1999. "Review: Judith Butler and the Politics of the Performative." *Political Theory* 27, no. 4: 545–559.

European Commission. 2005. "EU Programme Management Office for Central Asia Border Management and Drug Control (BOMCA/CADAP): Response of the International Community to Assist the Government of Tajikistan on the Tajik-Afghan Border." Meeting minutes, February 15–16.

Ferguson, James, and Akhil Gupta. 2002. "Spatializing States: Toward an Ethnography of Neoliberal Governmentality." *American Ethnologist* 29: 981–1002.

Hansen, Thomas Blom, and Finn Stepputat, eds. 2001. *States of Imagination: Ethnographic Explorations of the Postcolonial State.* Durham, N.C.: Duke University Press.

Heathershaw, John. 2009a. *Post-Conflict Tajikistan: The Politics of Peacebuilding and the Emergence of Legitimate Order.* London: Routledge

———. 2009b. "Tajikistan's Virtual Politics of Peace." *Europe-Asia Studies* 61, no. 7: 1315–1336.

———. 2011. "Tajikistan Amidst Globalization: State Failure or State Transformation?" *Central Asian Survey* 30, no. 1: 147–168.

Held, David, and Anthony McGrew, eds. 2003. *The Global Transformations Reader: An Introduction to the Globalization Debate,* 2nd ed. Cambridge: Polity

International Crisis Group (ICG). 2007. *Central African Republic: Anatomy of a Phantom State.* Nairobi/Brussels: International Crisis Group, December 13.

———. 2009. *Tajikistan: on the Road to Failure.* Dushanbe, Tajikistan: International Crisis Group, February 12.

Isachenko, Daria. 2009. "'Symptoms' of Democracy in Transdniestria." *Security and Peace* 27, no. 2: 97–101.

———. 2010. "The Making of Informal States: Statebuilding in Northern Cyprus and Transdniestria." PhD diss., Humboldt University of Berlin.

Ismailbekova, Aksana. 2011. "The Native Son and Blood Ties: Kinship and Poetics of Patronage in Rural Kyrgyzstan." PhD diss., Martin-Luther-University, Halle/Wittenberg.

Jackson, Richard H. 1990. *Quasi-states: Sovereignty, International Relations, and the Third World.* Cambridge: Cambridge University Press.

Jones Luong, Pauline. 2002. *Institutional Change and Political Continuity in Post-Soviet Central Asia: Power, Perceptions, and Pacts.* Cambridge: Cambridge University Press.

———, ed. 2004. *The Transformation of Central Asia: States and Societies from Soviet Rule to Independence.* London: Cornell University Press.

Kassymbekova, Botagoz. 2011. "Humans as Territory: Forced Resettlement and the Making of Soviet Tajikistan, 1920–38." *Central Asian Survey* 30, nos. 3–4: 349–370.

Lavrakas, Tomas A., ed. 2004. *Tajikistan: A Guide to the 2005 Parliamentary Elections.* Geneva: Cimera.

Lawson, George. 2008. "Book Review of: Sassen, Saskia. Territory, Authority, Rights: From Medieval to Global Assemblages." *Democratiya* 8: 67–73.

Lewis, D. 2008a. *The Temptations of Tyranny in Central Asia.* London: Hurst & Co.

———. 2008b. "The Dynamics of Regime Change: Domestic and International Factors in the 'Tulip Revolution.'" *Central Asian Survey* 27, no. 3: 265–277.

Malekzade, J. 2005. Transcribed interview with the author, May 10.

Marat, Erica. 2006. "Impact of Drug Trade and Organised Crime on State Functioning in Kyrgyzstan and Tajikistan." *China and Eurasia Forum Quarterly* 4, no. 1: 93–111.

March, Andrew F. 2003. "State Ideology and the Legitimation of Authoritarianism: The Case of Post-Soviet Uzbekistan." *Journal of Political Ideologies* 8, no. 2: 209–232.

McMann, Kelly. 2004. "The Civic Realm in Kyrgyzstan: Soviet Economic Legacies and Activists' Expectations." In *The Transformation of Central Asia: States and Societies from Soviet Rule to Independence,* edited by Pauline Jones Luong, 213–245. London: Cornell University Press.

Megoran, Nick. 2008. "Framing Andijon, Narrating the Nation: Islam Karimov's Account of the Events of 13 May 2005." *Central Asian Survey* 27, no. 1: 15–31.

Migdal, Joel S. 1994. "The State in Society: An Approach to Struggles for Domination," In *State Power and Social Forces: Domination and Transformation in the Third World,* edited by Joel S. Migdal et al., 7–34. Cambridge: Cambridge University Press.

Mitchell, Timothy. 1999. "Society, Economy and the State Effect." In *State/Culture: State Formation after the Cultural Turn,* edited by G. Steinmetz, 76–97. Ithaca, N.Y.: Cornell University Press.

Navaro-Yashin, Yael. 2002. *Faces of the State: Secularism and Public Life in Turkey.* Princeton, N.J.: Princeton University Press.

Nourzhanov, Kiril. 2005. "Saviours of the Nation or Robber Barons? Warlord Politics in Tajikistan." *Central Asian Survey* 24, no. 2: 109–130.

Ong, Aiwa, and Stephen J. Collier, eds. 2005. *Global Assemblages: Technology, Politics and Ethics as Anthropological Problems.* Oxford: Blackwell.

Radnitz, Scott. 2010. *Weapons of the Wealthy: Predatory Regimes and Elite-Led Protests in Central Asia.* Seattle: University of Washington Press.

Reeves, Madeleine. 2006. "States of Improvisation: Border-Making as Social Practice in the Ferghana Valley." Paper presented to the annual meeting of the Central Eurasian Studies Society, September 29.

———. 2008. "Border Work: An Ethnography of the State at Its Limits in the Ferghana Valley." PhD diss., University of Cambridge.

Rubin, Barnet R. 1998. "Russian Hegemony and State Breakdown in the Periphery." In *Post-Soviet Political Order: Conflict and State Building,* edited by Barnet R. Rubin and Jack Snyder, 128–161. New York: Routledge.

Sassen, Saskia. 2006. *Territory, Authority, Rights: From Medieval to Global Assemblages.* Princeton, N.J.: Princeton University Press.

———. 2008. "Neither Global nor National: Novel Assemblages of Territory, Authority and Rights." *Ethics and Global Politics,* 1, nos. 1–2: 61–79.

Schatz, Edward. 2004. *Modern Clan Politics: The Power of "Blood" in Kazakhstan and Beyond.* Seattle: University of Washington Press.

Scott, J. C. 1990. *Domination and the Arts of Resistance: Hidden Transcripts.* New Haven, Conn.: Yale University Press.

Sloterdijk, Peter. 1993. *Critique of Cynical Reason.* Minneapolis: University of Minnesota Press.

Sodiqov, Alexander. 2011. "Moscow Blackmails Dushanbe to Return to the Afghan Border." *Eurasia Daily Monitor,* 8, no. 158: no pagination.

Teschke, Benno. 2003. *The Myth of 1648: Class, Geopolitics, and the Making of Modern International Relations.* London: Verso.

Thompson, Chad. 2008. "Epistemologies of Independence: Technology and Empire in the Post-Soviet Borderlands." PhD diss., York University.

Ubaidulloyev, M. 2003. "Ukrepleniye Grazhdanskovo Obshestva v Tadzhikistane" [Strengthening civil society in Tajikistan]. In *The Political Discussion Club.* Dushanbe, Tajikistan: United Nations Tajikistan Office of Peace-building / National Association of Political Scientists of Tajikistan [UNTOP / NAPST].

Urban Institute. 2003. *Local Self-Government in Tajikistan Viewed through the Basic Characteristics of the European Charter.* [Report]. USAID: Tajikistan Local Government Initiative II.

United Nations Development Program (UNDP). 2005. Official transcript of conference, "Response of the International Community to Assist the Government of Tajikistan on the Tajik-Afghan Border," Dushanbe, Tajikistan, February 15–16, 2005, no pagination.

U.S. Agency for International Development (USAID). 2009. "Dar Borai Makomoti Khudidorakunii Shahrak va Dehot [Law on Self-Governance in a Town or Township]." Dushanbe, Tajikistan: USAID.

Wæver, Ole. 1995. "Securitization and Desecuritization." In *On Security,* edited by R.Lipschutz, 46–86. New York: Columbia University Press.

Walker, Robert J.B. 1993. *Inside / Outside: International Relations as Political Theory.* Cambridge: Cambridge University Press.

Weber, Cynthia. 1995. *Simulating Sovereignty: Intervention, the State and Symbolic Exchange.* Cambridge: Cambridge University Press.

Wilson, Andrew. 2005. *Virtual Politics: Faking Democracy in the Post-Soviet World.* London: Yale University Press.

Wimmer, Andreas, and Nina Glick Schiller. 2002. "Methodological Nationalism and Beyond: Nation-State Building, Migration and the Social Sciences." *Global Networks* 2, no. 4: 301–334.

World Bank. 2011. *Migration and Remittances Factbook 2011,* 2nd ed. Washington D.C.: World Bank. Available at: http: / / siteresources.worldbank.org / INTLAC / Resources / Factbook2011-Ebook.pdf (accessed February 12, 2012).

Yurchak, Alexei. 2006. *Everything Was Forever, Until It Was No More: The Last Soviet Generation.* Princeton, N.J.: Princeton University Press.

Zartman, William I. 1995. *Collapsed States: The Disintegration and Restoration of Legitimate Authority.* Boulder, Colo.: Lynne Rienner.

Žižek, Slavoj.1991. *The Sublime Object of Ideology.* London: Verso.

2. Dialogic Authority:

Kazakh *Aitys* Poets and Their Patrons

Eva-Marie Dubuisson

Sponsorship in the *Aitys* Tradition

In this chapter I describe a living poetic tradition in Central Asia: the form of *aitys* among Kazakhs in Kazakhstan, which is a staged verbal duel between two figures of *akhyn*, or poets.[1] Speaking as and for regions, kin, ancestors, and audiences, poets claim to voice "the truth of the Kazakh people."[2] *Aitys* poets not only present a positive and inclusive model of cultural belonging, but they also criticize government for its failure to support its citizens. *Aitys* comes from the Kazakh verb *aitysu* (to talk to each other). This form of poetry itself is a back-and-forth, a dialogue, and the relationship between poets and their sponsors, who are typically national- and regional-level politicians, is also a two-way street.[3]

In the case of *aitys* (as well as many other philanthropic and "cultural" projects in the region), cultural sponsors from the ranks of the country's political and economic elite have stepped forward with practical monetary support for the performance tradition. That form of cultural patronage is quite common both historically and currently (Levin 1996; Prior 2000). It is a component of "patronage politics" (McGlinchey 2008, 2009), a way in which individuals can establish and reaffirm their position: by being "visible" in the culturally legitimated "places" occupied by the powerful.[4] Cultural patronage is also a mechanism by which individuals located outside the networks of wealth and privilege operating at the top tiers of the economy (centralized under authoritarian rule in Central Asia) can substantiate and build up positions within kinship networks, communities, regions, and political parties.

The *aitys* tradition embodies an idealized "khan-like" form of Central Asian leadership, where a strong ruler makes himself available and accountable to the people he governs. The arguments and examples given here exemplify the paternalistic relationship of the state described by Morgan Liu (2005, 2012), which characterizes Central Asia more broadly and which is rightly understood as a legitimate alternative (or challenge) to "democratic reform" in the region. This alternate form of authority is also described by Judith Beyer in her ethnography of *aksakal* (venerated elder) leadership: Beyer notes that authority is not given but earned and enacted in relationships over time (see Beyer 2010, and Beyer, this volume).

A paternalistic form of authority is operative in the sphere of *aitys* poetry in the performative relation of poets to contemporary leaders and in the activity of the tradition's wealthy sponsors. Taken together, I describe these here as a dialogic form of leadership: performance and sponsorship presume precisely an ongoing conversation between poets and leaders, to which both sides are accountable. Dialogism entails co-performance (Madison 2005). By characterizing these as "dialogic," I also intentionally include the multiple layers of voice and experience brought into any given interactive exchange by social relationships and roles compounded through history (Bakhtin 1981).

Here I describe the concept of poets' voice as particularly valuable in the context of censorship under a repressive authoritarian regime, where other voices of criticism or dissent are actively silenced.[5] I explain how members of the economic and political elite, even from the innermost circles of power, can effectively collude with poets in their criticism of government: poets draw upon sponsors' economic and political capital in order to stage their performances, while sponsors draw from poets' cultural and historical legitimacy in front of "the people" they both serve.[6] While sponsorship contexts vary, I argue that *aitys* is most successful in maintaining a cultural and critical "voice" when sponsors collaborate with poets: together they can demand accountability from government leaders, they can enact a "life-changing dialogue" (Attinasi and Friedrich 1995).

The largest threat to this dialogic form of leadership and critique offered by *aitys* poets and sponsors stems from the fact that money is involved: poets might "sell out," and their voice would be nothing more than a sound box for sponsors' interests.[7] The process of sponsorship is itself an exercise in the simultaneous accumulation and expenditure of social capital. The more wealthy and popular the sponsor, the more successful and consequential the sponsorship projects can become. However, because there is often a wide gap in wealth between typical sponsors and their poet counterparts, there is always the risk that sponsors will not support poets' *own* words or voice but rather tell them what to say and pay them to say it. In the figure of the sponsor lies a threat that what should be a complex and intangible relationship will be reduced to a moment of capitalist exchange: buying the "commodity" of *aitys* for money.

Ideally, beyond flashy prizes and cash ceremonially awarded to winning poets, money should remain but a side aspect of the mutual relationship: while cash or goods are always involved, what is actually exchanged is a mutual form of legitimacy—not currency.[8] The fear or threat of sale has, indeed, become part of the discourse among *aitys* poets both in private conversation and in performances. Here I argue that the real value of *aitys*, in the eyes of its supporters, is the voice of the oral tradition as a whole, which embodies a positively valued Kazakh cultural identity as well as sociopolitical criticism. *Aitys* represents a positive medium of belonging as well as a pragmatic means of participation in a climate of repression, censorship, and political violence. The threat of "sale" for this poetic tradition metaphorically represents the removal of an alternate form of dialogic leadership, even as a potential.

From "Words" to "Voice": Creating a Dialogic Performance Context

Poets themselves draw a distinction between their words or phrases (*suzder*), and the concept of having a voice (*un*). From an analytic perspective, the relationship between an *akhyn* and his or her *suzder* correlates to that between an utterance and the person who "animates" or actively produces that utterance (Goffman 1981). Poets want for their words to be beautiful and powerful not just so that they themselves (or rather, their poetic personae) become famous, but rather so that the words are memorable, iterable. Words that are remembered will be repeated in contexts ranging far beyond that of the immediate performance and will have an impact within a broader social world. Poets can create *suzder* that will be part of the *un*, the voice, of the *aitys* tradition.

Poets' individual and collective goal is to influence their audiences, to give them information but to do so in a compelling way. Here "audiences" has a telescopic meaning. *Aitys*, as a traditional folkloric art of the peoples during the Soviet period, continues to be routinely staged in regional city theaters, which can usually house between 300 and 500 people. Over the last two decades, *aitys* has most often been filmed and televised on regional and national networks, reaching an in-home audience of thousands more. Those shows are sometimes even broadcast live. Text excerpts from the shows are also usually printed in the Kazakh language newspapers. Finally, the *aitys* community has expended funds to print DVDs of performances and books of poets' words, which have a limited circulation primarily in urban areas.

But typically, film and text renditions of *aitys* performances are heavily edited and even censored in these contexts. That is why the moment of live onstage performance becomes critical for poets in fulfilling their duty to their audience: "It's of course important to inform authorities in our country, because

[here] you can't criticize openly. But [poets] try, of course, try to say something important for the people. If people hear it, about the problems they think about, they're very satisfied—you can tell from their reaction." Reflecting on this point, the poet Dauletkere (originally from Mongolia but living in and representing Astana) told me he likes it when people recognize him. "It's a great pleasure because they don't just recognize you, it means they recognized your words, it means you can influence people toward something." But on whom and how can a poet's words have influence?

There is no question for poets that their words are dialogic, that in the course of performance they are not single "authors" (where "author" is defined as "someone who has selected the sentiments that are being expressed and the words in which they are encoded," Goffman 1981). At a basic level, *aitys* literally means "shared talk," and all poets know that the success of any given performance depends on their dialogue with an opponent. All poets have at least one mentor and a group of peers with whom they perform and practice regularly. If they are old enough, they also have students. This group necessarily contributes over time to the quality of poets' words and phrasing, and if possible, they are usually present when the poet performs.[9] Further, as the poets explain above, the audience plays a great role in the success or failure of performance—the audible level of vocal enthusiasm and clapping (or lack thereof) encourages or discourages poets.

At any one competition, several pairs of poets compete, each establishing anew relationships with their audience that may be successful or not. And within the context of any one competition, there are also other types of "words" spoken regularly: a head cultural organizer sits on stage with poets and functions as an MC, inviting poets to perform and often commenting on the performance. After the poets have all sung, a jury sitting within the audience judges them. A representative of the jury often stands to explain who has "won" the competition and to offer the reasoning behind that decision. At the end of each competition, all poets reassemble on stage and prizes are handed out to the top performers. Particular sponsors, who often give a small speech about local politics and cultural affairs to the audience, hand out prizes. Poetic personae, audiences, cultural organizers, juries, mentors/students, and sponsors are all participants in the dialogic framework of performance and have various roles within that frame: as speakers, hearers, and ratified listeners (cf. Goffman 1986).

There is another level at which *aitys* is dialogic: as a basic tenet of performance, poets must inhabit multiple social relationships—territorial, familial, historical. Poets always speak of and for a region; they are known and called by their first names and their region of origin. In order to *aitysu,* to speak with or against an opponent, poets must verbally establish a fictive kinship relationship. Poets also are always speaking as members of a particular maximal lineage group or tribe (*ru*);[10] these groups are also loosely territorially defined. Another type of ancestry that poets claim is a connection with the famous *akhyndar* (poets) or *batyrlar* (warriors) who also come from their region. This process of progressively inclusive naming and claiming forms a "people," voiced by poets, who then have the legitimate authority to confront contemporary Kazakh leaders.

At this point in the contemporary Kazakhstani tradition, which over the last decades has become a televised and published national performance network, the question is one of cost. Theaters must be rented, costumes and instruments provided, and cross-country travel and accommodation taken care of, not to mention substantial prizes obtained for competition winners. Poets themselves, who generally eschew the accumulation of wealth as antithetic to their social and artistic ideals, are not in a position to pay for any of this. Nor are the majority of their audience, who tend to be middle- to low-income families.

Today the *aitys* tradition, its cycles of learning and mentorship as well the performance frameworks it can create, is part of a broader political economy. The final relationships poets must cultivate, with their mentors and/or through the offices of cultural affairs, are with sponsors. By the time most poets are successful enough to make it to the national circuit they have almost always established a relationship with one or more local or regional sponsors—local politicians, rectors of universities, or prominent businessmen. These relationships are, by and large, some successful form of the patron poet ideal discussed hitherto.

On the national level, however, sponsorship becomes far more elite, and the relationship between poet and patron becomes more distant. Whereas in regional sponsorship relationships poets and patrons tend to meet frequently and socialize within the same cultural circles, on the national level the two figures may live in different regions and may rarely (or never) actually meet. The national circuit thus introduces a threatening dynamic: unfettered by mutual acquaintances and a personal accountability, the influence of elite organizer-sponsors will predominate. Sponsors' interests might overshadow a poet's relationship with his or her audience, as well as with some imagined "Kazakh people." This dynamic could ultimately undermine a poet's relationship to his or her own words and to the voice of the oral tradition as a whole. If *aitys* is commodified, it is ultimately "the people" who are left without a voice.

Sponsorship: Having a Social and Political Voice

"Voicelessness" is one of the harshest criticisms poets hurl at politicians, particularly seated senate members. What they mean is the practical inability to effect change—impotence. Few people or groups in Kazakhstan today are in a position to call attention to, let alone criticize, the authoritarian and centralizing government, and those who do are usually silenced. At the time of my research, there was an ongoing series of arrests and jailings of opposition politicians and journalists. Two former members of the president's government, turned outspoken opposition activists, were murdered in 2005 and 2006. The second of these killings was that of Altynbek Sarsenbayev, the former ambassador to Russia and former minister of communication, who advocated democratic reforms and who unsuccessfully attempted to privatize the state's monopoly of the country's media holdings.[11]

Poets are not in such a conspicuous position as Sarsenbayev was; nor are they demanding the degree of change that this opposition leader was. Poets perform as part of a historic and ongoing tradition. They are not seeking democratic revolution but rather simply accountability and attention from government. Poets must be "the people" in performance—their audiences, ancestors, and sponsors alike—so as to have the strongest position from which to launch criticism. It is far easier to silence a dissenting politician than a dissenting citizenry, especially when that citizenry embodies an idealized (and inclusive) Kazakh cultural identity and historical legitimacy. So long as the conditions of performance are maintained in a practical sense, so too will poets have the literal platform to accomplish those cultural and political ends: this depends directly on external sponsorship.

As described above, sponsors are typically in a position to advance their political careers, and thus they patronize *aitys* (and other social projects) in order to garner cultural legitimacy before their constituency. The relationship between poets and patrons is ideally one of mutual legitimation: both sides need the other to achieve their public persona and the political voice it affords.[12]

This vision of the relationship among people, poet, and patron (or politician) stems from a mythic history of the *aitys* tradition in which poets were tasked with mediating the relationship between wealthy patrons, like the khans of Central Asia's great khanates through the centuries. This is a critical point, because it is precisely this type of mutually informed and dependent leadership that is modeled by contemporary poet-patron relations and that poets further advocate as a model of leadership for the contemporary government of the Kazakhstani nation-state.

Khandai

Poets' demands for accountability are, in the performance framework, couched within the figurative frame of poets speaking as and for "the people" to their khan. The khanates are romanticized by *aitys* poets as a time when a strong and powerful leader was also responsible toward and listening to the populace under his stewardship. When successful sponsors are named or involved in poets' performances, the implicit message is that these men are, or have the potential to be, *Khandai,* khan-like. As I noted in the introduction, such leadership can and should be seen as characteristic of the region. Attention to paternalism at multiple levels reveals that the country and its regions do not function under a totalitarian regime. Rather, politics is a space where many forms of social authority (and attendant spheres of social relationships) jockey for recognition (cf. Jones-Luong 2004; Liu 2005; Beyer 2010; Gullette 2010).

One of the tradition's foremost sponsors during the years of my fieldwork (2003–2006) is archetypical of such a model of success. Having headed the presidential party OTAN for three years, and leading one of the country's powerful holding companies based in Almaty, Amangeldi Yermegeayev (hereafter A. Y.) himself echoes the mythical khanate framework of *aitys* performances and his own role therein. He praises poets for their wisdom, their meaningful words, their "open eyes," and their refusal to back down in the face of power. Congratulating poets for their "sharp" criticism of contemporary government, including his own party, A. Y. quotes a proverb: whips break the skin, but words break bones.

In an extended interview,[13] in order to explain his point of view, A. Y. shifted to a generalized historical frame:

> Before, the most important khan was Ablai Khan.[14] And in front of him was Bukhar Zhyrau, who could tell him what even his highest commanders and advisors could never say straightforwardly. Sometimes the words [Bukhar said] were unflattering, even hurtful. But [these words] were what the people were saying, so Ablai Khan had to accept them.

The mythology of Ablai Khan and Bukhar Zhyrau is well known in *aitys* circles—indeed, poets often related themselves to Bukhar Zhyrau when explaining to me how they saw their role with regard to society and power. Here their sponsor A. Y. is also likening himself to one of the khan's inner circle—a position at once privileged and restricted. While A. Y. is powerful, he also cannot tell his "boss," Kazakhstani president Nursultan Nazarbayev, directly if he disagrees. By telling his experience metaphorically through that of Bukhar Zhyrau, A. Y. tries to blur what is a real distinction between *any* patron-client and *this* particular politician-poet relationship into a mythic history with no distinction. He further locates this dynamic in culture, writ large: "Kazakhs never say anything straight out. They start to speak and turn things around [such that] if you listen to the middle of what's said, you wouldn't understand." So too in *aitys,* he explains, do poets create "a chain of words and thoughts from the beginning," comprehensible only in its entirety.

A. Y. at that time dissented from his boss in one fundamental way: he was a Kazakh nationalist. This meant that he felt Kazakh language and culture should be a priority in this still-developing state. His (Herderian) point of view was quite clear: "The spine of the nation is language. Language, culture, traditions—these are the center of the nation, not eye color, not territory. A Kazakh might live anywhere—even religion doesn't change it . . . [but] if you lose language you lose everything. For us Kazakhstanis, if we lose our language then we lose our people's government (*yel*)."[15]

At that point in the country's post-Soviet history, however, despite an initial nationalist platform in the immediate post-independence period, President Nazarbayev had by the mid-2000s increasingly begun to support an internationalist vision of the country, which by virtue of its wealth of natural resources could act as a power among Russia, China, Europe, and the United States. In a forward-looking and economically based model of state power, rather than wasting financial or human resources on traditional or "backward" linguistic or cultural forms like Kazakh, internationalist leaders advocated knowledge of Russian, English, or Turkish languages as a better indicator of outward-oriented or global, practical progress.[16]

Nationalist politicians like A. Y. found a relatively easy union with the tradition of *aitys,* as it is inherently a celebration of Kazakh language and culture. During the years 2004 and 2005, parliamentary and presidential election years, respectively, when the president's political party OTAN was advertising itself countrywide, A. Y.'s affiliation with the poetic tradition was a widely publicized move. While sponsorship monies came directly from his own pocket, at performances large banners proclaiming OTAN hung prominently around the theater, such that the actual figure of sponsor was ultimately blurred.

Aitys performances at that time were well attended in the major city of Almaty, where a series of scheduled performances ran for nearly six months in 2004 but were also televised on the country's national television station Xabar (News), a main arm of the media conglomerate controlled by the president's daughter, Dariga Nazarbaeva. When poets began to criticize leaders in those performances, even directly targeting the president, A. Y.'s prominent sponsorship and inclusion of OTAN had contributed to a confusing context in which it was not easy to simply stop poets from singing (though it should be noted that performances were disallowed at the actual time of elections in the fall).

The example of A. Y. shows that while sponsors and poets have their own agendas and ambitions, in nationalist contexts they can collude productively to promote Kazakh language, culture, and history. Poets could describe poor national stewardship as characteristic of particular leaders' continued Russo-hegemonic worldviews, which they could contrast directly with the positive example of A. Y. (Dubuisson 2010). In this formulation, while at some point money is transacted, actual finances are somewhat beside the point. The more important creation of this collusion is mutually legitimated cultural and political leaders—co-advocates of a specifically Kazakh polity-in-the-world.[17] It is precisely this form of leadership—at once attendant and dependent, taking the form of an ongoing dialogue, ambiguously public in its paternalism—that best exemplifies "khan-like" authority in Kazakhstan.

Many sponsors do not (or can not) fit so nicely into this collaborative mold. One particular problem is that, as sponsors do tend to be members of the wealthy and powerful elite, they may assume their position of power a priori rather than as a product of an ongoing relationship with poets or other cultural figures. It is this misrecognition that makes the sponsorship relationship fail. Each failed sponsorship relationship, however, calls to mind a basic truism: the *aitys* tradition cannot continue or grow without practical support. A lack of understanding sponsors seems to signify a lack of powerful individuals who value poetry for its own sake. Bad sponsorship is characterized by an overly commercial quality; in the following extended example, it is possible to see how the "sale" of the tradition stands as a broad metaphor for the devaluation of Kazakh culture and people.

Poetry? Or Piety?

In 2006, Zhursin Yerman, the head of the national *aitys* circuit, came forward with a new primary sponsor. It was to be Akh Orda (White Horde), a burgeoning pan-Islamic movement headed by the president's nephew Kairat Satypaldy, an individual clearly located within the country's top circles of power. When Yerman and Satypaldy initially met to discuss this financial backing, Satypaldy explained that he was opening offices of Akh Orda in every region of the country, and that he needed help spreading the message of the movement. *Aitys* poets were to be enlisted in that project: in performance they were supposed to discuss and share the tenets of the movement, primarily *imanshylyk* (piety). Akh Orda would host a two-day *aitys* competition in every region over the course of the year, paying for theater rental and poets' travel and accommodations and providing cash and other large prizes.[18]

In the months prior to this *aitys,* leaders of Akh Orda had established a regional office and, in an initial meeting with local religious leaders, had firmly established the movement's own presence and agenda regarding the upcoming *aitys* performance: poets who were to perform were clearly instructed to propagandize the goals, activities, and underlying principles of Akh Orda. The performances were judged by Akh Orda leaders and their friends in the community. Akh Orda had also done the great honor of sponsoring a *hadj* (pilgrimage to Mecca) for the head organizer of *aitys* Zhursin Yerman, six poets from around the country, and the elderly parents of Bakhytzhan Ospanov, head of Akh Orda's regional chapter in Shimkent.

Ospanov referred to the task of his representation as *politika* (politics). The religious movement was quite transparently laying the groundwork to become a political party in the next few years, in order to prop up Satypaldy's possible ascension to the presidency after the end of Nazabayev's last term. Thus at the time, Akh Orda was actively pushing its philanthropy and piety message across the country, seeking to insinuate itself firmly in Kazakh life.

Akh Orda's focus on religion backfired in *aitys* performances in Shimkent, even though that area (particularly the city of Turkestan) is widely recognized to be a spiritual center for Kazakhs. The Akh Orda *aityses* were, in the opinion of audience members I interviewed, very preachy and less political than the form usually allowed. I attended two days of performances, ranging from three to six hours, and sat next to a large elderly woman named Mira Apai, who kept me company and fed me candies. She and her husband had traveled three hours by bus to attend, having saved money from the sale of *kymyz* (fermented horse's milk) on the roadside in their village. At the end of it all, she seemed deflated. I asked her what she'd thought. "I don't know," she said, "of course it's nice to see our culture and our tradition, but these . . . all they did was sing about piety. It wasn't a real *aitys*."

It is important to note that while a majority of Kazakhs would identify as Muslim, that category is a cultural one as much as a religious designation. Kazakh Muslim identity is largely centered on family and the figurative "hearth" of the home, and it includes ancestor reverence as well as a relationship with the natural world and its elements.[19] This culture tends to be inclusive and flexible, rather than orthodox, and so preaching about "correct" Islamic morals and virtues rubbed many audience members the wrong way. Further, it was culturally inappropriate that poets, rather than mullahs or muftis, were taking on the role of religious advisors, especially in the given performance genre of *Zhek-pe-zhek* (one on one), which is designed to encourage social and political commentary as well as interpersonal rivalry.

Poets in the region were conflicted about the role of Akh Orda and the type of sponsorship it represented. One of the region's most successful and well known poets, Karima, talked to me at length about the fraught situation in which contemporary poets find themselves. I asked her to compare what goes on today with the atmosphere when she first started, in the late 1980s. Answering me, she was clearly frustrated:

> In those times *aityses* weren't bad, they were good. Then in the best people's *aitys* performances there were poets like Aselhan and Taushen. They have their own beautiful words, which people still remember. They were stars of their time. In those times, what I really liked was that there wasn't any kind of bartering or unfairness—whoever had the fastest horse in the race won. But today [the prizes are] cars, they say that you can't stand your ground in the face of wealth, and so like that [poets are] not shy of their elders, they don't give you the road. As if winning that car was

> the meaning for them. As if it all ends in this life. They do everything for the car. And here's how they're forgetting about art, forgetting why they came. This isn't *aitys* but some kind of bargaining. In those times it wasn't like this. In those times prizes were like tea services, rugs. The most expensive prize was a TV. Now even students wouldn't take a TV. And then they gave us certificates. We're up to here in that kind of thing! Property has ruined *aitys.*[20]

The reason that the prize issue is such a sticking point for Karima and other poets is that prizes are provided by sponsors—they come hand in hand. But as was the case with the *Akh Orda aitys* I saw, sponsors and their important colleagues and friends are usually also the ones who sit on the jury to judge *aitys* competitions, so obviously those poets who best represent sponsors' goals will win sponsors' cars, money, and other prizes. Karima noted that sometimes a private sponsorship relationship develops, and it does happen that one sponsor can buy off an entire competition such that his or her poet will win. However, later in our conversation she gave a contradictory point of view, reflecting that, just because *Akh Orda* spent big money on prizes, even if all that money is called in from those higher up in the president's administration (*Nazarbayevting khozghalysy*), perhaps it is not inherently bad. As long as each poet considers equally his or her financial situation and "moral jaw" (*moraldykh zhaghy*), Karima ultimately decided, she can support them.

Karima and Marzhan: *Aitys* Is Not for Sale

Karima's frustration came out not just in her reflections on the situation but in her next *aitys* performance as well. It so happened that a little over a month after the performance sponsored by *Akh Orda,* the city government held a regularly scheduled *aitys* in honor of the Kazakh New Year, *Nauryz.* That is, the *aitys* was funded by public (government) sponsorship, where the bulk of the cost came out of the regional budget. The state ministry of culture typically allocates enough funds to sponsor one *aitys* in each of the country's regions per year. Zhursin Yerman and his elite cadre of sponsors did not participate in this *aitys,* which meant that the only extra prizes were small in nature and given to poets personally by local community leaders.

In that second *aitys,* Karima met her friend and colleague Marzhan in performance. The MC for the event was Karima's mentor, Sabit Agha, who is also the director of the school where Karima teaches young *aitys* students. Marzhan is a professor of Kazakh literature at the local university and sometimes lectures at the school. These two women are widely known and respected pillars of the regional cultural community. They are also good friends. While Karima is sometimes more humorous or daring in her performances, Marzhan is quite serious. Her dignified persona (and deep voice) command attention from her audiences and students alike. She considers it her priority as a poet to support and promote respect for the Kazakh language and traditions such as piety and respect for elders.[21]

Marzhan had recently returned from an Akh Orda–sponsored *aitys* in the far southwestern city of Aktau, Mangystau oblast' (region). While she certainly considers herself to be religious, Marzhan noted that she was not *hadjy* (someone who has taken the pilgrimage to Mecca) like many of her opponents, and so she prepared for the *aitys* by reading and memorizing passages from the Koran. The strategy apparently worked, as Marzhan took first place in the competition and returned home with one million Kazakh tenge (roughly US$8,000).

The New Year's *aitys* between Marzhan and Karima was largely cordial, until the last turn, which was Karima's, when she accuses her fellow poet of selling out. I would emphasize here that because these two are friends and collaborators, it is most likely that this performance was planned or anticipated in some way by both. Further, Karima here is using the figure of Marzhan to stand in as a general referent for any poet who may start to sacrifice poetic virtue for monetary value (more below). While winning poets almost always receive cash prizes, the problem was that Akh Orda's prize was far too large, giving Karima an opportunity to comment on its metaphoric inappropriateness and the general situation:

Karima Akhyn:

Saudalap bittik zherdi de,	*The riches of the land are appraised for sale,*
saudalap bittik turdi de	*the riches of* tur *are appraised for sale.*
Akhyndykhty endi saudalap	*So then poet-ness is being appraised—*
bolyp khalmaiykh sorgha endi.	*let's stop this grief!*
önerding zholy tar bolmai,	*The path of art will not be narrow,*
tonyghymyz lailanbai	*our clarity will not be muddied.*
Akhikhat bolsyn aitysta	*Let there be truth, like authority*
tarazygha teng saghandai.	*hidden in aitys.*
Laghynetten aulakh bolaiykh,	*Let's be cursed further,*
adiletten syidy alghandai	*confusion just takes away from fairness.*
Arynyz taza bop khalsyn	*Let honor keep clean,*
bes kündik myna zhalghandai	*this kind of unity, five times a day.*
Arzan sözge barmaityn Marzhan dese	*Let Marzhan not go to cheap words.*
Marzhansyn	*You, Marzhan,*
baskhany bilmeimin	*I don't know another one;*
men ushin baghasy biik zanggharsyn	*for me you are tall, steeped in value.*

arkhasynda aitystyng batys	*You have gone supported to the east and*
shyghys barghansaiyn	*west of* aitys.
Ongtustikke de barghansaiyn	*And to the south you also went.*
on segiz zhyl degende milliondy da alghansyn	*Your wish for eighteen years, you took a million.*
Sol millionnyng endi sen tym bolmasa	*But it is not to be entirely your million—*
zhartysyn	*you are only half.*
Aluan bizge khamdarsyn	*Different to us you are prepared,*
Yrysty bolsyn singlinge	*may you be happy within yourself.*
Zhoghysty bolsyn singlinge	*May you become close quickly with your younger sister.*
Isgilik senen zholgha alsyn	*Take a sacred path, [to where]*
Engbegindi baghalap	*your work is worth something.*
zholdasyn deimin angharsyn	*You are a friend, I say, a ravine—*
ongtustikting osyndai	*your south is like that.*
Akhkhydai khos khyzday	*Girls like swans, like sown fields*
Tanti etip yel zhortty	*satisfy the people's country.*
Halykhty bugin tang khaldyrtsyn	*It is the people you are making blossom today.*
Zhuldyzymyzdyng saulesi ol	*The light of our stars,*
khyzdarymyzgha zhalghansyn	*you join to our girls.*
Halykhtan bolyp khoshemet	*May there be respect from the people,*
Zholymyz bizding ong bolsyn.	*may our road be the right one.*[22]

Partly due to time constraints, Sabit Agha stopped their duel at this point and so Marzhan was literally unable to answer Karima. Rather, in this case, Sabit himself had the last word, because as Karima finished singing, she was looking not at Marzhan or at the audience but directly at him. Sabit picked up the cue, and, after the audience finished wildly applauding, affirmed that Karima's words were right, that "we" should never bargain for our art. Their collusion trumped Marzhan, and in fact Karima did win.

Karima's *aitys* is multi-layered. At broad strokes she is describing the meaning of what *aitys* does for "the people." She uses several different terms to name the latter—*yel* (country), *zhort* (public), *halykh* (people and / or nationality), and *biz* (us). Karima names the elements of this world that belong in this nation: land, poetry, cleanliness, respect, fairness, honor, and unity. One of the elements Karima plays with in her poem is the idea of *baghy* (value). In the first four lines of song, she uses the term to appraise (1) the riches of the land, (2) *tur* (see below), and (3) poet-ness (*akhyndykh*). Karima articulates the concern that these standard bearers of cultural value are being transformed from unifying concepts to commodities. Karima and other *aitys* poets continually bemoan the removal of both resources and the absence of clear material benefits for their people.[23] Indeed, to take resources without caring for the land or its people is a base affront in a cultural mythology predicated on a nomadic herding lifeway, a ripping apart of "traditional" values and systems of sustenance and support.

Tur in particular expresses the indignity or inappropriateness of invasion, as it is also the spot within a Kazakh home of highest value, the spot farthest within, farthest away from the door, given to guests as a deep sign of hospitality. Keeping them away from the door demonstrates the host family's willingness to feed and shelter their guest, no matter what the period of time might be. Land, poetry, *tur*—these are all aspects of a Kazakh world to which it should be impossible, by cultural and historical standards, to attach a price tag. But yet it is happening, and Karima worries on behalf of some general "we" whether poetry itself could be commodified and sold like other vital resources of the people.

Karima has even characterized Kazakh unity in spiritual terms: let us keep our honor clean, this kind of unity, five times a day. Here she refers to the practice of reading *namas,* Muslim prayers. She exhorts Marzhan to "take a sacred path [to where] your work is worth something" and here she means a place clearly of cultural, rather than strictly monetary, value. The metaphor of a pathway is a very common one in *aitys: Akh Zhol* (the white way)[24] means a path to religious clarity and goodness in a broad Islamic context, but in Central Asia it also means, more colloquially, the virtuous path. The metaphoric path could be characterized in many ways, but it has at its core themes of ancestry, respect, and obligation. That is, it is a path "we" take together. The fear expressed in Karima's *aitys* and the very real threat that exists continually in cycles of sponsorship and performance is that the tradition itself could become, literally and figuratively, a "sell-out."

Turetam

What counters the threat of selling out, then, is the successful sponsorship of leaders at all levels of government (national, regional, municipal). In the *aitys* tradition as a whole, the forms of patronage described by poets in performance and embodied by politicians in real life are tied clearly to a quality of leadership. A "successful" patron is one who is accessible and accountable to the people. There are many ways to be *Khandai,* the benevolent benefactor, as a cultural sponsor of *aitys.* This may mean being highly visible and involved, as in the case of the national sponsor A. Y. discussed earlier. Or, by sponsoring *aitys,* a leader may also make himself present to his people in the conditions of performance, simply by making *aitys* possible and by emphasizing the relationship of poets and audiences (rather than himself or his interest group). The final example I give here is of precisely that: a quiet patron behind the scenes.

In June of 2006, I was fortunate to travel to western Kazakhstan for the last *aitys* of my field research. Together with Kyzylorda's regional cultural organizers, I went to a small town on the territory of Baikonur. Baikonur, the missile launch site of the former Soviet Union, is now federally Russian territory,[25] and so our entire group had to arrange visas and special permits to travel there. But Kazakhs call the area or town Turetam, also the name of the train station there, a stop on the Moscow-Tashkent line. *Ture* is a generic term for a person in the lineage of a khan—something akin to having royal ancestry. The president of Kazakhstan has suggested more than once that he, too, is *ture;* it is a way of staking and/or legitimating political authority that pointedly far precedes Russian rule. *Tam* means home; in a metaphoric sense then, this *aitys* did not take place in Russia but in the home of the Kazakh khan.

Aitys was coming here for a simple practical reason. A former employee of the regional cultural affairs office in the city of Kyzylorda had become head of the cultural administration for the Baikonur region, and she maintained close ties with her former office. She came to meet our group when we arrived, like so many arrivals in Kazakhstan, seemingly in the middle of nowhere on the steppe, after a five-hour bus ride. One of the first things she joked about was her workload: "Here we have to celebrate all the holidays—Russian holidays, Kazakh holidays, there's a holiday every time you turn around! But we have to fulfill them all equally." She came with the *akim* (mayor) of the town, who was single-handedly sponsoring this event as a part of his political self-legitimization—he had just become mayor the previous year. They came with a small caravan of black SUVs, into which we clambered for the short sojourn to the territorial border.

In the classic fashion of Kazakh hospitality, we had just dropped our bags in our hotel when we took off again to the home of a former *akhyn,* Turoly, who now works as a *tamada* (improvisational host of major events like weddings). He was to serve as MC at the following night's *aitys.* Having also been there to greet us in the steppe, he now received us in his home, a modest three-room apartment in a local block. His wife, her sister, and three female neighbors were cooking for this night. After a generous multi-course meal and conversation, the poets regrouped in the living room with Turoly Akhyn. When I realized our company had become divided, I went to see what they were doing. I found the group of poets comfortably lounging together on *kurpes* (floor pillows), watching videos of *aitys* performances from over the years. They were animated and happy, talking to each other about each competition, which poets had gone and what they'd said. They repeated the words of their friends and laughed together at their jokes. Older poets explained to younger poets about their colleagues' performances and styles. In the life of these busy artists, who are constantly on the road working or teaching, it was a great chance to relax and share one another's company. When we finally left it was nearly midnight, and we rejoined the cultural organizers to finalize preparations for the following day.

The Turetam *aitys* was a bit unusual in that it was to be held in the central square outside, rather than in a theater. By early evening on the day of the performances, nearly eight hundred people had assembled; benches and chairs were found for community elders in the front "rows" nearest the stage, adults found standing room behind them, and children played around, in, and through the crowd. Typically a smaller regional *aitys* competition lasts two or three hours, but this night's performances began at dusk and lasted eight hours, and the crowd remained for its entirety. The performances remained relatively nonpolitical, focused instead on poets' interpersonal relations and mastery of the Kazakh cultural canon. A few poets, like Marzhan who had come from Shimkent, commented on our strange political geography only in a passing joke: It is fine for Kazakhs to read Pushkin, as long as Russians read Abai.[26] The evening outdoors felt very special, and it was a fantastic success for this small Kazakh community. The crowd cheered, laughed, and clapped all night.

When the *aitys* finally drew to a close in the wee hours of the morning, most of the group (poets and cultural organizers) headed back out for a *dastarkhan* (table of hospitality) at a local restaurant. This tuckered ethnographer took a bus home with the town's vice-mayor, a small ebullient woman in her mid-fifties. I asked her what she thought, remarking how amazed I was that everyone stayed so long, even though they had to stand outside. She laughed, "They're still enthusiastic! Tonight they forgot about eating dinner, forgot about washing the floor. It was remarkable! Something like this has not happened here before." She seemed to echo the poet Marzhan who, when we arrived and saw the amassed crowd, said, "A free *aitys* is a huge gift for the people."

The man responsible for this "free gift," Turetam Akim (mayor) Kenzhibek, remained behind the scenes the entire time. He was present at our *dastarkhans* but didn't take a seat of honor. His sponsorship was mentioned in passing during the course of the night by the master of ceremonies, Turoly Akhyn, but no one made much of it. This was highly unusual, given how generous he had been (he had funded the entire night by himself), and that he'd done so specifically in order to legitimate himself in front of the community. It was a risk for him, to host what could be perceived as a Kazakh nationalist event in the immediate eye of Russia; that he did so was much appreciated by his constituents. Some cultural organizers managing the event also speculated that because Kenzhibek Akim was ethnically half Tatar, he also had a personal investment in publically enacting his "Kazakhness."

In contrast to most regional leaders I met over the years, who tend to be showy (even brusque or inaccessible) in their power, Kenzhibek was a different example. This may be in part because at the time he was a relatively new leader, one who did not feel as comfortable in a dominant role but rather needed to demonstrate cooperation and respect to other community elders and leaders. Whatever his reasons, his sponsorship of this *aitys* event was successful. Indeed, the mayor's generosity and enacted modesty allowed the primary focus of the event to be on the relationships between poets themselves and with their audience, rather than on political pageantry.

The night in Turetam was an opportunity for an enthusiastic audience to meet and greet beloved poets—children clamored for autographs, adults came to shake hands and to extend their congratulations. A great deal of attention was directed toward one poet in particular: Kenzhibai Akhyn. Having performed in the region for several decades, he was well known and respected. As an older poet, he serves as a mentor and leader in the *aitys* community and beyond because he is deeply committed to carrying through a sense of Kazakh history and culture in the area.

Kenzhibai himself also has personal sponsors, including his regional *akim* and others whom he does not personally know. The night of the Turetam *aitys*, a private individual gave him a special prize of 150,000T (approx US$1,200). A similar thing had previously happened after an *aitys* in Almaty in celebration of Rayunbek Batyr,[27] where an anonymous individual gave him a new car. Kenzhibai found out later that this person was actually someone very well known, a personal friend of the president.

Reflecting on this incident in a later conversation with me at his home, Kenzhibai explained the perceived relationship between his sponsor and the country's president like this: "My sponsor addresses [Kazakhstan's] president as '*sen, Nursultan*.'" In other words, the sponsor uses the informal you, *sen* (as opposed to *syz*, formal you) and the president's first name, which implies both closeness and equal footing. When Kenzhibai told me this story, he quickly followed it with that of Bukhar Zhyrau.[28] "If anybody wanted to know what was going on in the region," Kenzhibai explained, "they knew they could ask Bukhar and he would tell the truth." Kenzhibai hopes that one day the president will call all the poets to him, saying, "you can come to me and tell me all the truth about all the regions."[29]

Kenzhibai here echoed the national sponsor Amangeldi Yermegeayev described above in his invocation of mythic history and the figurative role of the poet to his leader and his people. In his hometown in western Kazakhstan, Kenzhibai very much enacts this responsive and personal form of leadership: he is an active and well-loved community leader, every day in conversation with members of his village, organizing events, encouraging relationships.

On a more local and modest scale, Kenzhibai also defines the model of dialogic authority I describe here: it is a relationship not of dominance but of involvement and communication.

Performance and Political Participation

When I returned to visit in the summer of 2011, Kenzhibai Akhyn was deflated. Confirming what other colleagues and informants in the *aitys* sphere had been telling me recently, he explained that for the past two years, *aitys* had been effectively "closed from the top," by which he meant metaphorically from the president's offices. This does not mean any direct order or overt censorship of the tradition: performances still regularly occurred in the country, including in Kenzhibai's region of Kyzylorda. In fact, the offices of cultural affairs there celebrated the publication of a research volume on historical and contemporary *aitys,* an elaborate effort funded in large part by government monies. What had changed, gradually, was more subtle: it was the tone of performances and the increasing pressure against critical political content. That pressure may have come from the president, or those who control his popular and cultural image, but it was diffused through many different lines of access, media, cultural organization, and financial support. An informant in Almaty noted that performances had been closed after (and perhaps because) one poet had said *Nur Otan yemes, a Ury Otana* ("Not the light of our fatherland, but the thief of our fatherland") in reference to the president's political party, renamed in 2007.

Cultural performance is one way in which expression organizes experience, how we come to see and know ourselves; it is an "explanation of life itself" (Turner 1982). In their study of cultural performances (like the oral tradition *aitys*), anthropologists have emphasized the spaces of exception that these "framed"[30] encounters necessarily create, where social mores are revealed, held suspended, and either reinvigorated or challenged (cf. Conquergood 1998). These spaces allow flexibility and change in the social order, and they become vehicles for the emergence of new or alternate critical "voices" in culture (cf. Fabian 1990). Culture itself is dialogic, requiring continual collusion in social interaction (Tedlock and Mannheim 1995). Thus even in routinized traditions, cultural performances are emergent and therefore unpredictable. In performance there is always both a powerful potential and the threat of complete failure.

In the case of *aitys* in Kazakhstan, limiting the practical conditions of performance hinders its content, and thus its dialogic potential. While not as overt or extreme as the murder of an opposition politician, this, too, is a form of silencing. That the state has acted to silence this oral tradition reflects the poetry's potency as a vehicle of expression and experience. In poets' claim "to voice the truth of the people," there are two aspects: cultural unity and socio-political critique. What is enabled by this voice is ultimately a demand by "the people" for accountability on the part of government leaders. It is a way to participate, however minimally, on a national political stage.[31] Performances are addressed to state leaders who fail to listen and take care of the very people they purport to represent.

The *aitys* tradition presents precisely such an alternative model of leadership to the uncaring and authoritarian state. Poets' performances and their more successful relationships with sponsors invoke and enact a dialogic leadership, where "the people" can voice their concerns, and where leaders are present and responsive. In this sphere, "the people" are Goffman's principal figure, a unified "someone whose position is established by the words that are spoken, someone whose beliefs have been told, someone who is committed to what the words say" (Goffman 1981, 144). The principal cannot be reduced to any one set of participants in the tradition (ancestors, poets, audiences, cultural organizers, sponsors); rather all these together contribute continually toward the figure. The principal is someone who is always coming into being. Over time, the principal of *aitys* is engaged in with government officials as an "addressed recipient" (ibid., 133), in a conversation that thousands of people are ratified to hear, a conversation with a thousand "shadows" (cf. Crapanzano 1988; Irvine 1996).

The inclusive and participatory politics that *aitys* embodies is very much part of the "value" of the tradition of which Karima and other poets speak; it is this value that is threatened by the sponsorship relationship. If sponsors' interests dominate, the precarious relationship of mutual legitimacy with poets is tipped out of balance and the people are left without a voice. By contrast, a successful collaboration between poets and sponsors results in the enactment and emergence of a particular dialogic form of authority, one of mutual respect and legitimacy where both parties are active and accountable to one another. When we consider that both sides, in their representative capacity, make claims to represent "the people," that dialogic relationship becomes political.

In that sense, cultural patronage is a form of political activity and authority that is very common to Central Asian communities more broadly. These are relationships in which governance is embodied and performed. Further, when poets and sponsors collude, the framework is created for them, together with the people, to speak to contemporary leaders of the nation-state and to demand of those leaders the same level of presence and accountability. The dialogic model I present here is at once a literal and a metaphoric performance of an idealized state: a possible present of participatory politics.

Notes

1. All italicized words in text are in the Kazakh language, with English equivalents given in parentheses.

2. *Aitys* is a contemporary legacy of Turkic-Mongol oral and epic traditions performed from Turkey to Mongolia and Western China, and as *aitysh* in Kyrgyzstan.

3. The ethnographic research and writing presented here was made possible with the support of a Fulbright-Hays Research Grant in 2004, a Wenner Gren Individual Research Grant in 2006, and the Social Science Research Council Eurasian Dissertation Fellowship 2008–2009. I would also like to thank Judith Beyer and Zhanara Nauruzbayeva for their careful reading, suggestions, and support.

4. The culturally legitimated places of the powerful could be the front of a crowded auditorium at an *aitys* performance, the front of a celebration or political gathering (Ismailbekova, this volume), "claiming a seat" that is respected by others during a village court session (Beyer, this volume), or being present at an exclusive spectacle performance (Adams 2010).

5. As an analytic, the concept of voice I present here is social and political, most akin to Goffman's principle—those committed to what is said (1981); I address this point further below and in the conclusion.

6. Daniel Prior (2000) provides in-depth examination of how those relations of patron and poet shifted in the early Soviet period to become less personal and instead nationalistic. Current sponsorship conditions are an admixture of both, the argument being that Soviet authorities clearly recognized and specifically sought to control the "propaganda potential" (Prior 2000, 9) of epic (and improvisational) poetry.

7. Some critics of the national tradition feel that *aitys* is no longer authentic, as its soul has already been sold (Kendirbaeva 1994; fieldnotes and interviews from the Institute of Literature and Art named after Mukhtar Auezov, spring 2004).

8. This relates more broadly to economic relations among kin networks, which operate according to the principle of a revolving credit system: kin networks mobilize to provide cash or goods for some members, with the understanding that those members will in turn do the same at another time. In that configuration, money is at once a necessary but minimal aspect of the relations of social obligation (cf. Werner 1999).

9. A poet's group will usually be in the audience, but in several performances I witnessed, members of the group actually came on stage to sit behind the poet where he or she could consult with them during competition.

10. The Kazakh tribes normally invoked are the six of the middle horde: Arghyn, Naiman, Kipshak, Khongyrat, Uakh, and Kereu.

11. Former mayor of Almaty Zamanbek Nurkadilov, who in an open letter demanded the resignation of the president in 2005 for corruption, was killed in November that year.

12. In her chapter on "performing authority," Judith Beyer (2009) has shown that the same dynamic exists among politicians and elders (*aksakals*) during political events in Kyrgyzstan.

13. Personal interview, June 27, 2006.

14. Eighteenth-century khan responsible for the unification of the three Kazakh *zhuz* (Kishi, Orta, Ulken) on the territory of Kazakhstan (cf. Soucek 2000; Grousset 2002).

15. Interview June 2006; the sense of the term *yel* in Kazakh is most like the English "country."

16. At the time of this publication, the country's internal linguistic politics and popular culture have shifted somewhat, and there seems to be a renewed interest in the de-

velopment and promulgation of Kazakh language as both a government and common language. Throughout the post-Soviet period, knowledge of Kazakh language has been used strategically in the nationalization of government offices throughout the country (cf. Cummings 2005; Dave 2007).

17. Sponsors can also be local or regional politicians and businessmen, whether established or trying to solidify their career, but a nationalist agenda tends to characterize those who are most successful.

18. Personal interview with Zhursin Yerman, June 2004.

19. See Privratsky 2001 for a detailed ethnographic description of Kazakh Muslim cultural identity.

20. Personal interview, March 3, 2006. I thank Akbota Anuzkhanova for help with this translation.

21. Personal interview, March 23, 2006.

22. Karima Akhyn, Shimkent Regional New Year's *Aitys,* March 18, 2006. Any faults in translation are entirely my own.

23. Kazakhstan's economy is largely based on natural resource extraction, primarily oil and gas, but also including coal, uranium, and gold. Profits from that industry remain centralized under the President's government elite.

24. It is also the common name of political parties in both Kazakhstan and Kyrgyzstan.

25. Kazakhstan's government agreed to lease the active site to Russia until 2050 for US$17 million per year. See Werner and Purvis-Roberts's chapter, this volume, for further information on the post-Soviet weapons and testing landscape between Kazakhstan and Russia.

26. Abai Kunanbaioly (1845–1904) was a late Russian-era poet, writer, and leader who has been canonized in Soviet (and now nationalist) Kazakh folk mythology as a great cultural hero.

27. The Kazakh hero credited with freeing Kazakhs from Dzungar rule in the mid-eighteenth century.

28. The poet of Abylai Khan, the seventeenth-century ruler, mentioned above.

29. Personal interview, June 2006.

30. The concept of an interpretive frame was developed as a rubric of sociological analysis by Goffman (1986). In his classic treatise on verbal art (1977), Bauman identified interpretive frame as a basic (metapragmatic) condition of performance.

31. One article exclaimed, "Kazakh Folk Poetry Slams Corrupt Establishment!" http://www.cacianalyst.org/?q=node/4465 (accessed September 26, 2012).

References

Adams, Laura. 2010. *The Spectacular State: Culture and National Identity in Uzbekistan.* Durham, N.C.: Duke University Press.

Attinasi, John, and Paul Friedrich. 1995. "Dialogic Breakthrough: Catalysis and Synthesis in Life-Changing Dialogue." In *The Dialogic Emergence of Culture,* edited by Dennis Tedlock and Bruce Mannheim, 33–53. Urbana: University of Illinois Press.

Bakhtin, Mikhail M. 1981. *The Dialogic Imagination.* Translated by Caryl Emerson and Michael Holquist. Austin: University of Texas Press.

Bauman, Richard. 1977. *Verbal Art as Performance.* Prospect Heights, Ill.: Waveland Press.

Beyer, Judith. 2009. "According to *Salt.* An Ethnography of Customary Law in Talas, Kyrgyzstan." PhD diss., Martin-Luther-University, Halle-Wittenberg.

———. 2010. "Authority as Accomplishment: Intergenerational Dynamics in Talas, Northern Kyrgyzstan." In *Eurasian Perspectives: In Search of Alternatives,* edited by Anita Sengupta and Suchandana Chatterjee, 78–92. New Delhi: Shipra (Maulana Abul Kalam Azad Institute of Asian Studies).

Conquergood, Theodore. 1998. "Beyond the Text: Toward a Performative Cultural Politics." In *The Future of Performance Studies: Visions and Revisions,* edited by Sheron J. Dailey, 25–36. Washington, D.C.: National Communication Association.

Crapanzano, Vincent. 1988. "On Self Characterization." In *Working Papers and Proceedings of the Center for Psychosocial Studies, #24.* Chicago: Center for Psychosocial Studies.

Cummings, Sally. 2005. *Kazakhstan: Power and the Elite.* London: I. B. Taurus.

Dave, Bhavna. 2007. *Kazakhstan: Ethnicity, Language and Power.* New York: Routledge.

Dubuisson, Eva-Marie. 2010. "Confrontation in and through the Nation in Kazakh Aitys Poetry." In "Performing Disputes: Cooperation and Conflict in Argumentative Language," edited by Valentina Pagliai. Special issue, *Journal of Linguistic Anthropology* 20, no. 1.

Fabian, Johannes. 1990. *Power and Performance: Ethnographic Explorations through Proverbial Wisdom and Theater in Shaba, Zaire.* Madison: University of Wisconsin Press.

Goffman, Erving. 1981. *Forms of Talk.* Philadelphia: University of Pennsylvania Press.

———. 1986. *Frame Analysis: An Essay on the Organization of Experience.* Boston: Northeastern University Press.

Grousset, Rene. 2002. *The Empire of the Steppes: A History of Central Asia.* Translated by Naomi Walford. New Brunswick, N.J.: Rutgers University Press.

Gullette, David. 2010. *The Genealogical Construction of the Kyrgyz Republic: Kinship, State, and "Tribalism."* Kent, UK: Global Oriental.

Irvine, Judith T. 1996. "Shadow Conversations: The Indeterminacy of Participant Roles." In *Natural Histories of Discourse,* edited by Michael Silverstein and Greg Urban, 131–159. Chicago: University of Chicago Press.

Jones Luong, Pauline, ed. 2004. *The Transformation of Central Asia: States and Societies from Soviet Rule to Independence.* Ithaca, N.Y.: Cornell University Press.

Kendirbaeva, Gulnar. 1994. "Folklore and Folklorism in Kazakhstan." *Asian Folklore Studies* 53: 97–123.

Levin, Theodore. 1996. *The Hundred Thousand Fools of God: Musical Travels in Central Asia (and Queens, New York).* Bloomington: Indiana University Press.

Liu, Morgan. 2005. "Post-Soviet Paternalism and Personhood: Why Culture Matters to Democratization in Central Asia." In *Prospects for Democracy in Central Asia,* edited by Birgit Schlyter, 225–238. London: I. B. Tauris.

———. 2012. *Under Solomon's Throne: Uzbek Visions of Renewal in Osh.* Pittsburgh: University of Pittsburgh Press.

Madison, D. Soyini. 2005. *Critical Ethnography: Method, Ethics, and Performance.* London: Sage.

McGlinchey, Eric. 2008. "Patronage, Islam, and the Rise of Localism in Central Asia." PONARS Eurasia Policy Memo No. 2.

———. 2009. "Searching for Kamalot: Political Patronage and Youth Politics in Uzbekistan." *Europe-Asia Studies* 61: 1137–1150.

Prior, Daniel. 2000. "Patron, Party, Patrimony: Notes on the Cultural History of the Kirghiz Epic Tradition." Papers on Inner Asia 33. Bloomington: Indiana University, Research Institute for Inner Asian Studies.

Privratsky, Bruce. 2001. *Muslim Turkistan: Kazak Religion and Collective Memory.* Richmond, UK: Curzon Press.

Soucek, Svat. 2000. *A History of Inner Asia.* Cambridge: Cambridge University Press.

Tedlock, Dennis, and Bruce Mannheim, eds. 1995. Introduction to *Dialogic Emergence of Culture,* edited by Dennis Tedlock and Bruce Mannheim, 48. Urbana: University of Illinois Press.

Turner, Victor. 1982. *From Ritual to Theatre: The Seriousness of Human Play.* New York: Performing Arts Journal Publications.

Werner, Cynthia. 1999. "The Dynamics of Feasting and Gift Exchange in Rural Kazakhstan." In *Contemporary Kazakhs: Social and Cultural Perspectives,* edited by Ingvar Svanberg, 47–72. London: Curzon.

3. Performing Democracy

State-Making through Patronage in Kyrgyzstan

Aksana Ismailbekova

Based on fieldwork in a northern Kyrgyz village in 2007 and 2008, this chapter focuses on the interplay of localized democracy and patronage. Specifically, I draw on ethnographic materials to explore how the state was performed locally during the 2007 parliamentary electoral campaign, culminating in election day in December of that year. I discuss how an indigenized understanding of democracy was fostered through the activation of patronage networks and how, through the performance of the election, the democratic state came to be enacted. By learning the rules of the new electoral system—distributing merchandise such as calendars and hats with party logos, clarifying which documents were needed for the elections, and "dressing up" for the occasion—the villagers took an active part in the electoral process and thus in performing the state. But they also exercised their agency in performing democracy by circumventing and even violating the state's procedural norms. Realizing that the officials in charge of the election were not impartial, those villagers who wanted to vote against the ruling party bribed the officials to ensure they would not manipulate the vote. The candidate of the opposition party was not only the favorite politician of the villagers; he was also a fellow villager and a local "big man" to whom most constituents were linked through patronage relations. While villagers acknowledged that the election itself was thus flawed, it was their active participation and moral investment in the event as such that constituted their sense of being part of a larger collective project of making the state.

Inspired by recent approaches in political anthropology, particularly the anthropology of the state, I explore how the state becomes an object of moral investment and desire in rural Kyrgyzstan. Recent anthropological contributions have shown that, far from being given, the state emerges in a multitude of often discontinuous practices (Das and Poole 2004; Ferguson and Gupta 2002). I contribute to this argument by showing how the performance of, and active participation and intervention in, the electoral process help to manufacture and sustain the contemporary state in Kyrgyzstan. This is the actual "doing" of politics. I employ Jonathan Spencer's notion of the political domain as "a complex field of social practices, moral judgments, and imaginative possibilities" (Spencer 2007, 22) in order to examine people's agentive involvement in the election; and, following John Comaroff and Jean Comaroff (1997, 123), I shed light on specific local processes of building democracy. What might "democracy" actually mean in post-Soviet rural Kyrgyzstan? How do people constitute democracy in their own ways? How do practices of patronage and discourses of corruption affect the process of constructing a democratic state (Roniger and Güneş-Ayata 1994)? How are democracy and the state indigenized (Appadurai 1998)? And finally, what does the state that emerges in these highly contingent processes look like?

Resonating with chapters in this volume by Dubuisson, Beyer, Reeves, and Liu, this chapter directs attention to the ways in which the state comes into being in people's imaginations and through their actions during national electoral campaigns and on the day of national elections. Up to now, comparable events have usually been portrayed as examples of the absence or the malfunctioning of democratic processes in Kyrgyzstan. I show in this chapter that from an emic point of view it is precisely such events that foster a local sense of democratic participation in state processes.

The Study of State and Democracy

In a new slant on the anthropological study of the state, Veena Das and Deborah Poole (2004) and Akhil Gupta (1995) argue that instead of thinking of the state as a distinct and distant entity, we should see it as constructed through everyday formations, the imagination and everyday practices of people. In their exploratory article, James Ferguson and Gupta (2002, 981) identify two principles that are key to state spatialization: verticality (the state is "above" society) and encompassment (the state "encompasses" its localities), and argue that "perceptions of verticality and encompassment are produced through routine bureaucratic practices" (ibid.), undertaken by state officials and invoked in daily life. In the case of Kyrgyzstan mundane encounters with representatives of state power foster an awareness of the state as something distant and unattainable at the same time that they question the usefulness or integrity of particular state officials. While Gupta and Ferguson stress the role of the state as one amongst several agents of governmentality, other authors have shown how the state should also be seen as object of fantasy, a site of hope, and the focus of often intense emotion (Navaro-Yashin 2002, 2003; Spencer 2007). As Begoña Aretxaga (2003, 393) notes: "despite transformations in the character of the state in an age of globalization, news of its demise is certainly exaggerated. . . . Invested with a kind of meta-capital, the state remains a crucial presence, a screen for political desires and identifications as well as fears." From this follows the question: "How does the state become a social subject in everyday life, examining the subjective experience of state power and tracing its effects on territories, populations, and bodies?"

To gain some ethnographic purchase on this question in my field site I have found Spencer's approach particularly fruitful. Spencer urges fellow researchers to operate with a more "expansive" account of the political—one that "gives as much weight to the expressive and performative aspects of politics as to the instrumental" (2007, 17). According to Spencer (2007, 22), "the political has emerged as a complex field of social practices, moral judgments, and imaginative possibilities." In this chapter, I employ Spencer's notion of the political domain to better understand the local processes of building democracy in rural Kyrgyzstan. Viewed from this perspective, democratic elections are never simply rational technologies for expressing political preferences but rather are distinct social and political practices that legitimate state governance through citizen participation and symbolically authorize elected candidates to govern. Following Comaroff and Comaroff's seminal work on alternative imaginaries of representation in Africa (1997), I view the election in Kyrgyzstan as a matter of democratic principles colonizing local practices, leading to the emergence of a localized democracy.

Patronage Networks

Patronage is key to understanding the dynamics of this process. Following Luis Roniger and Ayşe Güneş-Ayata (1994), I argue that modernization does not make clientelism irrelevant, just as patronage does not disappear in the process of democratization. Rather, patronage has evolved and persisted along with other forms of party and kinship in the Kyrgyz context. In the political realm, patronage involves the particular use of public resources often in relation to the electoral arena. It also involves clients providing their support and voting during election time. In return, the patron is expected to provide his or her clients with jobs and other benefits. This is another means of winning elections and building client support. It is a stratagem of biased political recruitment that differs entirely from the ideal type of electoral recruitment (Roniger 2004, 354). Self-interest shapes the nature of patron-client relations and is the reason why such relationships are formed, bound by the moral system of the society in which they are based (Campbell 1974). Thus, patronage and politics is not just the utilitarian pursuit of material interests but a form of moral action, intervention, and statement.

Patronage is an important mechanism through which those involved in it mutually benefit and one that selectively distributes resources. While patronage runs against the universal principle of democracy and a free market economy, it is nevertheless responsive to local sentiment, local norms and practices, and local identity. Moreover, patronage may solve people's basic needs; provide access to jobs, hospitals, and universities; and serve the community—in the case of my fieldwork, within the framework of appeals to the "native son." Yet all these characteristics are still usually considered, in policy and academic literature alike, as "inappropriate"—that is, as amounting to corruption. Despite this fact, patronage remains very much alive, and for all its negative qualities, such as the uncertainty and disappointment it can sometimes foster, patronage is also capable of tailoring itself to addressing or resolving moments of uncertainty and instability. It thus provides an alternative form of socio-political structure, one that guarantees stability and provides protection.

This argument takes my analysis in a different direction from the majority of scholars who write about politics and patronage in Central Asia. Political scientists have tended to approach patronage in Central Asia in terms of an oversimplified notion of "clan politics" and thus as detrimental to the development of democracy (Collins 2002; Juraev 2008; Khamidov 2006; Radnitz 2005, 2006; Schatz 2004). Here, by contrast, I show that political loyalties cannot be transposed in any simple way onto "clan" loyalties and that an analysis premised upon clan identification obscures more than it reveals in post-Soviet Kyrgyzstan. Instead, I develop a broader argument about the ongoing significance of patronage, suggesting that from an emic perspective patronage relations do not so much hinder as facilitate local democracy.

Kyrgyzstan: An "Island of Democracy" in Central Asia?

Kyrgyzstan's post-independence experience serves as a productive point of entry for exploring the forms and local meanings of democracy in post-Soviet Central Asia. On March 24, 2005, fourteen years after it gained independence, the government of the country's first president, Askar Akaev, was overthrown in a bloodless revolt known as the Tulip Revolution. For my informants in rural northern Kyrgyzstan, the Tulip Revolution signified the exercise of "people power" and offered some hope that there would be democratic change in Kyrgyzstan after a decade of increasing political and economic stagnation and an ever more visible concentration of resources in the president's hands. As its popular name suggests, the "Revolution" was generally peaceful (Hiro 2009), although there was some localized violence and a night of looting in the capital city of Bishkek. Following the Tulip Revolution, a presidential election was held in July 2005, as a result of which a southerner, Kurmanbek Bakiev, was elected to power.

To avoid the division of the country along regional lines and to prevent civil war, a coalition was formed between Felix Kulov (from the country's north) and Bakiev (from the south). In this political union, Bakiev, one of the opposition leaders, became president, and Kulov became the prime minister. Limited access to resources and a power struggle motivated this discourse between the south and the north.

It is in this polarized political context that the election that I describe occurred. The election of December 2007 was held to elect a new parliament following the revolutionary upheaval of 2005. The widespread hope at that time, both inside Kyrgyzstan and beyond, was that this new election would steer Kyrgyzstan back toward a "normal" political future after months of demonstrations, road closures, and political assassinations. Various parties were contesting the election, but the campaign was dominated by the newly formed Ak-Zhol party, which had been established by Bakiev just two months before the election, as an explicitly pro-presidential party. To my informants in the village of Vostok, in Kyrgyzstan's northern Chui oblast', Ak-Zhol was seen as a party of the country's south, just as President Bakiev was a southerner. By contrast, northerners led the party that came to dominate in the village, the Social Democratic Party of Kyrgyzstan (SDPK).[1] Crucially, moreover, as I explore below, it was the party through which the village's long-standing patron, Rahim, had sought to ballot for parliament. This provided the setting for the dynamics of political contestation in the village, to which I now turn.

The Election in the Village

I encountered Vostok village for the first time in 2007. Located in a mountainous region, the Vostok economy is based on agriculture, but the villagers also breed cattle for subsistence. In the autumn of 2007, the announcement of early parliamentary elections immediately ruptured the everyday routine of the village, and people began to hold lively discussions about the party system, expressing their desire to reconstitute a "normal" politics after years of political instability. As one of my informants later noted: "at election time men stop their normal working activities. Instead, they talk only about politics and read a lot of newspapers. But the good thing was that this year, the election was in the winter, not at harvest time."

During previous political campaigns, politicians had typically shown up in the village for short meetings and public speeches before disappearing again.

In anticipation of this, and after extensive meetings, the elders decided to demand "useful items" from politicians for the village during the party campaign, such as a yurt, cattle, or a mill. This signaled a more ambitious request than the bags of flour that had already been distributed to select villagers in return for party loyalty. People anticipated the arrival of the same old politicians that they were used to seeing and listening to the same old speeches as before. However, this time, they were prepared to make new demands, such as a request that the politicians buy an old store in the village and turn it into a café, which could then be used for ceremonies on the occasion of life cycle events. For the people of Vostok the election campaign thus constituted a short period during which people's concerns could be heard, taken into consideration, and realized in practice. This could also be a divisive time, however, during which the fabric of the village could split as people's loyalties were divided and commitments came into conflict. There were even reports of fights between husbands and wives as a result of politics, with some ending in divorce.[2] As Spencer (2007, 85) found in Sri Lanka, politics had "provided a new idiom in which villagers could express the kinds of division that had long existed." In other words, social cleavages that existed before came to be animated in new ways.

For all the expectations that this would be a time to make material demands of visiting politicians, the village was in fact visited little by politicians during the election campaign. Vostok village was promoting its *öz bala* (native son), Rahim, a member of the SDPK, in the political arena.[3] Other politicians therefore assumed that they should not waste their largesse on a village that was unlikely to return them the desired vote, and the village elders' hope for a new café was consequently frustrated.[4] In the election two years earlier, Rahim did not receive enough votes to become a member of parliament. However, this time he promised that as a prospective leader of the SDPK he would be able to represent his voters. Other candidates again saw no point in coming to the village, because it was assumed that the villagers would vote for their "native son."[5] Rahim secured the loyalty of the whole community by promising both economic security and reinforcing social values (respect, honor, loyalty), which were integrated into the overarching ideology of kinship *tuugan* (relatives). This served to justify and legitimize both the system and how it operated.

I arrived in Vostok on December 16, 2007—parliamentary election day—at around six o'clock in the morning, so as to observe the election in its entirety in the village. Although a citizen of Kyrgyzstan, my position at the election was that of an "international observer." I had travelled from the village of Orlovka, my first site of field research, reaching Vostok within an hour by car. The day before the election, I attended training conducted by the International Centre Interbilim, where I had been taught how to observe an election for irregularities and to write a protocol. At that training I had been asked to make sure that

I was present in the village before members of the electoral commission arrived at the village club to open the sealed packages containing the ballot papers.[6] When I arrived, the temporary election office was still closed. After two and half hours, the commission members began to arrive at the polling station.

At first sight, the difference between Vostok and Orlovka was striking. In Orlovka diverse ethnic groups living in the village had built different types of house, whereas the housing in Vostok was largely uniform in style and unrenovated. What made me want to observe the elections in this village, rather than in Orlovka, was the fact that this village was nominating its "native son" for the election. However, this same fact provided the representative of the electoral commission, as well as the community itself, with a challenge: the state representative was supposed to support the pro-presidential party, Ak-Zhol, whereas the villagers were supporting the SDPK. I was interested to see how these social actors negotiated the rules of the election and how they bargained with the state. The state representative in this case was a widow named Ainura, who at the time of the election was working as the chairperson of the electoral commission.

I introduced myself to the commission members at the polling station as an independent observer. However, there were several other election observers present, each representing either Ak-Zhol or the SPDK, these being the better represented of the twelve political parties running in the election.[7] My primary aim was to observe the activities of the commission members: how they counted, compared, and labeled the ballots. The commission consisted mainly of women. They compared the number of eligible voters (just over one thousand) with the number of ballots that had actually been cast. They had been struggling to keep counting and labeling the ballots. Two local police officers stood outside the polling station, which was the village's former house of culture (cf. Grant 1995; Donahoe and Habeck 2011), in order to manage the crowds at the door. Upon entering the polling station, there were two men present who were responsible for marking people's thumbs with indelible ink (and checking voters' fingers for traces of ink to prevent multiple voting). Eki, a brother of Rahim and a village political leader, voted first and complained that the pen for writing on the ballot papers was not working properly. Eki was anxious to make sure that everything inside the polling station was accurate and properly prepared for election day.

I spent the first three or four hours sitting in the cold polling station, watching to see what would happen. Whenever local villagers entered, they greeted each other using kinship terminology, as *eje* (older sister) or *aga* (older brother), *singdi* (younger sister) or *ini* (brother), respectively. The commission members consisted exclusively of young, newly married women of the village. Although their role was to direct and regulate the voting process (including prohibiting villagers from voting if they failed to produce the necessary documents), as *kelinder* (daughters-in-law) these women were structurally subordinate to the majority of villagers who were coming to the club to vote. They had been allocated these roles by elders of the village's council of internal affairs and were confronted with something of a dilemma when faced with elderly people who had not presented the right documents to vote. Asymmetrical expectations of honor respect were often in tension with the demands of electoral law: should they insist that an elderly person return home and bring the requisite identification, or should they allow the person to vote without an ID? It seems that young women may have been deliberately appointed by the commission in order to regulate the election process, as a way of making sure people could still vote even without the right documents. Changes to Kyrgyzstan's passport system meant that many villagers were not in possession of the military record, pension book, or passport that they needed to document their identity. Others who considered themselves to be village residents found that they were not on the list of voters because they were not registered as owners of assets such as land or a house. Those who could not vote were very angry, shaking their heads, debating their mistakes. They often quickly went home and brought back different documents to make sure that they could still vote.

During this intensive phase of voting, I met with various people who had come to the club to vote. As we chatted about their thoughts and expectations outside the club I saw that Oroz, wearing a blue cloth cap and a scarf with the SDPK emblem, was greeting voters before they entered the polling stations by shaking their hands. Oroz asked the villagers to vote for a candidate that they believed in but also made rhetorical appeals to solidarity and unity, insisting that *köngülübüz tüz* (we understand each other), *kaaloobyz bir* (we have one aim), and *tilegibiz ak* (we have the same good purpose). Oroz is a very close friend and distant relative of Rahim and works on Rahim's private farm. His responsibilities include managing Rahim's business, as well as campaigning for him during the election. Voters and their families approached the club, dressed in their best outfits, congratulating each other on the holiday with the expression *mairamyngar menen*! (happy holiday). Whereas women and their children quickly returned home after voting, men remained near the polling station, to discuss politics, the president and his programs, and the outcome of this election day. There was a celebratory atmosphere in the village with many people gathering on the streets to drink and talk politics.

Oroz stopped voters on their way home, asking them to remind those who had not yet voted to come to the club to cast their ballot. Meanwhile, Oroz's family had prepared some food and drinks for the commission members and election observers. While we were having our lunch, he called university students from the capital, 60 km away, to ask them to return to their village to vote, promising to reimburse the cost of their transport. He also tried to contact those who could not reach the polling station for health reasons, quickly mobilizing young men from the village to bring elderly or disabled people with them in their private cars. His ability to administer people in this way increased the number of votes and exerted some control over the election process. Those who were unable to reach the station were meant to state in advance and request a special mobile ballot box so as to cast their ballot from home. But many villagers had not known how or where to do this. So Oroz asked young men to bring people to the polling station, dividing them according the lineage of the village: first Ak-Zhol, then Karasakal, and so on.

After the election, Oroz told me that he had been so worried about the election that he had forgotten to eat that day. His informal negotiations with Ainura, the chair of the electoral commission in the village, had made it possible for the election process to run very "smoothly" for the Vostok villagers. First of all, he had persuaded Ainura to provide him with a list of those who were eligible to vote but who did not have the necessary documents, by giving her some money. Ainura in turn later permitted people to vote using other kinds of documents including library cards (literally "closing her eyes," as she put it, to this electoral violation: *köz zhumup koidu*). Ainura, however, was personally in a difficult position. As the *ökül kyz* (goddaughter) of Tyrmyshbek, who in turn was married to a sister of the village headman, Ainura was expected to support the pro-presidential party, Ak-Zhol. Indeed, it is very likely that precisely this presumed party loyalty was the reason why she had been appointed to chair the electoral commission in the village. Rumors circulating during the election also alleged that Ainura had once received a plot of land from the village headman for her two young married children and that she was obliged to repay this gift by voting for the presidential party.[8] Ainura had married in to Vostok from another village, where her father was the village head and an Ak-Zhol supporter. There were thus multiple pressures on Ainura to vote for the presidential party. What is interesting, however, is that even though Ainura and her family voted for Ak-Zhol, she also took money from the SDPK and allocated them 50 unused ballots at the end of voting, a phenomenon to which I return below. Ainura's case illustrates vividly how different kinds of commitments shaped her behavior on electoral day, but also how others assessed her navigation of these competing obligations. For Oroz, Ainura was "doing nothing but making money all the same" (*ona nichego ne delaet, no po khodu p'esy babki delaet*), suggesting that the job of the chairperson is easy and profitable because many party members sought to bribe her.

There was a further complication of party loyalties in Vostok. For Ak-Zhol, meaning bright or open path, is not only the pro-presidential party; it is also the name of one of the village's lineages. People would say that "our lineage is

Ak-Zhol, and we are on the bright way and will achieve successes," but that in order for the Ak-Zhol lineage to achieve success in politics, they first had to destroy the Ak-Zhol party by literally "walking all over them" (*Ak Zholdun üstünön basysh kerek*).

The outcome of the election at a national level was assumed by most of my informants to be a foregone conclusion: the party supporting the president would take the majority of seats in the parliament. This was deemed obvious because the Ak-Zhol party was forcing state officials to vote for it at the risk of losing their positions. One policeman, for instance, an SDPK supporter, told me that fifteen thousand policemen had been told to vote for Ak-Zhol. At a village level, however, the actions of Oroz and others were very important, not only because they increased voter turnout but also because they persuaded the majority of local voters to choose the SDPK and therefore demonstrate their support for their "native son." Such pressures could be considerable. When a community member called Baktybek, for instance, wanted to start campaigning for the Ak-Zhol party, he was asked to stop and was demonstratively not invited to the lifecycle event of one of the community members. Consequently, local villagers did not distribute pro-presidential Ak-Zhol party posters to community members, instead hanging caps, scarves, posters, and calendars with SDPK slogans in every house. People would try to get as many caps and scarves as they could in order to wear them in the street. As Coles (2004, 554) states, "election day, as a ritual and viewed as 'signifying practice,' might be thought to symbolize the changing values of democracy." For people in Vostok, election day was seen as a positive event that signaled hopes for change in the country's political fortunes. Their main concern was for their village son to get a seat in the parliament.

If election day was celebratory, the business of preparing for it was also an important education in "doing" democracy. Elders would tell each other for hours about changes to electoral politics, rules, codes, and procedures learned from newspapers or Radio Free Europe. They would constantly switch their conversations from election techniques to the political agenda, the future perspectives of the SDPK, and the promise of democracy. At a meeting I attended, one of the elders of the community read out the program of the party system in general to the audience in a loud voice: "The party system was designed to avoid kinship division and regionalism in the country; instead it should decrease the price of bread and electricity, and increase people's salaries and pensions."

Elderly people—the *aksakals* of the village—were also actively involved in mobilizing people and getting them to vote by ordering the younger generation to be more proactive within their community. The campaigners asked people to vote for *öz kökürök kychygybyz* (our son, our brother, our dignity, and our foal); someone who was better than any outsider and *eldik kishida, eldin*

Figure 3.1. Local people support the Social Democratic Party during the parliamentary elections in the village of Vostok, Kyrgyzstan, December 16, 2007.

kishisi (a man of the people). Private farm workers also worked very hard to get people to vote. Some of these employees were election observers themselves, who monitored and managed the voting situation in other parts of the region at the district (*raion*) polling stations. These followers returned to their own polling station to vote, arriving in their village at 7:30 p.m., before the polls officially closed. One of Vostok's private farm workers, Maria, who went to observe the election in the neighboring village of Orlovka, complained to me that the people of Orlovka were ungrateful. Rahim supported them by buying their private, bankrupted kolkhoz and repairing their schools and hospital, she told me. And yet Orlovka had voted for another party all the same! Maria also told me of her nervousness: nobody had slept properly that day, she told me, because some of the voters followed the car with the used ballots in it to the capital in order to be sure that the car arrived safely. Others had been calling each other and asking about the results, concerned about possible falsification of the results in Bishkek.

By the end of the day, hundreds of men had gathered outside the polling station in order to observe the process of vote counting. The windows of the polling station had been covered with material brought by Ainura, perhaps to prevent prying eyes. As chairperson, Ainura asked observers to monitor the counting procedure but not to touch the ballots. She proceeded to give a formal speech, thanking those who participated in the election and announcing to the audience that 700 out of a total of 1,007 had voted, leaving 307 unused ballots. She said that the remaining ballots should now be ceremoniously destroyed in front of the audience. Suddenly, her speech was interrupted by Oroz, who instead asked her to distribute the unused ballots between the party members present. Ainura immediately agreed, as if she had been expecting this request. She then went on to give a speech in which she stated that she would accept the request on the condition that she, too, be allowed to take an extra 50 votes for herself. Amongst her other responsibilities, Ainura was responsible for distributing the salary to other young commission members. As women who were newly married, recently arrived in the village, and financially dependent upon Ainura, none of the young commission members who had been appointed to oversee the conduct of the election opposed Ainura's request.

After thirty minutes of discussion, Ainura finally handed her 50 of the unused ballots, with which she voted for the Socialist Party (instead of Ak-Zhol party or even SDPK). The reason for this was that while she had been appointed to the position of chair because of her loyalties to the Ak-Zhol party, she had also received money from the Socialist Party. In this way, she enacted her own complicated interpretation of party loyalty. The party observers filled in the remaining unused ballots, voting for their respective parties (Ak-Zhol and SDPK). In the end, almost 90 percent of the local population had voted for number six of the voting list, the SDPK, and Rahim. Every ballot was counted to ensure that the total number of ballots matched the number of registered voters. The package containing the ballots was then sealed, stamped, signed, and sent to the district headquarters.

During this procedure there was some discussion as to whether I, as an "outside observer," should be given 50 of the unused ballots too. Instead of deciding myself (and ignoring the fact that I was officially an "international observer" for an organization committed to reducing electoral fraud), Oroz decided for me by claiming that I belonged to his village (I was *svoi*)[9] and that I therefore supported this village's candidate. I told them that I was not interested in any ballots, and after a long discussion, I was not given a vote. My role here was quite different from that of the other "observers" who, since they were observing on behalf of a particular party, were each eager to take unused ballots to mark for their desired candidate. My observations of this process of collective ballot stuffing posed a tension between my role as outside observer and insider-fieldworker. For although I was in the village as a representative of Interbilim, the very fact that I was given access to this process of allocating unused ballots reflected the fact that I was seen by many in the village as an "insider" and unthreatening.

This had not always been the case: when I first arrived in the village some in Vostok were quite suspicious of my presence. I heard later that people thought that I had come to the village to inspect whether the Ak-Zhol party calendars and newspapers had been properly distributed. Indeed, when I wanted to take a picture of Ak-Zhol newspapers that had been scattered all over the place and were ready to be burnt, I was not given permission. Party membership in this polarized field thus became crucial to acceptance in the village. When I later returned to the village from Bishkek with a registration document attesting to my membership of the SDPK I was welcomed very differently. People addressed me as "a member of their community" and recounted their hopes and expectations. Although my position as a woman and a researcher meant that I was never admitted to the inner circle of political discussion, my (notional) party membership meant that I came to be treated as a village "insider" during the election period.

Part of the reason for this politicization of life was that the stakes were so high. One of the village leaders of the SDPK told me that if they did not get a seat in parliament, his people were prepared to express their dissatisfaction publicly, taking their cause to the streets. His reference point here was the (flawed) parliamentary elections of 2005, which had been a crucial catalyst for the eventual overthrow of Akaev in the spring of that year. Spontaneous demonstrations in the months leading up to the revolutionary ouster of Akaev consumed the main streets of the capital, and protestors had blocked the main road between Bishkek and Issyk-Kul. For my interlocutor, this had been a struggle over justice, community, and political rights: the 2007 parliamentary election was seen as crucial in sustaining those principles in the face of an increasingly authoritarian presidency.

We learned the next day that the village candidate had come out on top of the list in the local electoral district and was to receive a place in parliament. His SDPK party received 6 percent of the general vote and eleven seats in parliament; however, the pro-presidential Ak-Zhol party gained seventy-two seats, giving it a clear parliamentary majority. As with many Kyrgyz elections, there was a distinct regional pattern to the voting. The majority of the votes for the SDPK had been cast in the Kemin region, a cluster of twenty villages in the northern Chui oblast', as well as in the Chui valley, Naryn, and Issyk-Kul regions. There was very little that was "private" about the elections. Villagers knew who had voted for whom and how many ballots had been distributed, to whom, and why. Everyone knew, for instance, the one person who had voted for the Socialist Party, the same party that Ainura had voted for when allocated her extra 50 ballots. They were tolerant of his actions, claiming that his brother was a member of the Socialist Party from a different district. However, there were ten votes for the Ak-Zhol party, excluding Ainura's additional 50 votes,

Figure 3.2. The audience has been waiting in the cold for three hours to hear party representatives speak at the rayon center of Yssyk Ata in December 2007.

and much discussion of who these ten traitors might be, as the whole village was supposed to vote for the SDPK. It later emerged that it was Ainura and her family who had voted for Ak-Zhol, as she had been against the SDPK from the very beginning.

People had drawn their own conclusions as to who the traitors might be, based on kinship relations and their distant relatives within and outside the village. People in Vostok were aware of who was related to whom and why they had voted for Ak-Zhol rather than the SDPK. What is striking, however, is that while people were aware of the distribution of extra ballots at the end of the election, this did not get moralized as "fraud" since the initiator had been Oroz, Rahim's right-hand man. Indeed, it was legitimated by creative appeal to principles of democracy: this had been a "fair" distribution of the extra votes, one that had allowed each of the election observers to cast an extra 50 ballots for the candidate of his or her choice.

Speculation over who voted for whom lasted for about a week, until Rahim's inauguration, guaranteeing their deputy obtained a stable position in the parliament. From the perspective of people in Vostok their efforts had paid off: they had refused to be "bought" by other candidates (in the form of money, sugar, vodka, and tea, regularly distributed at election time), instead opting for long-term gain (the resources that were perceived to accrue from having their son in parliament). This was also seen as a victory for their region in a context where the president was identified as a "southerner." The SDPK was seen as a part of northern Kyrgyzstan, and having their native son in parliament was a major coup for the village. Soon after election day, the SDPK's local victory was marked with the slaughtering of a sheep. Two months later, the patron whom they had supported sponsored a feast at a café in the town of Tokmok to which more than a thousand people were invited and a special toastmaster was appointed to say toasts to the community and to the SDPK.

Corruption or Native Son?

For international organizations, the election as it was conducted in Vostok is symptomatic of a democratic "failure" of the principle of one person, one vote (this had, after all, been an election day characterized by bribery, fraud, and ballot stuffing). The Organization for Security and Cooperation in Europe (OSCE) noted numerous voting irregularities, and other international organizations slammed the election as flawed and corrupt, noting the falsification of votes and the role of bribes (Human Rights Watch 2009; UNHCR 2012). Since the 1990s, international organizations have dedicated considerable resources to anti-corruption campaigns in Kyrgyzstan, including the International Centre Interbilim, which trained me as an international observer. Reports on electoral irregularities in Kyrgyzstan have become common following parliamentary and presidential elections, bolstering a broader narrative of Kyrgyzstani state weakness.

Anthropological perspectives show how such accounts often ignore the complexity of social life and the mutual obligations it entails. Cynthia Werner (2000) notes how corruption has been deemed a serious threat to political stability and economic prosperity in Kazakhstan, even as ethnographic research highlights the "security of mutual indebtedness" between rural households at a time of economic shortage. Gupta (1995, 377) has shown in an Indian context that corruption is not understood locally to be anti-political but instead "seen as simply a different, and no less functional, mode of political action." Smith (2001, 345; 2008) likewise shows how people socially reproduce the patterns of corruption for which Nigeria is notorious. For example, people approach their distant relatives to find them jobs, thereby undercutting competition and the possibility of an equal chance of obtaining employment.

In a Kyrgyzstani context, diagnoses of corruption fail to account for the complexity of social life and the degree to which it is structured by mutual obligations, exchanges, and the demands of community membership. Perhaps more importantly, they fail to explore what elections mean from actors' own perspective: why it is that people still vote for "corrupt" state officials or protective patrons. My analysis has shown how the social roles, status, and hierarchies that are conferred as part of the kinship system mattered to the election process. "Democracy" was not merely a cover or an empty claim in this process. The election mobilized a particular local idiom of democracy as fairness (thus everyone should be given the same amount of ballots at the end), loyalty (thus elderly men should not denied the right to vote even if they cannot formally document their identity), and solidarity (we are proud to support "our son"). Crucially, moreover, this performance of democracy derives from a significantly different notion of "representation" than that espoused in Western democratic theory. For the people of Vostok, citizens are not represented in the form of their individual personhood, via an elected deputy who is answerable to them as individuals. "Our son" is seen as representing the village as a whole, rather than a constituency of individuals who share a similar set of interests. Villagers ensure representation not by legally "pure" votes but by ensuring that their big man is able to engage with the centers of power through a parliamentary position.

Here I seek to extend this analysis to focus on the crucial relationship that the election served to reaffirm: that between a patron, Rahim, and the community from which he hails. In developing this analysis I aim neither to deny the existence of patronage in formal and informal contexts nor to underestimate the social salience of loyalty and trust. My concern, rather, is to elucidate the way in which patronage functions and how people perceive their relationships with their patron (that is, the native son) and their respective justificatory strategies ("a native son is better than an outsider"). My argument suggests that a focus on anti-corruption measures at the local level, if it fails to understand the social and political constraints to which patronage relations respond, risks undermining what is in fact a crucial mechanism of social protection. To understand the dynamics of this process we need to turn to the broader political field in which it occurred.

Potential politicians are aware of the fact that an honest person cannot enter into politics, and therefore create his or her own strategies by becoming involved in "fraud." They do this in order to enter into the "corrupt" system of politics with the hope of having access to resources and a better life. The illegal actions of the patron (giving money to state authorities, starting the campaign process earlier than permissible, etc.) strengthen his position in public life since it marks his ability to deal with the corrupt system of the state. In this case, it is not only donor organizations that claim that Kyrgyz politics is corrupt but ordinary people too. In this rhetorical move it is always "others" who are corrupt.

People perpetuate corruption (from the donor's perspective and that of social actors themselves), but they do not consider it as corruption if common people themselves get involved. Olivier de Sardan (1999, 34) argues that "the real borderline between what corruption is and what is not fluctuates, and depends on the context and on the position of the actors involved." Thus, the Vostok voters did not view the election in their village as corrupt. Rather, people found ways to justify their actions and legitimated their behavior through social networks of reciprocity and out of obligation and loyalty to their son, and as a result of community cohesion. This is reflected in proverbs that served to moralize their action, which circulated widely at the time, such as *öz bala küiöt* (our native son will always be with us). In this context, patronage was viewed as a coping strategy, constituted through interpersonal trust and profoundly important to the exchange of goods and services. People in Vostok were committed to supporting Rahim because, in the contemporary Kyrgyz context, their patron offers political protection, the chance of greater investment in the future, and someone who could mediate their interests to the government.

To note this is not to suggest that people were oblivious to the technical violations that were occurring. People in Vostok know the boundaries between legal and illegal are blurred in relation to state bureaucracy, just as Rasanayagam's Uzbek interlocutors did (2011). For example, in the case of the absence of ID papers, people knew that it was not possible to vote without proper documents. But they also knew that it would be possible to bribe the chairperson or to negotiate with her subordinates to be able to vote nonetheless. As well as participating in such actions themselves, they identified others' actions as being "corrupt"; they noted the "constant negotiation with state officials" and the need to "speak their language." There was general recognition of the vote as fraudulent (*zhazalgan*), even as people were involved in sustaining such practices themselves (through buying votes, accepting bribes, and ignoring the rules of the election). This was moralized locally, however, as being the only way they *could* vote: in a context of economic volatility, having a "son" in parliament who would protect their interests alongside his own was seen as the best guarantee not just of economic development but of political voice and ultimately, of political integrity.

So was this all merely an exercise in political pragmatism or a cynical (and ultimately empty) enactment of a ritual in whose authenticity no one really believed? My analysis suggests that this would be too reductive a reading. For one thing villagers saw the promotion of Rahim as a sincere demonstration of political participation and democratic intent. For all the procedural violations, people were still performing a localized version of democracy: the intense discussion of electoral rules; the active process of campaigning and distributing merchandise; the act of dressing up to participate in the election—all these were sincere gestures of political commitment; a belief in the significance of this event and of their role in shaping the outcome. Secondly, and equally significantly for thinking about the performance of politics in Central Asia, is the way in which, through such actions, villagers also upheld a normative image of the state as properly the locus of moral authority: a source of order and stability as well as a guarantor of basic economic protection. In this context—a context, as Humphrey notes (1998), in which party, state, and people are understood as properly fused in ways that might be considered problematic in the liberal imagination—participating in an election can also be read as a hopeful act: a reassertion of the authority of the state as such in a context where statehood had been dramatically undone by two years of revolutionary upheaval.

Conclusion

Much academic and policy analysis in recent years has been dedicated to diagnosing the failures of political institutions in Central Asia, the destabilizing effects of regional or kinship loyalties (Collins 2002; Schatz 2004), or the "temptations of tyranny" (Lewis 2008). In this chapter, I have sought to explore what electoral democracy means in rural Kyrgyzstan through a focus on the performance of one particular ritual of contemporary Kyrgyz politics: the parliamentary election. Following Comaroff and Comaroff's call to pluralize the study of democracy, I have argued that we need to understand democracy in Kyrgyzstan as a situated local practice, one that is both molded by, and which in turn serves to shape, understandings of community, obligation, and respect, and one that is crucial to performing the state into being in rural Kyrgyzstan.

This is so in a double respect: on the one hand, we need to pay attention to the ways in which an election is seen as providing a vehicle for voicing collective political claims, less through the expression of individual preference than by propelling "our son" into parliament as the best guarantee that local demands will be heard in the halls of power. I have suggested that much of the anti-corruption rhetoric prevalent in Kyrgyzstan misses this critical role that patrons play in translating local village concerns into government action and fails to ask why, in a context of weak state institutions and a polarized party landscape, having "our son" in parliament can be seen as the best guarantee of political voice. On the other hand, we need to remain attentive to the ways in which elections themselves, as dramatizations of political and social difference, can also serve to crystallize lines of difference that are often diagnosed as the source of Kyrgyzstan's problems.

Rather than seeing "traditionalism" or kinship loyalty as an essential trait or obstacle to Western-style electoral democracy (Juraev 2008; Khamidov 2006), we need instead to ask how regional or kinship loyalties are hypostatized by the fact of electoral politics—turned from a relatively fluid and situational aspect of village life into a dramatic line of demarcation: Are you with us or against us? Are you for Ak-Zhol or the SDPK? Ainura's dilemma, if we can call it that, is precisely that she has multiple commitments to multiple communities of obligation, based on ties of kinship, marriage, and work, and yet the election demands a single gesture of party (here read as "community") loyalty. This has consequence for the growing literature on "clan politics" in Central Asia: rather than a pre-existing frame that corrupts "pure" democracy, regional or kinship loyalties should perhaps be conceived as in part a product of electoral party politics. As Spencer found in the Sri Lanka of the 1980s, party politics "had become braided into the very fabric of local sociality" (2007, 33) such that local disputes came to be articulated in the language of party political difference.

There is a further argument that I have developed here, which concerns more centrally the relationship between democracy and the state. It is tempting to read the fraudulent parliamentary election that I have analyzed as a mark of disillusion with, or disregard for, the state and its political future: the response of a cynical citizenry toward a state that has "failed." By taking seriously the sincerity of my informants' participation in this ritual, I have developed a rather different interpretation, showing how the state is precisely reproduced through such performances—how, in a context of political turmoil, such activities serve to reanimate the state as ideal and site of popular participation. There is a huge popular investment, as I show, in performing the state—not just in the sense of "acting at" or "pretending to be," but in the sense of bringing in to being. This enactment of electoral democracy, for all that it was flawed, was significant precisely in asserting a connection to a state "out there": invoking the state as locus of ongoing authority in the wake of political crisis.

Notes

1. Interviews with Vostok schoolteachers, December 2007.

2. In Kyrgyzstan, women usually move to their husband's village upon marriage. Sometimes it happens that the wife's natal village has its own candidate and members of that community (*torkyn jak*), try to influence their daughters through the mediation of their parents. As a result there is often a debate between the side of the in-laws (*kuda jak*) and that of one's own kin (*öz jak*), and respect is often shown toward this most important group of relations by taking the side of one's in-laws rather than that of one's own kin at election time.

3. The local term is *öz bala*—the direct translation is "our own son," but it also refers to the "community son." In this context, I decided to call him a "native son" to stress the degree to which he is locally perceived to be of and for the community as a whole.

4. Rahim was invited to join Ak-Zhol but he refused because SDPK was considered part of the northern zone since its founder, Almazbek Atambaev, is a northerner. The founder of Ak-Zhol, Kurmanbek Bakiev, is from the south of Kyrgyzstan.

5. Local people also wanted the native son to represent them as northerners and defend their interests in the political arena vis-à-vis southerners, whom they saw as monopolizing politics through the Ak- Zhol party.

6. Interbilim International Centre is a non-governmental organization with a mission to strengthen civil society in Kyrgyzstan. The electoral commission is an independent agency charged with regulating the electoral process.

7. Since the party system in Kyrgyzstan is only weakly developed, the majority of parties were not able to send observers to all of the electoral districts.

8. The village headman was appointed to be the leader of two villages (Vostok and Trud) and was thus responsible for all of the village lands. The village headman, using his authority to distribute lands for Vostok, encouraged those who did not have land to vote for Ak-Zhol; otherwise, he claimed their land would be distributed amongst his own followers. By law the head of the village has the right to distribute land to young married couples but not to distribute the land belonging to the *National Land Fund* (FPS). http://www.landreform.kg/ (accessed February 12, 2009).

9. In this context, my "belonging" does not mean being born in their village; rather I was seen as taking their side by supporting their patron.

References

Appadurai, Arjun. 1998. *Modernity at Large: Cultural Dimensions of Globalization*. Minneapolis: University of Minnesota Press.

Aretxaga, Begoña. 2003. "Maddening States." *Annual Review of Anthropology* 32: 393–410.

Campbell, John Kennedy. 1974. *Honour, Family and Patronage: A Study of Institutions and Moral Values in a Greek Mountain Community*. New York: Oxford University Press.

Coles, Kimberley A. 2004. "Election Day: The Construction of Democracy through Technique." *Cultural Anthropology* 19, no. 4: 551–580.

Collins, Kathleen. 2002. "Clan, Pacts, and Politics in Central Asia." *Journal of Democracy* 13, no. 3: 137–152.

Comaroff, John, and Jean Comaroff. 1997. "Postcolonial Politics and Discourses of Democracy in Southern Africa: An Anthropological Reflection on African Political Modernities." *Journal of Anthropological Research* 53, no. 2: 123–146.

Das, Veena, and Deborah Poole. 2004. *Anthropology in the Margins of the State*. Sante Fe, N.M.: School of American Research Press.

de Sardan, Olivier J. 1999. "A Moral Economy of Corruption in Africa?" *Journal of Modern African Studies* 37, no. 1: 25–52.

Donahoe, Brian, and Otto Habeck. 2011. *Reconstructing the House of Culture: Community, Self, and the Makings of Culture in Russia and Beyond*. New York: Berghahn.

Ferguson, James, and Akhil Gupta. 2002. "Spatializing States: Towards an Ethnography of Neoliberal Governmentality." *American Ethnologist* 29, no. 4: 981–1002.

Grant, Bruce. 1995. *In the Soviet House of Culture: A Century of Perestroikas*. Princeton, N.J.: Princeton University Press.

Gupta, Akhil. 1995. "Blurred Boundaries: The Discourse of Corruption, the Culture of Politics, and the Imagined State." *American Ethnologist* 22, no. 2: 375–402.

Hiro, Dilip. 2009. "Kyrgyzstan's Tulip Revolution Wilts." http://www.guardian.co.uk/commentisfree/2009/jul/24/kyrgyzstan-election-tulipdemocracy, July 24 (accessed August 17, 2009).

Human Rights Watch. 2009. "World Report 2009. Kyrgyzstan: Events of 2008." http://www.hrw.org/world-report/2009/Kyrgyzstan (accessed September 17, 2012).

Humphrey Caroline. 1998. *Marx Went Away, but Karl Stayed Behind.* Ann Arbor: University of Michigan.

Juraev, Shairbek. 2008. "Kyrgyz Democracy? The Tulip Revolution and Beyond." *Central Asian Survey* 27, no. 3: 253–264.

Khamidov, Alisher. 2006. "Kyrgyzstan: Kinship and Patronage Networks Emerge as a Potent Political Force. A Eurasia Net Commentary." http://www.eurasianet.org/departments/insight/articles/eav112106a.shtml (accessed March 9, 2010).

Lewis, David. 2008. *The Temptations of Tyrrany in Central Asia.* London: Hurst.

Navaro-Yashin, Yael. 2002. *Faces of the State: Secularism and Public Life in Turkey.* Princeton, N.J.: Princeton University Press.

———. 2003. "'Life Is Dead Here': Sensing the Political in 'No Man's Land.'" *Anthropological Theory* 3, no. 1: 107–125.

Radio Free Europe/Radio Liberty. 2007. "Kyrgyzstan: Amid Protests, Ruling Party Seen Winning Elections in Landslide." http://www.rferl.org/content/article/1079270.html (accessed February 8, 2009).

Radnitz, Scott. 2005. "Networks, Localism and Mobilization in Aksy, Kyrgyzstan." *Central Asian Survey* 24, no. 4: 405–424.

———. 2006. "What Really Happened in Kyrgyzstan?" *Journal of Democracy* 17, no. 2: 132–146.

Rasanayagam, Johan. 2011. "Informal Economy, Informal State: The Case of Uzbekistan." *International Journal of Sociology and Social Policy* 31, nos. 11–12: 681–696.

Roniger, Luis. 2004. "Political Clientelism, Democracy, and Market Economy." *Comparative Politics* 36, no. 3: 53–375.

Roniger, Luis, and Ayşe Güneş-Ayata. 1994. *Democracy, Clientelism, and Civil Society.* Boulder, Colo.: Lynne Rienner.

Schatz, Edward. 2004. *Modern Clan Politics: The Power of "Blood" in Kazakhstan and Beyond.* Seattle: University of Washington Press.

Smith, Daniel Jordan. 2001. Kinship and Corruption in Contemporary Nigeria. *Ethnos* 66, no. 3: 344–364.

———. 2008. *A Culture of Corruption: Everyday Deception and Popular Discontent in Nigeria.* Princeton, N.J: Princeton University Press.

Spencer, Jonathan. 2007. *Anthropology, Politics, and the State: Democracy and Violence in South Asia.* Cambridge: Cambridge University Press.

UN High Commissioner for Refugees (UNHCR). 2012. "Freedom in the World 2012: Kyrgyzstan." http://www.unhcr.org/refworld/topic,4565c22538,4565c25f455,4ff542d928,0,,,.html (accessed September 17, 2012).

Werner, Cynthia. 2000. "Gifts, Bribes, and Development in Post-Soviet Kazakstan." *Human Organization* 59, no. 1: 11–22.

4. "There is this law . . ."

Performing the State in the Kyrgyz Courts of Elders

Judith Beyer

"We don't have a state here anymore!" This was a common expression among the villagers of Aral and Engels.[1] The claim referred back to Soviet times, when their joint kolkhoz had been part of a dense network of agricultural units that spanned the country. As the two villages were subject to the policies of Communist Party officials in Moscow and Bishkek, "the state," apparently, had been there but must have left some time after the country became independent. While state institutions have never gained access to the private sphere of the household in rural Kyrgyzstan to the extent that has been reported for other postsocialist settings, "the state" was a dominant and present actor in daily kolkhoz life, manifest in its officials, its bureaucracy, and its institutionalized means of enforcing order (*tartip*). Looking back at the Soviet state, my informants stressed that there had been order because there had been strong individuals in the kolkhoz who "made people work." After independence, many people in the village complained that the kind of order that existed in Soviet times was never restored. Not only have the labor opportunities in the kolkhoz disappeared; the controlling and nurturing state has also vanished. State officials have little to offer to the village population these days if they are not financially affluent. In order to sustain their own positions as heads (*bash*), they either need to cooperate with businessmen, become businessmen themselves, or tap the resources of international organizations. While the state is increasingly perceived as absent, villagers invoke its presence situationally by appropriating language, rituals, and symbols that they associate with it. In this chapter I investigate these invocations and performances, focusing on the role of state law in relation to customary law (*salt*). Since the state is "an idea" more than "a system," as Abrams

(1988, 75) and Graeber (2004, 65) have convincingly argued, I investigate how and where these ideas about the state are voiced and performed by exploring village bureaucracy as "official pronouncements where personal identity and state authority are aligned" (Herzfeld 1992, 37; Das and Poole 2004, 6).

In the village courts of Elders (*aksakal sottu*), for example, the elders phrased their perceived statelessness in terms of the lack of interest state judges had in their activities. Feeling left to their own devices, they had to handle their new role as judges by themselves. In court sessions they tried to create the appearance of a state court, and introduced procedures they claimed were derived from state laws. They also invoked the state as a threat specifically when people did not want to heed their decisions. While the institution of the *aksakal* court had been explicitly set up in each village of the country to allow adjudication according to *salt,* an imagined state law (Benda-Beckmann 2005) nevertheless played an important role in the institution.

Introducing the *Aksakal* Courts

Since 1993 the *aksakal* courts have been mentioned in all versions of the country's constitution. Their assignment has been amended several times: from having been incorporated into the judiciary in 1993, to forming a part of the local self-governance structure in 2003, to being subsumed under the section on "citizenship" in 2007, where they remain in the most recent version of the constitution (2010).[2] Art. 39 of the 2010 constitution postulates that citizens have the right to organize *aksakal* courts, and then refers to a separate law on the *aksakal* courts.[3]

The law was made more specific in 1995 after disturbing news reached the Kyrgyz public and international organizations about a number of serious offenses involving some *aksakal* courts. In Talas, a Kyrgyz citizen was allegedly stoned to death by fellow residents after the local *aksakal* court had pronounced him guilty of extortion. In other places *aksakal* courts had permitted the whipping of culprits. Amnesty International was furthermore concerned with "extralegal militias operating under the authority of *aksakal* courts [that] have subjected people to illegal detention and ill treatment and have administered punishments handed down by the *aksakal* courts" (Amnesty International 1996, 7). Since then international organizations have called for effective supervision and monitoring of *aksakal* courts and for special protection measures to ensure that *aksakal* courts fully apply the principles and provisions of international rights.[4]

Local non-governmental organizations (NGOs), on the other hand, demanded the immediate abolition of the institution (see, e.g., Anon. 1996). One of the leading activists of that time recalled the beginnings of the institution in an interview that I conducted in Bishkek:

> It was a big mistake. They were really hastily organized because it was an initiative from above. And awful things started happening. They started putting people in *zindani*. *Zindan* was the kind of prison people in Central Asia used to have in the Middle Ages. They are usually deep in the ground. They used to keep people there.

While this example refers to one particular case only, the activist presented the instance in a way that reflects the general resentment toward the *aksakal* courts among activists in the 1990s. Intensive lobbying by local NGOs and the pressure of international organizations elicited a reaction from President Akaev. But rather than abolishing the courts as some organizations had urged, he redefined the limits of their jurisdiction in a separate law and continued to lobby for them. The "Law on the *aksakal* courts," which underwent revision in 1995 as a result of these incidents, consists of eight sections and thirty-seven articles. Art. 1 defines *aksakal* courts as "societal organs that are formed voluntarily and on the basis of elections and self-governance." Arts. 2 and 3 emphasize that *aksakals* should be guided in their decision making as well as in the instructions they give to the people by "historically established Kyrgyz customary law." The court is supposed to consist of five to nine members (Art. 8), who are elected for a period of three years. Court sessions are scheduled on demand. Each municipality can have one *aksakal* court. In towns, one court for every 25,000 people should be established. The courts have to be registered with the local administration (Art. 12). A judge is not allowed to preside over cases that involve direct relatives (Art. 13). *Aksakals* are allowed to decide over family disputes, property issues, and disputes involving irrigation and overgrazing (Art. 15). Having established the guilt of an accused, they can issue a verdict and by way of punishment take one of the following actions: a) issue a warning; b) require a public apology to the victim(s); c) administer a public reprimand; d) require the guilty party to compensate for material damages; and e) fine the guilty party an amount not to exceed the equivalent of three months' salary at minimum wage. They can also sentence the guilty party to community service. If the court cannot reconcile the parties in a property- or family related case, it makes a decision on the question under consideration. If necessary, the *aksakal* court is empowered to hand materials over to the regional courts.

According to the law, court sessions are supposed to be free of charge for the disputing parties (Art. 23). A judgment made in the *aksakal* court must be based only on the evidence obtained during the court session (Art. 26), and it is legally binding when a simple majority has been reached (Art. 25). The case is to be transferred to a state court if the required quorum of judges is not present (Art. 16). The decision of an *aksakal* court can be appealed by the losing party or by other persons participating in the case within ten days from the day the verdict was issued. Appeals are submitted to the district *(raion)* or city court that has jurisdiction over the territory on which the *aksakal* court was established. The cases, the session minutes, and the judgment need to be recorded in writing (Arts. 24 and 27). At least once a year the *aksakal* judges must report to state judges (Art. 35). References to the jurisdiction of *aksakal* courts can also be found in the penal and civil codes of the country, as well as in a number of other laws.

Following this attempt to clarify the legal position of the *aksakal* courts, negative reports about them have ceased to reach the public. In 2004 the *aksakal* courts, initially only a rural phenomenon, were established in the capital, Bishkek, and in the southern city of Osh as well. While in most rural areas the courts are staffed with male elders only, women form a large percentage in the city *aksakal* courts in Bishkek.[5]

Akaev's promotion of the institution of the *aksakal* court must be understood in the following context: first, *aksakal* courts were established as part of the decentralization efforts of the government, as they constituted an alternative to state courts. The government, with the financial and logistical help of the United Nations, has carried out various reforms aimed at decentralizing the state administration and thereby transferring responsibilities and rights to local regions. This policy started in 1996 when a new administrative unit, the municipality (*aiyl ökmötü*), was introduced in order to strengthen the regions' capacities to govern themselves. Nowadays, each *aiyl ökmötü* has one *aksakal* court. However, this policy, which is officially framed as "more rights to the regions," can just as easily be interpreted as "less work and expense for the central state." Regarding the *aksakal* courts, this has meant less work for the police and the state courts, especially the regional courts, to which claimants had addressed their problems before. The possibilities for citizens to apply to the legal institution of their choice have thus been limited. Issues that are regarded as "minor" by the police or the courts are now being sent, without the consent of the claimants, directly to the *aksakal* court of the claimant's home community. Even when claimants have managed to access state courts, the cases have often been sent back to the villages, thereby depriving actors of formal judicial expertise.[6] In this way, villagers were forced to interact with this institution first if they wanted to have their cases considered by state organs at all.

Second, the promotion of the *aksakal* courts allowed Akaev to use the institution as one of several tools in his nation-building efforts. Campaigns such as the proclamation of the uninterrupted existence of a Kyrgyz state for 2,200 years and the assertion that the *Manas* epic represented the history of all Kyrgyz served to build up a sense of national identity (see Van der Heide 2008). While he published a series of books about the Kyrgyz state, Akaev struggled at the same time not only to reform the country's economic, political, and legal system but also to define what it meant to be "Kyrgyz" in the first place. For this purpose, Akaev not only elevated the significance of certain places and historical figures but also related these to contemporary challenges that independence had brought with it. He addressed this in a speech to *aksakal* court members in February 2005, emphasizing the *aksakals'* strong links to their forefathers, the inherent "Kyrgyz" character of the institution, and its suitability for modern reforms:

> While I was writing my book *The Kyrgyz State and the national epic Manas,* I had to read and review the history of the Kyrgyz people through the whole 2,200 years of its existence. I determined that Kyrgyz people were a united force back then. They not only built on their spiritual nomadic civilization but also knew how to govern themselves. The Kyrgyz *aksakals* and their courts played a big role in this regard. This becomes clear when reading Kazybek's poem.[7] He said: "One word was said to those who overstep the limits. There were not any courts and no police, just *aksakals* working together, admonishing each other." . . . Since last year we have been working on local self-governance. This does not mean that we are copying Western countries, as some people think. These principles of self-governance were in the history of the Kyrgyz people. There have never been *aksakal* courts in the history of other countries.

Third, the establishment of *aksakal* courts also provided Akaev with advantages in dealing with international organizations, which had been highly critical of the courts in their initial years but more recently had started to refer to them as "democratic and responsible to their constituents."[8] They therefore came to be regarded as potential tools that could be used to meet the objectives of international organizations (see UNFPA et al. 2003, 5). According to these organizations, the courts were easily adapted to village life because their working principles were assumed to be based on "pre-Soviet traditional clan-based customs" (Simpson 2003), which were now being channeled through the institution of the *aksakal* courts. While international observers emphasized that "customs are slowly changing, but customs are more important than law in the villages" (Giovarelli and Akmatova 2002, 19), Akaev himself also aligned the courts with human rights discourses: "To my mind this unique national court system plays a great role in the development and the realization of the conception of the national idea that Kyrgyzstan is a country of human rights. . . . As you know, our constitution says that basic human rights and freedom are guaranteed for everyone. Thus we put human rights above all" (Akaev 2005).[9]

From this quote it becomes particularly clear that the existence of *aksakal* courts in today's Kyrgyzstan is presented as much more than just a "survival": *aksakals* are of significance for modern state reforms because, according to

Akaev, they had been institutions of local self-government long before Western reformers deemed them fitting for the country. Especially with regard to the current popular approach of alternative dispute resolution (ADR), *aksakal* courts could be presented as mediating bodies and effective dispute management institutions.

One month after he had given a speech at a festive event in Bishkek where he publicly honored "the best *aksakals* in the country," the president had to flee Kyrgyzstan. On March 24, 2005 a large group of protesters gathered in front of the president's administrative building and eventually took over the complex.[10] Kurmanbek Bakiev became interim president and—on July 10, 2005—the new president of the country. Former president Akaev had planned to further extend the responsibilities of *aksakal* courts in the years to come and even promised to pay them a salary (Akaev 2005). These possibilities were also discussed under the presidency of Bakiev, but no changes in legislation have yet been made. At present, *aksakal* judges still work for free, with the exception of those in Bishkek, where they operate under the control of the city administration.

In all these accounts the institution of the *aksakal* court is either characterized by referring to the "customary law" that it presumably applies, or viewed in terms of its compliance or non-compliance with human rights. In my fieldsite, however, the institution was until recently predominantly associated with the state. Thus, while state officials adopted the language of "custom" and presented *aksakals* as the "bearers of tradition," *aksakal* judges in turn appropriated official state rhetoric in order to accentuate their competence and their public role as officials. The state and state law are invoked as part and parcel of *aksakal* court performances, but at the same time written state law is never consulted in *aksakal* courts and is even for the most part unknown to the *aksakals*.

"There is this law . . .": A Divorce Case

I was sitting in the house of Kasym Ata,[11] the head of the *aksakal* court in Engels, along with my partner and my research assistant, Eliza. We were having tea and chatting about the latest village news. When I asked him if any new disputes had arisen during my two-week absence from the village, he suddenly remembered a letter of complaint (*aryz*) to which he had not yet reacted, and decided to resolve the case that very day. The fact that the petitioner was in the hospital and not currently in the village did not bother him: "We will summon her brother since he wrote the *aryz* in her name." He explained that the case was about the divorce of Ainura and Emil.[12] The couple had two sons and a daughter, Mairam, and had been living together with Emil's parents for nine years. Ainura, however, was mentally ill and was often incapable of caring for her husband and her children. Finally, Emil sent her back to her parents' house. He kept their two sons, whereas Ainura decided to take their daughter with her. Emil then found a new wife, who had already moved in with him and his parents.

Ainura's family now wanted Emil to divorce officially, and to give them Mairam's birth certificate and her share of the land. They were claiming neither land for Ainura nor the payment of alimony. Emil did not react to the demands, and thus the family turned to the head of the *aksakal* court for help. We left Kasym Ata's house to pick up Ainura's brother, but as he was not home, we took his wife, Sura, with us instead. Then we picked up Tülööberdi Ata (referred to in the following conversation as TüA), another *aksakal* court member, who had not been informed of the case. Together we visited Emil and his parents. There, on the street in front of their house, Kasym Ata (KasA) started talking to Emil and his mother (EmilMo). Askar Ata, another *aksakal* and a neighbor of Emil, joined the group.

KasA [approaching Emil]: I received a message from the policeman about you. I will save you. You married another woman without divorcing your wife. Do you want to go to the regional court? Or do you want to come to the mayor's office instead, so that I can save you [from the possibility of imprisonment]? Choose one of these options and be quick.

TüA [to KasA]: I will also divorce. Will you save me too? [He laughs.]

KasA [ignoring the comment; to Emil]: Did you understand me?

Emil: When?

KasA: Now.

Sura: And bring Mairam's birth certificate.

KasA: If you don't agree, I will just send my decision and the note from the policeman to the regional court and you will go there. The regional court will deal with you. [to TüA] He married another woman without divorcing his first wife and left her with three children.

TüA: When was this?

Sura [to Emil]: Generally one should get married *after* getting divorced.

Emil: I have my two sons with me.

Sura: You have them, but who will take care of your wife now?

KasA [to Emil]: Who gave birth to your children?

Emil: Why are you threatening me? I don't care. I can even die [in prison].

Sura: Who is talking to you like this? Are you stupid or something?

KasA: Hey, come on! I will save you peacefully.

EmilMo [to KasA]: Dear relative, I am halfway to my death and so is my husband. Don't talk bullshit. How long will you torture this guy?

Emil: I am ready to die.

Sura [to EmilMo]: Dear relative, let him divorce legally.
EmilMo: What do you know about legal things? He might die.
Emil [to both *aksakals*]: I can die and I will take one of you with me to my grave. I promise if I die, I will kill one of you two.
Sura [to EmilMo]: Dear relative, I have told you that we need to separate them in the *aksakal* court. That's it.
EmilMo: Shut up. Since then [when her son left his first wife] I feel really bad and so does my husband.
KasA [to EmilMo]: Relative, who is talking bad to you? Let's do it like this: send him and I will give him a paper that says he is divorced. I want to save him.
EmilMo: Yes, ok. He is in your hands, in the hands of our relative.
TüA: Let's just make them divorce.
KasA: Let the new daughter-in-law live normally.
Sura: Yes. We don't have any ill will toward his new wife.

Kasym Ata started the case with a threat. Should Emil not be willing to have his case considered by the *aksakal* court, Kasym Ata would have to inform the state court. The note he allegedly got from the policeman was invented in order to frighten Emil. This shows that the first image of the state that the *aksakal* deployed was a threatening one, and Emil was definitely daunted. But it also shows that the *aksakal* needs to invoke the figure of a policeman in addition to his own presence in order to ensure he gets his message across. The role of the local policeman is particularly important in this regard: on the one hand, he embodies the state, his police uniform visibly marking him as an official responsible for enforcing "law and order." On the other hand, it is through him that the absent state can be contacted. Here, the state is envisioned as residing somewhere outside the village in an institutionalized form such as the Talas city court.

When I did fieldwork in 2005–2006 there was no permanent policeman in the two villages. Instead, a young man traveled to the two villages when he was "invited" by the respective mayor to levy taxes or to be present at an *aksakal* court session. The two villages had been promised their "own" policeman in 2006, but they had to wait until the summer of 2008 for such an official to permanently assume residence.[13] Invoking the presence of a policeman, as Kasym Ata did in the divorce case, or having him attend court cases, was a measure frequently taken by the *aksakals* in order to give their performances an official appearance and to emphasize that they acted as judges who have state officials at their disposal (cf. Das and Poole 2004, 20; Friedman 2003; Fuller and Harris 2001, 25).

In the lower village, Kudaibergen Ata is less confrontational. He simply informs the disputing parties of their "right" to have their case considered in the state court. But all participants know too well that this "right" is not enforceable for two reasons. First, according to *salt* it is considered inappropriate to engage non-kin in one's problems. Villagers usually try not to let their disputes "come out" (*chyktyrba*), that is, they try to keep them "inside" (*ichinde*). This was also a well-known strategy during Soviet times, when villagers hid their affairs from Soviet officials.[14] While "inside" refers to the sphere of the household within the village, it extends to the sphere of the village once state courts come into play. Thus, what is perceived as "inside" and what as "outside" changes according to the situation (see Vite 1996; Yurchak 2006, 118). Transferring a dispute case to the state courts triggers expressions of shame-anxiety (*uiat*) in villagers, and might cause those responsible to be stigmatized afterward. Moreover, state courts are very often directly associated with imprisonment, as we have seen in Emil's reaction. Consider how a city judge from Bishkek presented the public image of state courts:

> People are afraid of state courts. They always think of the iron cages [where defendants sit during trials] and that it is *uiat* to go there. It is also expensive—you need a lot of documents, you have to travel there . . . all this is expensive. Here, in Kyrgyzstan, the *aksakals* decide. This is how it has been done since ancient times.[15]

The second reason why villagers do not enforce their right to bring their problems before state courts is not related to notions of appropriateness but to practicalities such as those the state judge mentioned: most villagers simply cannot afford to have their cases considered in state courts. Not only does the registration of a case require payment but the procedure as such is also known to bear hidden costs.[16] The documents I collected in my fieldsite also show that, particularly in the early years, state judges sent cases that they considered "minor" back to the villages for (re)consideration in the *aksakal* courts. These cases dealt mostly with animal theft, grazing transgressions, and land disputes—issues of fundamental importance to villagers who live off their land, from their animals, and with each other.

While Kudaibergen Ata in the lower village knows of all these obstacles and therefore does not even threaten to transfer cases to state courts, Kasym Ata's style of conducting court sessions is based on his estimation that villagers nevertheless fear state courts as such. However, in this particular divorce case, he underestimated Emil's aggressive reaction: his counter-threat to take Kasym Ata or the other *aksakal* present with him to the grave should the case be transferred to the courts.

Figure 4.1. *Aksakal* court session in the upper village. Kasym Ata reads out a letter of complaint.

Emil associated state courts directly with imprisonment, and imprisonment with having to die. This was not the *aksakal*'s intention; although he certainly provoked Emil's reaction by saying he would "save" Emil. Emil's mother felt equally threatened by Kasym Ata's behavior. She reacted very emotionally, appealing to the fact that she and her husband were old and near death themselves, and that they and the *aksakal* were relatives. When Sura tried to clarify things, she was told that she did not know about "legal things" and that Emil would indeed die if his case were sent to the state court. Only after several attempts at pacification was she finally willing to put her son's fate in the *aksakal*'s hands.

Kasym Ata's performance, in the end, was successful, and the accused party agreed to follow him to the mayor's office. While the old men led the way, it was Askar Ata, a neighbor of Emil, who accompanied Emil and his new wife to the mayor's office. The two looked intimidated. Since all the offices in the building were locked, there was no room to sit down to discuss the case. The *aksakal* and Sura took a seat on the window ledges in the foyer, and the couple crouched on the floor. It was cold and windy even inside the building because some of the windows were broken and the door did not close properly. The *aksakals* made sarcastic remarks to each other about these working conditions. Nevertheless, the court session began.

Kasym Ata first read the letter of complaint aloud. After a couple of questions about its content, the *aksakal* again explained the need to divorce first before getting married again. When interrogated, Emil was told to stand up in front of the court. After having answered, he was told to "sit down." After the accused was made aware of the issue at stake, Kasym Ata again emphasized that there was no need for a conflict and that after he signed the paperwork, their divorce would be legal and Emil could officially marry his new wife. Ainura, on the other hand, would then be able to receive the childcare allowance for her daughter because she would then be a single mother. The couple asked whether they would be allowed to register their marriage in Talas after the proceedings, and the *aksakal* confirmed that they would. Later, Kasym Ata wrote a note stating that Ainura and Emil had decided not to live together anymore, and that the *aksakal* court had taken notice of their decision.[17] The court session ended amicably and everyone got up to leave the hall.

Although the surroundings in which the court session took place were in no way comparable to a courtroom, the procedures that the *aksakal* applied mimicked state court procedures. Having the accused brought before the court, reading out the complaint, asking the couple to stand up when being questioned, and telling them when to sit down—all this was highly reminiscent of state court procedures. In this case as well as in other cases I took part in throughout fieldwork, it was precisely the procedural state court-like appearance the *aksakals* wanted to create. The legal basis on which they made their decisions mattered little. To further associate their work with the imprimatur of the state, court sessions usually take place in the mayor's office and not in a private setting. The mayors join these events and take an active role, thereby giving the event additional official sanction.[18]

In the lower village, Kudaibergen Ata makes his elevated role as judge visible to everyone by claiming the mayor's leather chair for himself, while the mayor sits in a regular chair. Having the right to sit where the mayor usually sits is in itself an important procedural element of the court session. During the court sessions it is not the mayor but the head of the *aksakal* court who is the most important individual. A court session starts when the head of the court has arrived and when at least one individual from one of the disputing parties is present. I have witnessed court sessions where either the plaintiff or the defendant was absent. In these cases, their relatives show up to substitute for them, which never seemed to pose a problem, as we have seen in the divorce case. Kudaibergen Ata also often told me that it would be good if everyone stood up when he entered the room (as people do for state judges), and if only they had robes—he used the Russian word *forma*—they would be respected even more: "Then people would see me as a real judge." He also showed me the official stamp and seal of the *aksakal* court, which the mayor's secretary, Kalipa Ezhe, keeps locked in her drawer in the *aiyl ökmötü* building.[19] He also always opens the court with a formal statement, as he did at the beginning of a court session in July 2008:

> In the presence of the people involved in this case and in the presence of the policeman, the mayor, the deputy, and the members of the court, I declare the *aksakal* court open. I remind you that according to the law, we will fine you 200 *som*[20] if you speak about things not related to the case or disturb the process by misbehaving. You can only speak when it is your turn and only about things related to the case.

In this statement Kudaibergen Ata invokes the policeman, who since 2008 has also regularly taken part in the court sessions, as the personification of the state. However, the policeman usually sits quietly through the session without getting involved unless Kudaibergen Ata or Kasym Ata directly asks him for his opinion, in which case he generally agrees with what the elders have said before. This serves to underscore the notion that *aksakals* claim and are granted all the authority in the court room, including the authority to control other people's communication and to dominate the proceedings with their own talk. Although the ideal image of *aksakals* prescribes that they should express themselves in a humble manner, in court they often raise their voices and sometimes shout down the parties should they behave inappropriately by interrupting or screaming at one another.

In the divorce case discussed above this was not necessary. Emil and his new wife were intimidated not only by having been brought before the *aksakal* court without notice but mostly because they were accused of not having their documents in order. The divorce case, as many other cases brought before the *aksakal* courts, centered on the presentation, discussion, and invocation of documents: a birth certificate that Emil's ex-wife needed to apply for child benefits; the letter of complaint written by the brother of Emil's ex-wife, who acted as her guardian; an extended discussion about what documents the new couple needed in order to be officially married. Villagers in my fieldsite encounter the state through documents such as identity cards, application forms for child benefits, pensions, and veteran's benefits, birth and death certificates, maps of land plots, written complaints, and tax forms. These documents bear the double sign of the state's distance and its penetration into everyday life (Das and Poole 2004, 15; see also Ssorin-Chaikov 2003). While such written evidence of the state stood at the center of the discussion during this and other court sessions, none of these documents (with the exception of the letter of complaint read out by the *aksakal*) was visible as such. This suggests that while documents

Figure 4.2. Kudaibergen Ata claims the mayor's chair for himself at a court session. The mayor (the man without a hat) sits in a regular chair next to Kudaibergen Ata during these events.

are considered extremely relevant as a means of arguing and legal reasoning, as well as of establishing the state's presence, it is not the actual presentation or the exact nature of these documents that is of importance but the verbal invocation of them.[21]

In Kudaibergen Ata's opening statement above, another important procedural element is mentioned: the right of the *aksakals* to impose a fine. In this case, Kudaibergen Ata is talking about 200 *som*. Three years ago it was 150 *som* in the lower village, but in the upper village, it has always been 100 *som*, and in a village on the opposite end of Talas it was already 300 *som* in 2005. While these fines are presented as being fixed according to state law, the amount charged is different in each *aiyl ökmötü*, and sometimes changes from case to case. Being able to fine others is a plausible way of performing "law and order" in the *aksakal* courts, where the ability to enforce decisions becomes visible in the financial transaction between the defendant and the *aksakal*. In addition, this can also be seen as a way of "paying respect."[22]

By drawing upon the resources, strategies, and rituals of state officials, *aksakals* try to create the atmosphere of a state court in their sessions, aligning their performances with what they imagine state judges would have done in their stead. People associate all these procedures and measures with the state because of how they remember the Soviet state. This, however, is not meant in a negative way: when they refer to the state as such, they very often compare the contemporary government to previous socialist ones, and complain that there is no order (*tartip*) these days. In Soviet times, order, with a positive connotation, was established through strict control and pressure by officials. Rather than criticizing this, people see in it the reason for the success of the kolkhoz: the stricter the heads of the kolkhoz were, the better people worked. Material well-being and success are directly linked to strict surveillance. This kind of disciplining order does not naturally emerge among the population but needs to be created and maintained by an individual head—in the past this was the *bii*, the *manap*, and the *uruu* elders. During Soviet times it was the kolkhoz directors, and today it is the mayor, the governor, and the president. However, when the head of a given unit is not capable of establishing and keeping order, "work stops," as one of my informants said.[23]

In light of the perceived statelessness, *aksakals* have come to invoke the state by conjuring images of "law and order." Several *aksakals* of the two courts told me that they initially thought themselves incapable of doing "the job," as they were comparing the new institution to a state-like court. They did not know about "law" and did not consider themselves "real judges." They emphasized that they did not have "the right knowledge" it takes to be a judge. Kudaibergen Ata, at the beginning of my stay, frequently told me that there had been only one judge in Talas province who "knew the law" (i.e., was a trained lawyer), and that all the other *aksakals* were only "honest people." They saw themselves as experts in the technical, agricultural, or educational sphere, who merely happened to be in good positions when the institution of the court was formed in the lower village in 1995. When they were "elected," they could continue working as part of the state at the same time that they were dismantling the kolkhoz.

That their self-image has obviously changed became evident to me after the divorce case was over. As the relieved couple was leaving the building, the head of the *aksakal* court approached the couple's neighbor, Askar Ata:

KasA [to AskA]: After court one has to pay 100 *som*. There is this law [Russ. *zakon*].
TüA [to KasA]: Now how will you explain this? Do you have this law?
KasA: That guy [Emil] has to pay 100 *som*.
AskA: All right, I can tell him.
TüA: Yes, tell him.
Judith: Why does he have to pay 100 *som*?
KasA: For our work. I will give 30 *som* to the mayor and with the remaining 70 *som* I will buy something to eat for the *aksakals*.

Figure 4.3. Contractor's shed in the upper village, where the *aksakal* judges eat after their court sessions.

TüA: I don't know whether it will work out or not.
KasA: We will make it work out.
Judith: I have not heard about this law.
TüA [to me]: There is such a law. Write down this law.

We left the hall together. The accused and his wife were sitting in front of the building, waiting for us. Askar Ata started to explain to them:

AskA: There is a law of theirs. I will explain it to you. Since the decision was made in your favor, you will get the decision [the document] after having paid 100 *som*.
KasA: 30 *som* for the mayor.
AskA: You will pay for the mayor.
KasA: And 70 *som* for me.
AskA: For the court's labor.
TüA: Then that's it.

As usual, the participants in the court session wound up in the small contractor's shed left over from Soviet times, which some villagers had rebuilt into a store and a place where men often sit down together to drink tea or vodka. The head of the *aksakal* court ordered tea and cookies for everyone and vodka only for himself, as the other *aksakal* did not drink alcohol. These things were paid for by the couple.

Emil went home immediately, while his wife stayed to serve food and drinks to the group, as a good *kelin* is supposed to do. Later, after she had left as well, the mayor of the village, together with the tax inspector, arrived from a meeting in Talas. They got to hear about the new law:

KasA [to the mayor]: Hey! From now on it will be like this: One has to pay 100 *som* before a court session starts. Thirty *som* for you and 70 *som* for the document.
Mayor [looking irritated]: Hmm?
Tax inspector: Before each court session starts?
KasA: Yes. Until one pays, the court session won't start.
AskA: He says that he has this law before opening a court session.
KasA: It is written inside the back cover of the book that I got from Akaev.
TüA: Do whatever you want, but don't forget to buy something for us.
KasA: Aren't you eating something right now?
TüA: But you started it only today.
Tax inspector: Yes, it would be nice to have tea after the court session.
Mayor: There needs to be tea after court, but I don't know . . .
KasA: From now on it will be like this: people will pay. Only then will we start a court session.

This is the third image of the state, invoked after the court session was over. It centered on the invention of a new law allowing the *aksakals* to impose a fee of 100 *som* for their services. Whereas the *aksakals* involved in the divorce case knew that there was no such law, no one really challenged Kasym Ata's assertion that there was.

The fact that he was once invited by the former president to receive an award for being one of the most successful *aksakals* in the country boosts his standing among his fellow *aksakals* and the village administration. He alone owns a copy of "the book," given to him by Akaev himself, on the back cover of which the law in question is supposedly written.[24] The head of the court was therefore playing both on the fact that you have to do what the law (i.e., "the book") tells you (which exonerates him from personal responsibility for his decision), and that he is the only one in possession of a copy of it. In the divorce case, however, Kasym Ata also employed language associated with the state. Immediately after the session he explained to his fellow *aksakal* that a fee had to be paid to the court, and that the money would go to the mayor and to himself to pay for their food. Later, however, he told the mayor that the fee is to be paid before a court session begins, and that the money would be for the mayor and for "the document."[25] In presenting the law and the distribution of fees differently to the mayor than to his fellow *aksakals*, he may have been trying to accommodate for the mayor's skepticism about the new law. The mayor, in this case, represented the state because he forms part of the local administration and was usually eager to remind villagers about state laws that enabled or "forced" him to do certain things (e.g., levy taxes). Thus, the head of the *aksakal* court explained his new law in terms that sounded as impersonal as possible.

Kasym Ata, however, does not have much to fear from the mayor, who once was his pupil. Their teacher-pupil relationship in many ways has not changed and, thus, the mayor often keeps quiet instead of voicing his opinion. The position of the other *aksakals* is also interesting. They sometimes ridiculed Kasym Ata and his way of running the court, knowing that his standing was largely based on the villagers' lack of knowledge about the state. But later they allied with him, dismissing my objection that I had not heard about this new law. Of course, they also stand to profit from it. The new law in the former president's name allowed Kasym Ata and the other *aksakals* to at least have tea and cookies after their work. By telling me to write down this law, they assigned the codification of the new law to the anthropologist—an appropriate thing to do given the fact that this had been the role of anthropologists in Central Asia throughout the history of the Russian conquest.

Aksakals "represent at once the fading of the state's jurisdiction and its continual refounding through its (not so mythic) appropriation of private justice" (Das and Poole 2004, 14). While the former president set up the *aksakal* courts in an effort to establish *salt* as a viable alternative to state law, those who were supposed to enact *salt* on the basis of this law chose instead to invoke and imitate state law. These performances eventually led to growing confidence among the court members, who began aligning their role as *aksakals* with those of state judges, thereby customizing the institution.

The Customization of the *Aksakal* Courts

The *aksakals* in my fieldsite have managed to turn the two courts of elders into an institution that is increasingly accepted by villagers as a substitute for state courts. Whereas a couple of years ago villagers were disappointed when their cases were sent back from state courts to the *aksakal* courts, today they do not even try to go to Talas for reasons I have outlined above. This general tendency of not waiting for state officials to take care of them is also reflected in an increasing acceptance of their "state of statelessness." This is not only the case for the staff of the local administration and for state officials from the district but equally so for average villagers like my host's son, Nazir Baike, who works as a farmer. He explained to me why he does not care about the work of the local administration in the village anymore: "We do not care. They can do what they want because we do not get salaries anyway. They do not work for people. If the *aiyl ökmötü* functioned well they would bring diesel for the people to harvest wheat. We do not care if they exist or not. People work themselves and survive."

The mayor, in turn, had already told me two years earlier that he himself does not rely on "the state" anymore:

> I am teaching people to solve village problems by ourselves. We will not go to the province. We will not go to the government. If they [state officials] want to help, they are welcome. But the rest of the work, we will do by ourselves. We have to fix our roads ourselves. We have to build a bridge ourselves. We have to do other work ourselves, too. Then we need to live in harmony (*yntymak*). But we pay great attention to attracting foreign investment. We must attract foreign investors and make connections with them. This is my first goal.

That the attraction of foreign investment was important was also the opinion of state officials from the district. During one of the few village meetings in the lower village where officials from the district of Talas were present, villagers bemoaned the fact that the water pumps on the main road were not functioning properly and that they had to use the old-fashioned hand-pumped wells again. In response to their complaint, the district governor replied: "I already told you that you should organize an association through which you could get money. Through an association write a project and try to get money from an international organization. The water pump could also be bought with this money. Our government cannot provide you with water pumps!"

These statements show that the state is increasingly perceived as unreliable, for even in the presence of its officials it remains only "spectrally present" (Das 2004, 225–252). While villagers have stopped expecting anything from their mayor, the mayor does not expect anything from the district or the province anymore. To justify new regulations that elicited criticism from the villagers, the head of the district referred to the capital. In general, new requirements, laws, or rules are usually presented as coming "from Bishkek," where the government sits.[26]

International organizations are today regarded as the main providers and caretakers in Talas. Indeed, foreign organizations and rich individuals from Saudi Arabia sponsor most of the major renovations going on in the two villages. Villagers consider this new development disconcerting. While they have experience with forming associations, they do not understand why they should apply for money if state officials could do so for them. In their eyes, it is the state officials' task to find money, bring it, and then tell them what to do with it, like they did during Soviet times. In these times of local self-governance, however, this does not happen anymore, and the only individuals "taking care" are rich villagers who reside in the capital or even abroad.

In light of this situation, *aksakals* were initially disappointed when they were forced to realize that state judges had no interest in educating them about "law," as had originally been promised. As Kudaibergen Ata put it in 2006, "They used to come and invite us to seminars and talks. They used to teach us about the law. But this was five years ago. Nobody has checked my documents since then. Nobody has come to ask me about my work."

The situation in 2008 was similar: state officials had not monitored either of the two courts. Neither their documents, their styles of decision making, nor their ways of applying law had been scrutinized. They were also not kept informed of the constant and often significant changes initiated by lawmakers in the capital. It was not in spite of but rather because of this situation that they had to develop confidence in their new roles as judges and in their ways of attending to villagers' problems. Their performances as judges have slowly come to be accepted as part of customary law (*salt*) in the eyes of the village residents, who are equally disappointed by state officials, as the earlier comment by Nazir Baike has shown. Thus, being "abandoned by the state" has not resulted in disempowerment, as is sometimes suggested in the literature on decentralization (see Francis and James 2003). Instead, it has led to the customization of the *aksakal* courts. Today, the work of these courts in my fieldsite is considered more effective and legitimate than the work of the state courts. This finding also stands in contrast to how Noori presents Uzbeks' perception of the *mahalla* committee, likewise staffed with *oqsoqols* (Uzb.), as "yet another bureaucracy" that is "unsuccessful in achieving its objectives" (Noori 2006, 155). The *aksakal* judges' new self-image is most vividly reflected in how they (re) conceptualized their relations with state officials. In 2008, Kudaibergen Ata explained to me why state judges do not come to his village anymore:

> They [state judges] do not come here because they were offended by us, because now we deliberate on everything here that was supposed to go to them. Since anyone who goes to the [state] court has to pay, they do not make money anymore. My work, however, is for free, and this is what people like about us—among other things. We also know everyone personally. We even know the person's fathers. State judges don't know a lot.

By portraying state judges as the greedy recipients of villagers' money and as now subject to the will of *aksakal* judges, Kudaibergen Ata turned the historical hierarchy—socialist as well as postsocialist—upside down: if the state does not give anything to the village anymore, the village might as well not give anything to the state. State officials are presented as craving people's money and as knowing nothing about life in the village. While there certainly is a lot of wishful thinking involved, Kudaibergen Ata's statement reflects not only his general disillusionment with the state but the increasing self-confidence of the *aksakals* vis-à-vis "the state" and state officials.

When people complain that they have no state, as villagers in Talas did during my fieldwork, they were—according to Herzfeld (1992, 10)—affirming their desire for precisely such a source of justice in their lives. While former president Akaev envisioned the court of elders as an institution where "customary law" would be applied as an alternative to state law, the *aksakals* associated the institution of the *aksakal* courts with the state. It is precisely because they have been turned into representatives of the state by state officials that they draw upon courtroom ceremonialism and etiquette in their legal proceedings, which usually invest state judges with authority (see Arno 1985; Just 2007, 117). *Aksakal* judges thus tried to appear as "state-like" as possible, and specifically referred to the non-customary repertoire of "state law" in their court sessions. By combining different legal elements into a new justification scheme, they engaged in combined lawmaking (see Benda-Beckmann 1983; Fitzpatrick 1983). Over the course of time, however, they developed a new self-image by aligning their new role as judges with their way of being *aksakals*.

This, together with the continuing failure of state judges to take care of villagers' problems and the *aksakals'* legal education, led to the growing acceptance of the *aksakal* court in my fieldsite. Today, (legal) reasoning, establishing evidence, and making decisions are increasingly carried out according to *salt* in the *aksakal* courts. This is visible in the elders' frequent invocations of harmony (*yntymak*), in the sharing of food after court sessions, in the way one head leads the sessions and makes a decision, and in the preference for keeping things "inside."

As if in response to this increasing customization and the general laissez-faire attitude of villagers vis-à-vis state officials, state officials are now trying to enliven the presence of the state in the periphery by transferring policemen to the countryside, by paying for the renovation of police stations, by donating Russian Niva jeeps to the most successful mayors (usually those who collect the most taxes), and by significantly raising the salaries of the administrative staff in the villages. My impression is that a Potemkin state is being created by piling up insignia of the state in the countryside, demonstrating its presence, while at the same time state officials are increasingly less responsive to villagers' basic needs such as clean water, electricity, health care, regular payment of pensions, and childcare payments.[27] These new and shiny images of the state thus do not align with the concrete performances of state officials anymore. Judging from the contemporary situation, I consider it very likely that a few years from now the institution of the *aksakal* courts will be regarded as an inherent part of *salt* in my fieldsite and as something "that has always existed" among the Kyrgyz. Ironically, this is exactly what Akaev argued when he established the institution after Kyrgyzstan gained independence.

Notes

1. This chapter is based on fieldwork data gathered between 2005 and 2010. Research was financed by the Volkswagen Foundation and the Max Planck Institute for Social Anthropology. I would like to thank my co-editors, Madeleine Reeves and Johan Rasanayagam, as well as Felix Girke and Brian Donahoe for their support and helpful advice.

2. *Zakon Kirgizskoi Respubliki: O novoi redaktsii Konstitutsii Kyrgyzskoi Respubliki*, no. 410. See also the version of February 2003: *Konstitutsiia Kirgizskoi Respubliki*. Between 1993 and 2003, the constitution was completely revised once more (in February 1996), but no changes were introduced in regard to the *aksakal* courts. See Arts. 85 and 95 of the *Konstitutsiia Kirgizskoi Respubliki*, Bishkek (1996).

3. *Zakon Kirgizskoi Respubliki: O sudakh aksakalov*, no. 158. Bishkek: July 30, 2003.

4. For example, the "Written Replies by the Government of Kyrgyzstan Concerning the List of Issues Received by the Committee on the Rights of the Child." Report to the United Nations. http://www.unhchr.ch/tbs/doc.nsf/898586b1dc7b4043c1256a450044f331/13bf9d3e9dfff9f5c1256eef003050ee/$FILE/CRC.C.RESP.63%20_Kyrgyzstan-English_final.pdf (accessed March 31, 2013).

5. Decree "On the Registration of *Aksakal* Courts in Bishkek," June 30, 2004. I conducted some comparative research on two *aksakal* courts in Bishkek. As it turns out, the courts are organized in fundamentally different ways than village *aksakal* courts: they have to report regularly to the district administration that coordinates the institutions of local self-governance (Russ.: *sektor po koordinatsii deiatel'nosti organov territorial'nogo samoupravleniia*). From there the judges also receive a small monthly salary and occasional "training" from state judges of the district courts. The most striking difference, however, is that the Bishkek *aksakal* courts are predominantly staffed with female members of non-Kyrgyz ethnic background (see Beyer forthcoming).

6. In this regard, the institution resembles the Uzbek *mahalla* community. See Noori (2006, 138).

7. The Kyrgyz poet Kazybek was born in 1901. Being the son of a rich man (*manap*), he was imprisoned during the Stalin era and died in 1936 (according to other sources, 1943). He is famous in Kyrgyzstan for his poems, some of which he wrote during his imprisonment.

8. Giovarelli and Akmatova (2002, vii), in reference to the World Bank.

9. "Kyrgyzstan—a country of human rights" was also the president's slogan for the year 2003.

10. The cause of the people's discontent seemed to be the devastating results of the parliamentary elections in February and March 2005, in which only six of seventy-five seats went to the opposition. While the son and daughter of President Akaev won seats, well-known opposition politicians such as Kurmanbek Bakiev (who was later propelled to power in the 2005 "tulip revolution") did not. The immediate cause of the uprising,

however, was not election fraud but long-standing discontent with Akaev and his family among the Kyrgyz population (see Beyer 2005).

11. All of the names used in this section are pseudonyms.

12. This court case is one of ten full-fledged court cases that I observed in Aral and Engels in the course of fieldwork in 2005–2006. I obtained data on how the disputes evolved before they reached the court, took part in the court sessions, and stayed in touch with all parties involved after the court cases were over in order to assess the post-trial stage. In addition, I took part in about forty smaller and larger cases—presided over only by the head of the court—that never became official. When I returned to the field in 2008 and 2010 for brief periods of follow-up research, I participated in additional cases. While I have copies of all protocols and other written documents issued by the two courts since their very inception (in 1995 and 1996, respectively), these materials cannot be presented here. Moreover, as these documents were mostly written on the assumption that they at some point would be read by state officials in order to check on the work of the *aksakals*, they reveal more about how the *aksakals* want to present themselves "to the state" than about how the *aksakal* court in fact operates.

13. The villages simply could not afford to have a policeman, as there was no money for his housing and living expenses. People joked that he could live with the mayor and his family instead.

14. See Beyer (2006) for examples.

15. While this judge knew about my research interests in studying the *aksakal* courts, I had come to her to participate in state court sessions in order to be able to compare the two styles of what I call "court-making." The judge not only summarized people's perception, which I had already gotten to know in both villages, but also related it to the *aksakals*, presenting them as a legitimate alternative to state legal adjudication.

16. It is no secret that the Kyrgyzstani judiciary is corrupt. These costs are also at play when villagers opt against officializing their documents in terms of land ownership.

17. In contrast to how the *aksakal* presented it, however, this is not the divorce itself but only the first step toward it. The actual divorce will have to take place in front of a state court. What is solved, however, is the question of how the property, the land, and the children will be divided between the couple. When I left in September 2006, the couple had not been to the state court. When I returned in 2008, the situation was still the same. In this case, people gave the same reasons they give in regard to why they do not officialize their documents: the costs are too high, the procedure is too time-consuming, and it is considered shameful (*uiat*) to bring one's disputes into the open.

18. This is done even though the mayor should not be part of the court procedure. Very often, however, the mayors act as if they are court members. In a few rare cases I was made a member of the court and my assistant was asked to take the minutes. As we were recording and writing down the sessions anyway, we simply made a copy and handed the original notes over to Kudaibergen Ata or Kasym Ata or the respective secretary, who filed them along with the other documents.

19. While these objects make *aksakal* court documents look more official, I found out that the village only received them in 2002. Each *aiyl ökmötü* was required to pay

for the manufacture of these two symbols of state bureaucracy, but because there had been no money in the budget, they were only recently paid for by the mayor.

20. One Kyrgyz *som* was equal to 2 euro cents in 2006.

21. This handling of written and oral legal evidence has quite interesting ramifications, especially as it aligns very much with how my informants talk about another document: the Qur'an. In fact, I have come across a striking similarity between how the constitution (often invoked as "the law" by *aksakal* judges as well as villagers in general) and the Qur'an are talked about and rhetorically employed as part of legal reasoning: in both cases, it is not the actual document but invocations of "the book" that form the centerpiece of many speech acts and practices. See Beyer (2013) for details.

22. This is even more so the case if the *aksakals* use the money generated in court sessions to buy food for themselves when the court case is over (see below). In none of the cases I took part in was the money handed over to the state courts as prescribed in Art. 29 of the law on the *aksakal* courts.

23. I also credit the local knowledge about how state courts operate to television programs such as the American series *Law & Order* (Russ. *Zakon i poriadok*). In a seminar they attended in Bishkek, some city *aksakals* told the overseeing state judge that often they learn about "how judges behave" from watching TV shows in which court cases are staged in front of an actor playing a judge (see Beyer forthcoming).

24. "The book" is a compilation of state laws about the *aksakal* courts and is in and of itself a symbol of bureaucracy. I checked it at a later point and found nothing written on the inside of the back cover.

25. The *aksakals* often complained about the fact that their work was not being adequately rewarded. They were of the opinion that their work should either be financially compensated or should at least entitle them to free transportation or discounts when buying certain products such as tea, sugar, and tobacco. That Akaev had planned to pay them a salary is well known to all *aksakal* judges in Talas.

26. I myself noticed how much the state is perceived as something "foreign" when occasionally people in my fieldsite who did not know me referred to me as being someone "from the district" (*raiondon*), that is, a state official.

27. In fact, the situation is quite the contrary: rather than giving villagers a stake in state-building processes themselves, new laws on local self-governance have significantly undermined villagers' participation in village politics. Since 2008, for example, the mayor can no longer be elected directly by the villagers but only by the members of the village council (*aiyl kengesh*), and only after the candidacy has been approved by the provincial administration. This led an informant of mine to comment that the current mayor was "elected by the governor."

References

Abrams, Philip. 1988. "Notes on the Difficulty of Studying the State." *Journal of Historical Sociology* 1, no. 1: 58–89.

Akaev, Askar. 2005. "Dear Respected *Aksakal* of Our Country." Speech given at the third Republican meeting of *aksakal* courts, Bishkek, Kyrgyzstan, February 2.
Amnesty International. 1996. "Kyrgyzstan: A Tarnished Human Rights Record." http://www.amnesty.org/en/library/info/EUR58/001/1996/en (accessed September 25, 2012).
Anonymous. 1996. "The *Aksakal* Court in Kyrgyzstan: An Instrument of Barbarianism and a Violation of Human Rights." *Nezavisimaia Gazeta*, January 30.
Arno, Andrew 1993. *The World of Talk on a Fijian Island: An Ethnography of Law and Communicative Causation.* Norwood, N.J.: Ablex.
Benda-Beckmann, Franz von. 2005. "Pak Dusa's Law: Thoughts on Law, Legal Knowledge and Power." *Journal of Transdisciplinary Environmental Studies* 4, no. 2: 1–12.
———. 1983. "Why Law Does Not Behave: Critical and Constructive Reflections on the Social Scientific Perception of the Social Significance of Law." In *Proceedings of the Symposium on Folk Law and Legal Pluralism, XIth IUAES Congress, 1983, Vancouver,* edited by Harald Finkler, 232–262. Ottawa: IUAES.
Beyer, Judith. 2005. "It Has to Start from Above: Making Politics before and after the March Revolution in Kyrgyzstan." *Danish Society for Central Asia's Electronic Quarterly* 1: 7–16.
———. 2006. "Revitalisation, Invention and Continued Existence of the Kyrgyz *Aksakal* Courts: Listening to Pluralistic Accounts of History." *Journal of Legal Pluralism* 53–54: 141–174.
———. 2013. "Constitutional Faith: Law and Hope in Revolutionary Kyrgyzstan." *Ethnos Journal of Anthropology.* iFirst doi: 10.1080/00141844.2013.841270.
———. Forthcoming. "The Customization of Law: The Case of the Courts of Elders in Kyrgyzstan."
Das, Veena. 2004. "The Signature of the State: The Paradox of Illegibility." In *Anthropology in the Margins of the* State, edited by Veena Das and Deborah Poole, 225–252. Santa Fe, N.M.: School of American Research Press.
Das, Veena, and Deborah Poole. 2004. *Anthropology in the Margins of the* State. Santa Fe, N.M.: School of American Research Press.
Fiitzpatrick, Peter. 1983. "Law, Plurality and Underdevelopment." In *Legality, Ideology and the State,* edited by David Sugarman, 159–182. London: Academic Press.
Francis, Paul, and Robert James 2003. "Balancing Rural Poverty Reduction and Citizen Participation: The Contradictions of Uganda's Decentralization Program." *World Development* 31, no. 2: 325–337.
Friedman, Thomas. 2003. "Imagining the Post-Apartheid State: An Ethnographic Account of Namibia." PhD diss., University of Cambridge.
Fuller, Chris, and John Harriss. 2001. "For an Anthropology of the Modern Indian State." In *The Everyday State and Society in Modern India,* edited by Chris Fuller and Veronique Bénéï, 1–30. London: Hurst.
Giovarelli, Renée, and Cholpon Akmatova. 2002. "Local Institutions That Enforce Customary Law in the Kyrgyz Republic and Their Impact on Women's Rights." In *Agriculture & Rural Development e-paper,* edited by the World Bank. Washington, D.C.: World Bank.

Graeber, David. 2004. *Fragments of an Anarchist Anthropology.* Chicago: University of Chicago Press.

Herzfeld, Michael. 1992. *The Social Production of Indifference: Exploring the Symbolic Roots of Western Bureaucracy.* Chicago: University of Chicago Press.

Just, Peter. 2007. "Law, Ritual and Order." In *Order and Disorder: Anthropological Perspectives,* edited by Keebet von Benda-Beckmann and Fernanda Pirie, 112–131. New York: Berghahn Books.

Noori, Neema. 2006. "Delegating Coercion: Linking Decentralization to State Formation in Uzbekistan." PhD diss., Columbia University.

Simpson, Meghan. 2003. "Whose Rules? Customs and Governance in the Kyrgyz Republic." *Local Government Brief,* June 2003. Available at: http://lgi.osi.hu/publications/2003/241/1.doc (accessed September 1, 2009).

Ssorin-Chaikov, Nikolai. 2003. *The Social Life of the State in Subarctic Siberia.* Stanford, Calif.: Stanford University Press.

United Nations Population Fund (UNFPA), United Nations Children's Fund (UNICEF), World Health Organization/International Labour Organization (WHO/ILO), and Institute of Equal Rights and Opportunities. 2003. *Pilot Project: Improving the Quality of Sexual and Reproductive Health Care through Empowering Users. Report of Baseline Study in Pilot Villages.* [Report]. 1–6.

Van der Heide, Nienke. 2008. "Spirited Performance: The Manas Epic and Society in Kyrgyzstan." PhD diss., Tilburg University.

Vite, Oleg. 1996. "Izbirateli—vragi naroda? (Razmyshleniia ob adekvatnosti elektroal'nogo povedeniia i faktorakh, na ee uroven' vliiaiushchikh)." *Etika Uspekha* 9: 58–71.

Yurchak, Alexei. 2006. *Everything Was Forever, Until It Was No More: The Last Soviet Generation.* Princeton, N.J.: Princeton University Press.

Part 2
Political Materials, Political Fantasies

5. The Master Plan of Astana

Between the "Art of Government" and the "Art of Being Global"

Alima Bissenova

Political scientists, sociologists, and urban theorists have long pointed to the changing function of the state in planning and regulating urban development in the neo-liberal market economy (Harvey 1989, 2000; Holston 1989; Caldeira and Holston 2005). Although from its inception, urban planning emerged as an "art of government" exercised by the modern interventionist state, under neo-liberal conditions, the urban-planning capacity of the state has often been disrupted by the imperative to accommodate the interests of capital. This accommodation can range from short-term strategies guaranteeing a return on investment in one-time projects to long-term strategies of making the city "attractive" so that capital keeps returning and circulating in the cityscape. The technologies of marketing the city to investors and consumer-citizens are often produced by a multitude of international institutions and organizations outside the state urban-planning apparatus. The problematic of governance in this situation is thus: what happens to the power relations between the international centers that produce urban-planning and architectural technologies and the national governments that engage them? What are the terms of their cooperation? Can it be that the state itself—despite being a traditional holder of power—has now become subject to the global regime of "soft power" that determines, in Flyvbjerg's words, "what counts as knowledge," what counts as legitimate cultural capital, and what counts as valid expertise (Flyvbjerg 1998; Lukes 2005)? In order to maintain and increase its political power, the state then attempts to acquire those forms of cultural capital and expertise that "work" and bring success on a global scale in what Anna Tsing (2005) calls the "economy of appearances" where "image is everything" and "perception is reality."

In this chapter, I explore these questions by analyzing the politics that have underscored the enunciation, elaboration, and implementation of the master plans for the development of Astana, the new capital of Kazakhstan. In particular, I will analyze the Kazakh officials'[1] strategy of extensively borrowing expertise (cultural capital) from the established brands and centers of urbanism: a strategy whose objective has been to achieve, for Astana, the status of a "global" and "modern" city. According to Bourdieu (1984), cultural capital is both an outreach and a disguise of economic capital. I argue, however, that the conversion of economic capital into legitimate cultural capital, when it is attributed not just to people but to institutions, is much more difficult and is not to be taken for granted, especially, in the view of both established global hierarchies and interests in the durability and global transferability of certain kinds of cultural capital, representing what Bourdieu would call "legitimate culture."

Saskia Sassen (2000, 2002, 2003) has often argued that globalization is embedded in national territory both geographically and institutionally and that economic processes that we call globalization do not necessarily weaken the state. Complementarities of the nation-building and globalization processes have been particularly evident in the ethos of building the new capital of Kazakhstan, which curiously blends statist nationalism with neo-liberal market ideology. On the one hand, the construction of Astana has been a state project; on the other, it has resulted in a gateway for national and foreign investment, as well for the global markets of construction, urban planning, and architectural finesse. In my research, I follow Ulrich Beck, who argues that "there is no need to investigate the global totally globally" (2002, 24), and Doreen Massey, for whom the "global" is always encountered in a local site and any site is a "product of interrelations—connections and disconnections—and their (combinatory) effects" (2005, 67). We can often find the global and cosmopolitan behind an institution or a phenomenon that is manifested as local and national. Following Beck's argument of "internalized globalization," I show how in Kazakhstan's urban governance (particularly at the municipal planning office of AstanaGenPlan, where I conducted my fieldwork), the "global" practice and expertise of "How they do it there" morphs into a constant frame of reference for national policy-making and planning.

Since the relocation of the capital to Astana, the Kazakh government has adopted the strategy of inviting and contracting well-known urban planners and architects. Landmark buildings by celebrity architects in Astana include a palace in the shape of a pyramid, and a shopping mall in the shape of a transparent tent designed by Norman Foster, a concert hall by the Italian Architect Manfredi Nicoletti, and an airport by Kisho Kurokawa, who is also considered to be the author of the Master Plan for the whole city. These are the buildings that become part of "postcard Astana" in promotions locally and abroad.[2]

Astana's experiments with international sources of architectural and urban-planning expertise reveal the aspirations of the Kazakh state and its people to acquire a cultural and symbolic capital that would enable them to ascend the ladder of established hierarchy and to catch up with modern cities in the developed world. At the same time, extensive borrowing and opening up to the creative potential of architects with different visions from various parts of the world has made Astana susceptible to the criticism that it is merely imitative, that there is nothing unique or authentic about it, and that it is, therefore, devoid of its own cultural merit. As Homi Bhabha (2004, 31) noted, "the West carries and exploits what Bourdieu would call its symbolic capital." Following Bhabha (2004) and making Bourdieu's theory (1984) of cultural/symbolic capital work on a larger scale—to sustain the global hierarchies of modernity—I argue that the Kazakh state with its petro-dollars is akin to a member of the nouveau riche who, having come into money, has now diligently set about acquiring and displaying status symbols. The nouveau riche also hires international experts (Bourdieu's "cultural aristocracy") in order to become "cultured" before he can enter the "high society" of modern nations.

Enunciation of the Master Plan

When the government made the decision to relocate the capital of Kazakhstan from Almaty to Astana in 1997, the first bid for the design of the new capital was announced among Soviet-trained Kazakh architects. The winner of this bid was a group headed by the famous Kazakh architect Kaldybay Montakhaev, renowned in Kazakhstan and the wider region for his design of the Republican Square in Almaty. However, there had been concern as to whether any Kazakh architect's vision and performance would allow the capital to benefit from "cutting-edge" developments in contemporary international urban planning. So, in 1998, another international bid was announced (in which Kazakh architects were also encouraged to take part) for the conceptual design (*e'skiz-ideia*) of the new capital. Twenty-seven projects in total were submitted for this bid, and, in 1999, the jury of experts, consisting of internationally acclaimed architects from the United States, Russia, and Turkey, as well as Kazakh government officials, chose a winner—a Japanese concept for the new city presented by the late Kisho Kurokawa[3] and his team. In September 1999, Kurokawa came to Astana to discuss the plan with the Kazakh urban-planning officials and the president, and, in October 2001, a contract was signed between the *Akimat* (municipality) of Astana and the Japan International Cooperation Agency for the development of the Master Plan. A team of Japanese experts then commenced a study to produce a comprehensive development plan for the City of Astana and its surroundings. Of the thirty-six experts listed as the authors and consultants of the study of the Astana Master Plan, only three had Kazakhstani names.[4] The plan was completed in eighteen months, and, in June 2001, four elaborately bound, hard-backed volumes were presented to the municipality of Astana and the president. The Master Plan, which had been designed as a long-term thirty-year plan tied to President Nazarbayev's "2030" national development program, was approved as a blueprint for the city's development.

During nine months of fieldwork in 2008 in the municipal office of Astana-GenPlan, where, among other things, I contributed to the 2008 Correction to the Master Plan (the second correction to the 2001 Japanese Master Plan), I came to learn of several reasons as to why the Japanese project had been selected and which factors influenced the jury's decision.

Firstly, the Japanese project was tied loosely to the Japanese government's forthcoming grants and loans to Kazakhstan, and the Kazakh government chose (or rather influenced the decision to choose) Kisho Kurokawa's bid in order to secure these loans. It is worth noting that the Japan International Cooperation Agency (JICA) provided the US$60 million grant for the development of the Master Plan. In 1998, it also extended a loan of about US$190 million to Kazakhstan for the construction of a new airport and the reconstruction of the old one. In addition, in 2003, JICA extended a loan of US$200 million for the development of sewage systems on the left bank of Astana. In one of the conversations I had with the officials involved in the bid they indicated that at the time there were more investments "in the picture."

The second reason for the selection of the Japanese Master Plan is what I call the discursive affinity between Kurokawa's philosophy and the Kazakh government's general vision for the capital. The government of Kazakhstan thought that adopting what was considered the best international planning expertise was crucial for the international recognition and future development of Astana; in other words, the government's hope was that this project could help Kazakhstan's capital achieve the status of a global city and help Kazakhstan as a nation to overcome provincialism. The government also intended that the new capital would symbolize a break of the state with its Soviet legacy and emphasize the birth of the new nation in a new city, which would be conceived, planned, and built by the new Kazakh government—not Russian or Soviet authorities. Edward Schatz writes, "The Astana move was symbolically to counter the criticism that Kazakhstan was fundamentally unprepared for independent statehood" (2004,128). So, in order to create and present a new Kazakh modernity to the world the state wanted to build a city that would be radically different from "old" Soviet cities and, at the same time, would be recognized as modern and global. Ironically, "global" expertise was needed for legitimating such a project.

British anthropologist and architectural critic Victor Buchli (2007) has pointed out that Kisho Kurokawa's own philosophy was a perfect ideological fit for the unfolding national project in Kazakhstan. Kurokawa had a pronounced post-modernist take on architecture and urban planning and a very critical perspective on so-called modernist European architecture. In his own writings, Kurokawa repudiated the principles of the modernist architecture and urban planning formulated by the prominent modernist architect Le Corbusier, particularly the idea of the town or the house "as a machine for living in" (French 1995, 43). He writes,

> The architecture and arts of the age of the machine have employed analysis, structuring, and organization to achieve a universal synthesis. This closely resembles the process of creating a machine, in which parts are assembled to perform a certain function. Ambiguity, the intervention of foreign elements, accident and multivalent elements cannot be permitted in a machine. (Kurokawa 1994, 23)

In opposition to the modernist architecture and urban planning of "the age of the machine," Kurokawa proposed architecture that, in his words, "heralds the age of life." In an interview with the Russian journal *Proekt Rossia*, Kurokawa maintained that his philosophy of symbiosis is "the antithesis of the 20th century, the century of Western hegemony" (2003, 23).

Theoretically, what Kurokawa's Metabolist movement in architecture and philosophy of symbiosis professes is a call of sorts for the decolonization of the imagination. Partha Chatterjee (1996) famously asserted that for post-colonial subjects, there is nothing left to imagine in the sphere of the material; they are "only consumers of modernity" and can attempt to create their own modernity only in the sphere of the spiritual. Kurokawa, on the other hand, claimed to be able to produce a new kind of materiality and a new kind of material-built environment that, rather than follow Eurocentic logic and universal standards "of the machine," expresses both difference (regarding national or cultural identity) and the plurality of life.[5] Although the claims of discontinuity between the urban-planning technologies of "the age of life" and those of "the age of the machine" are debatable, there is no doubt that Kazakhstan's government found Kurokawa's philosophy and vision well-suited to their goals and understanding of Kazakhstan's new place in the world.

The plan itself explains in great length the importance of the new capital for the Kazakh nation-building project. Quoting President Nazarbayev's speech "New Capital—New State—New Society" from June 10, 1999, the Master Plan states that the planned capital must be "Eurasian" in character, represent national tradition and history and, simultaneously, embody the future that Kazakhstan wants for itself (GP 2001, vol. 2, chapter 3, 9).[6]

Apart from the ideological reasons that made Kurokawa's philosophy attractive to the developing nation's potential self-image, another factor in Kazakhstan's decision was the ability of the Japanese experts to present the relocation of Astana as an economically viable business plan. Although, in relocating the capital, the government used the Soviet rhetoric of raising a "garden city" ("Gorod-Sad")[7] in the midst of the steppe, it realized that in a post-Soviet age the bare exercise of political will and enthusiasm was no longer enough to inspire such construction to be carried out.

The Kazakh government needed to justify the new capital's development project first and foremost as capital investment and to "sell" it as such to the country's public, as well as to foreign investors. So in terms of the logic of its conceptualization, Astana can be compared not only to political projects like Ankara and Brasilia, but also to capital investment projects like Las Vegas and Dubai. The Japanese Master Plan for Astana explains in detail that investment spent on the relocation of Kazakhstan's national capital and the development of the relocated capital's infrastructure would be economically feasible.

Since the relocation of the capital, the project of building in Astana has been widely criticized on the grounds that it is improperly lavish. Many in the political opposition argued that it would have been better to spread resources over various social programs across the country rather than spend so much money in one place.[8] It then became important for the Kazakh government to enlist the help of prominent foreign experts to prove to local opponents of the Astana-development plan that, first, Astana would be able to attract private investment and, second, that public investment made in Astana would create wealth in the whole region (the predicted benefits for the Akmola and Karaganda regions were particularly well illustrated in the Japanese Master Plan). In its analysis of the development of the new capital, the Master Plan identified three types of projects (highly profitable, moderately profitable, and non-profitable), and made a case that the government would have to invest only in non-profitable projects (creating such infrastructure as roads, bridges, public zones, and industrial zones) while the development of residential areas, entertainment districts, and shopping centers would rely entirely on private investors.

Astana is a simulacra of the old socialist utopia in the sense that it is not so much an ideological but a materialistic vision, a promise of order and prosperity that can be seen, felt, and touched; a kind of a visual tactile testimony to urban material progress. In a post-ideological world, in order for the developmentalist state to sustain the hope of development and modernization (for those still offering it), the state has to stage what Abidin Kusno (2010) in his ethnography of Jakarta's urban development calls "spectacles of order" through the creation of "exemplary spaces" and "exemplary centers."[9]

Following Abidin Kusno's "exemplary center" concept, I argue that Astana has been planned, built, and run as one such "exemplary center" to give citizens a sense of positive social change and order and to reaffirm that the goals of development, modernization, and progress are still being pursued by the state (see also Mateusz Laszczkowski's contribution to this volume). Also helpful in this function is Astana's role as the seat of central government, showcasing the "civilizing" power of government regulation. Astana's achievements in managing traffic, disciplining drivers,[10] maintaining order in public places, and growing greenery[11] in difficult climatic conditions are indeed supposed to set an example for the rest of the country. The message is that it is not an extraordinary investment of capital that makes Astana beautiful but the right kind of governance, culture and discipline.

In retrospect, despite the initial marriage of interests and visions between the Kazakh government and Kisho Kurokawa's team, a contradiction would inevitably emerge between the modernizing state's desire to create an "orderly" city and Kurokawa's post-modern urbanist vision of a city that embodies and makes peace with a certain degree of chaos. However, the purpose of this chapter is not just to explore the disagreements that emerged between Kurokawa's group and the local bureaucrats, and the gap between the plan and its implementation. More important is the exploration of how the Kazakh government adapted the Japanese Master Plan to its own vision (especially evident in Corrections to the Master Plan from 2005 and 2008) and what kind of material forms and effects as well as ideological critiques surfaced in the process of adaptation of the Master Plan to local realities.

Elaboration of Kurokawa's Principles

The major principles that Kurokawa advanced in his conceptualization of Astana are the principles of symbiosis, metabolism or the "metabolistic city," and abstract symbolism (GP 2001, vol. 2, chapter 3, 14–20).

The principle of symbiosis is the antithesis of high modernism's principle of "creative destruction." If critics considered modernist architecture and urban planning to be an attack on nature and tradition, Kurokawa contended that a newly built Astana could, as it developed, incorporate into itself nature, history, and even the region's national nomadic traditions. A symbiosis could be created between the city and nature, tradition and modernity, and also, importantly, between the "old" city on the right bank of the Ishim River and the newly built city on its left. The ideal of symbiosis between the "old city" and the "new city" was particularly important for Astana, which, despite the rhetoric of building a "Gorod-Sad" in the steppe, was not being built in an empty place. The builders of the new capital arrived in a city that was already a regional center and had a population of 270,000 in 1997 (it had actually shrunk from almost 300,000 in 1992). The harmonious incorporation of the "old city," built under Khrushchev in the 1960s, into the new city would be a desirable outcome for the city as a whole.

The second principle—the principle of metabolism—suggests that buildings and towns could always be in a dynamic process of growth and change, like living organisms. So the Master Plan's proposal was that Astana should be "an evolving" linear (as opposed to concentrated) city that, if needed, would stretch "naturally" in a linear pattern (GP 2001, vol. 2, chapter 3, 15). Kurokawa's implementation of the ideal of metabolism in architecture is rare; one such case can be found in his Nakagin Capsule Tower, which he designed and had built in 1972. The building has a permanent central structure, but capsules that are tagged onto the central structure can be changed when they wear out. Kurokawa's plan for the building was that the old capsules would be replaced in the future with new, more advanced ones, an event that unfortunately did not take place: the building is now scheduled for demolition.

The third principle—the principle of "abstract symbolism"—was Kurokawa's attempt at the "reinvention" of Kazakh tradition in architecture. He proposed that the architectural style of Astana should follow "simple discernable geometric figures which would express traditional cultural symbols of Kazakhstan" (GP 2001, vol. 2, chapter 3, 18). According to Kurokawa, simple figures like triangles, cones, and crescents, which characterize the traditional ornaments and traditional clothes of the nomadic people, would enable the capital city to express the cultural heritage of Kazakhs and would also help create a harmonious modern landscape (GP 2001, vol. 2, chapter 3, 19).

By 2005, however, all of these principles had attracted a certain degree of skepticism (although not outright hostility) from leading Kazakh architects. Some problems with the implementation of the principle of metabolism and a linear city model became clear almost as soon as the government accepted the conceptual project. Already at that early stage, consultations with local urban planners led Kurokawa to modify the linear model suggested in the initial concept. Whereas the initial plan submitted for the 1998 competition was distinctly linear, the second plan was already more "concentrated" and compact.

In 2005, the government adopted the Correction to the Master Plan, which was authored by the local architect Nurmakhan Tokayev and which clearly stated that, for transportation-logistical reasons, the city would have to develop in a radial pattern around an identified "core open circle" containing all the business and residential quarters and contained in the loose frame of the K-2 second ring road. According to the modified plan, "the basis for the city's architectural-spatial composition should be the system of the city roads" (GP 2005, vol. 2, 55).

When the Correction to the Master Plan went back to the concept of the radial "concentrated" city, it was essentially reverting to the old Soviet urban-planning goals of "a limited city size" and a "limited journey to work" (French 1995, 47). However, in order to counter Kurokawa's declared preference for a "symbiosis with nature," Kazakh architects characterized their preference for a radial, concentrated city not as a return to "good old Soviet planning," but as a layout that operates in accordance with nature and with the Kazakh historical tradition of settlement: the Kazakh nomadic encampment (GP 2005).

The head of the Department of Architecture and Urban Planning of Astana, the chief architect of the city and member of the Architectural Council under the president Sarsembek Zhunusov, said in an interview to the Moscow daily *Vechernyaya Moskva* that the harsh climatic conditions of Astana dictate this kind of concentration: "What do penguins do when they are freezing? They crowd close to one another," he pointed out. "In the construction of Astana we are following the same method—building offices, residences, schools, and entertainment-shopping centers within a walkable distance from each other" (Aviazova 2008).

Amanzhol Chikanaev, another leading architect and member of the Architectural Council under the president, also pointed out in many of his works and interviews (including interviews we had in November 2008 and March 2010) that the concept of symbiosis does not necessarily mean peaceful and harmonious co-existence even in natural conditions. "There are many parasites in nature that live off their host, eventually killing it to their own detriment," he explained.

To an extent, this idea of parasitic co-existence can be applied to the so-called symbiosis, proposed by Kurokawa, between the city and the river. In Kurokawa's reconceptualization of Astana as a "river-city" (the Japanese experts found that the Ishim River dividing the city today had formerly been underutilized), the river was designated to be a "center of life," the center of the city and of the new residential district. In a 2003 interview, Kurokawa said, "In the future Astana will stand on the banks of a wide river which, like the Seine in Paris or the Thames in London, will flow through the center of the capital. The Ishim will unite nature and civilization, creating a symbiosis between the city and landscape" (Kurokawa 2003, 22).

From the residents' and local experts' perspective, however, the river had always been the center of life in the town. It was a water source for irrigation; there were parks, beaches, and other public facilities on both riversides. In fact, in the 1962 Soviet Master Plan of Tselinograd (Astana's former name), which was authored by a group of Leningrad architects, the territory around the river was labeled a recreation zone (*zona otdyha*), which amounted to an open public place and natural park on the edge of the city, separate from the residential zone.

The Japanese Master Plan's language of making Ishim into the "center of life" and the center of residential neighborhoods essentially meant that this space was up for large-scale development. As a result of the implementation of this vision of "symbiosis," the right riverside has already become what many local experts argue is a high-density, overdeveloped residential area that takes a destructive toll on the river. Even if, according to the plan, the river has a buffer green zone in the form of a 300-m "eco-corridor," the water for irrigation of the greenery in this eco-corridor and in the rest of the city is now being taken from the Ishim River itself, which, unlike the Seine or the Thames, is a small steppe river and has a limited capacity. Curiously, Soviet modernist urban planning, criticized for its mechanistic treatment of nature, left the river mostly to nature, while the attempt to create a symbiosis between the urban landscape and the river has made it into a commodity.

The Implementation of the Master Plan

The principles of "symbiosis" and "metabolism," although criticized and significantly revised by local experts, are still considered to have worthwhile value and have been reworked and developed in the new Corrections to the Master Plan, first in 2005, by a group of architects under the supervision of local architect Tokayev, and then, in 2008, by the collective of the AstanaGenPlan. In Kurokawa's urban-planning philosophy for Astana, the most controversial aspect of the implementation of the three principles turned out to be the principle of abstract symbolism (see figure 5.1). Going beyond Kurokawa and his vision, the controversy ultimately rests on the core question of "Will Astana be a 'Kazakh' city?" (as formulated by Tokayev in his 2005 Correction to the Master Plan) and, perhaps more importantly, the central question of "What does it mean to be a Kazakh city?" with which officials and architects have to grapple. The whole problematic of the "expression of national identity" has become an easy target of criticism and more than an annoyance for architects and architectural bureaucrats. During my fieldwork at AstanaGenPlan, I once overheard the head of AstanaGenPlan respond with irritation to a Reuters journalist's question on national architecture by declaring, "There is no such thing as national architecture. . . . We can only talk about regional architecture, not national" (*o regional'noi arhitekture, ne natsional'noi*). The regional in this context meant something larger than national, something that would include all of Central Asia, Russia, and even wider areas; thus the architect was claiming the right to borrow cultural forms outside the territory of Kazakhstan and project a more cosmopolitan taste in developing Astana, which also happens to be in accordance with the ideology of Eurasianism. The 2008 Correction to the Master Plan dismissed abstract symbolism's culturalist claims: the authors ar-

Figure 5.1. Kurokawa's "abstract symbolism" concept, according to which all buildings in the city should follow a style of simple geometrical form that would express national culture and identity. Picture courtesy of the AstanaGenPlan.

gued that simple geometric figures, which Kurokawa characterized as a supposed expression of Kazakh national identity, are present in the art, architecture, and ornaments of many cultures and are not in any sense unique to the Kazakh nomadic tradition. The authors further stated that the adherence to an abstract symbolism approach would promote "stereotypes" and "superficial understanding of national culture" and would prove itself to be ultimately unproductive (GP 2008, 29, 30).

In his contribution to the 2008 Correction to the Master Plan, chief architect Sarsembek Zhunusov justified the retreat from abstract symbolism by arguing that many architects from different parts of the world should enjoy the freedom to exercise their creative potential in working in Astana. "We shouldn't constrain them by requiring adherence to one particular style," he wrote. "Astana should follow the Eurasian style—the synthesis of the best, which has been accumulated in contemporary urban planning and architecture" (Zhunusov 2008). Zhunusov further argued that openness to different styles and different ideas creates an environment in which Kazakh architects could work on developing their own school and tradition. He wrote, "Only in cooperation and in competition with the great architects of modern times can daring and creative Kazakh architects emerge . . . creating something that will make Kazakhstan famous and make the 'Kazakh style' recognizable in the world" (Zhunusov 2008). The mixture of styles in Astana is thus supposed to indicate the multicultural, international face of the city, underscoring that it is open to the interplay of culture, ideas, and the spirit of creativity as a modern Eurasian city should be. Beyond that, since architects are strongly tied to their investors/developers, it reflects the diversity of investors working in Astana and their tastes. Astana is, both temporally and spatially flat, as Amanzhol Chikanaev, whom I interviewed, emphasized. "We are in the steppe, we are circumscribed neither by landscape nor by historical tradition," he told me in one of our interviews, "in this sense we are different from many of the modern-day historical capitals and even from the former capital of Almaty, in the construction of which architects have to consider the *Alatau* mountains."

It needs to be emphasized, however, that bureaucrats from the municipal-architecture and urban-planning offices (most of them architects themselves) have had to formulate their own justification of the architectural eclecticism and their own "official" position on the "national tradition" in architecture in response to mounting criticism from local intellectuals and opposition leaders, as well as criticism from visiting foreign journalists and foreign experts, all of whom assert generally that Astana has no cultural merit of its own. In the words of a BBC reporter, the new development is just an "oriental extravaganza" of a "petro-state." An article in *Der Spiegel*, tellingly titled "The Kazakhstan Klondike," was even more condescending in its criticism of Astana, declaring "the images depict a Kazakh Disneyland, but what they fail to show is a sense of proportionality and good taste. Indeed, megalomania is the name of the game in Astana" (Neef 2006). The charge of tastelessness and inauthenticity is echoed in the local opposition press. In a series of articles published at the online newspaper zonakz.net and devoted to developing "the brand of Kazakhstan," author Arman Khasenov rhetorically asked, "Where is the uniqueness. . . . Where is innovation in Astana?" The conclusion was descriptive: "It is all . . . tinted glass windows, Turkish tiles and 'the blue domes of Samarkand'"[12] (2005). The critic seemed to imply that even the blue dome present in several government buildings in Astana and most obviously in the presidential palace itself is not a "native" architectural form but is yet another example of "mindless" borrowing.

Indeed, for some people, the mixture of the buildings of different styles in close proximity to each other, as on Millennium Alley, the axis stretching from the presidential palace Ak Orda to Khan Shatyr (see figure 5.2), produces a sense of "uncanniness" and disorder and perhaps goes against some cultural sensibilities. Should an egg-shaped national archive be in an ensemble of structures including a neo-classical national library? Should a blue-domed presidential palace be flanked by two futuristic buildings in the shape of spherical cylinders (see figure 5.3)? Can the funnel-shaped Khan Shatyr stand next to the neo-classical oval-shaped KazMunaiGaz building? But who can pronounce an

Figure 5.2. The Millennium Alley axis. Picture courtesy of Vladimir Kurilov.

ultimate aesthetic judgment? And what kind of "global hierarchy of value," to borrow Michael Herzfeld's term, would be implicit in such a judgment? The discourse about taste versus tastelessness and beauty versus ugliness in Astana's urban-scape thus can both reinforce and undermine relentless promotional efforts by the government to make Astana global and modern (Foucault 1990, 100–101).

When asked by a Kazakh interlocutor if the new buildings in Astana "look right," British anthropologist Buchli (2007) experienced a moment of uneasiness as he considered pronouncing a judgment that would "validate" the new buildings in Astana. "Does it look right"? his companion asked him. In his chapter on Astana in the *Urban Life in Post-Soviet Asia,* Buchli recollected the interchange: "He wanted to know what I made of these structures that were supposed to be Western and modern." Buchli continued, "He simply had no experience with these new forms." Buchli seemed to admit that, as a general formula, a society needs to accumulate certain experiences and to undergo a certain degree of acculturation before it can be sufficiently certain of its own capacity to be modern (particularly the capacity to possess modern tastes) and certain of its own "normality" in the context of modernity (2007, 64–66).

This theme of the necessity of acculturation and experience with new urban forms harkens back to Bourdieu's (1984) theory of cultural legitimation and "cultural capital," which along with the economic capital of the bourgeoisie sustains the status quo and the hierarchies of the bourgeois order. In the current world, these hierarchies exist not only in one society, but also across the globe, making "modernity" a goal that can be achieved only with the "right" kind of modern and global "cultural competence." The requirement of the acquisition of "cultural capital" for the project of modernity, then, can be extrapolated from individuals to organizations, bureaucracies, and even states.

Figure 5.3. The blue-domed presidential palace flanked by the two futuristic towers in the shape of spherical cylinders. Picture by Vladimir Kurilov.

The kind of criticism that Astana is facing today—criticism of its pretentiousness, its inappropriateness, its lack of a self-specific cultural and even functional logic (as a city built to impress, not to live in)—has been characteristically employed against other "spectacular" non-Western cities. For instance, on the eve of the Beijing Olympics, the *New Yorker's* architectural columnist Paul Goldberger wrote, "This is an Olympics driven by image, not by sensitive urban planning." He continued, "The city, however, has yet to build a public space as inventive as that of post-Olympics Barcelona, or to think of the impact of the Olympics in terms as sophisticated as pre-Olympics London" (2008).

In a similar vein, Goldberger questioned the very motivation behind the newest tallest building in the world—Dubai's Burj Khalifa Tower:

> Almost everything in Dubai is a kind of visual spectacle intended to make you gawk. But that's nothing new. . . . *That's just what Asian and Middle Eastern countries are trying to do now* [my emphasis]. You don't build this kind of skyscraper to house people, or to give tourists a view, or even, necessarily to make a profit. You do it to make sure the world knows who you are. (Goldberger 2010)

A recent overall positive *New Yorker* article on Astana echoes Goldberger's view that it is another "wannabe" city (the article is indicatively titled "Nowheresville") mindlessly following the fashion of modernist skyscrapers: "In Manhattan, the buildings get higher and higher because there is no room; in Astana, situated in one of the most sparsely populated areas on the planet, the buildings get higher and higher just because" (Gessen 2011). This condescending assumption that Dubai or Astana, though surrounded by abundant developable space, build skyscrapers "just because" is flawed on several levels. First of all, the height of Manhattan buildings such as the Empire State Building and the former World Trade Center was also driven by the image factor and by competition with skyscrapers elsewhere. Secondly, Dubai and Astana are not exempt from the real estate market's "location, location, location" rule of thumb. Yes, Astana has a vast "steppe" stretching out in all directions, but land on the waterfront or the dwellings within view of the presidential palace is limited; thus, the value of this land is high, in turn justifying the construction of high-rises.

This sometimes flagrant, sometimes subtle contempt for Dubai, Beijing, and Astana's modernist aspirations of "becoming" underline the fact that the achievement of economic modernization and the improvement of the material environment does not yet guarantee the achievement of "modernity," which requires modern cultural "sophistication" and "sensitivity"; thus, transformation of financial capital into cultural capital should not be taken for granted, especially in the view of established global hierarchies and interests in the durability and global transferability of certain kinds of cultural capital.

Apart from issues surrounding Kurokawa's philosophical principles and his architectural vision, the implementation of the Master Plan of Astana has illustrated once again the discrepancies between planned development of urban growth and concrete realities on the ground. The Master Plan's timeframe was tied to the president's "2030" program, so the plan had stated short-term development objectives for the period of ten years leading up to 2010, and long-term objectives for the period of twenty years leading up to 2020, and "prospective long-term" objectives leading up to 2030.

By 2005, however, only five years within the short-term period, a huge gap appeared between the projected plan and the reality on the ground. The pace of Astana's development had turned out to be much swifter than envisioned in the Master Plan. The plan had greatly underestimated population growth, growth in the number of cars, as well as the level of capital investment in the city. The plan projected that the population of the city would reach 800,000 by 2030. However, Astana already had 500,000 residents by 2005 and 616,000 by 2008 (GP 2005, GP 2008). This serious underestimation in the projection of the population growth stemmed from international experts' decision to base Astana's growth on Almaty's in the Soviet years, in addition to comparing and adjusting Almaty's growth with that of Ankara and Canberra after these two cities became new national capitals. However, Ankara and Canberra became capitals in different socio-economic conditions in countries already possessing several nodal points for industrialization-driven migration. Almaty, on the other hand, grew under the Soviet conditions of urban management and population control, which differ drastically from the conditions of neo-liberal market economies and the rapid deindustrialization experienced in the regions around Astana in the 1990s.

Thus, by the end of 2004, because of the gap between the Astana's projected growth and the reality on the ground, the Japanese plan was considered outdated and unworkable as a blueprint for city development (in addition to all the other criticisms of the plan's major urbanist principles). In 2005, based on a new population-projection study conducted by a group from the Kazakhstan Institute of Management, Economics, and Strategic Research, a new bid was announced by the government for the Correction to the Master Plan. After reviewing various bids, the government selected the one submitted by a group of architects headed by Tokayev. As noted earlier, the new plan changed the linear pattern of the city envisioned by Kurokawa into a radial pattern, which was seen as more desirable for the city for transportation- and communication-related reasons and also as more in accordance with natural conditions and traditional patterns of Kazakh settlement. Arguing that it is not functional to continuously "stretch" Astana, the Correction to the Master Plan introduced by Tokayev's team defined the territorial limits of the city, which could fit from 1.2 to 2 million people. The international evaluation of the 2005 Correction to the Master Plan contended that it was not just a mere "correction," but a "new Master Plan," a new conceptual vision of the city, which would now follow not an "organic symbiotic linear development along the riverbed as suggested by Dr. Kurokawa . . . but the development along the proposed perimeter" (GP 2005). According to the evaluation, the radial pattern will "artificially" tighten the "natural" territorial growth like a hoop (GP 2005). So, in the eyes of many experts, the Tokayev group's Correction to the Master Plan amounted to a drastic revision and a de facto new Master Plan. However, to save everybody's face and to show appreciation to the Japanese counterparts, the group labeled and the government adopted these revisions diplomatically—as merely a "Correction to the General Plan."

The continued reworking of the Japanese Master Plan for Astana has jeopardized the authority of global experts in the eyes of the Kazakh community of experts and bureaucrats, and has raised questions about the transferability and the value of global expertise vis-à-vis local knowledge. In these regards, a high-ranking planning official at the AstanaGenPlan told me, "The problem is that, apart from philosophers-demagogues, there are very few good urban planners in the world." Comparing local urban-planning expertise with foreign urban-planning expertise, he noted, "The Soviet Union was building more than ten thousand new settlements each year, but most of the foreign experts, including Kurokawa, who come to teach us have never planned new cities."

In the book *Architectural Symphony of the Great Steppe* (Chikanaev 2008), the AstanaGenPlan authors publicly expressed some cautious and tactful criticism of the Japanese experts' approaches to designing the Master Plan of Astana. The authors revealed, in particular, the dichotomy between the rhetoric of the post-modern philosophy of architecture and the methodology of real planning on the ground. "A declaration of principles is not enough," they wrote. "Unfortunately, in the study produced by the Japanese experts, we could not discern a coherent methodology that would lead to the achievement of declared goals" (2008, 114).

Despite this criticism, the place and the value of foreign expertise in burgeoning construction and real estate markets around the world remain intact not least because of the global hierarchy of knowledge, "cultural capital," and "brand politics." One of the reasons for this continued appreciation of global expertise and devaluation of the local is that the circuits of the knowledge economy, of which architectural and urban planning are part, are linked to the circuits of funding and foreign direct investment. According to Manuel Castells (1996) and Saskia Sassen (2000), the global informational economy is concentrated in certain locales, so-called "thick places," which also happen to be financial centers of the global economy. These networks of international expertise, in addition to providing knowledge and technologies to governments, provide what Sassen calls "the infrastructure of global connectivity." The accumulation of knowledge, money, and power is structurally intertwined. It is not that there is always a direct conditional link between expertise and investment, but there exists a cultural and structural configuration of globalization that connects international experts and the expertise that they provide to investment opportunities. Because international experts are culturally closer to investors than are local experts, international investors can better read the scripts and calculations produced by them.

By hiring celebrity architects and designers, the Kazakh government has not only mobilized their expertise, for which it has been widely recognized, but has also hooked into financial circuits that usually help underwrite these kinds of creative productions. As a certain Kazakh official told a Kazakh architect whose Astana hotel design proposal had been rejected by the tender organizers, "It is not that our architectural projects are worse than foreign ones; it is just that we need projects that will attract investment." So if, in David Harvey's words, "urban processes under capitalism are shaped by the logic of capital circulation and accumulation" (1989, 3), any countries' continuing use of global expertise can be considered a strategy of the entrepreneurial state to accommodate the interests of capital.

The Kazakh government's experiment with the Japanese Master Plan and with other sources of expertise also indicates a different kind of "accumulation" process—the accumulation of cultural capital. And, in this sense, to compare a developing oil-rich state to a member of the nouveau riche who is learning from the established "cultural aristocracy" can be very productive. Even in today's post-boom and (perhaps temporary) post-crisis situation, when the Kazakh state is no longer as dependent on foreign investment as it was at the end of the 1990s and when it can now launch its own sizable investment projects, the problem of transforming financial capital into cultural capital and creating a "Kazakhstan brand" remains high on the state agenda. During my time with AstanaGenPlan, I was engaged in several projects in which the government sought to "borrow" urban-planning expertise from the municipal plans and the regulatory-normative documents belonging to North American cities that were deemed closest to the climatic conditions of Astana (e.g., Toronto and Minneapolis). In order to achieve the goals of "progressive" urban planning, urban regulation, and gentrification, Kazakh bureaucrats were motivated to learn and apply the "best standards" of the "best cities" in the developed world to Astana. I was also asked to study city ratings to find out what makes cities rank highly on the "liveability" scale and how these rankings are produced. Bureaucrats were somewhat disappointed to find out that most of the ratings rested on "subjective" criteria such as polling the city dwellers regarding their opinions on the given city's "stability," "culture & environment," "education," and so on. The bureaucrats wanted something tangible against which to measure the quality of life in Astana—some clear, objective goals, such as "how many trees are planted annually in Toronto, and how many square meters of greenery do Torontans have per person?" "What is the per capita living space in Ottawa or Minneapolis?" "What are the curb-making, asphalt-laying, or snow-cleaning procedures and regulations in these places?" One result of the knowledge-transmission process from the "developed" world, however, is that while this extensive borrowing is taking place, important elements within the borrowing state's bureaucratic apparatus grow resistant to international expertise, which comes across not as superior to local capital but as just "beautifully packaged" rhetoric. "We didn't learn any useful urban-planning technologies per se," admitted a high-ranking planning official about the Master Plan developed by Japanese experts. "What we did is we borrowed from their brand."

This kind of "brand borrowing" strategy was recently reiterated to me by the administration at Astana's newly opened international Nazarbayev University, the schools and colleges within which are being set up as partnerships with well-established Western schools. "We need to borrow from their brands in order to establish our own brand" one of the administrators said. "But, of course, there is always a danger in such a transfer, a danger that instead of developing our own brand we will be throwing more money at their brand."

Indeed, there is only a certain degree to which "cultural capital" and somebody else's brand can be borrowed for one's one image making. The government created an image of Astana, delivering a spectacular visual and physical landscape. But this image is ambiguous, contested, and even misrecognized. "The cultural is continuously interpenetrated by the political and is thereby transformed into ideology," wrote Abner Cohen (1993, 8). In a sense, the construction of Astana can be seen as a sort of architectural-cultural performance for the public aimed at pursuing political power (Parkin 1996). In their attempt to justify Astana's eclecticism and mixture of style, official bureaucrats entered the field of struggle not just for cultural but also for political legitimation, and in turn, they have come under fire not just for their taste but also for their ability to create an order. Thus the charges of tastelessness easily become charges of an inability to execute effective practices requisite of strong modern states. Perhaps there is no point in arguing about taste, but a government should establish its cultural competency in order to prove its political efficacy.

Notes

1. I am referring here to the officials at the AstanaGenPlan—a governmental research institute (a branch of the municipal government) charged with developing and implementing urban-planning policies, regulations, and norms in Astana. It has high standing in the bureaucratic hierarchy. Several leading architects and urban planners from this office are members of the Architectural Council under the president. AstanaGenPlan has received several visits from the president (though not during my time there) and also has been a seat of the City Urban Planning Council, headed by the mayor. The council meets every month and makes decisions about land allocation for development projects, zoning, and the like.

2. It is worth noting, however, that the majority of the landmark government and residential buildings in Astana have been designed by local architects.

3. Kisho Kurokawa died in October 2007. He was a leading Japanese architect and one of the founders of the Metabolist movement in architecture and urban planning, which emphasizes the symbiosis between technology, culture, and nature.

4. These were urban planner Serik Rustambekov, ecologist Arkadii Fisenko, and forestry expert Victor Gribov.

5. In the spirit of non-Western materiality and technology, Kurokawa, for instance, suggested that when devising its energy policy, India should not simply follow the West and Western models but should also build on its own traditions (e.g., using cow dung as fuel). He wrote, "As [with] Indian energy policy, would it not be best to combine the use of atomic energy, hydroelectric power, and cow dung in the most efficient combination?" (1994, 25).

6. I will be using the abbreviation GP (*General'nyi Plan*) to indicate both the Master Plan and the ensuing corrections to the Master Plan: GP 2001 will stand for "The Master

Plan for the Development of the City of Astana," produced by the Japanese experts headed by Kurokawa in 2001 (see Japan International Cooperation Agency 2001); GP 2005 will stand for "The Correction to the Master Plan for the Development of the City of Astana," produced by a group of authors at the *AstanaGenPlan* headed by N. Tokayev (see Gosudarstvennoe Kommunal'noe Predpriiatie AstanaGen Plan 2005); GP 2008 will stand for "The Correction of the 1st Phase of the Master Plan," produced by the collective of the AstanaGenPlan (see Akimat Goroda Astany 2008).

7. Gorod-Sad here refers not to the garden-city concept and urban-planning movement per se but to the popular metaphor and rhetoric in the Soviet urbanization and industrialization ethos. The saga of raising a new city in the midst of a distant wilderness or steppe resounded well into the 1980s through Soviet high and popular culture (e.g., the famous poem by Mayakovskii *Gorod-Sad*).

8. For instance, an article entitled "Astana on the 'Needle' of Subsidies" contended that it is unfair that Astana enjoys unprecedented tax breaks and spends three times as much as the old capital Almaty per capita—74,000 tenge (about US$500 in today's money) while at the same time contributing very little to the republican budget (Askarov 2000).

9. Abidin Kusno borrows the concept of "exemplary centers" from Clifford Geertz's (1980) *Negara: The Theatre State in Nineteenth-Century Bali.*

10. A 2011 article in the *New Yorker* (Gessen 2011) attests to the fact that drivers in Astana are the most disciplined in the post-Soviet space.

11. Astana municipality pays special attention to cultivating green space inside and outside the city (the so-called artificial "green belt" around Astana). The soil of Astana is known to be difficult for growing trees because ground water is too close to the surface and the vegetation period is short. The commitment of Astana to uphold green standards despite the harsh climatic conditions of southern Siberia is comparable to other globally known green cities. As a point of comparison, the city of Toronto plants about fifteen to twenty thousand young trees a year through its Tree Advocacy Program. According to "Astana-Zelenstroi" municipal greening company, in 2006 and 2007 there were more than thirty-eight thousand trees planted each year in Astana. The company maintains a tree nursery of seven hundred thousand trees located in the village of Hersonovka, 90 km south of Astana (I visited this tree nursery during my fieldwork). Since the relocation of the capital to Astana, the green space inside the city (this is not counting the "green belt" trees outside the city) has increased almost tenfold and has reached 660 hectares with 8 square meters of green space per resident of the city.

12. "The blue domes of Samarkand" (*golubye kupola Samarkanda*) is also a refrain in several songs and poems in Russian and Kazakh.

References

Akimat Goroda Astany. 2008. *Korrektirovka general'nogo plana goroda Astany,* Tom I. Poiasnitel'naia zapiska. Astana, Kazakhstan: Nauchno-issledovatel'skii proektnyi Institut General'nogo Plana Goroda Astany.

Askarov, Tulegen. 2000. "Posadim stolitsu na 'iglu' dotatsii." *Internet-Gazeta Zona KZ,* November 28. Retrieved from http://zonakz.net/articles/11599 (accessed May 18, 2011).

Aviazova, Zhanna. 2008. "Stolitse Kazakhstana ispolnilos' 10 let." *Vecherniaia Moskva,* July 15. Retrieved from http://www.vmdaily.ru/article/60884.html (accessed May 18, 2011).

Beck, Ulrich. 2002. "The Cosmopolitan Society and Its Enemies." *Theory, Culture, and Society* 19, nos. 1–2: 17–44.

Bhabha, Homi. 2004. *The Location of Culture,* 2nd ed. London: Routledge

Bourdieu, Pierre. 1984. *Distinction: A Social Critique of the Judgement of Taste,* translated by Richard Nice. Cambridge, Mass.: Harvard University Press.

Buchli, Victor. 2007. "Astana: Materiality and the City." In *Urban Life in Post-Soviet Asia,* edited by Catherine Alexander, Victor Buchli, and Caroline Humphrey, 40–69. London: UCL Press.

Caldeira, Teresa, and James Holston. 2005. "State and Urban Space in Brazil: From Modernist Planning to Democratic Intervention." In *Global Anthropology: Technology, Governmentality, Ethics,* edited by Aihwa Ong and Stephen Collier, 393–416. London: Blackwell.

Castells, Manuel. 1996. *The Rise of the Network Society.* Oxford: Blackwell.

Chatterjee, Partha. 1996. "Whose Imagined Community?" In *Mapping the Nation,* edited by Gopal Balakrishnan, 214–226. London: Verso.

Chikanaev, Amanzhol Sh. 2008. *Arhitekturnaia simfoniia velikoi stepi.* Redaktsionnyi sovet: S. E. Zhunusov et. al. Astana, Kazakhstan: Delovoi Mir.

Cohen, Abner. 1993. *Masquerade Politics: Explorations in the Structure of Urban Cultural Movements.* Berkeley: University of California Press.

Flyvbjerg, Bent. 1998. *Rationality and Power: Democracy in Practice.* Chicago: University of Chicago Press.

Foucault, Michel. 1990. *History of Sexuality.* Vol. 1, *An Introduction.* Translated by Robert Hurley. New York: Vintage Books

French, R. Anthony. 1995. *Plan, Pragmatism and People: The Legacy of Soviet Planning for Today's Cities.* Pittsburgh: University of Pittsburgh Press.

Gessen, Keith. 2011. "Nowheresville: How Kazakhstan Is Building a Glittering New Capital from Scratch." *New Yorker,* April 18, 96–107.

Goldberger, Paul. 2008. "Forbidden Cities: Beijing's Great New Architecture Is a Mixed Blessing for the City." *New Yorker,* June 20, 78–82.

———. 2010. "Castle in the Air: Dubai Reaches for the Sky." *New Yorker,* February 8, 62–64.

Gosudarstvennoe Kommunal'noe Predpriiatie AstanaGenPlan. 2005. *Ekspertnoe zakliuchenie po kontseptsii korrektirovki general'nogo plana goroda Astany.* Astana, Kazakhstan.

Harvey, David. 1989. "From Managerialism to Entrepreneurialism: The Transformation in Urban Governance in Late Capitalism." *Geografiska Annaler* 71 B, no. 1: 3–17.

———. 2000. *Spaces of Hope.* Berkeley: University of California Press.

Holston, James. 1989. *The Modernist City: An Anthropological Critique of Brasilia.* Chicago: University of Chicago Press.

Japan International Cooperation Agency. 2001. *General'nyi plan razvitiia goroda Astana, Tom I and Tom II. Kratkii ocherk*. Kisho Kurokawa Architect & Associates, the Nippon Koei Co. Ltd., International Development Center of Japan.

Khasenov, Arman. 2005. "Brend Kazakhstan," Chast' 3. *Internet-Gazeta Zona KZ*, October 7. Retrieved from http://www.zonakz.net/articles/9866 (accessed May 18, 2011).

Kurokawa, Kisho. 1994. *The Philosophy of Symbiosis*. London: Academy Editions. Also available at: http://www.kisho.co.jp/page.php/292 (accessed May 18, 2011).

———. 2003. "Megapolis XXI veka nikogda ne ostanovitsia v roste." *Novye Stolitsy* 4, no. 30: 21–25.

Kusno, Abidin. 2010. *The Appearances of Memory: Mnemonic Practices of Architecture and Urban Form in Indonesia*. Durham, N.C.: Duke University Press.

Lukes, Steven. 2005. *Power: A Radical View*. New York: Palgrave Macmillian.

Massey, Doreen. 2005. *For Space*. Los Angeles: Sage.

Neef, Christian. 2006. "Central Asian Powerhouse. The Kazakhstan Klondike." *Der Spiegel*, September, 11. Available at: http://www.spiegel.de/international/spiegel/0,1518,447451,00.html (accessed May 18, 2011).

Parkin, David. 1996. "Introduction: The Power of the Bizarre." In *The Politics of Cultural Performance*, edited by David Parkin, Lionel Caplan, and Humphrey Fisher, xv–xl. Malden, Mass.: Blackwell.

Sassen, Saskia. 2000. *Cities in the World Economy*. Thousand Oaks, Calif.: Pine Forge Press.

———. 2002. *Global Networks, Linked Cities*. New York: Routledge.

———. 2003. "The State and Globalization." *Interventions* 5, no. 2: 241–248.

Schatz, Edward. 2004. "What Capital Cities Say About State and Nation Building." *Nationalism and Ethnic Politics* 9, no. 4: 111–140.

Tsing, Anna. 2005. *Friction: An Ethnography of Global Connection*. Princeton, N.J.: Princeton University Press.

Zhunusov, Saken E. 2008. "Arhitekturnyi oblik Astany: teoreticheskie voprosy stilia i obraza." Unpublished contribution to the 2008 Correction to the Master Plan.

6. State Building(s)

Built Forms, Materiality, and the State in Astana

Mateusz Laszczkowski

With bells tolling in the background, a cityscape of scaffolding and whimsically shaped buildings was conjured up on stage. A hundred young construction workers in neat dark blue overalls and orange hardhats danced among the buildings to a lively, rhythmic music, with the noise of work beating in industrial harmony. Sparks and smoke burst high up on the scaffolding, while the workers acted out an elaborate choreography and the facades of buildings took form from a jigsaw of pieces. Before the eyes of a thousand spectators seated in bleachers opposite, the cityscape of the new administrative quarter of Kazakhstan's capital, Astana, was conjured into life in a matter of minutes. A huge banner with the image of ancient Turkic warriors that had been the background to the construction scene slid away to reveal a new backdrop: an enormous green map of the city, with red letters reading "Happy Birthday, Astana!" The stage, with its scaffoldings and imitation buildings, and the workers now standing proudly in the middle, was flanked by real cranes, scaffoldings, and the tall concrete carcasses of construction sites several hundred meters in the distance. Thus, a curious mimicry effect was introduced between the stage and the surrounding cityscape.

This show was one of the highlights of the 2009 celebrations of Astana Day: formerly a local festivity elevated the previous year to the status of national holiday and now celebrated across Kazakhstan over many days. The city itself has been known as Astana since 1998, following the transfer of the capital from Almaty. Beginning in the 2000s Astana has become the site of unprecedented construction effort: the building of a spectacular, eclectic, conspicuously cosmopolitan and ostensibly super-modern quarter of administrative, commer-

Figure 6.1. Reenacting state-building through building work on stage, Astana Day 2009.

cial, and residential buildings and monuments, designed to become the new center of the capital. It was the construction of this district that was theatrically reenacted to the rows of seated spectators. Much more was being celebrated, however, than the building of a new district. In the ideological discourse of the regime, Astana's construction represents the edifice of the state, its cohesion and viability, and its achievements on the path toward a prosperous future. The building work represents a quite literal process of building the state.

In this chapter, I focus on this labor and on the "state-building through building work" metaphor as a means of introducing several interrelated questions about the relationship between "the state" and materiality.[1] How is the state encountered and produced through built forms and the process of construction? How does the local history of the state's materiality influence expectations of the state today? How do citizens interact with official representations and attributed meanings of this building work, and what is their role in constructing and maintaining the state? How are citizen subjectivities shaped in relation to the state and construction? What kinds of engagement with the state does the materiality of construction enable? How is the experience of the state affected when construction drags on or seems reduced to theatrics? And more generally, why is it that the materiality of built forms provides such a powerful idiom for articulating the state, both affirmatively and critically?

These questions will lead me to see the state as repeatedly deconstructed and reconstructed as a material assemblage as much as a fantasy. Crucially, during fieldwork in Astana "the state" appeared not only as a bounded apparatus of regulation or a container of power, but also as a process of ordering and framing social experience in which citizens' active and affective engagement was sought. Kazakhstan has a record of two decades of president Nursultan Nazarbayev's continuous rule through a sequence of rigged elections and referendums, practically neutralized opposition parties, quashed protests (as demonstrated in December 2011 in Zhanaozen where at least sixteen people were killed in a crackdown on striking oilmen), and the occasional imprisonment, exile, or unexplained death of a critic of the regime.[2] It is thus hardly a participatory polity in the sense of a pluralistic formal political system (see, e.g., Cummings 2005; Schatz 2009). However, I argue that the building-work metaphor offers individuals possibilities to experience state-building as an incorporative process. If the idea of "the state" serves effectively to preserve unequal power relations (Mitchell 1999), then this is all the more reason for a critical perspective on power and the state to acknowledge and examine the ways the imaginary reality of the state seduces citizens in part through promises of order and progress. Lest it appears, however, that I allow "the state" to be treated on "its" own terms, it needs to be emphasized that the state's existence is contingent upon citizens' willingness to comply with their imaginations and their participation. The state needs to be performed and it is at best only "subjectively objective" (Žižek 1997, cited in Aretxaga 2003, 403).

"The state" is invested with affects such as hope and desire for involvement, but also with feelings of loss and longing, or fears of disappointment or abandonment. The materiality of built forms: their processual construction, tangibility, impressive gestalt, and physical fragility make them a compelling manifestation of the state in all these affective dimensions. I argue that exploring the relationship between the state and materiality can help us to grasp the ways that the state can be apprehended as both magnificent and unstable, awesome and unreliable, simultaneously the object of reverence and resentment, desire and disappointment (cf. Aretxaga 2003).

This may be true in some sense everywhere but the Central Asian experience—where the (Soviet) state had been ubiquitous in material infrastructure, then fell to atrophy along with it, and has recently been eagerly reconstructed in sometimes extremely spectacular but often awkwardly labile new architectural forms—offers a particularly convenient prism to view these ambiguities of the state's entanglement with materiality. And within the Central Asian context, Astana is an outstanding case. Urban (re-)construction has been used to perform state- and nation-building ideologies in all of the region's new states (Šír 2008; Trevisani, this volume) and beyond (e.g., Agnew 1998; Bozdoğan 2001; Holston 1989; Vale 2008; Wanner 1998). However, fed by the international flows of oil-related capital, Astana has witnessed construction on an unmatched scale

(Bissenova, this volume). It has captured the imagination not only of Kazakhstani citizens, but also of the inhabitants of neighboring republics who look upon it as a vision of an alternative and much-desired development for their own countries (Laszczkowski 2011).[3]

State-Building through Building Work

The construction of the new district, represented rhetorically as the construction of Astana, as if the entire capital was being built on a clean slate, has become the central theme of regime ideology. President Nazarbayev's memoirs (2006, 335) suggest that the origin of this idea should be traced back as early as 1992, not even a full year after Kazakhstan's independence, as this was when it first occurred to him to transfer the capital to the city then known as Aqmola.[4] He states the ultimate reason for the decision as follows:

> The country needed a patriotic breakthrough, a feat . . . corresponding to the new realities: the strengthening of independence, the building of statehood, the deepening of socio-economic and political transformations. And we were convinced that the transfer of the capital to Aqmola would . . . facilitate the accomplishment of these goals. (Nazarbayev 2006, 350)[5]

Here and elsewhere (e.g., Nazarbayev 2005), the president equates the construction of new quarters in Astana with state-building. Moreover, concurrent claims are widespread in the media, public statements by officials and luminaries of various ranks, as well as in a broad stream of academic and popular publications. "The flourishing of Astana is the flourishing of Kazakhstan" or "Astana—the achievement of the Kazakh nation" are two of the most widespread slogans, found everywhere from state development strategies to schoolchildren's essays. Such slogans are commonly complemented with images of Astana's newly built cityscape and ongoing construction work. Billboards carrying these messages are found across the country.

The public event described in the opening lines of this chapter is a particularly compelling example of the application of the "state-building through building work" metaphor in today's official ideological production in Kazakhstan. Recent scholarship has tended to interpret state-organized mass celebrations of that sort either in terms of coercion and "orchestration of bodies" or in terms of cynicism and collective dissimulation. In the former view, state power is being deployed by forcing citizens to attend the senseless events and thus arresting their agency for hours, if not days (e.g., Verdery 1992). In the latter, the citizens act "as if" they believed there was some deeper sense to the celebrations because they realize such tongue-in-cheek complicity is a trade-off for relatively undisturbed passage through the topsy-turvy terrain of everyday sociopolitical relations (see, for instance, Wedeen 1999). Despite the merits of such approaches, in this chapter I seek to tread a different path: to treat more seriously the citizen-spectators' commitment to participate (see also Navaro-Yashin 2002, 117–154) and to unpack the "state-building through building work" metaphor. While admission to the show was generally by invitation (I managed to sneak in early, before the invitation regime started to be enforced) and usually organized groups of students or public employees were bussed in for similar events, there was also a large crowd of spectators who came spontaneously; those who swarmed behind the bars police had put up around the bleachers. The theatrical performance is simultaneously a performance of "the state" as an intersubjective framework that organizes experience—of the event and much of everyday social experience in general. The spectators are in fact key performers. It is through the exchange between the stage and the audience that performance acquires meaning and, in this case, "the state" emerges as a shared frame of intelligibility.[6] Similarly, it would be a mistake to disregard the "state-building through building work" metaphor as "mere ideology" meant to veil "real" politico-economic relations. Rather, the metaphor has real effects in orientating citizen subjectivities vis-à-vis "the state." I argue that this particular ideological image works, firstly, because of the intricate relationship between the state, space, and materiality, and secondly, because it corresponds to a particular "structure of feeling" (Williams 1977), a longing for the state as a totality of social and material connections. That longing, as I shall discuss in the next section, was produced by the post-Soviet experience.

Let me consider the state's relationship with space and materiality first. Timothy Mitchell, analyzing how "society" and "state" were historically *constructed* as abstract objects, remarks that in the modern order of things monuments, buildings, as well as other objects and practices, have come to be understood as signifiers of "a further realm—the realm of meaning . . . synonymous with the social" (1991, 127). "The state" has become a part of that "deeper" order represented by material forms. Mitchell draws attention to the way in which modern practices in fields as diverse as house construction, town planning, health supervision, education, and agriculture and industrial production have made it possible to imagine the state as what renders society ordered and viable. He calls that "the state effect" (1999). Scholars who followed Mitchell have recognized spatiality as a defining dimension of the state (Ferguson and Gupta 2002). Likewise, Henri Lefebvre calls the state "social space" (2003, 84) that is produced by means of certain transformations of "natural," physical space. Lefebvre lists three essential characteristics of state space: it is "homogenous," in the sense that all places within the space of a state, at least in theory, equally belong to it; it is "fractured," that is, put to a variety of different organized uses; and it is hierarchical—organized into centers and peripheries, better and worse areas (Lefebvre 2003, 94). As we shall see, the specificities of state space brought about by the concentration of particular material forms in the capital city are crucial to the "state effect" of Astana's construction. The production of state space requires the building of diverse infrastructures out of materials. While we can rightly speak of the state as socially "constructed," that process involves much actual, material crafting (Navaro-Yashin 2012, 5–6). The building of a road, for example, is one such material operation producing "state effects" (Harvey 2005). I argue that the construction of a capital city is another, paramount instance of such an operation, marked with an unmatched abundance of explicit symbolism. The state is performed, rather powerfully, through the labor of building—it is an important way in which the state is "mattered," rendered concrete, literally and metaphorically.

Apart from studies of "state effects" and the relatively scarce work on state materialities (e.g., Bennett and Joyce 2010; Reeves 2009), scholars have highlighted the imaginary, fictional, or phantasmatic aspect of the social reality of the state (Aretxaga 2000, 2003; Navaro-Yashin 2012; Taussig 1992, 1997). As Begoña Aretxaga argues, "the state, whatever that is, materializes not only through rules and bureaucratic routines (Foucault) but also through a world of fantasy thoroughly narrativized and imbued with affect, fear, and desire, that make it, in fact, a plausible reality" (2000, 52). By fantasy is meant here not "an illusory construction opposed to an empirical reality, but a kind of reality in its own right" (ibid.). I believe it is fruitful to combine the two approaches and explore how the material building of state infrastructures enables and directs the state's construction in the imagination. Crucial to my argument is the point that "the state" is here understood primarily not as a self-contained, technical governing apparatus, seemingly separate from "society"—an understanding that, as Mitchell (1999) and Paul Rabinow (1995, 345) demonstrate, came to dominate the twentieth-century socio-political imagination—but rather as an imagined, meaningful totality, embracing and holding together social relations. "The state" is a structural effect of governance practices, as Mitchell argues, but as such it is also a subjective fantasy of objective order, called into being by the imaginations and active involvement of individuals. Crucially, this fantasy is supported by material infrastructures and networks connecting individuals, collectives, and things. So understood, for the individual citizen, the state can be an object not just of submission, but also of desire, and when it appears lost—of longing.

Post-Soviet Kazakhstan may be one of those countries where recent history has caused a particular need for collective ordering action under the aegis of "the state." Importantly, as a later section will illustrate, in the case of the building of Astana, many individuals, not only those involved directly in construction works but also those who pursue better futures for themselves by grasping the educational or professional opportunities opened up by the development of the capital (see Laszczkowski 2011, 86–87), have a chance to experience this collective effort as incorporative and hence particularly meaningful for their lives. It is a material change that they directly experience, but it recreates the imagined reality of the state.

The Disconnected State

In Soviet days, the state was encountered as materially present in urban infrastructure (Alexander 2004; Buchli 2000; Humphrey 2005; Kotkin 1995). Social relations were mediated through different material elements—workplaces, apartments, health centers, dormitories, pipes, wires, and so forth—that were all known to belong to and represent the state. An individual's relation to a given piece of infrastructure depended on and assumed their relation to the state. The same was true of one's immediate social environment: the workplace collective, the inhabitants of an apartment block, a Komsomol or Party cell. It was the development of infrastructural networks, such as the heating system (Collier 2004), that had almost literally knitted the various dispersed localities together into that vast territorial and social whole, "the state." Human bodies were connected to the state in subtle yet essential ways: they inhabited state-built and state-owned dwellings, and they were supplied with heat, light, gas for cooking, and water from state-organized networks (Alexander 2007). As Stephen Kotkin (1995, 23) puts it, in the USSR there was "thought to be no separation between the spheres 'state' and 'society', . . . everything was formally part of the state." It is plausible that the extensiveness of today's local notion of the state in Kazakhstan—the notion that is my focus in this chapter—builds on that mindset.

However, the post-Soviet experience suggests that the practical meaning of "the state" may sometimes be cast into sharpest relief when its vital features, long taken for granted, are suddenly found lacking. When the connections between the different pieces of hardware were suddenly broken, citizens experienced that as the atrophy of "the state" itself (Alexander 2004). The majority of urban residents, previously employees of state enterprises, suddenly found themselves unemployed, which undermined any sense of one's personal identity vis-à-vis the social and material context. The relative values of things became unknowable while shops ran empty and money was commonly replaced with factory-issued coupons, practically inconvertible to any actual goods. Systems that had previously been thought of as indivisible wholes, produced, owned, and managed by "the state," such as electricity and water supplies, were now privatized—that is, split up and divided between a fuzzy host of new subjects, private owners. Citizens, who now had to learn to think of themselves rather as "consumers," needed to establish individual relations with each of them (Alexander 2007). As James Ferguson notes (1999, 238), being disconnected is an entirely different experience from never having been connected in the first place, and considerably harder to bear. For former Soviet citizens, the dismantling of infrastructures and the reshuffling of relations between people and things marked a moment of radical disconnection (see also Humphrey 2002).

In Tselinograd, as today's Astana used to be known between 1961 and 1992, a number of large industrial establishments, such as the agricultural-machinery producer TselinSelMash or the textile factory, were either divided into numerous small companies, the relations among which remained highly unclear, or closed altogether. In many cases their financial assets were appropriated by actors practically unaccountable, while their material infrastructures were left up for grabs, leading to the enterprises' physical, as much as legal, disappearance. This affected most of the population, not only because of job loss, but also because entire living quarters had been owned and managed by those enterprises. One especially conspicuous result of the crisis was that the construction of new buildings suddenly came to a halt. For many long months, entire neighborhoods of incomplete apartment blocks, uncanny in the bareness of their concrete carcasses, stood as a powerful epitome of the sudden incapacitation of the state. The experience of the early 1990s is still painfully remembered among all those who had lived through it, as much in former Tselinograd as elsewhere across the Soviet Union. The situation in numerous smaller towns, many of which had been entirely dependent on a single enterprise, was even more dramatic.

To former Soviet urbanites, memories of the post-perestroika period of changes coalesce into a single, most regrettable transformation: the quick decomposition of "the state." As one of my Astana neighbors—a chain-smoking retired operator of heavy construction vehicles—would frequently complain, post-Soviet Kazakhstan became a total "mess" (*bardak*) and a "dead state," "a laughingstock, not a state." Others among my interlocutors subsumed the situation they had found themselves in as a "real nuthouse" (*durdom, samoi nastoiashchii*). What was lost was the sense of connectedness to that unimaginably extensive network that had linked hardware, places and bodies. That, from the practical perspective of a citizen, had been the Soviet "state." This point is captured most succinctly and most clearly in the following words of another neighbor, who thus concluded her lengthy account of the post-perestroika fragmentation of property, rights, and relations between people and things: "Before, there used to be factories—take TselinSelMash. . . . Many people used to work there. Then the factories were stopped, dissolved, taken apart, and the people were left out of business. . . . Suddenly, there is no state! There used to be a state before" (cf. Beyer, this volume).

We can better understand the invocations of chaos, madness, or absurdity in recollections of the turmoil of the 1990s (see also Alexander 2009; Nazpary 2002) by drawing on Mitchell's work. As he reports (1991, 29–31), it was in very similar terms that European travelers to Egypt—before that country was transformed in accordance with modern disciplinary principles—described the bustling life of Cairo: to them, it was an ocean of confusion. Prepared to see every thing and every person as signifiers of an abstract order ("the social"), they were shocked and found the Orient disorienting. There, things were not *yet* organized as representations of an overarching order behind them. In towns such as Tselinograd in the 1990s, they were not organized that way any longer. If pipes and walls had represented the Soviet state as a framework of order, then that was now abolished, and things, including those that remained vital to survival, became in that sense meaningless.

Grazhdanstvennost': Citizen Subjectivity

The work of scholars such as Michel Foucault (1983) or Judith Butler (1997) has shown that subjectivity—which we may provisionally define as "the capacity to think and act on the basis of a coherent sense of self" (Hoffmann 2003, 45)—is produced by political relations, including the state. Let us, then, consider what impact on citizens' subjectivities the material dismantling of the Soviet state and the both literal and figurative reconstruction of the state in the 2000s may have had. Numerous historical and ethnographic studies of daily life in the Soviet Union (e.g., Hoffmann 2003; Kotkin 1995; Yurchak 2006) have shown that from the perspective of an individual citizen the Soviet order of social relations was cumbersome, perhaps, but navigable. The meanings of self and of all things were worked out in the process of acting in that social and material environment. Within the Soviet state, therefore, subjectivities could be meaningfully performed; with its collapse, the sense of coherent order that had framed that day-to-day performativity was no more.

The construction works in Astana are represented in official discourse as a massive, progressive, concerted effort taken up collectively under the leadership of the president to restore societal cohesion and economic vitality. The built forms are to represent the national future and the labor itself represents the nation-state in action. Thus, the reality and sustainability of the state, implicitly understood as an overarching ordering principle of society, may be reestablished in the eyes of the citizen-public. The narrative of construction builds upon the remembered experience of collapse and destruction in the

1990s. As Mitchell points out (1991, 82), disorder is a precondition for the conceptual possibility of ordering, so this retrospective projection of chaos is necessary to the forward-oriented narrative. This is by no means to question the feelings of loss and suffering that many former Soviet citizens associate with the post-perestroika period; it is, however, to take note of the structural role this retrospection has in supporting the new narrative of construction.

Importantly, "the state" being reconstructed is not an entity external to citizen selves. Rather, it incorporates and encompasses, reaches to and into them—much the same way that a pipe system reaches to and into apartments. As Catherine Alexander notes (2004, 254), representations of the state are related to notions of personhood. Thus, the labor of construction that (re-)creates the state is expected simultaneously to produce a specific kind of citizen-subject. It is a process in which citizens' commitment and active input is sought, thus providing an avenue for the performance of subjectivity. President Nazarbayev evaluates the outcomes of the "breakthrough" brought about by the capital relocation and underscores the coining of virtue through the labor of construction:

> The capital relocation became a turning point. . . . Nowadays Astana is becoming a symbol of the rise of the state. . . . Ideas of patriotism and civic virtue [*grazhdanstvennost'*] receive their content precisely owing to the example of the construction of this city. Thousands of young boys and girls go to the new capital in the quest for opportunity. . . . Citizens have developed faith in themselves and their strengths, as well as an awareness of the fact that the future . . . can and must be built with one's own two hands. (2006, 357)

The crucial term here is *grazhdanstvennost'*, which I have just rendered as "civic virtue." In fact, it is an almost untranslatable word. Even to Russian speakers, it sounds unusual, different from the more common *grazhdanstvo*, "citizenship." An etymologically faithful approximation of the meaning of *grazhdanstvennost'* in English would require recourse to a neologism: "citizenhood," the specific quality of self derived from the fact of being a citizen. *Grazhdanstvennost'* differs in meaning from "citizenship" insofar as *grazhdanstvennost'* connotes not a set of entitlements but rather an identity. Unlike *grazhdanstvo*, which refers to an ascriptive category (one's being a citizen of this or that state), *grazhdanstvennost'* carries the implication of affective or moral engagement. It fundamentally designates a postulated kind of individual subjectivity defined in relation to the state. The notion of *grazhdanstvennost'* in connection to the construction effort in Astana builds on the Soviet ethos, where labor, especially on grand projects such as the construction of new cities (Kotkin 1995), defined an individual's incorporation in the state and thus constituted a citizen's meaningful identity. Simultaneously, contemporary *grazhdanstvennost'* includes the idea of the individual citizen's self-responsibility, as manifested in the call to build the future "with one's two hands." I now turn to illustrate how these two aspects of *grazhdanstvennost'* find traction among Kazakhstani citizens.

Roza, a Kazakh woman aged around fifty, likes to announce that she "participates in the construction of Astana." Nostalgic as she is about the foregone collective working spirit of Soviet construction sites, Roza's story supports the point that besides the undeniably vital prospects for individual material improvement, to many Kazakhstanis an important thing lost with the USSR's breakup—and then regained with the construction of Astana—was a sense of the state as a meaningful order, coherent enough to pursue grand goals for the sake of the collective future. A construction professional, Roza spent most of her life in small to mid-size industrial towns in different parts of Kazakhstan. Like others, she remembers the 1990s primarily as a decade of things falling apart. Trying to make ends meet, she found herself traveling from one town to another, picking up different jobs, venturing into small-scale trade, and so on. She finally came to Astana in 2006, at a time when construction was at its highest. This is how she remembers her motivations at that point:

> I came here to find a job. . . . After all, in small towns jobs are a difficult issue. And . . . I also wanted to take part in the construction of the new capital . . . to be at the very heart of construction, so that later . . . in my old age, I would be able to say: You see, there was a time when I . . . built this city with my own two hands! . . . To add to the good . . . for memory to remain, and, so to speak, to add to the benefit of our society, for our future fellow citizens. . . . First of all, this was the capital, the new capital. . . . I wanted to really take my part in the improvement, the construction of our new capital.

Since settling in Astana, Roza has worked at a number of construction projects, the most prestigious among which was the Monument to the Kazakh Nation,[7] where the spectacle described above took place. What transpires clearly from her account is an orientation to the collective as the entity that is expected to render personal, individual experience lastingly meaningful. In the snapshot above, Roza is fashioning herself as a Soviet-style "collectivist individual" who, in the words of Oleg Kharkhordin (1999, 204) "espouse[s] collectivist values and repeat[s] the statements of collectivist discourse in which they had been socialized, [and] act[s] individually in order to support this collectivism."

In turn, the account offered by Olga and Sasha, a couple of ethnic Russians about the same age as Roza and, like her, construction professionals, sheds more light on how individual subjectivity itself develops through participatory enactment of collective ideals. Olga and Sasha arrived in Astana in 2000, coming from Temirtau, one of those industrial towns in Kazakhstan that had been the most badly affected by the collapse of the Soviet state in 1991. In Astana, they found rewarding employment—Sasha has supervised housing construction and Olga found a job with a company installing heating in the new district. But they also gained much more: a sense of reconnection to a viable system of social and material relations, enabling meaningful personal agency.[8] Olga and Sasha believe they have personally changed by working in the entrepreneurially spirited social milieu of Astana; they have developed a confidence in the possibility to "realize oneself," plan and pursue personal goals. Olga captures this change as an alteration in the "composition of the soul" (*sostoianie dushi*). In contrast, Sasha portrays their former friends who stayed behind in Temirtau as having "retrograded" and become "like frogs in the mud" in the stagnant, economically depressed town. Despite the degree of resemblance between the construction of Astana and the highly ideologized collective construction efforts of the Soviet period, there are also important differences. The Nazarbayev regime's rhetoric emphasizes values such as entrepreneurship and competitiveness (Adams and Rustemova 2009) and Astana is to be a decidedly capitalist capital, enhancing Kazakhstan's exchange with global markets. Correspondingly, citizens such as Sasha and Olga espouse an entrepreneurial individual ethic as they seek participation in the collective rebuilding. The distance from Soviet official values is perhaps most pointedly expressed in Sasha's telling of the following joke about a Soviet labor-heroine turned bad as a conclusion to his and Olga's narrative of self-transformation:

> A woman is summoned to a labor committee for trial: What happened to you, Valentina Ivanovna? You used to be our many-medaled weaver, we used to give you holiday trips to Truskavets, and pioneer camp vouchers for your children, and first-row tickets to major concerts . . . So say, how on earth did you become a hard-currency prostitute? She rises and breathes heavily: Guess I must've been lucky!

Undoubtedly, individual economic improvement—a job, some pay, a decent dwelling—were the fundamental benefits of starting "new lives" in Astana for Roza, Sasha, and Olga, as well as for the many thousands of others who followed suit.[9] More broadly, however, these personal examples shed light on how incorporative state-building, a process at once material and ideational, becomes a way to perform subjectivity. By this token, these stories also help to grasp the concept of *grazhdanstvennost'*. To Roza, Sasha, and Olga, the linking of their lives to the development of Astana has been an investment in being a citizen as an agentive commitment. Both accounts convey a desire for activity. Implicit in both, but brought to the fore particularly in Roza's statement is the fact that what makes that activity particularly meaningful and rewarding is the connection it offers the individual, through her hard labor, to the "imagined community" (Anderson 1983) of "fellow-citizens," projected beyond the spatio-temporal horizon of individual experience. Not only Roza, however, but also Olga and Sasha through the growth from the hopeless condition of post-collapse Temirtau to active subjectivity in Astana have developed an affective identification with the new state. While admitting a sort of nostalgic identification with the Soviet Union and its symbols, they declare themselves Kazakhstani patriots. Moreover, in both cases the investment in *grazhdanstvennost'* inscribes trajectories of personal development onto physical space: Roza, Olga, and Sasha as well as the hundreds of thousands of other migrants have moved across various distances to perform their citizenly connection. Thus, qualitatively differentiated time—the past out on a limb and the future of reclaimed connectedness—is translated into space, while the disparate locales of departure and arrival are linked to create a continuous state space in and through the individual experience. In sum, we can see how *grazhdanstvennost'* works as a subjectivity, an agentive and affective willing identification with the state.

Monumental Seduction

Grazhdanstvennost' also has another, less clearly goal-oriented and more submissive side. As Butler (1997) argues, subjection is at the core of subjectivity as formed by power. Recent work in anthropology and human geography has drawn attention to the affective impact built space and material objects may have upon human subjects (Gell 1999; Thrift 2008; Navaro-Yashin 2012). In this section, I consider how the materiality of spectacular built forms in Astana works to sustain among citizens a willing subjection to "the state."

While the first new high-rise buildings started appearing in Astana shortly after the capital relocation, that is around 1998–1999, construction works gained unprecedented momentum from 2002. Since then, a new cityscape of skyscrapers, palaces, residential estates and monuments has been created on previously undeveloped land across the river from the Soviet-era center and on the southeastern outskirts of the late-Soviet "sleeper districts." Together, these areas have been nicknamed the "Left Bank." This new development comprises all of what are today the architectural icons of Astana and, more broadly, of the Kazakhstani elites' ambitions of "modernity" (Koch 2010). The most spectacular and extravagant buildings are arranged along an east-west axis, from the Monument to the Kazakh Nation and the pyramid-shaped Palace of Peace and Reconciliation, across the river and then for a further 2.5 km along a pedestrian-only promenade, Nurzhol Boulevard, with fountains, flowerbeds, and a brick pavement.

Figure 6.2. Midday on Nurzhol Boulevard, the heart of Astana's "Left Bank."

From Main Square (*Glavnaia ploshchad'*) by the river to Round Square (*Kruglaia ploshchad'*) at the opposite end of Nurzhol, the area is overflowing with different colors and shapes and an eclectic mixture of architectural styles. Especially on a sunny day, it is awash in light multiply reflected on the smooth surfaces of the buildings, made of glass, aluminum, or polished artificial granite. Generous void spaces allow for broad vistas and amplify the monumentality of particular buildings. The buildings themselves take a variety of forms, from the massive, barbican-like House of Ministries or the blue-domed Presidential Palace, to the wavy silhouettes of the Northern Lights estate or the see-through "tent" of the Khan Shatyr shopping mall, much lighter in appearance though equally gigantic. The copper-colored tower of the Ministry of Communication and the deep-blue building of the national railways spike the sky, while the heavy forms of other buildings, such as the olive-green National Archives or the gargantuan headquarters of the KazMunaiGaz oil company, convey a powerful sense of stately grandeur. Some buildings, such as the Peking Palace hotel, styled after a Chinese pagoda, allude to particular architectural traditions of the world, while others—such as a pair of tall golden conical office buildings flanking the central promenade at one point—represent a universalist geometrical style. Among the residential complexes in this area, the Nur Saia, right on Nurzhol Boulevard, is particularly impressive with its light gray facade decorated with numerous pilasters, and with expensive stores and restaurants on the ground floor. Nearby, amid a vast brick-paved space, stands a 105-meter column of white metal lattice, topped with an orb of golden-hued glass. This is Baiterek, Astana's main architectural icon, serving as a symbol of everything the city's development is meant to represent, the Tree of Life and beacon of Kazakhstan's radiant future.

In the context of the built environment elsewhere in Kazakhstan, this architecture is dazzling, by virtue of the extravagant shapes and colors, the unusual materials, and the sheer size of the buildings. It contrasts most vividly with the uninspiring and frequently decrepit concrete Soviet-era neighborhoods or the notorious semi-legal, self-built adobe huts (*samannie doma*), that together constitute much of the country's built environment, with Astana no exception (Buchli 2007).

The affective impact of encounters with the Left Bank architecture was often powerful. Two young Kazakh women, one of whom was from a provincial town, the other born in the city but living in a run-down area of self-built houses, described the feelings of awe they felt on approaching these monumental buildings. "Even when you're only approaching Baiterek," says Aidana,

> The fact that it's so big, so high, this is already some interesting sensation. As if you were so small! And there you are, going to come closer, something so big, and . . . if you imagine that you're soon going to be up there at the top, that's, I think, that's . . . well, it's good, what can I say, it's good that Baiterek has been built!

The memory of the sensation leaves Aidana short for words, but it seems she is speaking of what Andreas Huyssen (2003) calls "monumental seduction," the arousal of being dominated by the gigantic. In a similar vein, literary critic Susan Stewart (1984, 90) likens monumental public space to "an eternalized parade," and a parade according to her is a mode of display that suggests a seamless social whole, vast beyond individual perception, and apparently well-functioning since it moves so smoothly. Clearly, one can imagine a walk along Nurzhol Boulevard, lined on either side with spectacular buildings, as a parade in reverse: it is the spectator who moves surrounded by the monumental forms, rather than watching a *passeggiata* of forms from a still vantage point. Yet that renders the monumental all the more overwhelming, evoking a bodily sense of submission and encompassment in the spectator.

As a comment made by Aidana's friend Botagöz indicates, those built forms and the affective states they evoke are associated with the idea of "the state," implicitly understood as an incorporative frame coextensive with a territorial entity, "the country":

> I have gotten to love this city. It was here that I became a patriot of my country. Some sort of patriotic feelings have appeared in me . . . precisely

> because I live here, because of moving to Astana. . . . Here I am in closer touch with our country's politics, with our country's life in general.

We have seen earlier, with Olga, Sasha, and Roza, how affective identification with the state was forged in the labor of building; now we may note how the buildings, when complete, continue to affectively shape citizen subjectivity. This observation echoes the point made earlier about mass participation in state-celebratory holiday events. Against the grain of scholarship that assumes that either coercion or cynicism must be the motivating forces behind popular attendance at this sort of event, the possibility that "ordinary" citizens might actually enjoy such celebrations of statehood should not be written off too easily. Yael Navaro-Yashin (2002, 154) argues that "there is a level of agency and spontaneity among the so-called people, a willing initiative to stand for the state," which motivates popular involvement in state celebrations. What a focus on architecture adds to this argument is that buildings provide concrete, material loci for that affective identification that Michael Taussig (1992) calls "state-fetishism." Monumental built forms in public space index "the state." By virtue of their material features such as size, color, shape, and texture they produce an imagination of the state as just as gigantic and sophisticated as they are, and as something agentive—capable of such spectacular construction.[10] In a demiurgic display of force, they mark the Lefebvrean transformation of "natural" space into "state space": "our country" is qualified space, identified with a political "imagined community," the nation-state. Built forms such as Baiterek anchor subjective feelings in that space. Thus, the political edge of "monumental seduction" is thrown into sharp relief: it is a powerful affective impact the state has on its subjects, afforded by the material presence of built forms.

However, the built forms' constructedness is an ambiguous quality and this should not be neglected. The fact that the buildings are constructed, not given, enhances the state's seductive force, because the state is experienced as a process, an activity of growth, rather than as merely a passive structure. The buildings are some of the sites where *grazhdanstvennost'* itself is produced. Yet, materialities can expose the fragility, contingency and built-in contradictions of "the state" (Harvey 2005). Roza's participation in the building of the Monument to the Kazakh Nation was a source of patriotic pride to her. But, at the same time, she was aware of substandard construction practices that had been deployed to complete the grandiose project in time for a "state-fetishistic" display—the monument was to be inaugurated on Astana Day 2008. In this connection, the rumored instability of the monument's central element—a 91-meter obelisk of white marble that allegedly swayed in the wind—marked the inherent unreliability of the state itself as a social construct. Moreover, the fact that enormous efforts and resources were spent to produce spectacular monuments at a period when there was an acute shortage of affordable housing in Astana (cf. Bissenova 2012), made Roza wonder whether the state worked equally for all citizens. With this in mind, I turn now to the ambiguous "state-effects" of protracted and uneven construction.

Sultan's Lesson

The materiality of buildings, to which the state owes much of its impressive gestalt, also allows for the state to be cut down to size, as the following story demonstrates. Sultan, a colleague of Aidana and Botagöz's, fits quite perfectly the stereotype of a recent Astana new settler: Kazakh, under thirty, from a rural area in the south of the country, and a low-paid state-employee—perhaps less typically, an x-ray operator (see also Laszczkowski 2011, 88). When I met him, he struggled hard to make ends meet, working on two state jobs simultaneously. He lived with his wife and a baby in a temporary house without sewerage, central heating or running water. They had been on the waiting list to receive an apartment under a special state program for quite a while. As Sultan admitted to me, he had migrated to Astana full of hope: he had been lured by the vision of radical material betterment, a clean good job, and a comfortable, modern home. He was now becoming disillusioned.

Particularly given the memory of Soviet welfare, a central anxiety about the state with regard to its relationship to material infrastructures is the question whether the state that promises will be able to provide (see McMann 2007). Sultan's waiting-list experience could therefore be seen as a test to the state. Many scholars have argued that it is through particular bureaucratic practices—being involved in a housing program, having a so-called state job—that the state is produced as an entity "out there" (e.g., Gupta 1995; Mitchell 1999). Sultan's story could seem to offer just another case to corroborate that view. His agency and his dreams seemed literally trapped within the slowly growing carcass of the multi-story apartment building that one housing-authority official had once showed him. It was visibly, tangibly there, but its completion seemed forever deferred. Through this concrete shell, Sultan's future was dependent on the performance—and the good will—of "the state."

Meanwhile, a new building was under construction for the medical clinic (*poliklinika*) where Sultan earned his principal salary. It was to be a large, modern structure with an elegant facade and spacious, functional interiors. The construction received some publicity in the local media as an example of the state's progress and the increasing standards of welfare it was reportedly able to provide to citizens. The latter, used to the drab realities of understaffed, underfinanced establishments of public healthcare housed in often dramatically inadequate old buildings, were particularly sensitive to a state-of-the-art neighborhood clinic as a symbol not just of progress but, importantly, of progress that would directly benefit "ordinary people." For the time being, while construction work was in progress at the new building, the clinic functioned in a smaller one, conveniently hidden from view behind the rising structure. There was a sequence of construction delays, but the staff and the patients believed the completion of the works was just a matter of waiting still a little longer. However, one day the deadline came and the new clinic was ceremoniously inaugurated by the mayor of Astana, assisted by several television crews and a small crowd of newspaper reporters. The ribbon was cut, the speeches were delivered, and the distinguished guests left for other important obligations, enabling the construction crews to come back and continue their job while the medical staff continued theirs—in the small building at the back. Sultan and others still believed they would move to the new building soon, but at that moment the Potemkin-village aspect of the ostensible development was made conspicuously clear. If the construction process was not quite what it was publicly held to be, the reliability of the state to which that construction gave substance was likewise put in question. Could Sultan count on the state to deliver on "its" promise of housing?

Yet the lesson Sultan learned from his waiting-list experience was different. He realized that the state, in so far as it was relevant to his current concerns, could be manipulated. It gradually materialized, along with the apartment building, but this process was to Sultan's advantage. As he told me at some point, as soon as he received the apartment he planned to quit the state job that had made him eligible for the housing program in the first place. A friend of his was a manager at a private hospital and had offered Sultan a position there that would be significantly better paid. According to the rules of the program, Sultan explained, an apartment once granted could not be taken away as long as the grantee paid the installments, and that was safely affordable. Sultan acted as if the state was a superior force he depended on, but he knew better. Ironically, the same material form that made the state present and seemingly able to arrest Sultan's agency enabled Sultan to reduce the state to a resource he could tactically manipulate to his own benefit.

Conclusion

In Central Asia there is a particular history of the material articulations of the state. In the Soviet period, the state found nearly ubiquitous material presence in the built environment; it was performed through social relations that produced and utilized vital material infrastructures. The collapse of the Soviet political system subsequently brought with it a breakup of those relations and material connections. Beginning in the mid-1990s, the local rulers who had emerged from the turmoil, enjoying more leeway in exercising their power than their counterparts in some other corners of the former empire, ventured to use the built environment once again to perform statehood. After a period when the coherence of the state had been seriously challenged, the goal was now to prove beyond doubt that the state existed and worked. Therefore, the material forms these efforts produced have been as spectacular as possible. Astana, owing to Kazakhstan's comparably advantageous economic potential, has become an outstanding example of this pattern.

Since the 1990s, scholars have focused on the state as an idea (Abrams 1988) and a discursive construct (e.g., Gupta 1995). Despite the undeniable merits of that approach, there seems to have been insufficient attention to the fact that the state, while a fictional, ideational, or imaginary reality, is also supported by an extensive and dense network of material connections (Navaro-Yashin 2012). It is not only the case that too much "stuff" is organized around the idea of the state for any citizen to afford denying the state's existence, even though they can "see through it," as suggested by those analyses that emphasize "cynical" tolerance for the "obvious" fiction of the state (Navaro-Yashin 2002, 171). I argue that attention to the material make-up of the state allows for a better understanding of non-cynical identification with it, exposing the agentive as well as the seductive side of the voluntary subjection that can be called, following Taussig, "state-fetishism." While the state is a "construct," there is a material reality to its construction. That material reality can exert on citizen-subjects powerful feelings of incorporation, mobilization, or seduction.

Yet materializing the state in and through the built environment is always an ambiguous undertaking. "There is obviously no Archimedean point from which to visualize 'the state', only numerous situated knowledges," writes Akhil Gupta (1995, 392). Accordingly, in this chapter I have looked at the Kazakhstani state from a number of perspectives, following my informants' experiences of the materializations of the state in built forms. On the one hand, the buildings and monuments offer the citizens evidence of the state's existence and functioning. Importantly, those structures do not just stand as passive signs of an equally passive entity, "the state" beyond and above the individual. Quite the contrary: through construction, they enable the performance of the state as a collective, incorporative process. As such, the state is, as I have suggested above, a subjective fantasy of objective order. Individual citizens embrace the image of order and actively strive to enact it and participate in its performance—as far as it suits them. They use "the state" as a frame of meaning to organize experience and to orient their actions, desires, and affective as well as material investments. If citizens are cogs in an "artificial machine" (Mitchell 1999, 89), they are cogs with a soul and with their own agendas. While state-building, with all the material crafting it involves, provides an avenue for performing subjectivity, the state simultaneously depends on the citizens' subjective identification with it.

On the other hand, the very constructedness of the state as embodied in built forms renders it just as fragile as they are. Recent history has proved that the state can quite literally decompose when the connections, semiotic, economic, and physical, between people and things are broken, producing feelings of loss, precariousness, and longing. Currently, ambiguities inherent in the process of (re-)construction are also evident. What we learn from Sultan's case is that the same state that impresses and seduces with spectacular construction may also betray by distributing its efforts unevenly, deferring the delivery on its promises, and applying a Potemkin-village logic to building. In a similar vein, Roza, the self-styled collectivist, commented that much of what was being built was "not for the people." She referred as much to the evident priority given in Astana to the construction of monuments and government buildings as to the fact that the bulk of high-end housing being built was simply unaffordable for all but the wealthiest Kazakhstanis. Her comment signaled a return of the separation between "the state" and "the people" (*narod;* cf. Ries 1997, 27–28). And in yet another twist, Sultan managed to turn the materialization of the state in housing to his advantage and reduce the state situationally to a manipulable bureaucratic provider of services.

Materiality allows the simultaneous encapsulation of seemingly irreconcilable states; it accommodates the inherent ambiguities of social life. "The state" can be simultaneously magnificent and unstable, the locus of awe, hope, desire, disillusionment, and trickery. When materiality is put in the focus of the political, for instance when built environment is used as a prime means to perform statehood, it is possible to observe how that happens.

Notes

1. Elsewhere (Laszczkowski 2011) I have referred to the same spectacle and used parts of the life-stories of some of the informants who appear below to make a broader argument about the reconstruction of society as a seeming coherent whole. Here, however, I focus more specifically on the social and material relations that make up "the state."

2. Opposition politicians Zamanbek Nurkadilov and Altynbek Sarsenbaev were shot within three months of one another in late 2005/early 2006.

3. The capital of Turkmenistan, Ashgabat, has been subject to reconstruction on a comparable scale and some of its new architectural forms seem even more extravagant than those found in Astana (Šír 2008). However, the idiosyncrasies of the Turkmenistani regime tending toward totalitarianism are too well known for Turkmenistan to be viewed by anyone as an example to follow. Kazakhstan, in contrast, is perceived as the

regional leader both in economic development and in terms of its relatively low levels of political violence. Moreover, Astana is an available destination for tourism and labor migration from Uzbekistan and Kyrgyzstan, while Ashgabat remains out of reach due to Turkmenistan's isolationist policies.

4. Akmolinsk 1830–1961, Tselinograd 1961–1992, Aqmola 1992–1998, Astana since 1998.

5. My translation from the Russian.

6. Laura Adams, in her book on mass spectacle in Uzbekistan, notes that spectacle is a particularly useful medium of ideological work, for it gets the official message across "without making the masses feel left out"; however, she nonetheless sees spectacle as a "one-way flow of communication, speech without response, which isn't really communication at all" (2010, 3). In contrast, I stress the incorporative aspect of performances.

7. *Qazaq eli*—the Kazakh noun *el* translates as "people" and "nation," as well as "land" or "country."

8. See Laszczkowski (2011, 83), for more details of Sasha and Olga's life-story.

9. The population of Astana increased from around three hundred thousand in 1998 to approximately seven hundred and fifty thousand at present due to migration from across Kazakhstan (Regiony 2012, 5; Tatibekov 2005).

10. It is interesting to note that many of the "Left Bank" buildings in Astana are in no simple sense "state buildings." Built by private companies with funds coming from private and often foreign, transnational sources (Bissenova, this volume) and in many cases housing private businesses, they nonetheless support the state-fetish.

References

Abrams, Philip. 1988. "Notes on the Difficulty of Studying the State." *Journal of Historical Sociology* 1: 58–89.

Adams, Laura. 2010. *The Spectacular State: Culture and National Identity in Uzbekistan.* Durham, N.C.: Duke University Press.

Adams, Laura, and Assel Rustemova. 2009. "Mass Spectacle and Styles of Governmentality in Kazakhstan and Uzbekistan." *Europe-Asia Studies* 61: 1249–1276.

Agnew, John. 1998. "The Impossible Capital: Monumental Rome under Liberal and Fascist Regimes, 1870–1943." *Geografiska Annaler* 80: 229–240.

Alexander, Catherine. 2004. "Value, Relations, and Changing Bodies: Privatization and Property Rights in Kazakhstan." In *Property in Question: Value Transformation in the Global Economy,* edited by Katherine Verdery and Caroline Humphrey, 241–273. Oxford: Berg.

———. 2007. "Almaty: Rethinking the Public Sector." In *Urban Life in Post-Soviet Asia,* edited by Catherine Alexander, Victor Buchli and Caroline Humphrey, 70–101. London: University College London Press.

———. 2009. "Privatization: Jokes, Scandal and Absurdity in a Time of Rapid Change." In *Ethnographies of Moral Reason: Living Paradoxes of a Global Age,* edited by Karen Sykes, 43–65. Basingstoke, UK: Palgrave Macmillan.

Anderson, Benedict. 1983. *Imagined Communities: Reflections on the Origin and Spread of Nationalism.* London: Verso.

Aretxaga, Begoña. 2000. "A Fictional Reality: Paramilitary Death Squads and the Construction of State Terror in Spain." In *Death Squad: The Anthropology of State Terror*, edited by Jeffrey A. Sluka, 43–69. Philadelphia: University of Pennsylvania Press.

———. 2003. "Maddening States." *Annual Review of Anthropology* 32: 393–410.

Bennett, Tony, and Patrick Joyce, eds. 2010. *Material Powers: Cultural Studies, History, and the Material Turn*. New York: Routledge.

Bissenova, Alima. 2012. "Post-Socialist Dreamworlds: Housing Boom and Urban Development in Kazakhstan." PhD diss., Cornell University, Ithaca.

Bozdoğan, Sibel. 2001. *Modernism and Nation Building: Turkish Architectural Culture in the Early Republic*. Seattle: University of Washington Press.

Buchli, Victor. 2000. *An Archaeology of Socialism*. Oxford: Berg.

———. 2007. "Astana: Materiality and the City." In *Urban Life in Post-Soviet Asia*, edited by Catherine Alexander, Victor Buchli and Caroline Humphrey, 40–69. London: University College London Press.

Butler, Judith. 1997. *The Psychic Life of Power: Theories in Subjection*. Stanford, Calif.: Stanford University Press.

Collier, Stephen J. 2004. "Pipes." In *Patterned Ground: Entanglements of Nature and Culture*, edited by Stephan Harrison, Steve Pile and Nigel Thrift, 50–52. London: Reaktion Books.

Cummings, Sally N. 2005. *Kazakhstan: Power and the Elite*. London: I. B. Tauris.

Ferguson, James. 1999. *Expectations of Modernity: Myths and Meanings of Urban Life on the Zambian Copperbelt*. Berkeley: University of California Press.

Ferguson, James, and Akhil Gupta. 2002. "Spatializing States: Toward an Ethnography of Neoliberal Governmentality." *American Ethnologist* 29: 981–1002.

Foucault, Michel. 1983. "The Subject and Power." In Hubert L. Dreyfus and Paul Rabinow, *Michel Foucault: Beyond Structuralism and Hermeneutics*, 208–226. Chicago: University of Chicago Press.

Gell, Alfred. 1999. "The Technology of Enchantment and the Enchantment of Technology." In *The Art of Anthropology: Essays and Diagrams*, 159–186. Oxford: Berg.

Gupta, Akhil. 1995. "Blurred Boundaries: The Discourse of Corruption, the Culture of Politics, and the Imagined State." *American Ethnologist* 22: 375–402.

Harvey, Penelope. 2005. "The Materiality of State-Effects: An Ethnography of a Road in the Peruvian Andes." In *State Formation: Anthropological Perspectives*, edited by Christian Krohn-Hansen and Knut G. Nustad, 123–141. London: Pluto Press.

Hoffmann, David L. 2003. *Stalinist Values: The Cultural Norms of Soviet Modernity, 1917–1941*. Ithaca, N.Y.: Cornell University Press.

Holston, James. 1989. *The Modernist City: An Anthropological Critique of Brasilia*. Chicago: University of Chicago Press.

Humphrey, Caroline. 2002. *The Unmaking of Soviet Life: Everyday Economies after Socialism*. Ithaca, N.Y.: Cornell University Press.

———. 2005. "Ideology in Infrastructure: Architecture and Soviet Imagination." *Journal of the Royal Anthropological Institute* (N. S.) 11: 39–58.

Huyssen, Andreas. 2003. *Present Pasts: Urban Palimpsests and the Politics of Memory*. Stanford, Calif.: Stanford University Press.

Kharkhordin, Oleg. 1999. *The Collective and the Individual in Russia: A Study of Practices.* Berkeley: University of California Press.

Koch, Natalie. 2010. "The Monumental and the Miniature: Imagining 'Modernity' in Astana." *Social and Cultural Geography* 11: 769–787.

Kotkin, Stephen. 1995. *Magnetic Mountain: Stalinism as Civilization.* Berkeley: University of California Press.

Laszczkowski, Mateusz. 2011. "Building the Future: Construction, Temporality, and Politics in Astana." *Focaal: Journal of Global and Historical Anthropology* 60: 77–92.

Lefebvre, Henri. 2003. "Space and the State." Translated by Alexandra Kowalski-Hodges et al. In *State/Space: A Reader,* edited by Neil Brenner et al., 84–100. Malden, Mass.: Blackwell.

McMann, Kelly. 2007. "The Shrinking of the Welfare State: Central Asians' Assessments of Soviet and Post-Soviet Governance." In *Everyday Life in Central Asia: Past and Present,* edited by Jeff Sahadeo and Russell Zanca, 233–247. Bloomington: Indiana University Press.

Mitchell, Timothy. 1991. *Colonising Egypt.* Berkeley: University of California Press.

———. 1999. "Society, Economy, and the State Effect." In *State/Culture: State-Formation after the Cultural Turn,* edited by George Steinmetz, 76–97. Ithaca, N.Y.: Cornell University Press.

Navaro-Yashin, Yael. 2002. *Faces of the State: Secularism and Public Life in Turkey.* Princeton, N.J.: Princeton University Press.

———. 2012. *The Make-Believe Space: Affective Geography in a Postwar Polity.* Durham, N.C.: Duke University Press.

Nazarbayev, Nursultan. 2005. *V serdtse Evrazii.* Astana, Kazakhstan: Atamura.

———. 2006. *Kazahstanskii put'.* Karaganda, Kazakhstan.

Nazpary, Joma. 2002. *Post-Soviet Chaos: Violence and Dispossession in Kazakhstan.* London: Pluto Press.

Rabinow, Paul. 1995. *French Modern: Norms and Forms of the Social Environment.* Chicago: University of Chicago Press.

Reeves, Madeleine. 2009. "Materialising State Space: 'Creeping Migration' and Territorial Integrity in Southern Kyrgyzstan." *Europe-Asia Studies* 61: 1277–1313.

Regiony. 2012. *Regiony Kazakhstana.* Astana, Kazakhstan: Agentstvo Respubliki Kazakhstan po Statistike.

Ries, Nancy. 1997. *Russian Talk: Culture and Conversation during Perestroika.* Ithaca, N.Y.: Cornell University Press.

Schatz, Edward. 2009. "The Soft Authoritarian Tool Kit: Agenda-Setting Power in Kazakhstan and Kyrgyzstan." *Comparative Politics* 41: 203–222.

Šír, Jan. 2008. "Cult of Personality in Monumental Art and Architecture: The Case of Post-Soviet Turkmenistan." *Acta Slavica Iaponica* 25: 203–220.

Stewart, Susan. 1984. *On Longing: Narratives of the Miniature, the Gigantic, the Souvenir, the Collection.* Baltimore: Johns Hopkins University Press.

Tatibekov, V. L., ed. 2005. *Migranty v novoy stolitse Kazakhstana.* Astana, Kazakhstan: International Organization for Migration.

Taussig, Michael. 1992. *The Nervous System.* New York: Routledge.

———. 1997. *The Magic of the State.* New York: Routledge.

Thrift, Nigel. 2008. *Non-Representational Theory: Space, Politics, Affect*. London: Routledge.

Vale, Lawrence J. 2008. *Architecture, Power, and National Identity.* London: Routledge.

Verdery, Katherine. 1992. "The 'Etatization' of Time in Ceausescu's Romania." In *The Politics of Time,* edited by Henry J. Rutz, 37–61. Washington, D.C.: American Ethnological Society.

Wanner, Catherine. 1998. *Burden of Dreams: History and Identity in Post-Soviet Ukraine.* University Park: Pennsylvania State University Press.

Wedeen, Lisa. 1999. *Ambiguities of Domination: Politics, Rhetoric, and Symbols in Contemporary Syria*. Chicago: University of Chicago Press.

Williams, Raymond. 1977. *Marxism and Literature.* Oxford: Oxford University Press.

Yurchak, Alexei. 2006. *Everything Was Forever, Until It Was No More: The Last Soviet Generation*. Princeton, N.J.: Princeton University Press.

Žižek, Slavoj. 1997. *The Plague of Fantasies.* London: Verso.

7. The Bulldozer State

Chinese Socialist Development in Xinjiang

Ildikó Bellér-Hann

This chapter explores ongoing modernization processes in the Xinjiang Uyghur Autonomous Region (XUAR) of the People's Republic of China (PRC). In recent years this region has been frequently labeled by the Western media as China's "restive region" or "most troublesome province." Situated in the northwest and constituting the largest administrative unit of the PRC, the XUAR has long been characterized by interethnic conflict between the Han Chinese and the Turkic-speaking Muslim Uyghurs. The latter constitute a *minzu*, a minority group recognized by the Chinese state; they view the Han as colonizers whose continuing immigration into the XUAR is aimed at the appropriation of the region's resources, at securing its international borders as well as its internal stability (Becquelin 2000). Following Mao Zedong's death in 1976, far-reaching economic reforms were implemented in the early 1980s. Decollectivization and the introduction of a market economy were initially accompanied by certain freedoms and privileges for the recognized minorities. This economic liberalization, however, did not mean political liberalization. Due to accelerated Han immigration, interethnic competition for resources, and above all ethnic discrimination on the labor market, Uyghur discontent with Chinese rule has been growing since the 1990s (Bovingdon 2004). Economic liberalization has continued uninterrupted, but in Xinjiang it has always been carefully harnessed to serve the stability of the region and Beijing's firm control over it, while cultural and religious policies have become increasingly repressive.

In 2000, in an attempt to redress the economic backwardness of the western provinces relative to the rapid development of East China and thereby to contain the discontent of the vast borderlands inhabited mostly by ethnic minorities, the "Develop the West" campaign was launched. This intensification of the modernization strategy initiated in the last decades of the twentieth century is viewed by the Uyghurs with a great deal of suspicion, since in the tense political climate all top-down policies are seen through the prism of ethnic polarization. Many Uyghurs fear that Chinese modernization is intended to eradicate Uyghur culture and to achieve their full assimilation into the Han mainstream. Under these circumstances the state tends to be conceptualized by the Uyghurs as omnipresent, omnipotent, heavy-handed and threatening, as an external force working against local society. In the Uyghur imagination this opposition corresponds to the ethnic divide: the state is Han Chinese, the Uyghurs are its valiant, victimized opponents, and the remaining eleven officially recognized ethnic groups of the XUAR are excluded from the picture altogether.[1] These dynamics form the background to this chapter, which focuses on how material forms of modernization bearing directly on Uyghur culture shape experiences and conceptions of the state in the local context.[2]

After earlier attempts to eliminate it as an object of scholarly enquiry, anthropologists have now for some decades been at pains to bring the state back into their purview (Mitchell 1999; Krohn-Hansen and Nustad 2005; Sharma and Gupta 2006). The rediscovery of the state as an object of ethnographic research has been accompanied by new theories to explore how the state is materially constituted through everyday social practice and discursively reproduced through popular talk about corrupt politicians (Gupta 2006). In Xinjiang, however, extreme forms of repression mean that one can hardly speak of a "discursive construction" of the state in public culture (Gupta 2006, 212). The voices of both Uyghur intellectuals and liberal Han Chinese are muted through censorship and self-censorship. Nevertheless, here as everywhere the state is "implicated in the minute texture of everyday life" (Gupta 2006, 211). It is imagined and articulated in multiple ways and forms: through cautious private discourse, through everyday bureaucratic practices, through ritual and symbolic performances, through the implementation of new policies that in the XUAR often assume the form of shocking intrusions in people's daily lives and practices, and, last but not least, through myriad forms of material presence.[3] This chapter elaborates upon the last of these, or what Penelope Harvey has called the "materiality of state effects" (Harvey 2005). She adapts the concept of state effect from Timothy Mitchell, who has argued that the state should be approached "not as an actual structure, but as the powerful, apparently metaphysical effect of practices that make such structures appear to exist" (Mitchell 1999, 89–90). For both authors, the binary opposition of state and society masks the complexities of those social practices that produce the opposition and confirm the nature of the state as an "external structure" to society.

In Xinjiang both Uyghur villagers and urban residents experience the state through a multiplicity of forms, the most extreme being the violence used by security forces in the summer of 2009 during and after the Urumchi "riot," in the course of which almost two hundred people lost their lives (Millward 2009).[4] Following this event, the presence of armed troops and police along major roads and in strategically important cities has become a permanent feature of everyday life, as has the increasing use of surveillance cameras. Other, less tangible "state effects" include the isolation of the region from the outside world through closing down internet communication and international telephone connections that lasted for almost one year. But state effects are also produced by top down projects represented as benign interventions to deliver modernization and development. This contribution will explore how these goals can lead to friction in the domain of culture, where they both divide and unite the local Uyghur community, demonstrating the cultural embeddedness of the complex relationship between state, space, and power.[5] Using the metaphor of the "bulldozer state," various spatial strategies employed by the Chinese state in the oasis center of Qumul will be explored, showing how state directives realized in acts of demolition, construction, preservation, and reclassification reflect the often ambivalent and wavering policies of the center toward its Uyghur periphery and to what extent the "state effects model" is applicable to extreme authoritarian conditions.

Developing the West: Creative Destruction?

The XUAR constitutes about one-sixth of the total area of the People's Republic. It occupies an important geostrategic position since it shares international borders with several Central Asian republics (Kazakhstan, Kyrgyzstan, Tajikistan), with Russia, Mongolia, India, Pakistan, Afghanistan, and internal borders with Tibet as well as the provinces of Gansu and Qinghai. Thus the internal stability of the XUAR is of paramount importance since ethnic unrest in such an important border area can pose a real danger to the state. The region is rich in oil deposits and other raw materials, but in addition to its natural resources it also offers an outlet for impoverished Han Chinese migrants who pour into the XUAR from China proper. Han immigration serves two purposes: first, it takes some of the pressure off the overcrowded inland and eastern provinces, second, it "dilutes" and therefore weakens Uyghur presence in the XUAR itself.

Official encouragement of Han immigration has antecedents in imperial policies under the Manchu Qing dynasty (1644–1911), when the region served as a buffer between China and Russia. For a long time the Manchus relied on indigenous elites to mediate between them and the subjugated Turkic-speaking Muslims, thus realizing their own brand of indirect rule, but the imperative to increase Han Chinese presence was soon recognized, especially in the north of the region (Millward 1998). The socialist state has renewed this stimulus.[6] Indirect rule has ostensibly been replaced by nominal autonomy with the Uyghurs as the titular group, but in practice the region is increasingly regarded not as a buffer with special characteristics but as just another integral part of the Chinese nation-state (Becquelin 2000, 67–68). From the Uyghur perspective, the demographic consequences of immigration policies have been disastrous: the pre-socialist ethnic ratio of about 5 percent Han Chinese to over 80 percent Uyghurs had by 2000 changed officially to 40.6 percent Han to only 46.6 percent Uyghur; in reality, if the floating Han Chinese population (i.e., the unregistered migrants) are also included, it is likely that Han now outnumber the Uyghurs (Toops 2004).

Economic development of the region was stepped up in the early 1990s through investment in infrastructure and the promotion of cross-border trade. These measures were intended "to bind Xinjiang more closely to the rest of the PRC: by neutralizing the impact of the new Central Asian states; by developing communications axes linking Xinjiang with the rest of China; by reinforcing military and paramilitary forces in Xinjiang, especially in the south; and above all through measures aimed at speeding up Han migration to the region" (Becquelin 2000, 67). The Develop the West campaign launched in 2000 is a continuation of these policies and can be seen as the fulfillment of the promise made by Deng Xiaoping in the early phase of the reform period to resolve the problem of regional inequalities (Lai 2002, 433). Alleviating economic disparities between the coastal regions and the inland provinces is intended simultaneously to defuse resistance to Chinese rule among the minorities of the western borderlands and to mobilize the natural resources of the west; special attention has been paid to the "one white, one black," that is, to cotton and oil production (Millward 2007, 298–306). Investments into infrastructure, roads and railways in particular, facilitated the movement of people and goods between Xinjiang and the rest of China. This massive development program has many other facets not discussed here, such as fiscal reform, new environmental policies, urbanization, land reclamation, the opening up of new Han Chinese settlements, the establishment of new industries and the upgrading of others. All this has been implemented through a careful balancing act by multiple agents considering both Han Chinese interests and the cultural rights of minorities. Foreign analysts agree that the political aims of the campaign supersede the economic ones. One has written of a political "Trojan Horse" which uses development as a vehicle to increase Han immigration into the XUAR (Moneyhon 2003), another talks about multiple senses of "staged development," describing it as:

> a temporally phased development strategy (by stages) as well as . . . the building of a new "theatrical stage," a horizon of untold riches which merely wait to be untapped, as well as the elaborate orchestration of symbols associated with this push westward, designed to foster nation building and, last but not least, bestow renewed legitimacy to Chinese Communist Party (CCP) rule. (Becquelin 2004: 361)

Of course modernization is not confined to the XUAR or to borderlands inhabited by ethnic minorities. Demolition of what has been deemed old, backward and outdated is going on all over China. The Three Gorges Dam on the River Yangtze and its tributaries is exemplary of these developments: the world's largest hydraulic project has required the flooding of numerous settlements and the resettlement of over 1.2 million people (Yardley 2007).[7] Urban demolition and renovation processes, but also increasing public criticism, are widely reported nowadays in the mass media.

Such development projects initiated in minority areas are understood locally as expressions of Chinese territorializing efforts, that is, as a spatial strategy to exert control over land, resources, and populations, simultaneously delineating territories and endowing them with social meaning (Sack 1986; Lefebvre 1991; Joniak 2009). Place and space are mobilized in support of "the practical, discursive, and representational aspects of power" (Radcliffe 2001, 143). The rulers initiated such control of space soon after the incorporation of Xinjiang into the Qing Empire, through the establishment of settler colonies and the construction of colonial cities outside but in close proximity to the native urban settlements. Spatial control was extended and stepped up at the expense of local space following the occupation of Xinjiang by the People's Liberation Army in 1949 and especially after the founding of the XUAR in 1955. Techniques included the building of new highways, land reclamation through the construction of irrigation canals and dams, the establishment of new industrial plants, the construction of new public squares and buildings, and of course the accompanying demolition of many old buildings. Such large-scale construction projects were a hallmark of the Great Leap Forward. Although the policies of this period were later officially discredited, mass mobilization of men and women were still mentioned with pride by my Chinese co-researchers and by local officials during my fieldwork in Kashgar in the mid-1990s (Bellér-Hann 1998). By contrast, villagers I talked to emphasized the suffering caused by these projects. In occasional unsupervised conversations I heard about singularly destructive interventions, typically focused on the demolition or desecration of mosques, shrines, or other historical buildings by Mao's Red Guards during the Cultural Revolution (cf. Loubes 1998, 174).[8] Following the Cultural Revolution, Chinese territorialization efforts prioritized infrastructural development, not only in towns but also in many villages where asphalt roads were built. Even if many villages in the XUAR have remained almost exclusively Uyghur to the present day, the new regularity and modernity represented by these roads constitute a "Sinicization of space" (Loubes 1998, 13–15). This may be partly explained by the fact that here road construction can only take place under state control. The Sinicized nature of road building is further reinforced by the fact that construction workers tend to be Han Chinese rather than Uyghur.[9] This ethnic bias in employment in the construction sector is all the more conspicuous because both men and women work at such sites. The employment of women in such hard physical work, widely criticized by the Uyghur population, is reminiscent of conditions under Maoism and therefore very closely associated with Chinese socialism.

The case of Kashgar has attracted international outcry.[10] As an article in the *China Daily* warned, redevelopment plans for one of the Silk Road's most celebrated cities, one that has strong symbolic relevance for Uyghur history and identity, were particularly unfortunate because, in Western eyes, they confirmed the stereotype of "Han people ill-treating ethnic minorities." The article highlighted the powerlessness of local communities to counter renovation plans all over China and demanded a more considerate and above all transparent policy from municipal authorities.[11] The reasons given for large-scale demolition in this case included the safety of the population, whose traditional adobe structures would be replaced by new, earthquake-resistant houses. Some of these would be built in Uyghur style to preserve Uyghur culture, but according to the plans many sections of the Old Town would be replaced with modern apartment buildings (Wines 2009). The international publicity surrounding the demolition of old Kashgar has drawn attention to the ambiguous role of Uyghur cadres, themselves residents of the Old Town, whose job it is to enforce evictions. Many Uyghur cadres find themselves in a position when they are simultaneously subjects and objects of state coercion, both within and outside the context of development policies.[12] Also controversial are the questions to what extent the threat of earthquake can be invoked to justify the planned renovations, and how far residents participated in the decision-making. Kashgar's absence from the list of cities that China is nominating for designation as a new Silk Road United Nations World Heritage site (Wines 2009) confirms suspicions that the demolition of the Old Town is not just another example of the aggressive development drive affecting the whole of China. The promise to reconstruct at least parts of the traditional Muslim quarters cannot disguise the reality that Uyghur cultural heritage will be replaced with Potemkin structures: invented, artificial and stylized, they can stand only for the Han vision of a folklorized Uyghur materiality.[13] The reinvention of Uyghur material culture can take place not merely within the parameters set by the Chinese (as a renovation would do it) but only on Han Chinese terms.[14]

Although assimilation policies are becoming less and less covert in Xinjiang, efforts to uphold appearances are sustained, if only for the sake of the international community. Development is projected as a socialist variant of "creative destruction," to borrow Schumpeter's concept originally coined to describe the dynamics of capitalism (Schumpeter 1934). However, the indigenous people of Xinjiang see these policies as a barely disguised vehicle to bind Xinjiang more closely to Beijing. In addition to fostering Han immigration to the region, language and educational policies have been amended to promote Chinese at the expense of Uyghur and other minority languages. Uyghurs are also critical of what they perceive to be the forceful recruitment of young unmarried women from rural areas of the XUAR to work in far away southern Chinese cities. Such measures are justified by the authorities in terms of development: better knowledge of Chinese will provide young Uyghurs with better chances on the job market, no matter that this can only be achieved at the cost of the mother tongue; recruiting young women to work in distant factories puts money in their pockets and may even enable them to support their families at home, no matter that this violates local custom and undermines local ideals of morality. Young Uyghur men are recruited too, but their recruitment is voluntary and is organized through agencies set up by the government. Uyghurs themselves wonder why they have to travel so far for factory work when more attractive jobs in the XUAR are available for Han immigrants. The simultaneous stepping up of religious repression and the continuation of family planning restrictions (admittedly more generous for the minorities of Xinjiang than for the Han Chinese) are further examples of how coercive state measures affect the biological and social reproduction of its minority subjects.[15]

Demolition and Construction in Qumul

Although Kashgar is the most infamous case of what I have dubbed "socialist creative destruction" in the XUAR, similar state effects are pervasive throughout the region. However, not all such schemes are so blatantly antagonistic to local cultural traditions. I turn now to consider an example of demolition and reconstruction from Eastern Xinjiang, from the oasis of Qumul, which took place in the first years of the Develop the West Campaign.[16] Even if Qumul had the same media and scholarly visibility as Kashgar (which it does not), this case has features that appear to distinguish it from the demolition of Kashgar or Lhasa. The projects implemented in Qumul reflect the same development impulse. However, here we can observe a subtler attempt to embed "socialist creative destruction" in Uyghur cultural understandings of what makes their oasis unique. This invites contestation within the Uyghur community, even if this is necessarily articulated within parameters set by central policies. The material state effects thus emerge as a consequence of censorship, self-censorship, and local visions of an idealized Uyghur cultural authenticity.[17]

In 2006–2007 I spent six months working in two villages in the oasis of Qumul, which have also seen a great deal of infrastructure development.[18] One fieldsite was situated on the southern edge of the modern city. Here urban and rural spaces are juxtaposed, demarcated by a wide boulevard completed in a burst of creative destruction around the turn of the millennium. The physical appearance of the urban space along the road is strikingly different from the rural settlement behind it: modern style panel architecture dominates at the roadside, while the houses just behind represent traditional Central Asian architecture, the same adobe structures that are being demolished in Kashgar. The road both divides and connects: many families in the densely populated rural settlements take advantage of the opportunities offered by the city, including access to the market, to jobs and to education. At the same time, residence regulations (*hukou*) here as elsewhere in China divide the population into rural and urban categories, each entailing its own set of entitlements, rights and obligations. In the XUAR these divisions inevitably have an ethnic flavor: modernity and urban space are dominated by Han Chinese. Some Uyghurs have come to share this urban space, but the adjacent village space remains predominantly Uyghur both architecturally and demographically.[19] The construction of this new road required the demolition of a significant part of an Uyghur cemetery.

This particular road is a rather special boundary, which is also indicated by naming traditions: the rural settlement is called Inner City (*Şähäriçi*) in Uyghur and Muslim City (*Huicheng*) in Chinese. At its heart stood until the 1930s the walled residence of the *wang*, the indigenous Muslim dynasty that ruled Qumul under the Qing from 1697 onward (Su and Huang 2001, 3). Like other colonial powers, the Qing set about constructing a colonial town (New Town) outside but close to the Muslim City (also known as Old Town). Although the distinction between the two has become increasingly blurred in the socialist era, it is upheld by the registration regulations and remains engrained in local memory and language use, in Qumul as in many other oasis centers.

What remained of the *wang* palace after the fall of the dynasty in 1930 was demolished later in the turbulence of the warlord period,[20] with only some parts of the old city wall surviving these and the later depredations of the Maoist era. An Islamic college (*madrasa*) is locked up and a dervish cloister (*xaneka*) is in a similarly neglected state, awaiting renovation. Apart from these material traces, many people know where the palace, its treasury and the city gates were situated, and such historical memories anchored in space seem to be passed down to the next generation. *Wang* rule is prominent in local historical awareness and in local publications.[21] These are mostly the work of Uyghurs but some Chinese authors writing on the subject are also read by teachers and young educated villagers, mostly in Uyghur translation. Thus scholarly knowledge trickles down and becomes incorporated into the transmission of oral tradition concerning the personalities and governing style of the dynasty. Official versions of history project the local rulers as feudal exploiters of the poor Uyghur population; but oral tradition and local intellectuals' censored and self-censored publications provide more nuanced accounts, an unofficial discourse laden with contradictions. While some vilify the dynasty in general and the last ruler in particular, echoing the official version of history, others emphasize its good governance and attribute *wang* benevolence to their having been "one of us," although it is often unclear whether this identification has an ethnic (Uyghur) or religious (Islamic) basis or both. Some individuals tried to strike a balance between all these possibilities.

Even the official version of local history is not free of contradictions, since the *wang* were both rulers over the local population and close allies and supporters of the Qing dynasty (Qumul Wilayitlik Täzkirä Komiteti 2005, 1428–1440). The latter probably explains why the new road that the bulldozers drove through a large segment of the Uyghur cemetery used by families residing in *Şähäriçi* did not infringe on the family tombs of the *wang*, which have been restored to form an impressive museum complex, the city's principal tourist attraction. Two hundred meters further down the road the *wangs'* palace was reconstructed in 2005 and linked to the shrine complex. This palace, according to local people, has little in common with the original palace that used to stand about a kilometer away. The problem for Uyghurs my research partner and I talked to was not only that reconstruction did not take place in situ but also that the Chinese style of the architecture was considered as lacking authenticity. When architects were invited to submit plans for the reconstruction, those proposing exclusively Central Asian Islamic architectural features were rejected. The plan accepted and realized displays the typical pagoda style of Chinese imperial architecture. In the course of an informal guided tour, an Uyghur cultural official was at pains to explain the symbolism of the various styles employed: according to him, the style of the buildings was eclectic, reflecting a mixing of Chinese, Mongolian,[22] and Muslim traditions and thus representing the unity and harmonious co-existence of all nationalities, which echoes the official ideological stance increasingly imbued with Confucian values.[23] Locals see the reconstructed palace as a colorful creation for the benefit of outsiders: a handful of foreign tourists mostly from Japan and Korea, but mainly Han Chinese visitors.[24]

Figure 7.1. View of the *wang* mausoleum complex.

Historical facts have little significance in the unofficial discourse: for Uyghur residents of the vicinity, who had lived in or around the Muslim dynasty's residence, the reconstructed palace museum is alien, inauthentic and another symbol of Han Chinese hegemony. During an informal conversation one Uyghur teacher expressed these sentiments by saying that the palace reconstruction was the Chinese interpretation of history that Uyghurs disagreed with, which also explained the choice of the Chinese architectural style. Several residents of the nearby village pointed out that to look for history in the palace museum is a waste of time, since real history is located in the village itself.

The renovated *wang* mausoleum, by contrast, boasts original buildings dating from the late 18th and 19th centuries, some of which, including a vast mosque, represent Central Asian Muslim architectural styles in unadulterated forms. Like the reconstructed palace, this complex is a museum and is visited by the same tourists who traipse around the palace museum, but Uyghur visitors are also more frequently seen here. Although they consider the shrines a holy place that they would like to visit regularly, villagers do not do so because the entrance fee of 20 *Yuan* (2 euros) is high for them. One woman, resident in the village, who claimed to be a descendant of the former ruling family, expressed indignation at the idea that she would have to pay to fulfill her religious obligation to pray at the tombs of her dead ancestors. She also added that a few indi-

Figure 7.2. Worshippers at the mosque on the premises of the mausoleum during the Festival of Sacrifice.

viduals are in practice allowed in without payment whenever they wish since the ticket collectors, being local people themselves, know them and have sympathy for their feelings. In saying this she was not necessarily expressing respect for the *wang* themselves, but rather protesting at the state's appropriation of what they consider to be communal sacra.

The old cemetery nearby also belongs to the communal sacra, parts of which had to be bulldozed down in order to build the new road. That the mausoleum and the cemetery have been perceived as a spatial and sacral unit is testified by the fact that the same name is used for both: Altunluq (Golden Mound). At the time the plans for the demolition became clear, protests were waged by the inhabitants of the Inner City whose dead were buried there. As an Uyghur teacher explained, one of the most memorable means employed by the local government in reaction to the protests was to enlist the support of the leading Imam of Inner City, who issued a *fatwa* (legal opinion) to legitimate the act, by declaring that it is legal to destroy a Muslim cemetery after forty years had passed (following the last burial). Locals had no way of checking the legal basis of the *fatwa*, but they had no doubt that the Imam acted under great pressure.[25] Thus, legitimation remained shaky and it was fear that persuaded inhabitants to accept.

As elsewhere in Central Asia and much of the Muslim world, the veneration of the dead is an overriding principle of Uyghur religious belief and practice. The spirituality emanating from the mausoleum complex confers on it a shrine-like status, even in the eyes of those who do not hold positive opinions about the *wang*. Twice a year, on the first day of the two major Islamic holidays, Rozä and Qurban, the gates are opened and thousands of male believers enter to participate in the communal service. On these occasions the site ceases to be a museum and state property; it assumes a sacred character. The mosque is unable to accommodate the crowd, which fills the large courtyard and then spills out onto the pavement and even onto the new asphalt road. A few police cars are positioned here, ostensibly to control the traffic to ensure public safety, but one suspects that the state needs to be alert when so many Uyghurs gather. For these holiday prayers loudspeakers (normally forbidden for mosques in the XUAR) are allowed. Participants are exclusively Uyghur, since Chinese Muslims attend their own mosque.[26] The authorities' decision to allow the temporary transformation of the museum into sacred space, and even to encroach into the public space of the new road, can be interpreted as a reversal in Victor Turner's sense (1995). The "normal" territorial arrangements are temporarily lifted, the state museum reverts to Uyghur sacred space and for a few hours Sinicized modernity gives way to Uyghur sacra.

The renovation of the mausoleum in the same neighborhood where not long afterwards ordinary cemeteries were razed reveals a double irony. The *wang* are vilified as feudal exploiters of the poor people, but it is *their* burial place that is renovated and turned into a museum, to which access is assured by bulldozing the graveyards of the downtrodden. While many local people embrace the same negative rhetoric concerning the *wang,* some through internalizing the official discourse, others perhaps reflecting the oral traditions of their families at the time of the Islamic festivals, this burial complex is wholeheartedly embraced as communal sacra. In contrast, the reconstructed palace of the same *wang* is unanimously rejected as lacking authenticity, as a falsification of local history.

Socialist creative destruction in this part of town did not stop there. On the other side of the road, equidistant between the mausoleum complex and the fake palace and again on land formerly occupied by graves, a monumental building has been erected to house an Uyghur cultural center. This is dedicated to the Uyghur musical tradition known as the twelve *muqam*. Today this large musical canon is listed in UNESCO's intangible heritage program, one of 29 items from China. The *muqam* tradition has many local variations, among which the Qumul *muqam* is one of the most famous; this has given local officials an opportunity to capitalize on the prestigious UNESCO listing, and the new cultural center is a spinoff of their efforts. Architecturally, the building de-

Figure 7.3. The Qumul Muqam Heritage Centre.

fies clear-cut classification. It lacks explicit Chinese characteristics and can be described as modern but with some echoes of traditional Central Asian styles. In any case its raison d'être is unmistakably underlined by the oversized sculptural representations of traditional Uyghur musical instruments in the forecourt. At the time of my most recent visit in 2009 the internal decoration was not yet complete, although some office workers had already moved in ahead of the formal inauguration. Local officials were proud of the fruits of their lobbying, but I had no opportunity to ask local Uyghur residents what they thought about this imposing tangible idealization of authentic Uyghur culture.[27]

Locating the reconstructed palace and the new institution for researching Uyghur folk music along this road is at one level, the level perhaps of most tourist visitors, in harmony with the old Uyghur cemetery on the edge of the city. What the tourists do not appreciate is how these interventions have disturbed relations between the living and the dead, which are of such central importance for Uyghur social relations (Bellér-Hann 2001, 2008; Schrode 2007). In Qumul, male family members are expected to pray at the graves of their ancestors on the eve of the major holidays,[28] but many communities also perform weekly rituals there.[29]

Given this context, this building can also be seen as yet another form of state intervention through spatial territorialization and transformation of public space. Yet this building is undeniably a monument of Uyghur tradition. The *muqams* have been revised and institutionalized "to craft an image of the Uyghur Twelve Muqams as a treasured artistic canon from the Uyghur past that belongs to all Uyghurs" (Light 2008, 26). Nathan Light has shown how the *muqams,* even in their reworked and reedited versions still retain elements of Sufi poetry and the Central Asian romantic epics, the *dastan*. Moreover the editing took place offstage, "largely outside of the sphere of Chinese government interests and cultural management" (Light 2008, 298). The canonization of the *muqams* therefore belongs to the intimate zone of Uyghur cultural autonomy. It is the work of Uyghur scholars rather than the result of Chinese state policy. Yet in spite of this Uyghur agency, the final products of national culture are highly contingent. Light is critical of works that, in focusing on the production of cultural representations and their connectedness to structures of domination, tend to essentialize power and homogenize the groups exercising it. In the Xinjiang context this inevitably means endorsing the dichotomy of Chinese state versus Uyghur society (Light 2008, 294–298).

The Qumul *muqam* is only one of several regional *muqam* traditions, and musically it is not linked to the central corpus of the twelve *muqams* at all (Harris 2007, 78). The very label "Qumul *muqam*" is therefore a misleading "recent coinage applied to suites of local folk songs" (Harris 2007, 79). This makes it all the more remarkable that Uyghur officials in Qumul should assert their contribution to the idealized twelve *muqam*. It was no doubt the only way in which they could legitimate their share in that slice of Uyghur intangible heritage that has been recognized by UNESCO, while simultaneously promoting their own regional variant.[30] Informal interviews implied that the promotion of the twelve *muqam* in Qumul as idealized Uyghur heritage, to which the Qumul *muqam* is a regional contribution, has taken place in a sphere of Uyghur "cultural intimacy" (Light 2008; Herzfeld 1997); this sphere has at least a degree of autonomy from direct Chinese state interference.[31] This public recognition of a sanitized, canonized, approved version of the *muqam* might be conceived by the uninformed as the promotion of a purely national tradition at the expense of regional and religious traditions. Yet locals are well aware of the religious connotations of the *muqam* as well as its potential for political symbolism; at an informal evening gathering of local intellectuals working in government offices or schools, the performance of some romantic epics of the Qumul *muqam* clearly conveyed a message of social discontent and even resistance; although most of the epics sung on this occasion are available in the bookshops in Uyghur-language folklore anthologies, many of the verses performed contained variations that had been left out of the censored publications, in line with the *muqam* tradition, which welcomes improvisation. But even without such additions, the themes of the songs relating the heroic fights of local people against the enemy or the sufferings of the prisoner were perceived as symbolic of the Uyghurs' plight within the Chinese nation-state. Significantly, this particular evening entertainment had the mixed atmosphere/aura of secrecy and anxiety. In my experience, both villagers and urban residents cherish traditional folk music (equated with the *muqam* tradition) and many villages boast some tradition bearers who benefit from occasional small grants distributed by Uyghur cultural officers. Even those may benefit whose engagement is not necessarily in the field of music but, for example, in skillful embroidery of folk garments characteristic of the oasis of Qumul, or in creative writing that may reach local literary journals. For some, such support may be essential for their livelihood, for others the prestige of such public recognition outweighs the importance of the material benefits. At the time of my last visit there was no doubt that the activities of the offices moving to the new premises were generally approved by those who were aware of them. Therefore attitudes toward this building are likely to remain less antagonistic than those harbored toward the reconstructed palace. But it is common knowledge that the road and these new structures serving cultural purposes replaced the ancestors' tombs, which may explain the reluctance of some people to express an opinion about the building, while others saw in it the recognition of Uyghur cultural achievements.

The Bulldozer State

To what extent does the concept of "state effect" help in understanding the state under authoritarian conditions? It remains useful for conceptualizing the state as a structural effect, even in circumstances when it is used for spectacular, large-scale spatial reorganization, as described here, rather than for everyday, mundane arrangements (Mitchell 1999, 89–90). The ideological underpinnings of the demolition of Kashgar emphasized the existential danger for citizens: the threat of earthquake is eliminated by a benevolent state that protects its citizens against natural disaster by means of sending in the bulldozers. This representation also makes the inevitability of the demolition absolutely clear. This rhetoric avoids any reference to ethnic belonging. The case of Qumul is more intricate, since modernization here has affected communal sacra, local culture and local history and involves complex forms of demolition, (re)construction, and preservation. Protests against the demolition of the cemetery were countered by the state by enlisting religious legitimation. However, if we question the distinction between ideology and practice, the two cases are very similar in a number of ways: they both fit well in the nation-wide project of development, which in itself contributes to creating the illusion of a unified state. They both touch a nerve through interfering with important and intimate dimensions of everyday life: through the destruction of traditional dwellings and with it a way of life, and through erasing ancestral tombs. In both cases state effects are created in at least two ways: first, through the appropriation of citizens' decision making power and the enforcement of this decision through mobilizing machinery and technology, themselves the symbols of the very modernity and development the Chinese state is trying to promote; and second, through the territorialization of intimate spaces. Although the case of Kashgar ostensibly builds upon the struggle between people and nature, development projects in their everyday manifestation are ethnicized in both oases since the booming construction industry mostly employs Han Chinese workers: the bulldozers are more likely to be driven and operated by Han Chinese than by Uyghurs, and modernization is widely perceived as top-down development.[32] Thus modernization reinforces not just the externality of the state but the externality of the Chinese nation-state that defines itself against its internal others. In both Kashgar and Qumul, bulldozers are sent in to reinforce state presence in a territory the external borders of which are sufficiently secured; it is therefore not so much geopolitical sovereignty which they aim to achieve, but "internally oriented justifications and explanations of territory" (Radcliffe 2001, 143–144).[33] Bulldozers may well symbolize development and simultaneously pursue a legitimation quest, justifying the presence of the Chinese state through good governance but also through measures that define and shape local culture and tradition.

The bulldozer state is not an emic metaphor but I believe that it could potentially find resonance with many local actors. It conjures up images of irreversible, irresistible destruction and violence, which inevitably accompanies destruction. It also lives up to the term's original usage, which referred to "a person who intimidates by violence."[34] Violence is a state monopoly, and the Develop the West campaign that provides the framework for large-scale development projects in contemporary Xinjiang has been initiated and sponsored by the central government. The symbols of development, the three-dimensional materiality of bulldozers also implies change. Inasmuch as the bulldozer state promises something new in the form of new building, renovation or reconstruction, it also stands for good governance. But bulldozers also represent the imposition of non-negotiable state control, the disruption and irreversible transformation of existing spatial organization. They also represent the technology and knowledge necessary for modernization, and thus reinforce the self-image of the Chinese state as carrier of a *mission civilisatrice* in frontier regions inhabited by "backward minorities." They are the material embodiment of the state, which physically invade, colonize, and reorganize space. The metaphor of the bulldozer state implies the physical power of the state to rearrange space, which can be achieved through a number of regulations, ranging from literally sending in the bulldozers to introducing administrative reclassifications, such as degrading an urban quarter into a village or turning a Muslim shrine into a museum. Through their materiality bulldozers remind minority citizens of the power of the state and thus contribute to the making of the state in space (Radcliffe 2001,123).

Metaphors include numerous but not endless possibilities for interpretation, and one possible deficit in this case is that it attributes a privileged role in the development of Xinjiang to the state and to its local representatives, bureaucrats, planners, builders, and architects, leaving little room for Uyghur agency. This deficit could be made good by an ethnographic exploration of the workings of the extreme authoritarian state. However, the very nature of authoritarianism renders such a venture very difficult; it could be achieved only by risking the safety of local actors. It also impedes expressions of Uyghur agency publicly in the form of social movements, public debates, NGOs, and delegates it to the sphere of "hidden transcripts" (Scott 1990). My preliminary work suggests that, like the *muqam,* informal and semi-formal Uyghur discourses on local history are also produced within the intimate zone of Uyghur cultural autonomy. What from the point of view of the bulldozer state appears as making concessions to the subject population, from the Uyghur point of view may well appear as the expressions and result of the workings of Uyghur agency: when on the Islamic holidays the mausoleum complex turned into a museum reverts into a shrine, when the authority of a local Muslim religious dignitary is enlisted to legitimate the demolition of a Muslim cemetery, when homage is paid to a local Muslim dynasty through reconstructing its palace (albeit in Chinese style), when an Uyghur musical tradition is sponsored and promoted. Furthermore, such acts may well be attributed to the fear of the center of further antagonizing a sizeable troublesome population. However, local interpretations of central directives also suggest that many of these outcomes are achieved by the (ethnographically still insufficiently documented) activities of Uyghur representatives of state power on various administrative levels, whose co-option by the bulldozer state rarely becomes complete: they do not operate the bulldozer and when they do, they may well mobilize their local knowledge and familiarity with the terrain to modify its route. State effects result not only from a rigid implementation of top-down policies but also from their interpretations by state officials whose vision of authentic culture is constantly being reworked—of course within political parameters that they do not control.

Conclusion

In this chapter I have considered some of the material aspects of how the state is performed into being in two localities in the XUAR. The relatively small stretch of a new road in Qumul reveals a great deal about the complexities of what at first sight appears to be the benign implementation of a nationwide modernization drive combined with the promotion of local history and culture in the light of official minority policies. The boulevard and the modern buildings alongside it where it approaches the city center are the products of a singularly Chinese modernity that divides urban (Han Chinese) from rural (Uyghur) space and in the process redefines them, diminishing the old Muslim city to rural, second-class space. This bureaucratic degradation of the Old Town into a village, which physically pushed its inhabitants to the margins of the city, can be compared to the demolition of Kashgar Old Town, which pushes large numbers of Uyghurs to the new housing estates away from the traditional center. It can also be taken as a reflection of the continuing uncertainty surrounding the evaluation of the role of the *wang* in local and national history, oscillating between vilifying them as feudal exploiters of their own people or glorifying them as faithful allies of the Qing against common enemies of the Chinese empire. Yet for local people a third possibility may also be attractive; recognizing the *wang* as an Uyghur Muslim dynasty who existed as a buffer between them and the alien colonizing power. It is unlikely that such a view can be embraced overtly in the foreseeable future, not only because of censorship but also because local reminiscences (influenced by censored publications) are contradictory, but the possibilities of salvaging elements of this past remain available, a potential resource that can be mobilized.

Taken separately, the old Uyghur cemeteries, the reconstructed Potemkin palace of the *wang*, the renovated mausoleum complex of this Muslim dynasty, and the *muqam* center all embody local history and tradition. But each is at the same time the product of state territorialization. Their juxtaposition along a short section of a new road shows how state effects come into being, replete with contingencies, uncertainties and ironies. The conditions of field research did not permit enquiries into how the various decisions concerning the demolition of the cemetery, the renovation of the mausoleum and its classification as a museum, the reconstruction of the palace and the building of the *muqam* center were made. Even if local Uyghur officials conceived many of the details, they had of necessity to conform to guidelines, which allow certain forms of national expression and repress others. The appropriation and partial demolition of Uyghur sacra (the cemetery) has been used to promote a facet of Uyghur culture that fits with official, reductionist visions of ethnic minority representations ("the Uyghurs who dance and sing") and is also compatible with global projects as epitomized by the prestigious UNESCO listing of the Uyghur *muqam*. Unlike Kashgar, in Qumul the bulldozers have been followed by projects of preservation and renewal in which members of the local Uyghur elite have been actively involved or co-opted. They are complicit in creating a new vision of what Uyghur culture should be, within the framework of a singularly Chinese vision of Uyghur modernity. What is presented by the Han Chinese as the destruction necessary to modernize a "backward" society becomes an arena of contestation over cultural authenticity and the right to control an ambiguous, unruly past. The resulting transformation of the cityscape has immediate consequences for people's everyday lives and ritual practice, but it also shapes their notions of identity and cultural heritage. As in Kashgar, in Qumul, too, the bulldozers are both the instruments in the decentering and marginalizing of the Uyghur within the Xinjiang Uyghur Autonomous Region and a blunt reminder of the reach of Han Chinese power.

In the increasing absence of any real means for Uyghurs to go along the road of grassroots democratization, the threatening pace of the bulldozers on their way of modernizing Xinjiang and Sinicizing the Uyghur has one unintended consequence; it further strengthens Uygur ethnic nationalism at the expense of traditional regional loyalties in the face of the bulldozer state. The realization of central directives effectively contributes to the further externalization of the state, which, however, does not remain a distant abstraction but is experienced in its materiality through its attempts to appropriate and control local space.

Notes

1. Although the multi-ethnic nature of the XUAR is formally acknowledged, few analysts have addressed the predicament of other groups such as Kazakh, Kyrgyz, Hui, and so forth.

2. This chapter is based on observations made in the course of joint fieldwork focusing on social support carried out with Chris Hann in Eastern Xinjiang in 2006–2007. I thank Chris Hann and the three editors of this volume for their helpful comments and suggestions.

3. Due to increasing authoritarianism, much of the recent scholarly literature on the XUAR bears the imprint of the literature on resistance, emphasizing a sharp division between the (colonial) state and local society. In Jonathan Spencer's words, "In the literature on resistance, the state is never a resource, or a place to seek justice, let alone a zone of hope, however distant or deferred, in the political imaginary. It is, if it appears at all, an 'absolute externality,' a source of coercion, violence, or fear; and thus the only theoretically correct response to the state is resistance" (Spencer 2007, 45–46). Local intellectuals are unable to elaborate their views and foreign scholars work under difficult circumstances, typically under the watchful eyes of appointed "minders" within the parameters set by them (Mitchell 1999, 89).

4. The Urumchi riot was the culmination of a series of violent "incidents" initiated by Uyghurs since the early 1990s. Initially these were typically labeled in the Chinese media as examples of "splittism" and treated by and large as a domestic problem. After

9/11 they were upgraded as the acts of "Islamic terrorists" and thus of international concern.

5. This chapter does not aim at a comprehensive account of the ways in which Uyghurs come into contact with the Chinese state. Experiences and conceptualizations vary enormously according to regional and professional affiliation, residence status (rural vs. urban), income source and level, gender, age, and other factors. As I showed in research in rural Kashgar in the mid-1990s, abstract concepts such as state (*döwlät*), government (*hökümät*), and Communist Party (*partiyä*) may be conflated and used interchangeably to denote a central, omnipotent authority, but when emotions run high, centralized power is condensed into an ethnic category: the discourse turns against the Han Chinese. Depending on the context, village- and even township-level cadres may be blamed for corruption as agents of the state or classified as fellow victims of state aggression. But different forms of authority may be conceptualized in similar ways: villagers also habitually drew on parallels from the religious realm to explain the workings of the state, for example, the mediation of cadres and their meting out of punishment if obligations were not fulfilled (Bellér-Hann 1997).

6. This recent emphasis on stimulating Han migration to the west to achieve homogenization and promote national unity amounts to a "paradigm shift in the national minorities doctrine" of the early socialist decades. The strategy has been dubbed "The Peacock Flying West"; see Becquelin (2004, 373–374); Millward (2007, 309).

7. In 1992, plans were announced to relocate approximately 470,000 of those about to lose their homes to Kashgar in the XUAR. Following protests both by the villagers and by Xinjiang officials, the plans were withdrawn (Millward 2007, 309–310 n. 34).

8. More recently, bulldozers have been used with purely destructive intent in the case of those buildings in Urumchi that belonged to Rebiya Kadeer, once the most successful female entrepreneur of the XUAR, who, however, after falling out of favor and eight years of imprisonment, has now become one of the leading Uyghur dissidents. See Millward (2007, 356–361).

9. A recent study of the provincial capital, Urumchi, suggests an ethnic division of labor between the Han, mostly employed in construction, and the Uyghur, mostly employed in demolition (Hopper and Webber 2009, 187). I have not found any evidence for a comparable ethnic division of labor in Qumul or Kashgar. In some Uyghur villages in the oasis of Qumul Han Chinese laborers were brought in to take care of both demolition and construction.

10. For a summary see, for example, Hammer and Brown (2010).

11. "In the Name of Renovation" (2009).

12. They are under stricter measures of state surveillance and control than ordinary Uyghurs since they are supposed to be model citizens: for disobedience they may lose their jobs and may be subjected to harsher forms of sanctions. As agents of enforcing unpopular policies they frequently become targets of popular resentment. High-level cadres and religious dignitaries perceived as collaborators of the Chinese state and therefore traitors of the Uyghur cause have been victims of violent attacks; low-level cadres are more typically accused of corruption. Those who use their position to protect fellow villagers' interests in the face of state coercion have to tread carefully and

take enormous risks. For a more detailed account of the ambiguous role of Uyghur cadres in the rural context, see Hann and Bellér-Hann (1999).

13. Other aspects of reconstruction include the question of surveillance: the maze of small, winding streets and courtyards of the Old Town made policing difficult, while the modernized, regular street plan of the reconstructed neighborhoods will facilitate the functioning of security cameras.

14. Since the winter of 2009 this work has been well under way; the information presented here is derived from official government pronouncements, newspaper articles, and internet blogs (see Delius 2009; UHRP 2009; Summers 2009; Sainsbury 2010). It is too early to know how Uyghurs who lose their homes in the Old Town and are relocated will take to their new, modern, earthquake-proof lodgings. While some will no doubt enjoy the mod cons offered by the new houses, for others the new Potemkin houses, constructed in fake Uyghur style, will be an unwelcome imposition. For a scholarly treatment of the reconstruction of Kashgar, see Dillon (2011).

15. For a similar example of the tactical mixing of repressive measures with development in Uzbekistan, see Trevisani, this volume.

16. The Chinese name is Hami.

17. For an elaboration of idealized cultural authenticity in the context of Kazakhstan, see Dubuisson, this volume.

18. For road-building activities in the oasis of Qumul during the socialist period, see Qumul Wilayitlik Täzkirä Komiteti (2005, 848–862).

19. In recent years a few Han enclaves have also appeared in the village, mostly market gardeners who have been allocated plots near the city.

20. That is, the Republican period (1912–1949).

21. An analysis of these materials is in progress. Apart from Su and Huang (2001) and the *Qumul Wilayitlik Täzkirä Komiteti* (2005), most of these articles have appeared in publications clearly marked as "for internal use only." This means that allowing foreigners access to these works is in itself a criminal offense. The fact that several local people were prepared to share these materials with me was in itself a sign of resistance. This in turn illustrates the extreme political conditions characteristic of the region, which renders fieldwork increasingly difficult and even ethically questionable. In this chapter I have adopted a generalized tone in order to protect the many people who talked to me and shared their views and knowledge of the past and present with me.

22. He may have meant Buddhist architectural tradition, though he kept on referring to the Mongols rather than Buddhism.

23. On the growing importance of Confucianism in contemporary China, see, for example, Bell (2008).

24. At the time of fieldwork Qumul had very few Western visitors since it was not included in popular tourist guides such as the Rough Guide or Lonely Planet.

25. Religious dignitaries are in a very similar position as Uyghur cadres described above. Those appointed as "official Imams" are under close surveillance, have to regularly participate in reeducation meetings, and are often used as conduits of state policies. Perceived by some as ethnic traitors, a number of such co-opted religious dignitaries have been attacked and even killed by fellow Uyghurs (Dillon 2004, 70).

26. They are also exclusively male since local custom forbids women entering the mosque. The only women to be seen around the mausoleum at the time of the Islamic festivals are beggars who stand outside the gates and receive alms from the men after the prayers.

27. For a discussion of the architectural complex described here in the context of secularism, see Hann (2012).

28. I heard disapproving comments about the desecration of cemeteries in several other villages. During a visit to a saintly shrine in the Tianshan mountains, I was told how it had been destroyed during the Cultural Revolution by Red Guards recruited from local youth. My guide, an elderly man and self-appointed guardian of the isolated shrine, commented with satisfaction how the saint had later punished all those who took part in the destruction, all of whom died young.

29. The integration of the dead in the community of the living through communal ritual focusing on graves is not only fundamental to local religious beliefs and practices, but all such land is considered sacred even after the bones have been removed, as long as the site is remembered as a cemetery (Bellér-Hann 2008, 289). In one rural settlement farther away from Qumul I observed how religious communal rituals continued to be performed by local men on the site of a former cemetery, which no longer contained any graves.

30. A certain regional rivalry has persisted and in certain ways even intensified during the decades in which modern Uyghur ethnic identity was effectively disseminated (Rudelson 1997).

31. This supposition remains speculative, since I was unable to inquire into the exact processes of planning approval and financial allocation. I am certain that final decisions were taken in the provincial capital Urumchi, but I do not know if Uyghur as well as Han were involved. It is well known that, since the early 1990s, the editors of Uyghur scholarly journals and literary publications have sometimes sought to publish "hidden transcripts" that escape the Chinese censors' attention.

32. Although Chinese-driven bulldozers may well reinforce the ethnic coloring of the antagonism toward development, the occasional Uyghur driver is likely to be seen as a clog in the machine.

33. Although on occasion, as is the case of Kashgar, internally and externally oriented elements may be inextricably connected.

34. http://www.etymonline.com/index.php?term=bulldozer (accessed on November 9, 2010).

References

Becquelin, Nicolas. 2000. "Xinjiang in the Nineties." *China Journal* 44: 665–690.

———. 2004. "Staged Development in Xinjiang." *China Quarterly* 178: 358–378.

Bell, Daniel A. 2008. *China's New Confucianism: Politics and Everyday Life in a Changing Society.* Princeton, N.J.: Princeton University Press.

Bellér-Hann, Ildikó. 1997. "The Peasant Condition in Xinjiang." *Journal of Peasant Studies* 25, no. 1: 87–112.

———. 1998. "Work and Gender among Uighur Villagers in Southern Xinjiang." In "Les Ouïgours au XXéme siècle," edited by Françoise Aubin and Frédérique-Jeanne Besson. Special issue, *Cahiers d'Études sur la Méditerranée Orientale et le Monde Turco-Iranien* 25: 93–114.

———. 2001. "'Making the Oil Fragrant.' Dealings with the Supernatural among the Uyghur in Xinjiang." *Asian Ethnicity* 2, no. 1: 9–23.

———. 2008. *Community Matters in Xinjiang 1880–1949: Towards a Historical Anthropology of the Uyghur.* China Studies 17. Leiden: Brill.

Bovingdon, Gardner. 2004. *Autonomy in Xinjiang: Han Nationalist Imperatives and Uyghur Discontent.* Washington, D.C.: East-West Center.

Delius, Ulrich. 2009. *Save Kashgar's Old Town! Treasure of Silk Road in Danger—China's Authorities Ordered Destruction.* Göttingen, Germany: Society for Threatened Peoples.

Dillon, Michael. 2004. *Xinjiang: China's Muslim Far Northwest.* London: RoutledgeCurzon.

———. 2011. *Xinjiang and the Expansion of Chinese Communist Power: Kashghar in the Twentieth Century.* London: Routledge.

Gupta, Akhil. 2006. "Blurred Boundaries: The Discourse of Corruption, the Culture of Politics, and the Imagined State." In *The Anthropology of the State: A Reader,* edited by Aradhana Sharma and Akhil Gupta, 211–242. Malden, Mass.: Blackwell.

Hammer, Joshua, and Michael Christopher Brown. 2010. "Demolishing Kashgar's History." Beijing Cultural Heritage Protection Center, http://en.bjchp.org/?p=1884 (accessed November 10, 2010).

Hann, Chris. 2012. "Laiklik and Legitimation in Rural Eastern Xinjiang." In *Varieties of Secularism in Asia: Anthropological Explorations of Religion, Politics and the Spiritual,* edited by Nils Ole Bubandt and Martijn Van Beek, 121–142. London: Routledge.

Hann, Chris, and Ildikó Bellér-Hann. 1999. "Peasants and Officials in Southern Xinjiang." *Zeitschrift für Ethnologie* 124, no. 1: 1–32.

Harris, Rachel. 2007. "Situating the Twelve Muqam: Between the Arab World and the Tang Court." In *Situating the Uyghurs between China and Central Asia,* edited by Ildikó Bellér-Hann, M. Cristina Cesàro, Rachel Harris, and Joanne Smith Finley, 69–88. Aldershot, UK: Ashgate.

Harvey, Penelope. 2005. "The Materiality of State-Effects: An Ethnography of a Road in the Peruvian Andes." In *State Formation: Anthropological Perspectives,* edited by Christian Krohn-Hansen and Knut G. Nustad, 123–141. London: Pluto Press.

Herzfeld, Michael. 1997. *Cultural Intimacy: Social Poetics in the Nation State.* New York: Routledge.

Hopper, Ben, and Michael Webber. 2009. "Migration, Modernization and Ethnic Estrangement: Uyghur Migration to Urumqi, Xinjiang Uyghur Autonomous Region, PRC." *Inner Asia* 11: 173–203.

"In the Name of Renovation." 2009. *China Daily,* May 30, 4. http://www.chinadaily.com.cn/cndy/2009-05/30/content_7953396.htm (accessed November 10, 2010).

Joniak, Agnieszka. 2009. "Xinjiang Uyghur Autonomous Region (People's Republic of China) and Chinese Territoriality." Paper presented at the 19th ASEN annual conference *Nationalism and Globalization,* London School of Economics, March 31–April 2.

Krohn-Hansen, Christian, and Knut G. Nustad. 2005. "Introduction." In *State Formation: Anthropological Perspectives,* edited by Christian Krohn-Hansen and Knut G. Nustad, 1–26. London: Pluto Press.

Lai, Hongyi Harry. 2002. "China's Western Development Program: Its Rationale, Implementation, and Prospects." *Modern China* 28, no. 4: 432–466.

Lefebvre, Henri. 1991. *The Production of Space.* Oxford: Blackwell.

Light, Nathan. 2008. *Intimate Heritage: Creating Uyghur Muqam Song in Xinjiang.* Halle Studies in the Anthropology of Eurasia 19. Berlin: LIT.

Loubes, Jean-Paul. 1998. *Architecture et Urbanisme de Turfan. Une oasis du Turkestan chinois.* Paris: L'Harmattan.

Millward, James. 1998. *Beyond the Pass: Economy, Ethnicity, and Empire in Qing Central Asia, 1759–1864.* Stanford, Calif.: Stanford University Press.

———. 2007. *Eurasian Crossroads: A History of Xinjiang.* New York: Columbia University Press.

——— 2009. "Introduction: Does the 2009 Urumchi Violence Mark a Turning Point?" *Central Asian Survey* 28, no. 4: 347–360.

Mitchell, Timothy. 1999. "Society, Economy, and the State Effect." In *State/Culture: State Formation after the Cultural Turn,* edited by George Steinmetz, 76–97. Ithaca, N.Y.: Cornell University Press.

Moneyhon, Matthew D. 2003. "China's Great Western Development Project in Xinjiang: Economic Palliative, or Political Trojan Horse?" *Denver Journal of International Law and Policy* 3: 491–519.

Qumul Wilayitlik Täzkirä Komiteti, ed. 2005. *Qumul wilayiti täzkirisi* I.-II. Ürümçi: Xinjiang Xälq Näşriyati.

Radcliffe, Sarah. 2001. "Imagining the State as a Space: Territoriality and the Formation of the State in Ecuador." In *States of Imagination: Ethnographic Explorations of the Postcolonial State,* edited by Thomas Blom Hansen and Finn Stepputat, 123–145. Durham N.C.: Duke University Press.

Rudelson, Justin. 1997. *Oasis Identities: Uyghur Nationalism along China's Silk Road.* New York: Columbia University Press.

Sack, Robert David. 1986. *Human Territoriality: Its Theory and History.* Cambridge: Cambridge University Press.

Sainsbury, Michael M. 2010. "Uighur Tensions Persist as Kashgar's Old City Is Demolished." *Australian,* January 6, 2010. http://www.theaustralian.com.au/news/world/uighur-tensions-persist-as-kashgars-old-city-demolished/story-e6frg6so-1225816713997 (accessed November 10, 2010).

Schrode, Paula. 2007. *Die Totengeister der Uiguren: Beobachtungen zu Islam und Gesellschaft in Ostturkestan.* Berlin: Schwarz.

Schumpeter, Joseph A. 1934. *The Theory of Economic Development.* Cambridge, Mass.: Harvard University Press.

Scott, James. 1990. *Domination and the Arts of Resistance: Hidden Transcripts.* New Haven, Conn.: Yale University Press.

Sharma, Aradhana, and Akhil Gupta. 2006. "Introduction: Rethinking Theories of the State in an Age of Globalization." In *The Anthropology of the State: A Reader,* edited by Aradhana Sharma and Akhil Gupta, 1–41. Malden, Mass.: Blackwell.

Spencer, Jonathan. 2007. *Anthropology, Politics and the State: Democracy and Violence in South Asia*. Cambridge: Cambridge University Press.

Su Bei Wei and Huang Jienxua. 2001. *Qumul, Turpan uyğur wangliri tarixi* [The History of the Uyghur Wangs of Qumul and Turpan]. Ürümçi: Şincaŋ Xälq Näşriyati.

Summers, Josh 2009. "Kashgar's Old Town Bulldozed; Is Uyghur Culture in Danger? Travel and Life in China's Far West Province Xinjiang." *Far West China*, May 19. http://www.farwestchina.com/2009/05/kashgars-old-town-bulldozed-is-uyghur.html (accessed November 10, 2010).

Toops, Stanley W. 2004. "The Demography of Xinjiang." In *Xinjiang: China's Muslim Borderland*, edited by S. Frederick Starr, 241–263. Armonk, N.Y.: M. E. Sharpe.

Turner, Victor 1995. *The Ritual Process: Structure and Anti-Structure.* New York: Aldine de Gruyter.

Uyghur Human Rights Project (UHRP). 2009. "Kashgar Demolition Is a Serious Political Issue." http://www.uhrp.org/articles/2348/1/Kashgar-demolition-is-a-quotserious-political-issuequot-official-document-reveals-aggressive-nature-of-propaganda-work-used-to-enforce-Kashgar-resettlement-/index.html (accessed November 10, 2010).

Wines, Michael. 2009. "To Protect Ancient City, China Plans to Raze It." *New York Times*, May 28.

Yardley, Jim. 2007. "Chinese Dam Projects Criticized for Their Human Cost." *New York Times*, November 19.

8. The Time of the Border

Contingency, Conflict, and Popular Statism at the Kyrgyzstan-Uzbekistan Boundary

Madeleine Reeves

The river falls steeply in the upper Sokh valley, where Kyrgyzstan and Uzbekistan meet: a thin strip of grey-blue surrounded on both sides by densely planted garden plots, apricot orchards, and adobe houses nestled amidst sheer rocks.[1] Several kilometers downstream, the river irrigates a band of rice, wheat, and barley, stretching down toward Rishton and Qoqon in the fertile Fergana basin. Up here, where the largely unmarked and sporadically policed border between two neighboring states runs along *mahalla* (neighborhood) streets and water channels, crossing courtyards and through fields, it is the mountains that dominate the landscape, dividing villages into upper and lower halves, sunny and shady sides. "Our spirits are magnanimous here," Temirbek-agai, a retired farmer from the village of Sogment, would tell me, comparing the mountain-dwellers to the cotton-growers in the valley floor below, "because our heads are closer to the sky."[2]

It is in this bucolic setting that a conflict occurred in the spring of 2005 that briefly flashed into national news headlines, in Kyrgyzstan at least. (In Uzbekistan, where societal conflict is a muted theme in state media, the incident went unreported for over a year.)[3] Over the course of several days in early May a tense and sustained local stand-off occurred between men from the villages of Sogment and Charbak, located on the southern, Kyrgyzstan side of the border, and the larger village of Hushiar, spatially contiguous with its Kyrgyz neighbors but administratively part of Uzbekistan.

By all local accounts, the immediate trigger for the escalation of tensions across this rural stretch of international boundary was an altercation between Kyrgyzstani conscript soldiers who were stationed to man the border here, and two eleventh-grade school boys from Hushiar. The boys had illegally crossed the unmarked state border into Kyrgyzstan with their cattle—common practice here in the spring, as Hushiar, hemmed in by a triangle of mountains and the border, has no grazing lands of its own. The boys were asked for some form of identification by the border guards, and when they admitted to having none on their person, a verbal, and then physical conflict ensued, leaving the two boys hospitalized.[4]

During the following week, at the height of the spring planting season, this local incident of border violence morphed into displays of open hostility between young men from the villages of Sogment and Charbak, on the one hand, and Hushiar on the other. Relatives of the injured boys demanded an apology from the commander of the Kyrgyz border unit, stationed in a converted teahouse at the bottom of Sogment village. Two days later, at the weekly market that straddles the border, Kyrgyz traders who were selling their wares on the southern, Charbak site, were taken hostage by a group of men from Hushiar in retaliation for the behavior of "their" border guards. Three Kyrgyzstan-registered cars parked near the entrance to this section of the market had windows broken, and sections of a water pipe that provided Charbak with irrigation water from the Sokh River, constructed as part of a USAID-sponsored Peaceful Communities Initiative, were destroyed.

Over the next hours and days, military reinforcements from Uzbekistan and Kyrgyzstan were sent to the scene, joined by officials from regional and district administrations, policemen, and members of the security services. Several hundred men from Hushiar and Sogment gathered on either side of the Baiaman Bridge, the informal border marker between the villages, armed with spades and sticks. Delegations arrived from the respective provincial capitals, Batken (Kyrgyzstan) and Fergana (Uzbekistan), consisting of governors and their assistants along with military corteges from the respective interior ministries. In this moment of stately escalation, each of these delegations met with village elders from "their" side of the border to discuss their grievances. At stake were several issues: the allocation of water from the spring that provided both Charbak and parts of Hushiar with irrigation water; the presence of the Kyrgyzstani border post that had been stationed between the two villages since 2000 and was much resented by people from Hushiar; the use of grazing lands in Kyrgyzstan by citizens of the neighboring state, and the status of several areas of "contested territory" at the edges of the two villages. During meetings between the crowds gathered on the Baiaman Bridge and local officials, elders from the Kyrgyz villages demanded that the state boundary be "unambiguously determined" (*chetko oboznachit'*) and requested that the number of soldiers at the Kyrgyzstani border post be increased to provide protection. Meanwhile, a group of Hushiar elders petitioned their regional governor to remove the Kyrgyzstani border post altogether, and asked that an earlier schedule for water allocation, which had existed prior to 2002, be reinstated.

Within days of this escalation, the incident took shape in proliferating conflict analyses and news reports as a recognizable entity: an "interethnic conflict" over resources; the latest in a catalogue of violent conflicts at the southern fringes of the Fergana basin, where new international borders between Kyrgyzstan, Uzbekistan, and Tajikistan have come to transect villages, pastures, and waterways, transforming shared landscapes into strategically important—and sometimes openly "contested" (*spornaia*) territory (Megoran 2002, 2010; Reeves 2008, 2009; Bichsel 2009; Abashin et al. 2011). By dint of its geographical and demographic complexity, the Sokh valley has often been identified in policy and academic literature as particularly vulnerable to trans-border conflict (Mercy Corps 2003; Osmonov 2010; see also Nazarov and Shozimov 2011 on the history of land exchanges around Sokh). The Sokh district (*So'x tuman*), an administrative entity of 23 *mahallas,* is Central Asia's largest geographical exclave at 238 square km, administratively part of Uzbekistan's Fergana oblast' but entirely surrounded by the territory of Kyrgyzstan. Although citizens of Uzbekistan, the vast majority of Sokh's inhabitants are Tajik speakers and identify as ethnically Tajik, with many families having ancestral ties west and south to districts across the mountains in today's Tajikistan—places that both geographically and politically are largely inaccessible from Sokh today.

It is this ethnic and territorial complexity that provides the interpretative framework for the flurry of conflict analyses and news reports that surrounded the events of early May. Although I had spent much of the preceding few months conducting ethnographic research in southern Sokh, I first learned of the escalations of tensions in the valley by e-mail several hundred miles away, in the Kyrgyzstan capital, Bishkek. "URGENT! We have a conflict!" was the message from Umar, an engineer from Batken whose small non-governmental organization (NGO) was actively involved in conflict prevention initiatives in the border villages of southern Sokh. Inside, Umar's message, addressed to a number of conflict-monitoring organizations and donor agencies, fused analysis with a plea for continued funding for conflict prevention activities in the region: "Dear colleagues," the first e-mail read: "unfortunately it seems that it is too early to close the RDD [Regional Dialogue and Development] Project because conflicts and incidents of an inter-ethnic character still have reason to occur." The message described how law-enforcement officials of the two states had had to draw a "line of separation" to prevent an escalation of violence between Kyrgyz and Tajik crowds, who were grouped by that time on either side of the Baiaman Bridge. Employees of local NGOs, including Umar's own, were seeking to reach the conflict's "epicenter," the letter explained, in order to mediate between the two sides. The situation was at an impasse: all communica-

Figure 8.1. The Baiaman Bridge, Kyrgyzstan-Uzbekistan border, August 2005.

tion between the two villages had been "entirely blocked by the powers of RU [Republic of Uzbekistan] and KR [Kyrgyz Republic]."

Eventful Borders

This chapter explores this multiply mediated incident and its repercussions for the way that borders came to materialize in the Sokh valley during subsequent months. I revisit an event that reports at the time cast in familiar and localizing terms: an interethnic conflict, driven by resource shortage, waiting to occur. I question this determinist interpretation by situating the events that occurred in the spring of 2005 within broader contexts of political repression in Uzbekistan and political upheaval in Kyrgyzstan, which fostered radical uncertainty over the location of "law" and debate concerning the proper social, institutional, and spatial correlates of sovereign territorial statehood. As such I seek to repoliticize our understanding of "resource-driven conflict" in the Fergana Valley.

By foregrounding the political contexts of resource-based trans-boundary conflict, my aim is not to deny the relevance of ethnicity to the dynamics of mobilization. Nor should we ignore the acute pressures upon trans-boundary resources in this mountainous, irrigation-dependent region. Historical interdependence (as well as contemporary tensions) between Kyrgyz-speaking pastoralists and settled Tajik-speaking agriculturalists figure regularly in local accounts of the valley's distinctiveness, and population growth during the twentieth century has increased pressures upon a finite flow of spring water between upstream and downstream communities (Dzhakhonov 1989; Thurman 1999; Bichsel 2009). During the escalation that occurred in May 2005 the destruction of the neighboring village's irrigation channel and the demands that were pressed in meetings with the local authorities suggest that water distribution was centrally at stake in this conflict. The event occurred at the height of the spring planting season, when demands on a restricted flow of irrigation water are at their greatest. The single target of explicit collective violence during the events of May 2005—the "USAID pipe" that transported irrigation water to Charbak—was of huge symbolic and material resonance on both sides of the border. This conflict was thus, at some significant level, about differential access to resources. But it is the differential access and the political relations that have produced it that is crucial to understanding what happened; not the resource per se. To understand why people in Hushiar, on the Uzbekistan side of the border, were aggrieved by the distribution of irrigation water, we need to examine the divergent possibilities for lobby and appeal that had emerged over the preceding years in Kyrgyzstan and Uzbekistan, and what these reveal about the complex business of enacting stately limits after socialism.

In developing this argument I seek to extend this volume's analysis of the performance of politics in Central Asia in two particular ways. Firstly, I draw attention to the place of political contingency in the materialization of a state boundary. I suggest that the tendency to accord analytical primacy to the map—to treat borders as an a priori manifestation of their cartographic representation—has tended to divert attention from their eventful character: their capacity to erupt, crystallize, appear, and disappear with considerable speed. Drawing on arguments that have sought, in a kindred analytic field, to divert attention from "developmentalist" to "eventful" accounts of nationhood and identity, I argue that in taking the presence of borders as discrete spaces for granted, we have tended to ignore how and when (and indeed whether) they appear, in any material sense, on the ground. Or, put in more general terms, the complex and variable spatiality of borders has tended to attract much more attention than their variable temporality (Radu 2010; Green 2012). In the southern Sokh valley, a moment of violence caused a border to "happen" in new ways between Sogment and Hushiar. To understand when and why, we need to look beyond "ethnicity" and "water" to the complex intersection of contingent factors that disrupted an existing border ethic and prompted intense local debate about the bounds of legitimate violence and legitimate restriction upon borderland movement.

This points me, in turn, to the second argument that I develop here concerning the dynamics of popular statism: that is, the affective and material investment of ordinary border dwellers in the idea of having a "normal," territorial state, even when this institutional bounding, in the form of border guards, customs officers, policemen, and barbed wire effectively imposes a limitation upon their own mobility. Much of the important anthropological contribution to a comparative discussion of borders has drawn attention to the way in which people living in borderlands often challenge the logic of the territorial nation-state, by finding strategies of accommodation and subversion (Flynn 1997; Wilson and Donnan 2005; Chalfin 2010). This is undoubtedly true in Central Asia, where the intensification of border controls over the past decade and a half has led to ingenious new mechanisms for traversing and deriving a living from the economic differentials that such gaps produce (Megoran, Raballand, and Bouyjou 2005; Reeves 2007; Usmanov 2011). Such action, however, does not exhaust the way in which people relate to borders; nor should we necessarily interpret such practices of borderland pragmatism as representing a rejection of stately territoriality. Indeed, in contexts of uneven globalization, popular statism in the periphery may appear to marginalized subjects "the first step on the long road to social redistribution" (Cheah 1998, 34; Simone 2001; cf. Ferguson and Gupta 2002; Geschiere 2009).

I return to these concerns below. I begin, however, by returning to the contexts of the conflict itself to consider why it was that an altercation between school boys and border guards came to morph into a "trans-border" conflict in May 2005. I suggest that three aspects of this context are of note. The first concerns the shifting politics of resource allocation, which had left both upstream and downstream communities feeling aggrieved at the distribution of water from a shared spring; the second relates to the role of elite patrons, simultaneously within and beyond the law, in sponsoring and supporting land claims on the Kyrgyz side of border; the third to the increasingly asymmetrical pressures upon notionally balanced NGO partners. In important respects each of these pressures can be traced to an increasing divergence between models of state practice on two sides of the Uzbekistan-Kyrgyzstan border: the first, increasingly authoritarian and protectionist; the second open to various forms of non-governmental provision, but increasingly dominated by the interests of local patrons who perceived themselves to be above the law.

Allocating Irrigation

In the upper Sokh valley, villages on both sides of the new international border between Kyrgyzstan and Uzbekistan rely on shared sources of drinking and irrigation water. The canal infrastructure running between villages, built during the World War II and extended in the 1970s to accommodate sharp rises in population, transects the border, "knitting" the two former Soviet republics into a shared infrastructure network. In Hushiar, pump stations built in the mid-1970s take water from the Sokh River, located in a steep gorge below the villages, and require a regular supply of electricity to work. In all three villages, families rely primarily on spring-water for their drinking and irrigation needs. This flows from Sogment to lower-lying Hushiar and Charbak and is allocated on a daily schedule.

Until 2002, a nine-day cycle for distributing this spring water was in operation. Hushiar, with a comparatively large population (three times that of the Kyrgyz villages at the southern end of the valley combined) de facto had use rights for seven of those nine days, with the small hamlet of Charbak having use rights for the remaining two. The actual mechanism for irrigation regulation was a simple technology of selective sluices, which sent the water flowing downstream from Sogment in one direction or the other. It is a process that depends on a considerable degree of trust and mutual social control for its successful functioning, with a locally designated *mirob* or "water master" overseeing water allocation. In 2002, the existing schedule for allocating water was changed. Instead of Hushiar having use rights for seven days out of the nine, the distribution was changed to a weekly schedule, in which Hushiar would have use rights for five out of seven days, and Charbak for two (Protokol 2002).

Crucially, the 2002 protocol not only changed the substance of the intervillage agreement, but also the process of its negotiation. The timetable for water allocation went from being a spoken, non-codified arrangement between the elders of neighboring villages to a stately act of regulation, which was to be signed and sealed by the respective regional governors. There is a long history of informal water regulation in the Sokh valley (Dzhakhonov 1989, 44–47; Abdullaev 1991), just as there is of progressive stately involvement in the regulation of irrigation over the course of the twentieth century (Thurman 1999). In Hushiar, there was occasional speculation that the reason for the renegotiation of the water schedule "in favor of Charbak" said as much about the dynamics of relations between district- and oblast'-level governors in the two states as it did about real changes in the demand for water on both sides of the border. The district governor of Sokh, newly appointed at that time, was keen to "prove himself" to his regional superior, I was told by one Hushiar elder, by showing that he could take unpopular decisions at home and still maintain order in his district. Whatever the veracity of this claim, the 2002 agreement was, for my interlocutors on the Uzbekistan side of the border, indicative of far more than an "unfair" agreement: it was rather a material reminder of unequal powers of lobby and appeal.

By May 2005, recent events had given new intensity and salience to these "unequal powers." To friends and acquaintances in Sokh, events over the preceding few weeks provided a vivid and sobering reminder of the oft-repeated adage that "in Uzbekistan the state is rich and the people are poor; in Kyrgyzstan the people are rich and the state is poor." Kyrgyzstan's first post-Soviet president, Askar Akaev, had been ousted less than six weeks earlier in what the media (and even many previously cynical citizens in Kyrgyzstan) were calling a "people's revolution" (*eldik revoliutsiia*). This was a time of dramatic implosion of central power, but also of tremendous (if short-lived) hope. In Bishkek at the time, former university colleagues who had been indifferent to political engagement were euphoric about the possibility of real popular change. Ad-hoc live broadcasts from parliament and hastily convened press conferences were suddenly the most compelling drama on television, and provided a constant narrative backdrop to the business of getting on with life in a city that had been looted to the core (Marat 2006). Shops, offices, and public space became covered, in the space of hours, in the *leitmotif* of this so-called "Tulip Revolution": "we're with the people!" (*biz el menen!*)—a sudden, dramatic affirmation of multitude in the face of the president's ouster. In the spring of 2005 there was a palpable, if short-lived, feeling that that opportunities were wide open (often painfully, disconcertingly so), and that everything was potentially "up for grabs": power, property, fame, influence, jobs, contracts and above all, land.[5]

It was this sudden shift in the quality of land—a public resource that demanded just allocation—that was the most visible spontaneous reaction to the shifts in the political landscape. Illegal land seizures consumed Kyrgyzstan's two largest cities, Bishkek and Osh, closing roads and sending shock waves through these cities' normally quiescent microdistricts. Property rights were being reconfigured; normally muted debates about "autochthonous" and "arrived" (*priezhie*) populations were suddenly thrust into the mix of discussion over claims to property, contestation was everywhere, and the administration of justice was often very rough indeed.[6] As the headline of the usually sober *Vechernii Bishkek* newspaper asserted in one mid-April edition, addressing the new powers in the White House: "You grabbed power. Now give us land" (Soltoeva 2005). The "revolution" had made seizure legitimate; "grabbers" (*zavkhatchiki*) were, for a brief moment, turned into national heroes.

Patrons and Politics

These events in no way can be said to have caused the conflict that occurred in southern Sokh in early May 2005. The ripples from political storms in Bishkek and Osh were weaker here, and most people were far too preoccupied with the business of sowing corn and weeding fields (and still more, leaving to work for another season in Russia) than with "grabbing" Akaev's land around Bishkek. But among the villagers of Sogment and Charbak, on the Kyrgyz side of the border, there was, nonetheless, a sense that this was their revolution too, and that their role in propelling a new, southern, elite to power deserved recognition and reward. Key to understanding why this was so is the figure of Baiaman Erkinbaev, with whose money the bridge that proved the conflict's epicenter had been built three years earlier, and in whose honor it was named. Erkinbaev, known in southern Sokh simply by his first name, Baiaman, was a wrestler turned businessman turned Olympic committee chair who was rumored to have control over much of the drug trade through Osh as well as a controlling stake in Kyrgyzstan's largest wholesale market in Kara-Suu. Although aged only thirty-nine, he had already thrice successfully balloted for parliament as a way (many suspected) of ensuring parliamentary immunity for his business interests. He was indisputably one of the country's wealthiest men.

When he balloted as parliamentary deputy in February 2005, Erkinbaev was one of only three candidates in the country to run unchallenged. In Sogment and villages farther up the valley, which fell within his constituency, he received 95.5 percent of the vote;[7] at the time of the conflict in early May 2005, he was busy balloting for president.[8] His background in wrestling, his straddling of "legal" and "illegal" economic domains, his notoriously rough manner of speech with misogynist and nationalist overtones inspired fear and awe in equal measure. A macho "strongman" who combined disdain for law with heavy-handed paternalism, Erkinbaev tapped into a particular post-Soviet gender ideology in which new configurations of power are naturalized through reference to highly traditionalist gender norms (cf. Uehling 2007).

In this context of patriarchal provisioning, it is perhaps unsurprising that for the people of Sogment and Charbak, Erkinbaev had the status of local hero. As Christine Bichsel notes (2009, 94), as far as many people in Sogment were concerned, Erkinbaev's provision of "humanitarian aid" made him little different from the various non-governmental development projects operating in the village, except that the conditionality of the aid was different. Given his notoriously heavy-handed style in resolving conflicts of interest, it is also not hard to see why the very bridge on which informants from Sogment often asked to be photographed would be read by people in Hushiar as a site of divide. Erkinbaev, after all, was a staunchly, self-consciously Kyrgyz hero.

During the events of early May 2005, Erkinbaev, while not personally present, was a significant figure in absentia for understanding the dynamics and escalation of conflict. For the people of Sogment and Charbak, he was known to be both a powerful and intimate friend of the village and a source of ultimate political authority: a patron whose successful performance of stately authority (a presidential candidate, no less) would enable him to overturn and override any unpopular decisions taken by lesser stately figures (compare Ismailbekova, this volume). Indeed, he is reported to have remarked at the time that he would "take matters into his own hands" if "the authorities" should fail to resolve the conflict between Sogment and Hushiar (Bichsel 2009, 94): a striking discursive move that signals both the extent of his own power and its ambiguous status within a realm of law. He was both within the state and outside it; both an embodiment of "legitimate" authority and outside or above the law. In the specific dynamics of early May, he was crucial in ensuring that the newly appointed governor of Batken region (a figure whom he had helped propel to power), responded immediately to the demands of the villagers in Sogment and Charbak, arriving soon after the conflict began, noting villagers' demands, and promising to "raise issues" with the Fergana governor in Uzbekistan.

Non-governmental Mediations

In these complex blurrings of the boundaries between "state" and "society" it is important to consider also the role of non-governmental governmentality. Many previously state functions in southern Sokh of provision, of lobbying, and of representation are now performed by non-governmental organizations; and civil society, especially in its trans-national variant, has been accorded discursive (and often material) primacy in conflict prevention in the Fergana Valley (Young 2003; Kluever 2004; Bichsel 2005; Maasen et al. 2005). In the narrative accounts of program documents there is often a seductive symmetry to their activities. Two local NGOs, *Yntymak* (Harmony) and *Mehr* (Mercy), for instance, while independent organizations subject to different governmental legislation, banking rules, and reporting requirements, had been sponsored by the Swiss government to collaborate in joint cross-border events. Indeed the second of these two NGOs had been founded by Mercy Corps precisely so as to implement projects through its Peaceful Communities Initiative. The rationale is that while each organization is embedded in its own community, it could successfully mobilize populations for the undertaking of joint tasks such as canal-cleaning, and collaborative social events, such as the sponsored volleyball matches that were a regular feature of Sokh life in 2004–2005. It is a model premised upon balanced powers of mobilization and representation.[9]

By May 2005, however, the gulf between nominal institutional symmetry and the practical asymmetries of their operation was vast. In the days before I received the first e-mail about the tensions that had turned violent in Sokh, I had been attending, along with many of Batken's conflict analysts, Kyrgyzstan's "All-National Forum of Civil Society" (*Obshchenatsional'nyi forum grazhdanskogo obshchestva*) in the National Philharmonic Hall in Bishkek. The gathering was vast and the atmosphere euphoric. Even the setting was significant: as the opening speaker noted, this was the first time that the organizers had been able to demand where the forum be held, rather than appealing to the authorities for public space. This was a time of palpable excitement for Kyrgyzstan's non-governmental sector. As one young speaker at the conference noted, "for the first time we are a free republic. For the first time we are able to develop a strong state. This is civil society's tulip revolution" (fieldnotes, Bishkek, April 2005).

The spatial ordering of the *grazhdanskii forum* made very visible what was occurring in more subtle ways elsewhere in Kyrgyzstan. Members of non-governmental organizations were often being given significant governmental power. In Batken, the Kyrgyz provincial capital, members of one of the region's largest non-governmental organizations, the Foundation for Tolerance International, had played a very visible role in mediating between "governmental" and "opposition" factions for control of the city administration, and one of their employees (a conflict analyst who had done much of the ground work for materializing the USAID pipe in Charbak) was invited to become deputy governor of the oblast' after the revolution. Local television, like its national counterpart, threw "civil society" into the spotlight in Batken: volleyball matches conducted as part of NGO-sponsored "preventive development" initiatives were now the stuff of regular local news reports; public buildings in Sogment were briefly covered in signs proclaiming, to the chagrin of Uzbekistani citizens across the border that "Kyrgyzstan is the jewel of democracy in Central Asia!"

The buoyancy felt by Kyrgyzstani NGOs immediately after the "Tulip Revolution" stood in stark contrast to the anxiety felt by their colleagues in their partner NGO across the border, Mehr. This was already a dreadful year for any organization daring to call itself "non-governmental" in Uzbekistan. New fiscal regulations made the receipt of grant funding harder and many organizations were curbing activities that could be construed as having a "political" component. Mehr's director talked frequently about giving up his politically risky work and leaving for a building site in Russia (something he eventually did in 2007; see also Goldenbaum et al. 2006, 20). In a speech in January 2005, Uzbekistan's president, Islom Karimov had promised to rid the country of "alien ideologies," reserving particular criticism for the "various so-called open society models" espoused by non-governmental organizations (Karimov 2005). During the days of May tension in Sokh, employees of Mehr, far from being sought out for advice or interviewed on national television, as was occurring with their Kyrgyz counterparts, were often subject to accusations from the regional and oblast' administrations of having *exacerbated* the conflict between Hushiar and Sogment. Threats and accusations ("lack of patriotism," "collusion" with Kyrgyz partners) were used to enact a boundary between state and society, law and its violation, placing Mehr firmly outside the bounds of state. The relationship between two collaborative partner organizations on either side of the border, therefore, could not have been more imbalanced.

Figure 8.2. Revolutionary border work on a Sogment shop. "Kyrgyzstan is the jewel of democracy in Central Asia! K. Bakiev is the hero of the revolution!" Sogment, July 2005.

Events and the Work of Separation

The broader context that I have described here does not explain the conflict that erupted in May 2005, but it may help us to account for the incidents that triggered it and the dynamic of its escalation. In particular, it may help us to make sense of why the Kyrgyz border guards ignored an established border ethic (according to which children from Hushiar regularly take their cows to the fields beyond Charbak to graze) to enforce the law, violently, to its limits. And it may help us to see why the "USAID pipe" that was destroyed in the violence was overdetermined as a symbol of difference and discord. As such it offers an instructive lesson for the narration of "interethnic conflict" and its triggers in the Fergana Valley, and in particular, the need to bring the active, contested, intensely political work of enacting stately limits into our frame of analysis.

This empirical case also provides material for reflection in a more theoretical direction, however, on the significance of "events" for the production of state borders; for attending to their variable salience, intensity, and material presence. My lead here comes from a related field, the study of nationhood and identity, which has sought to redirect analytical concern from development to event. One of the clearest statements to this effect comes from Rogers Brubaker who, in an exploratory paper, notes that in studying nationhood "we must give serious theoretical attention to contingent events and to their transformative consequences" (1996, 21). Brubaker's account developed from an initial sense of dissatisfaction with existing theoretical accounts of nationhood (and, in more recent work, ethnicity), which failed to make sense of the experience of being "overcome by nationhood" during the Yugoslav wars of secession. Conventional, "developmentalist" accounts of nation-formation and the building metaphors implicit in much constructivist literature simply do not allow us to grasp the way in which nationhood can come, suddenly and contingently, to structure social relations. Brubaker's earliest statement of this concern is perhaps the most evocative:

> I know of no sustained analytical discussion of nationness as an event, as something that suddenly crystallizes rather than gradually develops, as a contingent, conjuncturally fluctuating, and precarious frame of vision and basis for individual and collective action, rather than as a relatively stable product of deeply developmental trends in economy, polity, or culture. (Brubaker 1996, 20)

Three features of this critique are noteworthy. The first is that it directs attention from an ontological question ("what is the nation?") to a question of process ("how is nationhood institutionalized?"). The second is that it opens to empirical investigation the conjunction of conditions that dictate whether and to what extent social relations are structured along national lines. For Brubaker, ours is emphatically not "a world made up of nations," but rather "a world in which nation is widely, if unevenly, available and resonant as a category of social vision and division" (1996, 21). The third is that it reminds us that the everyday subjective awareness of ethnic identity cannot simply be "read from" the strength and outspokenness of official pronouncements. Indeed, Brubaker's recent empirical work has precisely sought to emphasize the divergence between nationalist political rhetoric and the everyday experience of ethnicity in social interaction (Brubaker et al. 2006).

What interests me here is the potential of invoking this particular conceptual shift for rethinking "stately" happenings too. This is not something that Brubaker addresses in his earlier article: indeed the state is rather the stage for action; its spatiality is taken for granted. What, though, if we were to take the contingency of the state and its limits seriously? What if we were to recognize the state to be a "work-in-progress" and for contingent events to produce quite dramatic shifts in the quality, not just of "nationness," but of "stateness" and "borderness" (Green 2009, 2010) too—that is, the lived sense of the state as a bounded, finite, integrated space, structured and authorized in particular ways, constituted by particular people and institutions?

Making this conceptual move demands a shift analogous to that argued for by Brubaker in his account of nationhood, from substance to process, from slow development to the "relatively sudden fluctuations" with which seemingly stable elements of the political landscape come into being (and potentially disappear); from category (nation) to quality of feeling (nationness) (Brubaker 1996, 20). But it is also harder in the case of "state" precisely because our categories of thought and language, as Bourdieu and Wacquant (1999) would say, have been "authorized" by the state. "Stateness" can be no more grasped within a vocabulary of citizenship than the lived experience of "statelessness" can be reduced to the categorical fact of being without a document or a formal claim upon citizenship. Indeed, the very fact that our vocabulary allows us to conceive of statelessness as an experiential condition, while the positive equivalent, "stateness" has the ring of a clumsy neologism is revealing. Living under the authority of the state is so much the default condition that we have few tools for grasping, analytically, its variable quality (see also Laszczkowski's discussion of *grazhdanstvennost'*, this volume).

This brings me back to the "event" and its significance.[10] It is precisely at eventful times, I suggest, that we may begin to gain some ethnographic purchase on this variable quality of stateness. When I returned to Sogment and Hushiar two months after the May conflict, the concrete institutional formations that we might seize upon to index state strength or weakness, boundedness or permeability had not shifted. There was still no barbed wire between Hushiar and its neighbors; the border guards were no greater in number; there were no visible material obstacles to movement; all traces of the barriers that had been mounted to block roads in May had been removed. The "state" as set of material institutions had not changed significantly. But there was a quite salient shift in what it meant to be subject to separate authority. In Sogment and Charbak, as in Kyrgyz villages farther upstream, there was a new, though not uncontested, discourse about the "need to define the border precisely" (*chek ara taktash kerek*) or to "put up wire" between villages on two sides of the border (*zym tartysh kerek*) (Reeves 2011). New, gendered limits were being placed on movement through informal social sanction and public commentary on behavior considered shameful (*uiat*). Most visibly, there were quite practical attempts to enact state spatiality in new ways: by appropriating the border guards and their "legitimate" violence for defense of private property, and by dividing a previously integrated market.

Each of these actions was symbolically resonant as well as materially significant. Separating the market between Hushiar and Sogment, for example, was a symbolic rupture of the institution that, historically, has been the central site of social exchange between Kyrgyz and Tajik villages in southern Fergana. In all three languages of this region—Kyrgyz, Uzbek, and Tajik, one finds the same expression: "if the bazaar doesn't live, the grave will get you!" (*Bazar tiibeseng mazar seni tiet*). And this process in turn incited other acts of demarcation. The building materials for the new bazaar were taken from the grounds of a sacred site located at the border between the two villages, the Khodjai Orif *mazar* (cemetery). This had been paradigmatically shared space: the resting place for a famous Sokh *Hajji,* whose village of birth is now administratively in Uzbekistan, and whose resting place, a site of pilgrimage for two communities, now lies just across the border, in Kyrgyzstan. Outcry amongst Hushiar elders at the felling of trees that had been collectively planted on the site of the mazar was met by practices of stately classification, officials coming and confirming that since this was indeed Kyrgyz territory, the Sogment elders could fell whichever trees they liked.

The shift in the bazaar's location, to a site more fully inside Kyrgyzstan, was not without opposition. The seventy-five families living in Charbak depended on the border-straddling bazaar as a major source of livelihood: virtually everyone in the village was involved in trade, and many home-owners made a small income by letting their houses as an overnight storehouse for traders from lower-lying villages. When I visited the previously bustling Charbak bazaar on market day in July, a few determined traders (mostly from Charbak itself) were still selling there, even though there were few customers and the market felt eerily silent with the ghosts of abandoned trade. Separating the market was neither straightforward nor uncontested, but this very contestation was productive: throwing the question of stately edges vigorously into public discourse, raising in new ways the question of what it meant to be a separate state.

If the market seemed to crystallize concerns over the proper spatial and economic correlates of being independent, another Sogment institution, the medical clinic, seemed more than any other to condense questions about the appropriate regulation of cross-border movement and the everyday meanings of having a "manned" border. Kyrgyzstani border guards had been stationed in the small tea-house just above the Baiaman Bridge since 2000, their posting a response to incursions across the mountains above Sokh in 1999 and 2000 by armed militants seeking to enter Uzbekistan. By 2005, however, the role of border guards in defending against incursion was rather more ambiguous. On the gravel track leading from Hushiar up to Sogment and the mountains beyond, there was little traffic, and virtually all of it was local. During previous fieldwork I had sometimes sat with the border guards on the small wooden bench outside their base, chatting and watching cars go past—a rate, usually, of no more than three or four per hour.

The majority of those passing on foot were women; heading, as the guards would often point out, for the Sogment medical clinic. This was a simple concrete building, sparsely furnished and with little in the way of medical infrastructure. What it did have, however, were skilled medical personnel, most of them young, on an initial obligatory posting following a two-year college training. They offered medical services to men and women from throughout the Sokh valley, accepting small informal payments to supplement their salaries. I had first heard about the clinic, and one woman in particular, Saltanat, several months earlier, when I lived lower down the valley, in one of Sokh's central mahallas. Saltanat was the clinic's gynecologist, and had, in a matter of months, become a source of friendship and information for many of Sokh's women. In the winter of 2004–2005, the whole of Uzbekistan's Sokh district, with a population of 57,000 had just two gynecologists, both of them men. As guardians of scientific knowledge about female fertility, these figures seemed to be feared and revered in equal measure. They were often invited guests at neighborhood wedding parties, and were two of the district's wealthiest men, capitalizing on the scarcity of their skill and the social value of their knowledge by setting up a lucrative private practice. In a context where there is enormous pressure on the young daughter-in-law to bear her first child within a year of marriage, and where female fertility becomes the index of family honor, this social standing is perhaps of little surprise.

It is in this context of symbolic and emotional overdetermination that Saltanat's care came to be known and appreciated—on both sides of the border. While her gender meant that she could be visited by women without arousing gossip, the fact that she was ethnically Kyrgyz meant that, for Tajik women from Sokh, she was outside the realm of mutual mahalla obligations according to which a local doctor might also become a family guest. For Mavliuda, the young daughter-in-law of the family with whom I lived in Sokh, Saltanat's "lack of connection" to her own mahalla heightened her feelings of appreciation: one could be close to Saltanat because, embedded in networks of kin that led elsewhere, she was socially distant.

Such lines of intimacy, however, had been challenged by the May conflict. Saltanat had previously treated women from the Uzbekistan side of the border on the same basis that she had seen those from Kyrgyzstan. She would treat whoever walked through her door, expecting no fee but gratefully welcoming gifts. During the May conflict such connections had been disrupted, physically and discursively. For not only did it become impossible for women from Sokh to cross through the (male) crowds on the Baiaman Bridge that provided the only way up to the clinic; even after the barricades were removed Saltanat was reputedly instructed by fellow villagers not to treat any Tajik woman from

Sokh. Her prized knowledge was, briefly and publicly, transformed into a means for enacting a social and stately boundary.

By July, when I returned to Sokh for the first time after the conflict, such extreme prohibitions had diminished. Indeed, when I crossed the border from Hushiar to Sogment that summer it was with a group of Tajik women who were on their way to visit Saltanat. They were visibly nervous at crossing the Baiaman Bridge and passing the border guards sitting on the bench at the far side. It was with scarves pulled over mouths and eyes trained down that they passed the soldiers, half-walking, half-running, passports in hand. When we settled to a walk on the other side, they told me that this was the first time they had gone to Sogment since the conflict six weeks earlier.

Saltanat, then, was being cautiously, nervously visited by women from Sokh again. There were no physical obstacles to their reaching her, and the border guards at the Baiaman Bridge did not bother to ask any of us for our documents. But like issues of trade, transport, and water use, the question of medical care and its proper ownership had become a site of intense social commentary. The availability of Saltanat's skill seemed to crystallize more than any other issue the tension between an ethic of borderland conviviality and the business of upholding the law. For what was at stake was not simply the accessibility of her care (should citizens of Uzbekistan be charged differently from those in Kyrgyzstan for seeing the doctor in "our" clinic?) but the proper limits of stately verification in a context of highly coded gender relations. Should women be asked for their documents and the purpose of their border crossing if to do so might cause embarrassment and undermine a delicate ethic of mutual recognition? How to maintain a culture of gendered respect (*urmat*) and nonetheless uphold the law? Quite what are the border guards posted here for when threats to local peace seem to emanate from far beyond?

These discussions were an integral element of the border work occurring in Sogment in the summer of 2005. What was taking place was not a sudden closure of space: the dramatic territorialization of the kind that had occurred in May, which makes news stories and shapes images of the Fergana Valley as a peculiarly conflict-prone site. What was occurring, rather, was a moment of intense discursive production concerning the territorial correlates of stately difference in a context of profound historical interdependence and considerable strain on shared resources. In southern Sokh the events of May (and, I would venture, the political turmoil of the preceding few months) had served to crystallize in new ways the question of what it meant to live "on two sides of the border" and social boundaries of ethnicity and gender were central to articulating and navigating these shifts. Questions about the proper limits of stately authority were mediated through, and in turn served to fix previously far more fluid social boundaries. It was precisely by articulating who ought to be allowed where (can our elders go to "their" mazar? Can their women use "our" medical clinic?) that stately territoriality was being enacted. At this moment of deliberation, the production of "stately" limits and "social" ones were fundamentally intertwined.

Conclusion

In this chapter I have sought to argue for an eventful account of bordering, drawing attention to the variable quality and salience of borders, even as their physical and institutional traces on the landscape remain unchanged. By exploring the escalation of stately violence at a moment of trans-border tension, I have sought to question the tendency for instances of conflict at Central Asia's new borders to be explained in terms of enduring resource-driven competition between ethnically polarized communities. Ethnicity can be a generative and powerful framework for social mobilization and political action, just as it provides a ready template for political and media interpretations of violence. But an analysis of the dynamics and escalation of particular instances of conflict at the southern borders of the Sokh exclave reveals a far more complex picture of political contingency, elite manipulation, imbalances in political representation, and competing assertions of sovereignty than an account framed in terms of resource-led conflict allows. As Kathleen Kuehnast and Nora Dudwick (2008) have argued in a study of local sources of borderland tension, it is often precisely the multiplicity of competing authorities that makes social life fraught: the problem, not just of knowing what the rules are, but of knowing "whose rules rule."

In exploring this incident of borderland conflict and its performative aftermath, I have also sought to stress the need for greater attention to the temporality of bordering: to explore "border" as quality rather than as thing, as verb rather than noun. To recognize this is not to suggest that borders are not also experientially real and often viscerally present in the life of borderland dwellers. But it is to leave open the question of how and when (and whether) the line on the map comes to equate a limit on the ground. In his programmatic reflections on nationhood as "event," Brubaker leaves questions of process largely unelaborated. He asks us to "think theoretically" about the experience of being "overcome by nationhood" (1996, 20), yet the mechanism whereby this happens remains rather mystical in his account.

Moments of dramatic political change are clearly significant to the argument (the example he cites is the feeling of being "sucked into" Croat-ness during the Yugoslav wars); yet quite how events bring about quite sudden, dramatic fluctuations in our sense of political belonging or our imagination of the state-as-institution is left tantalizingly open. The deliberations that I describe here demonstrate the extent to which a previous event incited a proliferation of talk about the boundaries of political community. Alongside the practical business of moving markets and felling trees, this narrative proliferation was integral to territorializing the state; conversations, rumors, and deliberations actively sedimented borders; served to render them experientially real.

This has implications for the broader concerns of this book. Ethnographic attention to the work of bordering highlights the need to explore the tempos and intensities of producing "state effects." The incident I explore in this chapter was one where the processes of "spatial organization, temporal arrangement, functional specification, supervision and surveillance" through which the state is produced as an autonomous structure went from being "mundane," as Mitchell depicts it in his account of state effects (1999, 97), to being highly charged and the site of considerable popular discussion and pragmatic claims making. These were dynamics, moreover, that were both appropriated and contested in consequential ways. Quite how or whether low-ranking border guards, non-governmental conflict analysts, elders' councils, big-man sponsors, regional governors, state security officials, or village leaders spoke and acted with "stately" authority was contested and variable. At stake was the question of what the entailments of "territorial integrity" should be in a context of historically deep interdependencies between upstream and downstream communities that now happen to be divided by an international border. The conflict that I explore here, while exceptional within the ongoing dynamic of trans-border relations in Central Asia, is instructive precisely in illuminating the work entailed in making borders come to appear a social and geographical "given." Moments of upheaval reveal the radical contingency of law's legitimacy, or what Asad (2004, 287) has referred to as "the arbitrariness of the authority that seeks to make law certain." Borders, as a stately limit point, are privileged points of access for probing these concerns ethnographically.

Notes

1. Research for this chapter was supported by the Economic and Social Research Council and a Research Councils UK post-doctoral Research Fellowship. I would like to thank Judith Beyer, Johan Rasanayagam, and Sarah Green for their valuable feedback on earlier drafts.

2. All names used throughout are pseudonyms.

3. I have explored the conflict and its narration in more detail in Reeves (2008).

4. This narrative sequence is based on interviews in Hushiar, Charbak, and Sogment in the weeks following the events and on conflict analyses that were produced contemporaneously by the local non-governmental organizations, Mehr, Yntymak, and the Foundation for Tolerance International. Those used here include reports by FTI (2005); FTI, Mehr, and Yntymak (2005); and Yntymak Saiasaty (2005a, 2005b).

5. The sense of terrifying possibility is well captured in the oral histories in Tulegabylova and Shishkaraeva (2005); on the sense of the state being "up for impersonation" in the weeks following the March 24th seizure of power, see Kniazev (2006, 156–196). For the "official" (victors') version of the "people's revolution," see Kazybaev (2006); for the Akaev family narrative recounting of the "So-called Tulip Revolution," see Akaeva (2006).

6. This was a time, in Bishkek, when ethnicity suddenly became a salient mark of social "vision and division" in a way that, in this most comfortably cosmopolitan of post-Soviet cities, it normally emphatically is not. Particular ethnic groups (notably Uyghurs) had suffered disproportionately from the looting that followed the storming of the White House in Bishkek, and there were rumors (largely unsubstantiated, though socially consequential), of ethnic Russians having been targeted in domestic attacks. Certainly, for many urbanite Russophones (of all ethnicities), the *el* (people) of the revolution were perceived as remote from their own (urban, Russophone) social world. The people storming the White House, after all, were overwhelmingly rural and Kyrgyz-speaking.

7. All of the parliamentary election results were archived on the website of the Central Election Committee (www.shailoo.gov.kg), last successfully accessed in June 2007.

8. Erkinbaev subsequently withdrew, throwing his weight behind the eventual victor, Kurmanbek Bakiev.

9. See, for an explicit statement, the "principles of prevention" in Lubin and Rubin (1999, 14–17).

10. My discussion in this section of the everyday territorial enactments in which the people of Sogment were engaged draws on material previously published in Reeves (2011, 915).

References

Abashin, Sergey, Kamolidin Abdullaev, Ravshan Abdullaev, and Arslan Koichiev. 2011. "Soviet Rule and the Delineation of Borders in the Ferghana Valley, 1917–1930." In *Ferghana Valley: The Heart of Central Asia,* edited by Frederick Starr, 94–118. Armonk, N.Y.: M. E. Sharpe.

Abdullaev, Ulugbek. 1991. Traditsionnye i sovremennye mezhetnicheskie sviazy v sel'skikh mestnostiakh ferganskoi doliny. Avtoreferat. Candidate of Science dissertation summary, Academy of Science of the Republic of Uzbekistan.

Akaeva, Bermet. 2006. *Tsvety zla. O tak nazyvaemoi 'Tiulpanovoi Revoliutsii' v Kyrgyzstane.* Moscow: Mezhdunarodnye otnosheniia.

Asad, Talal. 2004. "Where Are the Margins of the State?" In *Anthropology in the Margins of the State,* edited by Veena Das and Deborah Poole, 279–288. Santa Fe, N.M.: School of American Research Press.

Bichsel, Christine. 2005. "In Search of Harmony: Repairing Infrastructure and Social Relations in the Ferghana Valley." *Central Asian Survey* 24, no. 1: 53–66.

———. 2009. *Conflict Transformation in Central Asia: Irrigation Disputes in the Ferghana Valley.* Abingdon, UK: Routledge.

Bourdieu, Pierre, and Loic Wacquant. 1999. "Rethinking the State: Genesis and Structure of the Bureaucratic Field." In *State/Culture: State Formation after the Cultural Turn,* edited by George Steinmetz, 53–75. Ithaca, N.Y.: Cornell University Press.
Brubaker, Rogers. 1996. "Rethinking Nationhood: Nation as Institutionalized Form, Practical Category, Contingent Event." In Rogers Brubaker, *Nationalism Reframed: Nationhood and the National Question in the New Europe,* 13–22. Cambridge: Cambridge University Press.
Brubaker, Rogers, Margit Feischmidt, Jon Fox, and Liana Grancea. 2006. *Nationalist Politics and Everyday Ethnicity in a Transylvanian Town.* Princeton, N.J.: Princeton University Press.
Chalfin, Brenda. 2010. *Neoliberal Frontiers: An Ethnography of Sovereignty in West Africa.* Chicago: University of Chicago Press.
Cheah, Pheng. 1998. "The Cosmopolitical—Today." In *Cosmopolitics: Thinking and Feeling Beyond the Nation,* edited by Pheng Cheah and Bruce Robbins, 20–44. Minneapolis: University of Minnesota Press.
Dzhakhonov, Usto. 1989. *Zemledelie Tadzhikov doliny Sokha v kontse XIX–nachale XX v. (Istoriko-etnograficheskoe issledovanie).* Dushanbe, Tajikistan: Donish.
Ferguson, James, and Akhil Gupta. 2002. "Spatializing States: Towards an Ethnography of Neoliberal Governmentality." *American Ethnologist* 29, no. 4: 981–1002.
Flynn, Donna. 1997. "We Are the Border: Identity, Exchange and the State along the Benin-Nigeria Border." *American Ethnologist* 24, no. 2: 311–330.
FTI [Obshchestvennyi Fond "Za Mezhdunarodnuiu Tolerantnost'"]. 2005. "Kratkaia informatsiia ob intsidente mezhdu zhiteliami s. Khush'iar Sokhskogo Raiona RU i Charbak, Sogment Batkenskogo Raiona KR." Unpublished conflict analysis, May 3.
FTI, Mehr, and Yntymak. 2005. "Informatsiia o tekushchem konflikte mezhdu zhiteliami s. Khush'iar Sokhskogo Raiona RU i Charbak, Sogment, Gaz Batkenskogo Raiona KR." Unpublished conflict analysis, May 8.
Geschiere, Peter. 2009. *The Perils of Belonging: Autochthony, Citizenship and Exclusion in Africa and Europe.* Chicago: University of Chicago Press.
Goldenbaum, Mark, Justin Odun, and Kevin Grubb. 2006. "USAID's Peaceful Communities Initiative." http://pdf.usaid.gov/pdf_docs/PDACJ077.pdf (accessed September 30, 2012).
Green, Sarah. 2009. "Lines, Traces and Tidemarks: Reflections on Forms of Borderliness." Paper presented to the COST Eastbordnet Workshop, Nicosia, April 14–15. http://www.eastbordnet.org/wiki/Documents/Lines_Traces_Tidemarks_Nicosia_2009_090416.pdf (accessed September 30, 2012).
———. 2010. "Performing Border in the Aegean." *Journal of Cultural Economy* 3, no. 2: 261–278.
———. 2012. "Reciting the Future: Border Relocations and Everyday Speculations in Two Greek Border Regions." *HAU: Journal of Ethnographic Theory* 2, no. 1: 111–129. http://www.haujournal.org/index.php/hau/article/view/66/105 (accessed September 30, 2012).
Karimov, Islam. 2005. "Nasha glavnaia tsel'-demokratizatsiia i obnovlenie obshchestva, reformirovanie i modernizatsiia strany." Doklad Prezidenta Republiki Uzbekistan Islama Karimova na sovmestnom zasedanii Zakonadatel'noi palaty i Senata Olii

Mazhlisa. www.uzbekistan.pl/documents/ru/worddocs/nashaglavnajatsel.doc (accessed September 30, 2012).

Kazybaev, Pamirbek. 2006. *Kyrgyzstan: Eldik Revoliutsiia, 24-mart 2005. Narodnaia Revoliutsiia.* Bishkek, Kyrgyzstan: Uchkun.

Kluever, Anna. 2004. "Rol' Nepravitel'stvennykh Organizatsii v Predotvrashchenii Konfliktov." Paper presented to the Osh Media Resource Center/Index on Censorship conference on "The Role of the Mass Media in the Portrayal of Border and Inter-Ethnic Problems." Osh, Kyrgyzstan. May 1.

Kniazev, Aleksandr. 2006. *Gosudarstvennyi Perevorot. 24 Marta 2005g. v Kirgizii.* Bishkek, Kyrgyzstan: Obshchestvennyi fond Aleksandra Kniazeva.

Kuehnast, Kathleen, and Nora Dudwick. 2008. *Whose Rules Rule? Everyday Border and Water Conflicts in Central Asia.* Washington, D.C.: World Bank.

Lubin, Nancy, and Barnett Rubin. 1999. *Calming the Ferghana Valley: Development and Dialogue in the Heart of Central Asia.* New York: Century Foundation Press.

Maasen, Kristel, Bektemir Bagyskulov, Akyn Bakirov, Asylbek Egemberdiev, Anara Eginalieva, Abdygapar Karataev, Lubov Kolesnikova, and Abror Mirsangilov. 2005. *The Role and Capacity of Civil Society in the Prevention of Violent Conflict in Southern Kyrgyzstan.* Bishkek, Kyrgyzstan: Foundation for Tolerance International.

Marat, Erica. 2006. *The Tulip Revolution: Kyrgyzstan One Year After.* Washington, D.C.: Jamestown Foundation.

Megoran, Nick. 2002. "The Borders of Eternal Friendship? The Politics and Pain of Nationalism and Identity along the Uzbekistan-Kyrgyzstan Ferghana Valley Boundary, 1999–2000." PhD diss., University of Cambridge.

———. 2010. "The Uzbekistan-Kyrgyzstan Boundary: Stalin's Cartography, Post-Soviet Geography." In *Borderlines and Borderlands: Political Oddities at the Edge of the Nation-State,* edited by Alexander Diener and Joshua Hagen, 33–52. Lanham, Md,: Rowman and Littlefield.

Megoran, Nick, Gaël Raballand, and Jerome Bouyjou. 2005. "Performance, Representation and the Economics of Border Control in Uzbekistan." *Geopolitics* 10, no. 4: 712–740.

Mercy Corps. 2003. "Semi-Annual Report October 2002–March 2003. The Peaceful Communities Initiative. Conflict Mitigation Initiative in the Ferghana Valley." http://pdf.usaid.gov/pdf_docs/PDABY751.pdf (accessed September 30, 2012).

Mitchell, Timothy. 1999. "Society, Economy and the State Effect." In *State/Culture: State Formation after the Cultural Turn,* edited by George Steinmetz, 76–97. Ithaca, N.Y.: Cornell University Press.

Nazarov, Ravshan, and Pulat Shozimov. 2011. "The Ferghana Valley in the Eras of Khrushchev and Brezhnev." In *The Ferghana Valley: the Heart of Central Asia,* edited by Frederick Starr, 140–163. Armonk, N.Y.: M.E. Sharpe.

Osmonov, Joldosh. 2010. "Incident in Kyrgyzstan Actualizes Border Problems in Fergana." *Central Asia-Caucasus Analyst,* September 9. http://www.cacianalyst.org/?q=node/5348/print (accessed September 30, 2012).

Protokol. 2002. *Protokol o grafike sovmestnogo vodopol'zovaniia zhiteliami sel Charbak, Kungoi-Tam Kyrgyzskoi Respubliki i sel Khush'ier, Kyzyl-Kiiak Respubliki Uzbekistan.* Unpublished document.

Radu, Cosmin. 2010. "Beyond Border-'Dwelling': Temporalizing the Border-Space through Events." *Anthropological Theory* 10, no. 4: 409–433.

Reeves, Madeleine. 2007. "Travels in the Margins of the State: Everyday Geography in the Ferghana Valley Borderlands." In *Everyday Life in Central Asia Past and Present,* edited by Jeff Sahadeo and Russell Zanca, 281–300. Bloomington: Indiana University Press.

———. 2008. "Border Work: An Ethnography of the State at Its Limits in the Ferghana Valley." PhD diss., University of Cambridge.

———. 2009. "Materialising State Space: 'Creeping Migration' and Territorial Integrity in Southern Kyrgyzstan." *Europe-Asia Studies* 61, no. 7: 1277–1313.

———. 2011. "Fixing the Border: On the Affective Life of the State in Southern Kyrgyzstan." *Environment and Planning D: Society and Space* 29, no. 5: 905–923.

Simone, AbdouMaliq. 2001. "On the Worlding of African Cities." *African Studies Review* 44, no. 2: 15–41.

Soltoeva, Anara. 2005. "Vlast' vziali. Zemliu davai!" *Vechernii Bishkek,* April 8.

Thurman, Jonathan. 1999. "Modes of Organization in Central Asian Irrigation: The Ferghana Valley, 1876 to Present." PhD diss., Indiana University.

Tulegabylova, Nurjan, and Elmira Shishkaraeva, eds. 2005. *The Spring of 2005 through the Eyes of People of Kyrgyzstan: Anxieties, Expectations and Hopes (Oral Histories)/ Vesna 2005 goda glazami Kyrgyzstantsev: Trevogi, ozhidaniia, nadezhdy.* Bishkek, Kyrgyzstan: Tsentr izdatel'skogo razvitiia.

Uehling, Gretta. 2007. "Dinner with Akhmet." In *Everyday Life in Central Asia: Past and Present,* edited by Jeff Sahadeo and Russell Zanca, 127–140. Bloomington: Indiana University Press.

Usmanov, Seyitbek. 2011. "'Closed' Kyrgyz-Uzbek Border: A Recipe for Clashes." *Eurasia Daily Monitor* 8, no. 156, August 12.

Wilson, Thomas, and Hastings Donnan. 2005. *Culture and Power at the Edge of the State: National Support and Subversion in European Border Regions.* Münster, Germany: Lit Verlag.

Yntymak Saiasaty. 2005a. "Informatsiia o konflikte ot 1–3.05.2005 goda v regione Sokh KaraTokoi." Unpublished conflict analysis, May 3.

———. 2005b. "Informatsiia o konflikte ot 1–3.05.2005 goda v regione Sokh Kara Tokoi. Na 19:00 vechera 04.05.2005 Goda." Unpublished conflict analysis, May 4.

Young, Anna. 2003. *Ferghana Valley Field Study: Reducing the Potential for Conflict through Community Mobilization.* Portland, Ore.: Mercy Corps.

Part 3
Moral Positionings

9. Reclaiming *Ma'naviyat*

Morality, Criminality, and Dissident Politics in Uzbekistan

Sarah Kendzior

In May 2008, Uzbekistan's president Islam Karimov announced that he had penned a treatise on morality. Released three years after state military forces shot to death hundreds of citizens in the city of Andijan,[1] *High Morality—an Invincible Force* (*Yuksak Ma'naviyat—Yengilmas Kuch*) discusses the moral caliber of the Uzbek people and offers guidance on how Uzbeks can attain moral greatness in a world hostile to its development. The book was not Karimov's first foray into moral philosophy. Since taking office in 1991, the communist apparatchik turned fervent nationalist has published dozens of essays and speeches on *ma'naviyat,* a moral and spiritual quality that he sees as both intrinsic to Uzbek identity and under continuous attack from enemies seeking to harm the Uzbek nation. *Ma'naviyat* was the subject of some of Karimov's earliest essays and speeches, titles of which included "*Ma'naviy* Honor Is National Pride," "The Strength of Our *ma'naviy* Legacy" and "Let's Promote *ma'naviyat* and *ma'rifat* [enlightenment] to a High Degree," a task Karimov's team of ideologues undertook with aplomb.[2] In 1994 the state established the department of Ma'naviyat and Ma'rifat along with the Ma'naviyat television station and the Ma'naviyat publishing house, which issues state-sanctioned tracts on ethics and values. Hailed by Uzbek state officials as "the best book on philosophy and morality since the time of Socrates," *High Morality—an Invincible Force* soon joined Karimov's earlier works as required reading in Uzbekistan's high schools and universities (Najibullah 2008).

On the other side of the world, an exiled Uzbek dissident read about Karimov's latest work from his new home in Edmonton, Canada. Nasrullo Sayyid has been a fugitive since 2005, when he fled Uzbekistan for Kyrgyzstan after being arrested for allegedly distributing a protest song about the Andijan massacre. A former member of parliament—ousted in 1992 for his affiliation with the banned Erk opposition party—Nasrullo is now featured on wanted signs in his hometown of Bukhara, having been labeled a "religious extremist terrorist" by the state he once served. He was arrested for the first time in 1994, after *militsiya* officers broke into his home and claimed to have found a grenade hidden in his children's wardrobe. Jailed for two months and sentenced at trial to a year of manual labor and house arrest, he remained a target of state persecution until his exile in November 2005.

As Nasrullo read of Karmov's musings on morality, he began to reflect on his own experiences in Uzbekistan. He decided to write a book about his 1994 trial and contemporaneous incarceration and publish it on the internet. Entitled *Five Recollections of "High Morality"* (*'Yuksak Ma'naviyat' Haqida Besh Xotira*), the book begins as follows:

> Recently in Tashkent Islam Karimov published a new book. I read in a media report that the book is called "High Morality—an Invincible Force." I still haven't seen or read it, but I would guess that Karimov probably expresses his views of the "high morality" he has built in Uzbekistan over the past 18 years. . . .
>
> Nowadays Islam Karimov's apologists are preaching from their lofty tribunes, selling out with their nonsense about "high morality" [*yuksak ma'naviyat*] while Uzbek society sinks in the swamp of its own immorality [*ma'naviyatsizlik*]. I know that it is wrong to remain silent about this. The basis of Uzbek society has died—lies, deception, and corruption have diseased our nation's morality [*millatimiz ma'naviyat*], and there is no choice but to talk about how low we have sunk.
>
> Obviously the government of Uzbekistan has no interest in my opinions of Karimov's book, as I am a representative of the *muxolifat* [opposition]. For today in the Uzbekistan that Islam Karimov has built there is no tolerance for individual perspectives, for the opinions of someone like me. Therefore I don't intend to quickly find and read Karimov's book or to analyze it.
>
> I have instead decided to make this book about my recollections of five events which have happened over the past 18 years in Uzbekistan. I cannot ever forget these five events. Where I could write about this objectively, I did. Do not think it is a fabrication. This is the truth, as I am afraid of being liar and a sinner in front of our Creator.
>
> These recollections are about "high morality"—that which is covered up, the book that Islam Karimov did not print.[3]

In this chapter, I examine how the Uzbek state and the Uzbek political opposition (*muxolifat*) have invoked competing conceptions of *ma'naviyat* to make claims to political authority in Uzbekistan. As the lynchpin of Karimov's ideological apparatus, *ma'naviyat* is both revealing of how a state can coercively enforce its vision of nationhood and citizenship and of how individuals locate themselves in relation to the state in unexpected and contradictory ways. In Uzbekistan, discourses on morality are imposed by the state but also reflect genuine interests and concerns of Uzbek people. This uncomfortable overlap takes on new significance when examined in the context of the outlawed Uzbek political opposition, many members of which, like Nasrullo, served in the first administration of independent Uzbekistan and helped shape its national ideology. Through discussion of *ma'naviyat,* the state and its opposition make claims about what is acceptably, authentically Uzbek, and, correspondingly, what is immoral, criminal, and not truly Uzbek at all.

Like most Uzbek words concerning ethics or religion, the word *ma'naviyat* derives from Arabic and entered the language through Persian, its meaning transformed along the way. As Charles Kurzman (1999, 89) notes, *ma'naviyat* in the Islamic tradition is associated closely with faith and the acceptance of the words of God. In Uzbekistan, *ma'naviyat* has come to describe less a relationship with the divine than an essential, almost material moral quality that is innate in every Uzbek yet dependent upon the state for its cultivation.[4] Kurzman (1999) describes Uzbekistan's *ma'naviyat* as "politically neutered Islam," claiming it extends a Soviet ideology that justified individual sacrifice for the greater good while divorcing Uzbeks from their Muslim heritage. Though the imposition of the term *ma'naviyat* is arguably an attempt to distance Uzbeks from Soviet ideology and frame the Karimov regime as connected to Islam, the way in which it is taught in schools and other civic centers recalls Soviet practices on moral education, which promoted a rigid form of ethics tied intrinsically to the idea of Soviet citizenship (Medlin, Cave, and Carpenter 1971).

But while there are parallels between certain Soviet ideologies and Karimov's brand of nationalism—unsurprising given Karimov's roots as a Soviet apparatchik—it is important to view *ma'naviyat* not as a "failed" or "neutered" Islam but as a phenomenon that has taken on meaning outside of the propagandistic boundaries Karimov has drawn. As state ideologues and citizens have struggled to negotiate their relationship with Islam—one complicated by eighty years of Soviet atheism and the narrow state-sanctioned Islam that Karimov has imposed in its place—*ma'naviyat* has proven a convenient term with which to discuss morality while side-stepping the complexities of religious doctrine. The gulf between the way *ma'naviyat* is defined in Uzbekistan and its original use in theology may be wide, but there is a comparable gap between how Karimov employs *ma'naviyat* and how others in Uzbekistan, particularly those who identify with the *muxolifat,* negotiate its meaning.

The Uzbek *Muxolifat:* History and Background

Scholars of Uzbekistan have paid little attention to the *muxolifat,* or political opposition, which is often dismissed as ineffective, disorganized, and fractious: a characterization *muxolifatchilar* do not dispute.[5] Largely exiled from Uzbekistan since the 2005 Andijan events, *muxolifatchilar* today live in different countries, belong to different parties, and hold differing notions of the meaning of their dissident status. Some proudly note that they joined the ranks of the *muxolifat* in the 1980s; others claim they became aligned only inadvertently after having been accused by the government of alleged crimes: writing a poem, running a profitable business, being in the wrong place (Andijan's Bobur Square) at the wrong time (May 13, 2005). There is no *solidarność* of Uzbek dissidents, only a scattered body of disparate individuals connected by their enmity toward the Karimov regime—and by the internet, where they engage in intense and insular debate with each other. *Muxolifatchilar* have little say or sway in Uzbekistan, where their attempts to bring about political reform have failed. Though they give many reasons for this impotence, most trace their plight back to Karimov's co-option of the opposition platform in the late Soviet era, and his subsequent insistence that its precepts have been followed despite evidence to the contrary.

The Uzbek political opposition first emerged in the 1980s in response to Soviet policies and ideologies that they believed denigrated the Uzbek people. Political parties like Birlik (Unity) and Erk (Will)—fractious and feuding even in their infancy—called for a revival of Uzbek national culture and language, a return to Islam from atheism, and the ratification of a democratic constitution. Under Karimov, all these things have—on paper at least—come to pass. This has left the *muxolifat* in the awkward position of contesting a state that claims to support its ideological goals and that justifies brutal actions—in particular, the persecution and incarceration of anyone deviating from the narrow official interpretation of nationalist ideology—by invoking tropes and values that the *muxolifatchilar* themselves favor. *Muxolifatchilar* are no longer engaged in a battle with the government over ideology, as in Soviet times, but over public perception of ideology in practice, over the discrepancy between how the state describes Uzbekistan and how many Uzbeks experience it.

Theories of resistance suggest that in critiquing a dominating power—in this case, the Uzbekistani state—dissenting parties reaffirm the logic of its domination (Foucault 1977; Abu-Lughod 1990; Oushakine 2001). In such a formation, the state is a source of psychic attachment even for those who despise it, and this fantasy "does everyday maintenance work for the state" by regenerating its power (Navaro-Yashin 2002, 4). While this insight is helpful in understanding the dialogic relationship between the Uzbek government and the *muxolifat,* its assumptions are complicated by the unique manner in which the Uzbekistani state came into being. In Uzbekistan, the opposition existed *before* the state. Many of the same people who then opposed the Soviet system now oppose Karimov—who himself (in rhetoric tinged by the opportunism of hindsight, at least) also opposed the Soviet system and sought an independent Uzbekistan. Some *muxolifatchilar,* including Nasrullo, were members of parliament during the state's formative years, and served side by side with current government elites to shape a state-sanctioned Uzbek national culture, one distinct from that of the UzSSR and the surrounding Central Asian countries.

The relative newness of Uzbekistan as an independent state, and the complicated social relationships between the current administration and the opposition, make it hard to view Uzbek dissent in terms of traditional formations of "the dominant" and "the subordinate" (Scott 1990). Resistance is here not a clash of ideologies, but a way to occupy a position of moral integrity. The authority to dictate what is moral implicitly includes the authority to establish what is immoral, and, in many regimes, punishable by law. In situations where feuding parties lack obvious points of differentiation, accusations of criminality can serve to establish moral authority (Siegel 1998; Comaroff and Comaroff 2006). Such is the case in Uzbekistan, where the conflict between the *muxolifat* and the government is between two superficially similar groups: Uzbek versus Uzbek, Muslim versus Muslim, nationalist versus nationalist. *Ma'naviyat* is useful to state officials not only as a symbol of the government's moral authority in an uncertain post-Soviet environment, but as a way to designate who is outside state-sanctioned moral boundaries and thereby criminal. In police states like Uzbekistan, which oppress their own people, the production of the state and the production of its enemies are mutually dependent. Here, as Begoña Aretxaga (2003, 403) notes, "the criminal or terrorist or threatening Other is a familiar face, familiar but strange, strange in its familiarity."

Nasrullo Sayyid is such a familiar face—a former deputy featured on wanted signs in Bukhara. His story is relevant to this analysis not only because he publicly contests the official version of *ma'naviyat,* but because in doing so he refutes the state's parallel categories of criminality. Over the years state officials have called Nasrullo many things: a criminal, a religious extremist, a terrorist. Yet the off-hand way in which these attributes were assigned, with little differentiation between one allegation and another, echoes the Karimov administration's casual evocation of essential themes—morality, religion, national culture—in rhetoric that many, especially *muxolifatchilar,* feel is not only hollow but dangerously so. Karimov's rhetoric on morality and law flexes with the times yet remains legally impervious to contestation, highlighting what Asad (2004, 287) calls "the arbitrariness of the authority that seeks to make law certain." By publishing their articles online, *muxolifatchilar* like Nasrullo attempt to make this arbitrariness open, to strip state claims on morality and criminality of their authority by forcing events shrouded in secrecy into the light.

In Uzbekistan, political authority is often tied to a view of the leader as exemplar of moral standards (Liu 2006, 2012; Louw 2007). The relationship of the *muxolifatchilar* to Karimov offers the flip side to what Morgan Liu (2012) identifies as the "personhood" of the Uzbekistani state. While the Osh Uzbeks of Liu's study view Karimov positively as a paternalistic moral authority reminiscent of the glorious khans of Central Asia's past, *muxolifatchilar* like Nasrullo reject Karimov because he fails to embody the moral attributes of a worthy leader.[6] In their view, he is the "bad" khan—tyrannical, vindictive, unwise—disguising himself as the "good" khan, and he brings the territory with which he is identified down with him.

Official *Ma'naviyat:* "Historical Memory" and the State as Savior

Like leaders of other Central Asian states, Islam Karimov has a prodigious publishing output. Since taking office in 1991, he has opined on subjects ranging from the legacy of Amir Temur to the presence of Allah in our lives to how to solve the 2008 world economic crisis. Though Karimov's works have received relatively little attention from Western scholars, two significant analyses have been conducted by Andrew March (2003) and Nick Megoran (2008). March describes how Karimov's works have been used to justify authoritarianism by advancing an "ideology of national independence" from which Karimov's power and policies are assumed naturally to flow. Megoran, while largely agreeing with this characterization, notes that March, in criticizing Karimov's rhetoric, does not take into account how this ideology may have genuinely appealed to Uzbeks in the 1990s, or how individual Uzbeks have since interpreted it. These are critical issues in understanding the Uzbek dissident movement. Karimov's works are propagandistic screeds that provide pretext and justification for draconian policies, but that does not mean that their ideas do not resonate with much of the Uzbek population—not necessarily because they are imparted by Karimov, but because Karimov taps into pre-existing interests and values and adjusts his rhetoric to reflect changing political and social mores.

The Karimovian oeuvre has a cannibalizing consistency. Unlike, for example, the books of Turkmenistan's Saparmurat Niyazov, Karimov's works never descend into megalomaniacal lunacy or ignore contemporary problems—even (and perhaps especially) problems created by the Karimov regime. Karimov confronts threats by melding them into the mythology. In 1994, after cracking down on dissents and outlawing opposition parties, he released *Independence and Morality,* a compilation of essays and speeches emphasizing Uzbekistan's ingrained political unity and cohesion. In 1999, one year after shutting down thousands of mosques and jailing practicing Muslims whose allegiances he saw as a threat, he wrote *Allah Is in Our Hearts and Souls,* a pious paean to the virtues of Islam. In 2005, after the Andijan massacre had caused Uzbekistan to become isolated from the international community, he published *The Uzbek People Will Never Depend on Anyone,* which positions Uzbekistan as voluntarily outside a corrupt world order. One should not view Karimov's works merely as an expression of an ideology of national independence, but as a chronology of how that ideology has played out in practice, how the state rhetoric that shapes Uzbekistan was itself shaped by the events of his rule.

Karimov's definition of *ma'naviyat* has remained relatively consistent, in part because he has made it so broad that it easily encapsulates any concern on which he wishes to focus. However, since 1991 it has been augmented in three significant ways. First, *ma'naviyat* has been transformed from a quality describing social life and historical legacy into a quality denoting a mode of consciousness in an individual. Secondly, *ma'naviyat* now incorporates Islamic terminology. It is presented as the Uzbek embodiment of Islamic faith, not as its nationalist alternative. Finally, *ma'naviyat* has been given a special place in Karimov's discourse on danger. As Megoran (2005, 2008) notes, Uzbek state rhetoric asserts that Uzbekistan is constantly under threat from hostile forces. *Ma'naviyat,* the key to both Uzbekistan's spiritual sanctity and the state's political survival, is presented as similarly imperiled. The emphasis Karimov puts on *ma'naviyat* as a threatened value automatically places those who criticize his interpretation among a subversive, anti-Uzbek population. To understand the repercussions of this, an overview of how the definition of *ma'naviyat* has evolved along with state policies is necessary.

In early works, Karimov depicts *ma'naviyat* as both elemental and innate ("necessary like air or water . . . it is the milk from our mothers, the example of our fathers") and a quality that needs to be cultivated. (Karimov 1994, 8) This is because *ma'naviyat* is tied to "the people's memory" (*xalq xotirasi*), which at the time of Karimov's earliest writings was recovering from an eighty-year onslaught of amnesia known as the USSR. "*Ma'naviyat* is the history of our own people, its culture and deep knowledge of its obligations, and the transformation of this understanding into the utmost strength," he explained in a 1993 speech. "In appealing to history, we need to take into account the people's memories. Just as a person without a memory is incomplete, a people who do not know their history do not have a future" (Karimov 1994, 7).

As many have noted, the Karimov administration went on to "spur the memory" of the Uzbek people with a cultural rehabilitation often seen as contrived due to the speed and conspicuousness of its implementation. By evoking *ma'naviyat* as critical to Uzbek identity, Karimov was able to situate Uzbekistan's abrupt transformations—Karl Marx out, Amir Temur in—as part of a purposeful historical narrative. *Ma'naviyat* wove a consistent thread through the patchwork ideology of independent Uzbekistan. It sought to give Uzbeks assurance that their character derived neither from Islam nor communism but from something else, something intrinsically Uzbek, something already there. Independence in this light could be viewed not as a surprise twist in the story of the Uzbek people, but as its inevitable conclusion. While emphasizing *ma'naviyat*'s innate presence in the heart of every Uzbek, Karimov also claims that *ma'naviyat* requires state guidance and individual effort to reach full fruition. "*Ma'naviyat* is not a gift of fate," Karimov warned. "To perfect one's *ma'naviyat,* one needs to work with one's heart, conscience, intellect and hands" (Karimov 1994, 8). Karimov's depiction of *ma'naviyat* imbues the Uzbek people with an absent-minded superiority. They are programmed to walk toward a glorious destiny, yet they must continually look to the state for reminders as to where they are going, where they have been, and where they are.

Over time, Karimov's depiction of *ma'naviyat* became more elaborate. A 1993 definition reads like a series of unobtrusive buzzwords: "The meaning of *ma'naviyat* is very broad—land, family, parents, children, relatives, neighbors, the people (*xalq*), devotion to the independent state (*davlat*), respect for individuals, trust (*ishonch*), memory, conscience, freedom" (Karimov 1994, 7). In the late 1990s and 2000s, Karimov moved away from such enumerative descriptions and began to portray *ma'naviyat* as an internal spiritual state (albeit one enforced by an external police state). His definition of the term in 2008's *High Morality—an Invincible Force* reads as follows:

> *Ma'naviyat* is a person's spiritual purity, the maturity of their heart, a person's internal world, the strength of their will-power, the whole of their faith [*iymon-e'tiqod*], the boundless strengths of their conscience; it expresses every aspect of our lives today and in history . . . my understanding of *ma'naviyat* is that it is the full embodiment of our society's ideological [*g'oyaviy, mafkuravi*], educational [*ma'rifiy*], moral, ethical [*madaniy, axloqiy*] and religious [*diniy*] aspects.

Karimov's new emphasis on the private world of the individual is notable given the state's harsh crackdown on unofficial religious practice, a development that emerged contemporaneously with the inclusion of overtly religious terminology in state works on *ma'naviyat* in the late 1990s. (Above examples of such terminology include *iymon* [faith] and *din* [religion], which, while rarely included in early works, appear frequently in recent definitions like the one above.) In 1999's *Allah Is in Our Hearts and Souls,* Karimov declared that "[Uzbeks] cannot in any way imagine a separate condition from the holy religion of our own nation [*millatimiz*]. We have so absorbed this sort of religious character, these concepts of faith into our lives that without them we lose ourselves" (Karimov 1999, 5). Such self-contradictory description—the thoroughly absorbed faith in constant danger of being lost—typifies Karimov's later writings on *ma'naviyat,* which similarly oscillate between warning and bravado. *Ma'naviyat* and religion (notably a component of and not a source for *ma'naviyat*) are said to be innate to Uzbeks and in danger of extinction, and so the state, as arbiter of moral and religious standards, serves as both a reflection of the people and as their spiritual savior. *Ma'naviyat* justifies the existence of the Uzbek people: it is their "understanding of themselves," their heritage, their culture, their faith. Threats to *ma'naviyat,* on the other hand, justify the presence of the Uzbekistani state, which must act to protect it.

High Morality—an Invincible Force was published three years after *The Uzbek People Will Never Depend on Anyone* (2005) and echoes that volume's calls for vigilance. Unlike the earlier work—a rush job aimed at quelling inquiry over the Andijan events—*High Morality* attempts to situate contemporary anxieties in the context of pre-existing rhetoric on *ma'naviyat.* After stating that *ma'naviyat* is a complex subject often discussed in a shallow way, Karimov lays out his objective:

> This book came about as a result of the vital need to precisely define the conditions connected to the instruction on the upbringing and moral [*ma'naviy*] health of our future generations, to bring attention once again to these issues in the broader community and in our nation and land [*el va yurt*], to inform people of the dangers of the threatening and complicated times during which a new life and new community of our people are being built, to spread the word about the real dangers and attacks on our *ma'naviyat* that are being leveled and, finally, to discuss the importance of achieving high *ma'naviyat.*

He goes on to explain that *ma'naviyat* is subject to "secret and open attacks," an inevitable byproduct of our "complex and violent era." Karimov does not say much about these attacks other than that they are ominous, imminent and foreign in nature. He never mentions Andijan directly, but given his earlier framing of those events as largely caused by "people from other countries," one can assume that *High Morality* was written in part to give his explication of Andijan a philosophical foundation. In *High Morality—an Invincible Force,* attackers are never described as targeting the state or government. They instead target *ma'naviyat,* the substance and sustenance of the Uzbek people. Similarly, Uzbeks are never portrayed as expressing ire against the state, but are instead potential victims protected by the state from hostile alien forces. Karimov's portrayal of the Uzbek people is uniformly flattering. The people are the "caravan leading us down a holy path"; they pursue "worthy goals and understand every aspect of the road to development." While plagued by external enemies, the only real danger an individual Uzbek could pose to the state of Uzbekistan is that they may "lose their historical memory" if they "show indifference to *ma'naviyat,*" an unfortunate outcome that would impede the aforementioned road to development.

It is impossible, in Karimov's philosophical works, for an Uzbek to be portrayed as intentionally challenging his own government, for this would contradict Karimov's depiction of the Uzbek people as having a morality cultivated by and dependent on state logic. If every aspect of Uzbek identity—personal and political, spiritual and social—stems from a primordial consciousness, exemplified in *ma'naviyat,* that spurred the Uzbek people to their destiny as an independent state under Karimov, then those who deviate from this path must be recast as outsiders, as not really Uzbek at all. They are either actual foreigners or, when such a characterization is impossible, people who fall into categories outside the parameters of what is acceptably Uzbek: terrorists, religious extremists, and criminals. Here we turn to the life of Nasrullo Sayyid, the Uzbek *muxolifatchi* who has been deemed all three of these things, and who has attempted to refute these categories of criminality by challenging the authenticity and authority of Karimov's *ma'naviyat.*

Dissident *Ma'naviyat:* State Authority and the Erosion of Moral Integrity

In our conversations and in his written works, Nasrullo paints an image of himself as a constant in a world in which the stability of ethical concepts—"guilt," "morality," "conscience"—has steadily eroded.[7] That his name is now associated with political dissent and even criminality came about, in his view, not through changes in his politics but through the ways in which certain behaviors and values became defined as "criminal" by the ruling elite.

Five Recollections, published on the Yangi Dunyo ("New World") *muxolifat* website in 2008, is structured as a five-chapter autobiographical account of Nasrullo's 1994 arrest, trial and imprisonment. Like Karimov's work, his is an examination of *ma'naviyat,* shaped and centered by personal experience. Before and after his brief tenure in government, Nasrullo worked as a construction manager, running various projects in Bukhara until local officials shut his company down in March 2005. He also served as an Erk party leader in Bukhara until this time. In November 2005, a fellow Erk party member, Jamal Qutliev, was arrested for allegedly distributing a cassette by the dissident singer Dadaxon Hasanov featuring protest songs about the Andijan massacre.[8] Under duress, Qutliev was forced to sign a confession saying that Nasrullo had given him the cassette. On 16 November, the *militsiya* arrived at Nasrullo's home and ordered him to admit he had given the cassette to Qutliev. Nasrullo refused, and he was brought to the interrogation center in Bukhara, where they made him sign a *tilxat* (a written promise) saying he would not leave the city. After much pleading from his wife, who had called the office repeatedly, they allowed him to go back to his home in Vobkent.

Nasrullo returned home and, at three in the morning, snuck out through the back of a neighbor's house and made his way to the bus terminal, where he boarded a bus to Tashkent. At eleven in the morning on November 17, 2005, he entered Kazakhstan illegally. From Kazakhstan he crossed into Kyrgyzstan, where he lived in Bishkek until 2007. In June of that year, Uzbekistani internal affairs officers arrived in Bishkek to speak with Kyrgyzstani migration officers about extraditing Nasrullo to Uzbekistan. These events prompted Nasrullo to finally seek asylum in a third country, an avenue he had been reluctant to pursue since he viewed Kyrgyzstan to be part of his greater homeland of Turkistan. In September 2007 he was flown to Canada, where he currently resides.

Nasrullo, who prior to leaving Uzbekistan had never used the internet, chronicled the events of his exile in works published on Uzbek-language *muxolifat* websites. His works include poems, autobiographical narratives, and a three-part historical novel about post-Soviet Uzbek politics. ("The Tree of Death" and "Suspicious People" were published in 2008; a yet untitled third installment is forthcoming.) Nasrullo dismisses any notion that his writing is of literary merit—one of his best-known poems is called "I am not a poet"—and claims that he writes purely to console himself. However, by propagating his works through the internet, Nasrullo joined a growing body of online *muxolifatchilar* who consistently and loudly address themes of injustice, state violence, and morality in Karimov's Uzbekistan. *Five Recollections* exemplifies the tenor of these works.

Nasrullo positions *Five Recollections* as a response to Karimov's conception of *ma'naviyat*. In the book he does not explain the term, invoking it only to observe who lacks it (Karimov and the vast majority of Uzbek society). However, it is important to establish what he means by *ma'naviyat,* and why he chose to frame the events in his book—the events of his life—in relation to this concept. In our conversations, Nasrullo lays out his interpretation as follows:

> Let's not call the great being "Allah," "God," "Xudo," "Tangri" or other such names, he is, when it comes down to it, the great Creator. Everything in this world is divided into light [*oq*] and dark [*qora*]. Everything is in conflict with each other. In this world there is a struggle between Good and Evil [*Egzulik va Yomonlik*]. It is interesting that no one who is doing evil would say, "I am doing evil." Every murderer thinks, "I am acting in the name of justice." Karimov is now a tyrant, but he says he does what he's doing to bring peace to the people, to maintain peaceful condi-

tions in the country. In short everyone measures the world according to their own standard. And the importance of this standard is directly connected to the idea of *ma'naviyat*. A person's moral field exists wholly in a state of his choosing.

Ma'naviyat is not only the knowledge that a person holds. It is, in general, a complex concept—it is a person's nature, it is a person's understanding of his nature, it is a person's sense [*tuygu*] of his senses [*his*]. A person of high morality comprehends as much as possible the actions he takes and senses always that he is responsible for his own actions. A person's morality is generally not something a person talks about or writes about, it is measured in his actions [*amal*]. In action it is evident whether or not a person is at a low moral level.

A hundred years ago in our country people would purchase cattle at bazaars and bring them back home, leaving them out in the open. No man touched another man's cattle. Today it is considered foolish to do this. Because today everything that is left alone is taken by another person. Even 20–30 years ago we generally had a different kind of *ma'naviyat* than we do today. *Ma'naviyat* is changing everywhere, it is changing across the whole world. Every place has its own kind. Where a person of strong, pure *ma'naviyat* is the head of society, the *ma'naviyat* of the society is also beautiful. Where people of a low *ma'naviy* level are in power [*hokimiyatda*], all of society down is brought down.

Action is crucial to the *muxolifat* conception of *ma'naviyat:* while Karimov and his ideologues describe the concept as an internal state, Nasrullo emphasizes *ma'naviyat* in action so as to draw attention to the incongruities between how Uzbekistan is described and how it is experienced. Conversely, the actions of others can hold great sway over an individual's internal moral standards. While personal *ma'naviyat* draws from the ability to act according to one's own moral code, public *ma'naviyat* is bound to leadership. A bad leader can take the country down with him, yet the people have a moral obligation to consciously resist his influence.

Because *Five Recollections* is a lengthy work, I do not examine it here in its entirety. Instead I focus on two themes on which Nasrullo opines concerning *ma'naviyat* and authority: the dubious nature of the state's construction of guilt, or *ayb,* and a perceived erosion of the Uzbek people's morality as a result of corrupt state authorities. The narrative arc of *Five Recollections* is as follows: on February 20, 1994, Uzbek *militsiya* officers arrived at Nasrullo's home to search for copies of the Erk newsletter. They searched for hours to no avail until one officer announced that instead of the paper, he had found a grenade in the wardrobe belonging to Nasrullo's five children. In shock, Nasrullo was arrested and interrogated by a state official who pronounced him an *aybdor*—a guilty person—and recommended trial. While awaiting his day in court, Nasrullo spent two months in Bukhara's Otbozor prison, housed alongside drug addicts and murderers. His trial that April was a spectacle that drew hundreds to the courthouse. He was again pronounced an *aybdor* and sentenced to a year of labor and house arrest.

Ayb, or "guilt," is a key term for the *muxolifat*, as it is one of many words in the Uzbek legal system that carries an assumption of guilty until proven innocent (and often still even then so). The word *aybdor* combines the root *ayb* with *-dor*, a suffix indicating ownership or profession. The word for innocent is *aybsiz:* "without guilt." *Ayb* also forms the root of *ayblamoq*, "to accuse," and *ayblanuvchi*, "the accused," or as it is rendered more optimistically in English, "the defendant." In Uzbekistan's judicial discourse, *ayblanuvchi* and *aybdor*—the accused and the guilty—are often used interchangeably. Nasrullo was deemed an *aybdor* both before and after his trial. Throughout *Five Recollections* he scoffs at his guilty status, continually putting words related to *ayb* in quotes. When I asked Nasrullo about this, he explained:

> Everywhere else in the world, if they don't have evidence you will not go to jail. In these cases until the trial a person has a defense and the situation is tolerable. Because if a person is *aybsiz*, he will be *oqlanishadi* [cleared]. For us some people are *oqlanmaydi* [not cleared]. When they go to jail, it's because something is at work . . .
>
> The suffix on "aybdor," like on "mulkdor" or "amaldor," would be more accurate if it were "bor." [*Bor* is the Uzbek word for "to have" or "to be," depending on how it is modified.] Something like "aybibor"—this is a better understanding of the situation. Because for us a person who is investigated for guilt is, in actuality, the same as a "guilty person." Since they are already guilty their guilt is able to be divulged. In truth, "suspicious" [*shubhali*] means "guilty." The sin [*ayb*] of the guilty person is not precisely known. When someone is arrested, there is never any "fact" [*fakt*] or evidence of wrongdoing.

With these connotations of *ma'naviyat* and *ayb* in mind, let us return to *Five Recollections.* Following his arrest, Nasrullo was interrogated by a member of the Bukharan provincial branch of the security services (IIB). Nasrullo portrays this man as a fellow victim of the system, "an ordinary, plain person who was not in the peaceful business of fabricating 'criminals.'" Over the course of the interrogation, Nasrullo and the interrogator developed a rapport, and as the interrogator became convinced of Nasrullo's innocence, his commitment to the case began to wane. He suggested stating that Nasrullo was "partly guilty." Undeterred, Nasrullo insisted he was innocent and that the officer was obligated to admit this:

> I told him, "What's so difficult, just speak the truth. There's no evidence of my guilt [*ayb*], this is slander." He suddenly got very nervous and said, "You don't know, you don't understand what will happen. I could get fired, I could spend my life in jail. In the end there are politics behind this, Karimov is behind this. What did you do, getting mixed up in politics?" he screamed at me.
>
> Following this exchange, the interrogator claimed he had no recourse but torture, and the next day Nasrullo was severely beaten and then brought back to the interrogator, who, after cruelly mocking him with the possibility of release, gave his final verdict: "*Ayblanovchi* Sayyidov, I am aware that you have finished the work of the interrogation. I need to bring your file to the procurator tomorrow. I have found you to be *aybdor.* If you are *aybsiz,* prove it in court."

Nasrullo here describes a situation in which the term *ayb* is invoked in the name of politics. But it is an incoherent politics, one to which the person designating *ayb* has little direct relation. The interrogator is presented as a person aware of the political nature of his profession but determined to distance himself from the political arena. He knows that the terms of justice are being arbitrarily employed and is thus terrified that such arbitrary allegations could be aimed his way. Nasrullo views the interrogator's actions as appalling, at one point writing, "This event is lodged in my memory; every day for fourteen years the image of this interrogator and his disgusting words have flashed before my eyes."

This statement makes it quite startling when Nasrullo concludes the first chapter with the following:

> I'd like to add that this interrogator is today working as a lawyer, he seems to defend human rights, and for this reason I forgive him; I write this recollection knowing that his name will in history be marked as worthy.

Surprised by this, I asked Nasrullo to explain how he could have forgiven this man after what he had done. He responded:

> Today in Uzbekistan there are very many interrogators, court officials, *prokurors* and *militsiya* who issue false [*nohaq*] proclamations of guilt [*ayb*]. Why is this? Because the majority has a *ma'naviyat* in which God to them is work and money.
>
> The interrogator I wrote about stopped doing many things, and because he went into advocacy I forgave him. I think that perhaps he un-

derstands his mistakes. Because he defends people now, I forgive him. I say that people should become more and more forgiving. Being able to forgive someone is deeply connected to the issue of *ma'naviyat.*

Action is again the standard upon which evaluations of *ma'naviyat* are made, as action is all that remains when the terminology of justice and sin have been drained of integrity. In *Five Recollections, ayb* is a meaningless and arbitrary construct; *yuksak ma'naviyat,* as a phrase used by Karimov, is laced with hypocrisy. In a world of fabricated evidence, moral behavior becomes the only proof of moral character. Nasrullo continues this theme in a later chapter in which he describes his cellmate, a drug addict named Ilhom, and his relationship with the *militsiya.* Upon meeting Nasrullo, Ilhom attacked him, resulting in a scuffle that had to be broken up by the guards. Nasrullo recalls their conversation thereafter, included here as it similarly reflects skepticism of the language around which the state frames crime and justice:

"What are you in for?" Ilhom asked [in Russian] after our "battle" had ended and we were quiet.

"220, article 1," I answered [in Russian].

"Oooh, *terrorist*! *Terrorist*!" he said and for some reason calmed down. "And you?" I asked him in Uzbek.

"I have a life sentence and have done 15 years already," he said.

"They have slandered me, God willing I will get out of here now," I said.

"Oh yeah?"

"I'm a democrat [*demokrat odamman*], the higher-ups don't appreciate my honesty, that's why . . ." I said, but did not continue.

"Oh, a democrat! *Demokratiya* . . . ! *Dem-o-kra-tiya*!!" Ilhom said and began laughing, mocking me.

"Don't you smirk at me, do you even understand what it is?" I said to him.

Later that day, Ilhom was visited in the prison by a woman, who after giving money to the officers on duty, reached into her headscarf and pulled out a small satchel, which she passed to Ilhom. Inside the satchel was a syringe. Nasrullo writes of how the *militsiya* stood passively in the hallway, watching with amusement as Ilhom injected heroin. "You call me a '*terrorist*' and then send in a '*narkoman*'?" Nasrullo wondered to himself.

Ilhom began to shake uncontrollably, moaning that his heart was racing. Panicked, Nasrullo asked him what was happening. "Don't you know what this injection does?" Ilhom taunted him. "You say you are a democrat, don't you know what democracy really is?" Nasrullo asked the guards to take Ilhom away or move him into another cell. They ignored him and sat at a table in the hallway, drinking vodka. Soon another woman arrived at their cell. She was a prostitute. "I had seen a lot of lowliness in my life, but this was the first time I had seen such a revolting sin," Nasrullo recalls. The *militsiya* stood around watching and cheering. Nasrullo does not elaborate further on what transpired. "This smut I cannot say more about," he writes sarcastically, "because it does not conform to our 'high morality' [*yuksak ma'naviyat*]." He then reflects on the *militsiya*'s role:

> I was really astonished by the events with the *militsiya* officials. They acted like this was an ordinary situation. This dreadful scene—did the *militsiya* consider this spectacle of a man acting like a beast to be an ordinary turn of events? Perhaps some of them did consider this ordinary.

However, in the next paragraph, he assumes a more sympathetic stance:

> I am far from the view that all of the *militsiya* in Uzbekistan are like this. It's true that in Uzbekistan there are *militsiya* of high morality [*yuksak ma'naviyat*], and I think that work is being done to clean out the impure people [*nopok shaxslar*] from the ranks of the *militsiya*. But those *militsiya* who participate in corruption and accept bribes are today in Uzbekistan the deep roots of our most awful disease.

As in his prior depiction of the interrogator, Nasrullo takes pains not to castigate all *militsiya* officials, despite the fact that he has been engaged in a struggle with such officials for eighteen years. Life in Karimov's Uzbekistan, like life in the UzSSR before it, is a juggling act, a constant compromise of beliefs and values in the aim of getting by. The *militsiya* become the "roots of the disease" because they are the men of *action,* the Kalashnikovs behind Karimov's curtain. But even their worst actions are portrayed as rooted in fear and struggle more than adherence to an ideology or to the government. Nasrullo's outrage is less with specific individuals, or even specific institutions like the *militsiya,* than with the net effect of corruption on the *ma'naviyat* of Uzbek society of which the *militsiya* is part, and that this corruption is buried under a regime advertising itself as the pinnacle of an unblemished nation.

In a later section that describes his April 1994 trial, Nasrullo depicts the *militsiya* officials who testified against him as ignorant victims of a country in decay. There is Ahmat, "an irresponsible man who did not understand his own actions . . . when I think about the image of a 'typical Uzbek', Ahmat-*aka*'s picture always comes to mind." There were the "slaves of Uzbekistan" and "puppets of the administration" working in the security services, unable to extract themselves from the corruption of their occupation. One testimony came from the head of a regional security services branch who turned out to be a former friend of Nasrullo's from college: "As time passed he turned into a government-trusting person [*xukumatning ishonchli odam*] and I became an 'enemy of the people' [*xalqning dushmani*]. It is a joke of fate that we were to meet again in this situation." With the exception of Karimov, there is never a clear enemy in this story, because the slide into enmity and back is so easy, and the terms of criminality and morality so riddled with fraud.

Nasrullo concludes *Five Recollections* with a brief commentary on *ma'naviyat* aimed, like Karimov's, at the Uzbek people. "I did not write this book with the intention of making it about my persecution or incarceration, but to show how the *ma'naviyat* of Uzbek society has plummeted off the precipice," he writes. He goes on to describe "the great *ma'naviyat* of our ancestors" as a quality now plagued by "disgusting disease." This desecration of morality has in turn caused the lifestyle (*turmush*) of the Uzbek people to decline. Once again, the emphasis is on action, on the observable traces of low morality as evidenced by actual experience. Nasrullo has no illusions that his book will have influence; in contrast to Karimov's book, written out of an "urgent need" to inform the public, Nasrullo refers to his own work as something that "initially seemed like a pointless endeavor." Referencing *High Morality—an Invincible Force,* Nasrullo notes, "My commentary is worthless to those who deeply pore over that sort of book, but I hope that those who have read this work have a better picture of what happens on the streets." He closes *Five Recollections of "High Morality"* with a tribute: "This book is dedicated to the 18th anniversary of the ratification of the democratic constitution of Uzbekistan."

Conclusion

For Karimov and his opponents, the state of morality and the morality of the state are intertwined. Both employ *ma'naviyat* as a way of situating a broader discourse on criminality, and both connect *ma'naviyat* to the concept of threat. For Karimov, threats to the Uzbek nation are external and target not state apparatuses, but *ma'naviyat* itself. Uzbek *muxolifatchilar* such as Nasrullo are never discussed in his propaganda, but instead are labeled (and tried) as criminal, unworthy even of explicit entry into the discussion of Uzbek *ma'naviyat.* It is notable that so many *muxolifatchilar* have been forced into exile and thus literally imbued with the foreignness with which they have already been metaphorically ascribed. For Nasrullo, the greatest threat to the Uzbek nation is the state and its immoral leadership. Because political authority is so closely tied to the setting of moral standards, corrupt leaders produce a corrupt society (*jamiyat*), exemplified in the pernicious practices of *militsiya* officials. It is important to note that Nasrullo never disregards *ma'naviyat* as itself an invention of state propaganda. In fact, he sees it as essential to Uzbek identity in much the same way Karimov does.

At the heart of the debate on *ma'naviyat* are the Uzbek people, or *xalq*. Karimov links the state, *ma'naviyat* and *xalq* together by presenting the government as a source for precious historical knowledge that would otherwise be lost. If *ma'naviyat* is in the "heart of the people," as Karimov claims, then the state is their relentless defibrillator, continually jolting them back to life through rhetoric and regulation. The *muxolifat* presentation of the state as that which corrupts the people's *ma'naviyat* relies on depictions of actual events, on reportage of *ma'naviyat* in practice. In writing a story that is equal parts what he endured and what he witnessed, Nasrullo presents Uzbek morality in a condition of crisis; the Uzbek people (himself among them) as victims of their leaders' moral decay. Though his works praise the *xalq* and convey great love for the homeland, Nasrullo's portrayal of the Uzbek people is far more complicated, and contradictory, than that offered by the state. Whereas Karimov and his ideologues praise the people's valor, deeming their illustrious heritage equal to their current state of glory, the *muxolifat* details every flaw of contemporary Uzbekistan in excruciating detail.

Karimov's monopolization of *ma'naviyat* and use of violence to suppress alternative perspectives has left the *muxolifat* with little recourse but to argue their moral position from the perspective of personal experience. Their positive feelings for Uzbekistan—in particular, their love of homeland, faith in Islam, and desire for freedom—are echoed hollowly in the pronouncements of Karimov, who claims to have achieved for Uzbekistan everything the *muxolifat* claims the country lacks. Unable to argue on the grounds of ideological difference, the *muxolifat* attempts instead to drain Karimov's rhetoric of moral authority by contrasting it with descriptions of the immortality and criminality they have witnessed. In doing so, they recast the terms of their own criminality by questioning the right of the state to make claims on justice and guilt. High morality is, in both state and *muxolifat* accounts, a potent force. The question is who in Uzbekistan has the authority to wield it.

Notes

1. On May 13, 2005, Uzbek state military forces fired on protestors and onlookers in Andijan's Bobur Square, killing hundreds of people. The crowd had gathered following the controversial trial and imprisonment of twenty-three local businessmen accused by the government of being terrorists. For more detailed analyses of the 2005 Andijan events, see Kendzior (2007); Khalid (2007); and Liu, this volume.

2. These titles were taken from 1994's *Istiqlol va Ma'naviyat* (Independence and Morality). *Ma'naviy* is the adjectival form of *ma'naviyat,* translated here as "moral."

3. Nasrullo Sayyid, *Yuksak Ma'naviyat' haqida besh xotirasi*, Yangi Dunyo website, www.yangidunyo.com. The work was later renamed *Terrorchi Deputat* (The Terrorist Deputy). Translations from Uzbek to English are my own.

4. Though *ma'naviyat* is translated in English by both Western scholars and Uzbek state ministers as "spirituality" (Kurzman 1999; Hanks 2004), a more apt translation is "morality," particularly since many Uzbek authors draw a distinction between *ma'naviyat* and *ruhiyat*, a word that more directly references matters of the spirit (*ruh*).

5. This statement is based on four years of research on and observation of the Uzbek *muxolifat* in exile, including a daily reading of *muxolifat* web publications and print works and interviews with self-identified *muxolifatchilar* from various regions, of various professions, and from various parties (the majority from Birlik, Erk, and Birdamlik).

6. The view of Karimov held by Osh Uzbeks has changed since Liu's original study, as reflected in his piece on the Andijan events for this volume, and is currently undergoing yet another transformation in light of the violence in southern Kyrgyzstan in the summer of 2010.

7. I interviewed Nasrullo multiple times over a six-month period from January–June 2009. This account of his life is based on our conversations and his many published works.

8. For more on this case, see Kendzior (2007).

References

Abu-Lughod, Lila. 1991. "The Romance of Resistance: Tracing Transformations of Power Through Bedouin Women." *American Ethnologist* 17, no. 1: 41–55.

Aretxaga, Begoña. 2003. "Maddening States." *Annual Review of Anthropology* 32: 393–410.

Asad, Talal. 2004 "Where Are the Margins of the State?" In *Anthropology in the Margins of the State*, edited by Veena Das and Deborah Poole, 279–288. Santa Fe, N.M.: School of American Research Press.

Comaroff, Jean, and John L. Comaroff. 2006. "Criminal Obsessions, after Foucault." In *Law and Disorder in the Postcolony*, edited by Jean Comaroff and John L. Comaroff, 273–278. Chicago: University of Chicago Press.

Foucault, Michel. 1977. *Discipline and Punish*. New York: Pantheon.

Hanks, Reuel R. 2004. "Religion and Law in Uzbekistan." In *Regulating Religion: Case Studies from Around the Globe*, edited by James T. Richardson, 319–332. New York: Springer.

Karimov, Islam. 1994. *Istiqlol va Ma'naviyat*. Tashkent, Uzbekistan: O'zbekistan.

———. 1999. *Olloh qalbimizda, yuragimizda*. Tashkent, Uzbekistan: O'zbekistan.

———. 2005. *O'zbek xalqi hech qachon, hech kimga qaram bo'lmaydi*. Tashkent, Uzbekistan: O'zbekistan.

———. 2008. *Yuksak ma'naviyat—yengilmas kuch*. Tashkent, Uzbekistan: Ma'naviyat.

Kendzior, Sarah. 2007. "Poetry of Witness: Uzbek Identity and the Response to Andijon." *Central Asian Survey* 26, no. 3: 317–334.

Khalid, Adeeb. 2007. *Islam after Communism*. Berkeley: University of California Press.

Kurzman, Charles. 1999. "Uzbekistan: The Invention of Nationalism in an Invented Nation." *Critique: Journal for Critical Studies of the Middle East* 15: 77–98.
Liu, Morgan. 2006. "Post-Soviet Paternalism and Personhood: Why Culture Matters to Democratization in Central Asia." In *Prospects for Democracy in Central Asia*, edited by Birgit N. Schlyter, 225–238. Istanbul: Swedish Research Institute in Istanbul.
———. 2012. *Under Solomon's Throne: Uzbek Visions of Renewal in Osh*. Pittsburgh: University of Pittsburgh Press.
Louw, Maria. 2007. *Everyday Islam in Post-Soviet Central Asia*. London: Routledge.
March, Andrew. 2003. "State Ideology and the Legitimation of Authoritarianism: The Case of Post-Soviet Uzbekistan." *Journal of Political Ideologies* 8, no. 2: 209–232.
Medlin, William K., William M. Cave, and Finley Carpenter. 1971. *Education and Development in Central Asia: A Case Study of Social Change in Uzbekistan*. Leiden: Brill.
Megoran, Nick. 2005. "The Critical Geopolitics of Danger in Uzbekistan and Kyrgyzstan." *Environment and Planning D: Society and Space* 23, no. 4: 555–580.
———. 2008. "Framing Andijon, Narrating the Nation: Islam Karimov's Account of the Events of May 13, 2005." *Central Asian Survey* 27, no. 1: 15–32.
Najibullah, Farangis. 2008. "Uzbekistan: Authoritarian President Publishes Tome on 'Morality,'" May 19. http://www.rferl.org/content/article/1117512.html (accessed September 28, 2012).
Navaro-Yashin, Yael. 2002. *Faces of the State: Secularism and Public Life in Turkey*. Princeton, N.J.: Princeton University Press.
Oushakine, Serguei A. 2001. "The Terrifying Mimicry of Samizdat." *Public Culture* 13, no. 2: 191–214.
Sayyid, Nasrullo. 2008. *Yuksak Ma'naviyat haqida besh xotirasi*. Also published as *Terrorchi Deputat*. Formerly published on Yangi Dunyo, http://www.yangidunyo.com. Currently unavailable.
Scott, James C. 1990. *Domination and the Arts of Resistance: Hidden Transcripts*. New Haven, Conn.: Yale University Press.
Siegel, James T. 1998. *A New Criminal Type in Jakarta: Counter-Revolution Today*. Durham, N.C.: Duke University Press.

10. The Reshaping of Cities and Citizens in Uzbekistan

The Case of Namangan's "New Uzbeks"

Tommaso Trevisani

Two decades after Uzbekistan's independence, this chapter focuses on the emergence of the "New Uzbeks," a governmentally promoted citizenry that marks a shift from the early, unsettled period of postsocialism to a more consolidated phase of government rule over society in the second postsocialist decade. Situated in between the elites and the poor, the New Uzbeks refer to those segments of society who have come to terms with and found a place in President Karimov's Uzbekistan. Rather than a coherent and cohesive social entity, they should be seen as the ambivalent outcome of an ongoing political project whose impact on the urban landscape of Uzbekistan has so far received little attention.

In this context, I discuss a government policy in which the reshaping of cities and the propagation of a new model of (non-liberal) citizenship form part of a state project of hegemony. Presented as necessary steps upon the "Uzbek path to development" by government officials, these policies seem to be readily welcomed by a significant part of Uzbek society. The reality, however, is more complex and must take shifting areas and mechanisms of coping into consideration.

I argue that in order to adequately frame this emerging phenomenon it is necessary to shift from the modernization framework underlying official state discourse on national development to the realm and language of legitimacy. While keeping a focus on the ambiguities of the New Uzbeks' attitudes toward the state, I want to problematize the relationship between the rulers and the ruled in independent Uzbekistan that so far has been mostly conceptualized in terms of power discrepancies, fear, and coercion.[1] I suggest that this relationship has been portrayed in too simplistic a way, and that coercion and compliance, coping and consent all play a role therein to different degrees.[2]

Methodologically, a hitherto little attempted ethnography of consent in Uzbek authoritarianism poses problems at various levels, not least one of access. Fieldwork conditions in Uzbekistan are restrictive, which limits possibilities for conducting ethnographic research in depth.[3] Moreover, as Matveeva rightly notes: "in authoritarian states it is difficult both for outsiders and insiders to interpret the extent to which citizens identify with the political order" (Matveeva 2009, 1096). Yet these difficulties should not translate into avoidance or neglect of how citizens relate to the political order, as this is essential for understanding state-society relations in present-day Uzbekistan (Jones Luong 2004). Consequently, by adopting Megoran's plea to use ethnography to gain more insights into the everyday "politicization of national belonging in independent Uzbekistan" (Megoran 2008, 28), I pay attention to local discourses justifying the state and the rulers' modus operandi toward society. In these discourses ambiguity and ambivalence emerge as distinctive qualities, contradicting simple models opposing support to resistance that see compliance as mere submission to coercion.

Post-Soviet Namangan

My particular vantage point is the city of Namangan and its surroundings, in the Uzbek part of the Fergana Valley. Namangan is a symbolically resonant place since, in the first decade of independence and following prolonged turmoil and anti-government protests, it came to epitomize the confrontation between the post-Soviet government and Islam. Its region-wide notoriety is rooted in the early 1990s Adolat movement (*adolat* means "justice" in Uzbek), a militant Islamic group established in Namangan ostensibly to fight corruption and speculation, uphold public order, and to promote Islamic mores.

Karimov's rancorous relationship with Namangan goes back to the personal humiliation he experienced in that city during winter of 1991–1992, at a time when Adolat effectively held power over the city and exerted growing influence over the whole Fergana Valley. Under the pressure of the "street," that is of mass rallies organized by Adolat followers, Karimov was pulled into a public meeting with the leaders of the movement, where he was treated disrespectfully and requested to turn Uzbekistan into an Islamic state (Khalid 2007, 140–141). Although Karimov eventually overcame this crisis and was able to reassert control over the city in the months that followed, on that occasion he felt vulnerable and personally threatened to a degree he had not experienced before or since. A watershed moment for him, this experience strengthened his convictions and decisively influenced his future policy toward Islam and toward the Fergana Valley.

Consequently, struggles for legitimacy permeating the religious sphere were even more tangible in Namangan than elsewhere in Uzbekistan. Protracted tensions between government and Islamist political groups characterized the early years of independence.[4] In the years of state reconquest of the Islamic sphere, control over mosques and communities became markedly more rigid and effective. At the same time an Islamic clerical establishment responding to a centrally commanded national bureaucracy was built up and consolidated.[5] Bringing together moral conservatism with national values it embodied the position of a state Islam able to reconcile secular and material orientations with moderate religious vocations.

A central trigger of the government's reaction was its perception of an Islamist threat. This perceived threat has, in various ways, become instrumental to the government's legitimization strategy, whether through its ability to successfully instill a climate of "everyday vulnerability" amongst believers (Rasanayagam 2006), or by distracting from the essential competition over legitimacy; competition, that is, "between local religious leaders who enjoy growing grassroots support and . . . a central leadership whose one power is its promotion of an environment of fear" (McGlinchey 2007, 316). Ousting any form of non-conformist religiosity, the state became excessively concerned with any manifestation of religious piety and popular devotion in private and public realms. By the time this long-smoldering conflict was won by the Karimov-dominated state, Namangan's public image, such as that produced in the state-controlled media, had gone from that of an Islamist bulwark to that of a devoted and loyal city.[6]

This façade should not conceal that relations between this very city and Karimov are still characterized by deep mistrust and resentment. Local narratives of residents saying that "Karimov hates Namangan" relate back to the events of the early 1990s, and the new turn of politics cannot fully cover up the delicacy of this state of affairs. So, for instance in Namangan the centrally appointed state-trained clergy, which by and large everywhere in Uzbekistan has supplanted the previous generation of elder, self-educated community dignitaries (the latter enjoyed community esteem but were viewed with suspicion by the authorities), is conspicuously young and ostentatiously informal.[7]

In the spring of 2009 my fieldwork coincided with a very particular moment for the city, which was characterized by a high degree of uncertainty amongst its inhabitants. I arrived at a time when the effects of the so-called credit crunch of 2008 were beginning to reach Uzbekistan, threatening the fragile veneer of normality that had been finally reestablished in the Fergana Valley in the years following the Andijan massacre of 2005.[8]

During my first visit to Namangan, which goes back to 1997, I was interested in the local social institution of the *mahalla*, a traditional neighborhood community that has received growing attention and been increasingly formalized through government policy.[9] I returned again in 1998 and in 2001 for relatively short periods of research, with a continued interest in the local dynamics at the interface between Islam, traditional society and local government (Massicard and Trevisani 2003). The idea to revisit Namangan several years later originated from my wish to revive long neglected relationships with those who at that time had shared their homes and thoughts with me. By revisiting Namangan the most obvious interest for me was to see what had happened to the people and places I knew from before. I ended up looking at what I call Namangan's New Uzbeks, a variegated social entity, with disparate backgrounds, yet increasingly sharing common aspirations and sensibilities.

Voices from Society's "Middle"

In Namangan entrepreneurs and businessmen, low- or mid-level state employees, militiamen, professionals, doctors, university teachers, and journalists all represent a new, more or less successful group of actors who embrace new orientations and consumerist desires and who today play a crucial role in the state-led project of modernization. Although the government emphasizes the "middle class-ness" of this variegated group, the term "middle class" in this context appears to be problematic, as it imposes a unitary label on a group that lacks self-consciousness and homogeneity. Just as with Jennifer Patico's post-Soviet middle classes, we can use this term to refer "not to a demographically locatable category of people but to a set of moral and material aspirations and orientations" (Patico 2008, 12). Without overstretching the comparison, analogies exist with South and East Asia's much emphasized emergent middle classes in the recent past, seen as agents of rampant development and carriers of social modernization, while at the same time remaining apolitical or politically quiescent within non democratic regimes (Funabashi 1993, Jones 1998, Ahmad and Reifeld 2003), and these analogies help frame what should be seen as a new phenomenon for Uzbekistan. More importantly, unlike the New Russians (Humphrey 2002), enriched but illegitimate elites, the New Uzbeks are neither the new rich, nor the political elites, but society's mainstream that buys into the government's ideological project and at the same time constitutes its backbone.

Over the 1990s and early 2000s scholars have been much concerned with the growing discrepancies opening up between the "new poor" and the "new rich" in the post-Soviet space, which according to many, left little scope for the development of a middle class (Silverman and Yanovitch 2000; Patico 2008, 66). In Central Asia things started to change with the second half of the second post-socialist decade, as the emergence of a relatively large stratum of actors moving in between the formal and informal economy, who have been able to successfully transit out of poverty into a viable existence, could not remain unnoticed any longer. Oil rich Kazakhstan was the first Central Asian country in which an embryonic middle class, principally defined in relational terms by its level of income and capacity of consumption, and not by the nature of labor, has emerged (Daly 2008). Less rich and liberalized Uzbekistan also set out in this direction. Here the social background of those who occupy the field in between the rich and the poor has its roots either in the public sector—schoolteachers, medical staff, engineers, and other public administration employees, who at least in part can be traced back to the Soviet category of "mass intelligentsia" (Shlapentokh 1999)—or in the local bazaar economy, and in the variegated, and today little studied, practices of "voluntarism and autonomy under Soviet rule" that made Central Asians "adept at identifying and exploiting small zones of independence and self-management" (Starr 1999, 32).

Tohirjon,[10] a university teacher in his early 50s, is indicative of those emerging social strata in Namangan who express aspirations for more material well-being but at the same time show support and understanding for the necessity of the government's strong-handed policy. Neither rich nor poor, yet educated and traveled, he represents the state servant who supports the status quo, who acknowledges problems with the present yet remains confident in the future:

> We are in Asia here, not in Europe. Democracy does not work here. In your country, if a politician does something wrong the media will bring him trouble. Not here. Look at Kyrgyzstan. They said without democracy there will be no development, but they got democracy and this has only led to chaos. People here experienced democracy in the early years of independence. But people also realized that if there is no Karimov, there will be the "wahhabists,"[11] there will be anarchy: this is no alternative. Ours is maybe not a democracy, but we have our freedoms. During the Soviet period we were even afraid to build large homes or to own cars. The security organs would come and ask you: "where did you get the money from? How can you afford it?" Today nobody asks you such things anymore: this is freedom. Today we can use our language: this is freedom. Think about the Uyghurs in China, they do not even have a passport. We are happy with our independence.

Taken as a representative of the New Uzbeks, Tohirjon does not articulate political demands, but rather is satisfied with the new economic opportunities and material freedoms that have become available to him under Karimov. To him these opportunities largely outweigh the loss of those—in his account—dangerous freedoms that people experienced during the early years of independence. Yet feelings toward the political order are not so clear-cut, as exemplified by another conversation with Rustam. A father of three born in 1974, who graduated from university and now works as a taxi driver, he holds a different view on the current condition of his country:

> Today there are many problems, as compared to the Soviet Union. Once there was the mafia here. But the mafia took and gave. Today the mafia is the militia. They only take, without giving back. There are many more militiamen today than during the Soviet Union.
>
> At that time everybody lived equally, at the same level. Not so today. People have economic problems, everything is more expensive, and many cannot afford to buy meat anymore. You know what meat means to our people. For this reason the people are not so hospitable anymore—if you cannot afford meat you don't invite the guest.
>
> But today it has become also fine. It is getting better again. Maybe before, during the Soviet Union, life was easier. There was abundance and peacefulness. People did not need to think so much. The state created all conditions; today people must create them by themselves, and must work independently. This is also right, but harder.

Rustam's statement combines an awareness of the problems of the present with a sense that the situation has become more difficult and precarious for the average person, and with the acknowledgement that—compared to past standards—the yardstick by which membership of society's "middle" can be measured has lowered significantly. Mirroring a widely circulating understanding he uses the affordability of meat as an index of wealth and poverty and points out that wealth has become more unequally distributed, as the state (or in his words the militia) has become more overtly extractive. Yet recognition of the flaws of the current political order does not prevent him from acknowledging what he considers to be a positive evolution, namely that people, now more than in the past, must take their destiny in their own hands.

Both statements of Rustam and Tohirjon testify to opposing, and yet very commonly held attitudes, which often coexist or can be expressed in a combined form. Oscillating between the positions of Rustam and Tohirjon, society's "middle" remains essentially ambivalent in relation to the political order.

Namangan in the Late 1990s and in 2009

A newly traced distinction between two temporal periods in the city, those of *mustaqillik* (literally meaning independence but colloquially used to refer to the early years of Uzbekistan's independence) and *yangi davr* (a term used in the government propaganda, literally meaning new epoch, colloquially used to refer to the years of consolidated independence) was one of my first discoveries emerging from conversations with some of my interlocutors in Namangan. In the words of Ahadjon, a shuttle-trader in his mid-30s, a perceived shift between early and consolidated independence, or early and late postsocialism, occurred at some unspecified point after the turn of the millennium. He put it as follows:

> *Mustaqillik* has become history by now. We are now in a new epoch (*yangi davr*), in which a new person is being created (*yangi davr odam*). The difference now is that we all have become less naïve and simple (*sodda*), more cultured and educated (*madaniyatliroq*).

Such differentiation between two distinct phases of independence echoed popular narratives on the state-led path of development that recurred during my last visit in 2009. The issue of development, intended as progress, or modernization, an issue particularly important to the government, was often highlighted with pride in conversations with my acquaintances. "'There has been much progress, development" (*rivojlanish katta*) I was often told when people begun to tell the story of the modernizing society, in which cell phones have spread, a multitude of locally manufactured cars have poured out into the once half-empty streets, and the one-story clay-plastered *hovli* houses have given way to multi-story buildings with house fronts made of glass and aluminum. In narratives such as these, the recurring leitmotiv of construction was often also accompanied by the belief that the new generations were more educated and more cultivated, and that these merits were to be attributed to the policy of the president.

This recurring narrative seemed to be an already familiar one about the city growing and modernizing and the village moving to the city and imposing its color on it, as elsewhere in Central Asia, where the city has not yet had the time to dissolve rural culture (cf. Alexander and Buchli 2007), but at the same time, where new types of urban dwellers and urban dwellings are increasing the city's complexity. As in other Central Asian cities (see, for instance, Liu 2007 for the case of Osh) over the last decades of the Soviet Union Namangan's residential areas had developed, divided between a traditional, Uzbek-speaking sector composed of *mahalla* neighborhoods, and a predominantly Russian-speaking modern Soviet sector referred to as *mikroraion* (Russian, meaning "micro-region"), an apartment block community built of multi-story prefabricated buildings made of concrete slabs (Liu 2007, 74). If in Namangan the dichotomy between "traditional *mahalla*" and "modern *mikroraion*" still had some validity during my first visit in the late 1990s for reflecting on the post-Soviet city's cultural recombination and mixture, in 2009 new residential projects, new peripheries, many new bazaars, far fewer mosques, and a quite altered composition of the population, have rendered this dichotomy fairly outdated.

Compared with the late 1990s, new peripheries have emerged at the margins of the city, turning land grown with family run agricultural small plots (called *tomorqa* land) into residential areas.[12] The city's administrative boundaries have been enlarged and now incorporate some nearby villages. New residential projects were underway in the city center. Some city center streets have been enlarged, cutting into old residential quarters. New bazaars have been established, and those existing before have grown in size and importance. At the same time, new administrative buildings have appeared, along with many newly opened shops and cafés.

According to official statistics, between 1996 and 2008 Namangan's population had grown from ca. 310,000 to around 440,000 inhabitants (more than half of them aged twenty-four or less), thus surpassing Samarkand to become the second largest city in the country.[13] The problems related to demographic pressure that were already critical in the 1990s have become even further exacerbated and are frequently identified by the government as a threat to stability. In an attempt to stem rural out-migration, 2009 was officially declared the "year of rural wealth and development" (*qishloq taraqiyoti va farovonligi yili*). The main measures initiated by the government were a nationwide redirection of a significant share of agricultural land devoted to cotton, the country's main agricultural crop and a crucial foreign currency provider, toward wheat production, and the announcement of a large construction scheme of schools and colleges in the countryside.[14] These measures were respectively aimed at reducing Uzbekistan's dependency upon grain imports with a view to stabilizing bread prices, as well as a way to provide a stimulus to the local economy. In spring 2009, Karimov's answer to the credit crunch was published as a booklet, in which he explained why "the crisis" (*inqiroz*) could not and would not touch the Uzbek people, Uzbekistan being less exposed in terms of debt to international markets and more protected from the risk of contagion by a vigilant and protectionist government (Karimov 2009). These episodes fit into the larger history of the Uzbek path toward industrial development and welfare, which, in the words of a functionary I met, is "deemed to replicate South Korea's and other Asian countries' success."

Yet in spring 2009, against all official denials, people perceived themselves to be threatened by the "crisis," as new and tangible signs of an economic slowdown in the city were generating new anxieties. While for some the crisis started with independence—when the large factories closed, state services and salaries ceased to be paid out, and with them, the moral and material certainties of Soviet life faded away (Yurchak 2003)—and has since then never ended, others had managed to profit from the economic possibilities of the new post-independence environment and eventually reach a degree of economic security.

At the time of my fieldwork, traders in the bazaars of Namangan lamented the standstill of transactions, while the salaries of public employees were again being paid out with delays or just "virtually" on debit cards, restricting access to cash for bank account holders.[15] Over the years before my last visit a re-strengthened state budget had been able to support a more regular payment of wages and pensions. Many perceived the return of delays in wage payments as an alarm bell recalling the turbulent 1990s. People were feeling insecure and nervous about the crisis, and friends often asked me if there was such a crisis in my country; whether it was hitting us hard; and when I thought the crisis was going to end. Everyone I spoke to had one or more family member who had gone to Russia in search of work but who was now waiting, jobless, to see how the situation would evolve

Coping with the Crisis

The 2009 crisis represents an arrest in the long period of gradual economic recovery distinguishing the second from the first decade of independence. I could not access any economic statistics, but the common perception was that the economic recovery had brought a veritable, although very unevenly distributed prosperity into the city. Labor migration, cross-border smuggling and the privatization and reorganization of formerly state-owned enterprises and property played a major role in augmenting the city's economic vitality. Also, they provided powerful impulses to the other economic sectors and thus to the city's overall economy.

At the outskirts of the city, the subsidiary household plots (*tomorqa*), which every family can apply for, turned into expensive building land exchanged for thousands of dollars. For many ordinary families this had become a source of wealth and an unexpected asset and many experience a discrepancy between their supposed wealth in terms of real estate, and their everyday poverty at the bazaar. Debt servicing and money lending through unofficial channels had strongly increased as compared to the 1990s and early 2000s. With it, besides a growing number of poor and debt contractors, it has also created hidden wealth and hidden opportunities for gain and profit. In a *mahalla* neighborhood I was acquainted with this was the case with a wealthy shop owner with a past in the militia who, thanks to connections in his former job, successfully reinvented himself as a businessman after early retirement and managed to make a fortune as a money lender.

The families' post-independence hybrid income generation pattern, featuring a mix of petty trade, car-driving, state-employment, labor migration and agriculture, has been further consolidated and is now at best cushioning the effects of the crisis. But making ends meet absorbs so much of people's time and energy that, as one small hotel-owner put it to me evocatively, "people end up being tied up without there even being a rope." Ergash, aged fifty-nine at the time of my fieldwork, fits well within this image. He has a son who had recently returned from Russia and who was now without work. As an English language teacher, Ergash works ten hours a day every day of the week, splitting his time between his *tomorqa,* work at college, and extra lessons after work.

> During the Soviet Union I used to earn 143 rubles a month, now I can make 600,000 *so'm*. But in that [Soviet] time I managed to arrange seven *to'ys*,[16] now this is even insufficient to feed my family. I am worried for my grandchildren. What will they do? How will they live? I don't see anything better in the future. Who will pay for their *to'ys*? Who will build a house for them? Not my son, he will be poorer than me.

Such anxiety is widespread and does not leave room for many other thoughts. If Ergash could be stylized to be, at least according to his social background, *o'rtacha* (literally: medium, average), the perceived reality of his situation proves otherwise. Yet at the time of my last fieldwork, a redirection of the household's economic activities was underway: after inconclusive studies at the language faculty and a similarly inconclusive period of labor migration in Russia, Ergash's son had been convinced by his father to open a joinery on the parental household compound with the money that his father borrowed from a moneylender in the *mahalla*. Thanks to Ergash's seniority and connections to the education department the micro-enterprise started with rich commissions for the refurbishing of two newly built rural colleges. This did not offer many future certainties but was a good start and provides an insight into the way in which the local government ameliorates the economic needs of its affiliates. Yet, Ergash, who was a devout Muslim and a former Soviet Army officer, had now arrived at the end of his career and could not conceal his bitterness for the turn of history:

> Various times the Islamic people have tried to seize power, but they failed. Maybe they have no capacity to do so; maybe it was God's will. Maybe Lenin was right: "a revolution without blood is a revolution without fruits." You might think that I am not patriotic enough. Or that I am not a good Muslim. But I must work more than ten hours a day, seven days a week, to feed my family, and now I don't care about anything else.

Accordingly, when toward the end of May news of a terrorist attack in neighboring Xonobod and Andijan filtered into the city, unsettling the precarious peace restored after the Andijan Events of 2005, it was received with diffidence, if not with indifference.[17] "Those who protest against the government have no skills (*layoqat yoq*)," my acquaintances could only criticize. "If they rule, we will have a government pursuing only worthless deeds (*befoida ishlari*)." These reactions that I recorded from two friends of mine were in some sense typical. Whether or not spoken out of fear, these attitudes suggest that, somewhere between opportunism and fear, or between acceptance and acknowledgement of the need of a strong-handed government, coping was the prevailing response.

> Today the task of the government is to unify the country, to build the country. Between the young and the old today there are many differences; the young are happy, the old, those who grew up under the Soviet order, are angry. We from the government try to keep the two things in balance: westernization and tradition. A difference with the Soviet period is that at that time we had just to carry out the plan, we did not need to think for ourselves. Today we have become the owners of our problems. What we need in order to fix them is technology, and people with new thinking.

As in the example above, taken from a conversation with the mid-level government official Baxtiyor, officialdom's answers to people's disorientation habitually invoke a conciliatory language, in which metaphors such as "building," "mediation," or "bridging gaps" often recur. Yet on the way to its implementation this language often translates into harsh and divisive reality, as I observed just a few weeks after this conversation.

At the beginning of July 2009, President Karimov's rapid stopover in Namangan abruptly ended the atmosphere of suspense that had been created over the last months by rumors of the global financial crisis and by news of recent terrorist attacks in the valley.[18] The day after his visit dozens of houses along the main streets were demolished, leaving behind a landscape of debris. Many more were to follow in the coming days. Lutfullo, the owner of a copyshop in the city center, a father of three in his thirties, explained to me that Namangan was to become totally modernized within three years. Billions of *so'm* from the state budget had been allocated in the form of credits and investments into this project. A commission of architects instructed to oversee the program targeted everything that obstructed the straightening of the city's streets: crummy *hovlis*, old Soviet era buildings, irregular outbuildings of shops, but also newly built illegal buildings, and possibly even trees on the sidewalk—hereby anticipating, for the same reason, what was to happen with the wholesale removal of trees on the country's most prestigious square in Tashkent just a few months later.[19]

Lutfullo, describing this new turn of events, explained that the president did not like the traditional plane tree (*chinar*), but favors the pine tree (*archa*), thus implying that the two symbolized mutually exclusive, divergent underlying visions of the world—where the "archa" stands for the new and the "chinar" for the old. Lutfullo sympathizes with the "chinar," but he also recognizes the validity of the government's master plan. He too, perceives the colonial and Soviet period buildings as something that is "just old," that must be overcome. The same applies to the old *mahallas*, which are giving way to newly-built modern residential areas.

For Lutfullo, all this is well, on the one hand: "the city must be orderly" (*shahar tartibli bo'lish kerak*). But on the other hand "people suffer" (*halq qiyinaladi*). From one day to another people have had to demolish their own source of livelihood and restart from scratch. This fate can hit anyone, as it did with a wealthy trader, who had built a large supermarket costing thousands of dollars, demolished the morning after the President's visit. Many in the city are furious and resigned; they feel like victims of heavy injustices—but then, in the implicit acknowledgement that the government's national path of development is something good and necessary, and that some sacrifice is unavoidable on the way toward it, they go on doing their business as usual as long as there is enough space left for coping. Problems posed by the impasses of a veritable modernization drive, such as scarcity of jobs, agricultural land and housing, that had so far been mitigated by the remittances of migrants must now be addressed locally, for instance by undertaking construction work and local handicrafts. No matter how ineffectual these measures are for solving the underlying problems, they result in people being kept busy with work.

New Citizens

Seen from the perspective of Namangan, one effect of the events of Andijan in 2005 was that this neighboring regional capital city took over the reputation of the valley's most troublesome town—a reputation that had previously lain firmly with Namangan. This changed the government's original plans to dignify Andijan as the showpiece center of the valley,[20] representative of an epoch, as Kokand was for the pre-Tsarist era or Fergana was for the Soviet period. It also ended its ostracism of Namangan, whose city elites are now eager to polish its image of a loyal subject.

The government's firm response to the city's recalcitrance and to its Islamic vocations can be subsumed under the binary of "repression and development." People have learned to fear both. In front of the Chorsu bazaar, in the center of Namangan, where there once used to be traditional *mahallas* said to host many "wahhabists," an entire new quarter of expensive, four- to six-story European-styled houses is being built, anticipating the future homes of the New Uzbeks. This measure follows the logic to appropriate places and meanings perceived to be threatening by turning them into ones in line with the rulers' master plans.

In similar fashion, the former "wahhabist" mosque "Gumbaz" has been turned into the regional center for Islamic higher education, and the former madrasa "Mullo Qirghiz" into a museum.

This new urbanism corresponds with and anticipates its use by a new, modern citizenry. The new Uzbek families have fewer children,[21] they arrange their conspicuous weddings in the *yangicha* (meaning newly, in a new style) way at cafés and restaurants if they can afford it; they have a "new thinking" concerning their expectations and demands toward the state, and they profess and practice an Islam that follows the dictates of the state. When they have a background in rural districts, they have moved into apartments in the *mikroraion,* into those flats left empty by the out-migrating first-generation dwellers (with European or mixed ethnic background). Otherwise, if they are from one of the city's old *mahallas*, they are building new *hovlis* at the outskirts of the city, some of them with the luxury of American-fashioned mansions, others very modest. There are increasing economic inequalities, but, regardless of these, there is also more awareness of (and pressure toward) consumption.

Supported by the growing role of migrants' remittances and the reorganization of the nation-state apparatus, post-Soviet social and economic relations have rapidly changed in Uzbekistan. So far little noticed by external observers, this phenomenon is most visible in the transforming cityscapes, where the appearance of new urban landscapes coincides with the appearance of a new type of citizen. Seen from Namangan, as compared to its equivalent of the 1990s, the new Uzbek citizen could be characterized to be as at once more sophisticated (*kulturnyi*), more conformist, nationally conscious and broadly apolitical; but also a consumer latently supportive of the status quo. Recalling the urban transformation processes that in the 1990s led to the emergence of an Asian middle class, caught in between "generalized dependency" and (individualized) "market rewards" (Tang and Parish 2000, 11ff.), this group is today the idealized target of the government-propagated Uzbek path to development.

Conclusion

According to an influential commentary on the recent history of Uzbekistan, the post-Soviet years of material hardship have fuelled people's disillusion with the political order. Thus, by undermining the implicit "social contract" that in the past had legitimized Soviet rulers vis-à-vis their local constituencies the years after independence have opened up a legitimacy problem for the country's new-but-old ruling elites (Kandiyoti 2002; 2003).

My evidence from Namangan offers a different reading of the situation. It suggests the existence of a partial, but nonetheless significant, post-independence social contract that rests on a larger basis than that entailed in the formula "obedience for security" (March 2003b, 321). It involves an ideologically and politically backed new type of citizen whose very existence redraws the boundaries between the areas of disaffection and those of consent in the current political order. Also, it offers an alternative explanation for Uzbek authoritarianism's successful consolidation in the transition from the early post-Soviet years to independence's "maturity"—one not exclusively concerned with the role of fear and coercion.

The social contract that characterizes today's *yangi davr* differs from the Soviet social contract revolving around the security of jobs, health and housing (Adam 1991; Cook 1993; Patico 2008, 64), as well as from its late socialist distortions entailing fraudulent diversions of welfare provisioning and of collective resources. Today's new epoch is characterized by coping, co-optation, and a degree of shared understanding between rulers and ruled concerning what should be the Uzbek path of development.

Engaging with post-Soviet Uzbekistan's ideological foundation, March (2003a, 2003b) has argued that Karimov is moved by the desire to "turn a merely unopposed authoritarianism into true hegemony" (March 2003b, 321), but that he falls short of his claim to achieve total hegemonic unification as he remains "particularly vulnerable to Uzbeks' expectations of increases in living standards" (2003b, 324). My findings from Namangan suggest that this statement needs qualification. One lesson drawn from Namangan's two last decades of development is that, despite hardship and anger, a significant proportion of the ruled have developed an ambivalent relation to the social order shaped by the new state, oscillating between attachment and compliance, and that this attitude sustains the asymmetric relationship between state and society.

Thus, contrary to the claims of some literature, Karimov's state has moved on from legitimacy struggles to hegemonic hold, and has become, in the words of Fontana (2006, 35), an "integral state": a state, that is "depicted as [the] embodiment of an ethical/cultural life reinforced by force and coercion," which, among its capabilities and purposes, is also able to "generate, proliferate and disseminate a given conception of the world" (Fontana 2006, 39). As once was the Soviet state, the Uzbek state is preoccupied with producing its own "set of values" and concerned with articulating its own "way of life" (Kotkin 1995, 23), for which it adopts a governance technique directed at controlling both the meanings and its materialization in people's lives, by virtue of a hegemonic use of power. In this respect, the government's claim of defining and controlling a certain path of development has something deeply reminiscent of the Stalin era, and today's efforts to promote the New Uzbek recalls the making of the "new Uzbek man" of the Soviet past (Stronski 2010, 174). However different the New Uzbeks are from their Soviet correlate, and however ambivalent they are in their relation to the current regime, today they increasingly mark Uzbekistan's urban landscape.

Notes

1. Many scholarly commentaries have highlighted the role of fear, coercion, or ideology (Lewis 2008; McGlinchey 2007; Liu 2005; March 2003a, 2003b). For Liu (2005), the Uzbekistani government relies on the binary "paternalism cum paranoia" as its dual basis of legitimization, which, he argues, ultimately rests on the government's capacity to exert threat and instigate fear within the population.

2. Noteworthy among the few to have recognized the role played by consent is the contribution of Adeeb Khalid, who has stated that we should not assume "that simply because the new regimes are corrupt they are unpopular" and who recognizes that the regimes "have banked on nationalism to acquire a substantial fund of legitimacy" (Khalid 2007, 130). A similar line of argument has been developed by Matveeva (2009, 1098), who argues that the legitimacy of Central Asian authoritarian regimes rests not on fear only but on a bundle of factors, including the accomplishments of "state building, order, stability, effectiveness and a degree of common interest between the rulers and the ruled." However, she sees the effectiveness of Central Asian regimes' legitimization strategies as still based on fragile foundations, as the common interest between ruled and rulers largely rests on the latter's capacity to manipulate the political landscape and "to portray an absence of meaningful alternatives" (Matveeva 2009, 1118).

3. Research for this chapter was conducted with support from the Institut Français d'Études sur l'Asie Centrale (IFEAC) in Tashkent. I undertook fieldwork in the Namangan region during the spring and summer of 2009. I also thank the Stiftung Wissenschaft und Politik, Berlin, and the Gerda Henkel Foundation for support and funding.

4. On this, besides Khalid (2007), see also Rasanayagam (2011, 127–129), and Lubin and Rubin (1999, 45–49, 52–54).

5. For a discussion of the creation of a state Islamic sector in post-Soviet Uzbekistan, see Khalid (2007), Kehl-Bodrogi (2008), Louw (2007), Rasanayagam (2011).

6. In a reconciliatory speech held by Karimov in Namangan sometime after the Andijan Events of May 2005, the city was termed *pok niyatli*, meaning "with pure, candid intentions" (personal communication to the author during fieldwork).

7. Everywhere in Uzbekistan many of the new, young Imams are genuine about their Islamic commitment but are obliged at the same time to accommodate to state policies. In Namangan, however, due to the particular political climate, the young generation of Imams has been exposed to more pressure than elsewhere. Fear of suspicion has led many to be overzealous in their reception and promotion of state-sanctioned Islam.

8. On this see Human Rights Watch (2005), Rasanayagam (2011, 1–2), Megoran (2008), and Liu, this volume.

9. After independence the Uzbek government promoted the incorporation of the traditional neighborhood community (*mahalla*) into the state structure and instrumentalized it for the purpose of its national ideology. See, indicatively, Koroteyeva and Makarova 1998, Arifkhanova 2000.

10. Here and elsewhere in the chapter I use pseudonyms to preserve the anonymity of my respondents.

11. Today the term is used indiscriminately by state authorities to refer to any form of Islamic religiosity that deviates from officially sanctioned practice. In Namangan, this use has been partly taken over in popular parlance and colloquially is employed to

refer to Islamic extremists or religiously defined state enemies. For a discussion of the term "Wahhabi" in the context of the Fergana Valley, see Hilgers (2009, 50ff).

12. *Tomorqa* (or *qo'shimcha tomorqa*) is a subsidiary small plot of agricultural land distributed to households. Its size can be up to 0.12 hectares of irrigated land. While *tomorqa* plots play a crucial role for subsistence in the countryside, they are also important for the city dwellers, who can also apply for them. Around cities *tomorqa* land is being increasingly converted into land for construction.

13. Information provided to the author by the Uzbek State Statistics Committee, Namangan region department, 2009.

14. See Presidential Decree on the "Year of Rural Wealth and Development," Nr. PQ-1046, January 26, 2009. Available on the website of the Ministry of Economics, www.mineconomy.uz/uz/node/287 (accessed August 17, 2012).

15. Public sector workers, whose salaries were now being paid to debit card accounts, were particularly affected by these measures. See on this Deirdre Tynan, "Uzbekistan: Cash Crunch Causing Retail Gridlock," September 20, 2009. http://www.eurasianet.org/departments/insightb/articles/eav092109a.shtml (accessed August 17, 2012).

16. *To'y* in Uzbek means life-cycle celebration, such as weddings and circumcisions.

17. "Two Killed in Attack on Police in Andijan Region," May 27, 2009. http://www.uznews.net/news_single.php?lng=en&cid=30&nid=10469 (accessed March 17, 2010).

18. On Karimov's visit to Namangan, see the official statement in *Xalq So'zi,* N. 132 (4795), July 3, 2009.

19. See "In Pictures: Tashkent Trees Axed," December 23, 2009. http://news.bbc.co.uk/2/hi/asia-pacific/8421479.stm (accessed March 1, 2010).

20. Uzbekistan's only car factory, originally a joint venture initiated with Daewoo, is located in the Andijan Province. Because of the high import taxes, most cars are produced locally, thus reinforcing the city's reputation for being a showpiece city for modern industrial development in Uzbekistan.

21. Cases have been reported in which persons were forced to have fewer children. On this see "Uzbekistan Favours Forced Sterilization over Condom Promotion," March 3, 2010. http://www.uznews.net/news_single.php?lng=en&cid=30&sub=top&nid=12706 (*accessed March 17, 2012*).

References

Adam, Jan, ed.1991. *Economic Reforms and Welfare Systems in the USSR, Poland and Hungary: Social Contract in Transformation*. London: Macmillan.

Ahmad, Imtiaz, and Helmut Reifeld, eds. 2003. *Middle Class Values in India and Western Europe.* New Delhi: Social Science Press.

Alexander, Catherine, and Viktor Buchli. 2007. "Introduction." In *Urban Life in Post-Soviet Asia,* edited by Catherine Alexander, Viktor Buchli, and Caroline Humphrey, 1–39. London: University College London Press.

Arifkhanova, Zoia. 2000. "Traditional Communities in Modern Uzbekistan." *Central Asia and the Caucasus* 4: 56–63.

Cook, Linda J. 1993. *The Soviet Social Contract and Why It Failed: Welfare Policy and Workers' Politics from Brezhnev to Yeltsin.* Cambridge, Mass.: Harvard University Press.

Daly, John C. K. 2008. *Kazakhstan's Emerging Middle Class.* Silk Road Paper, Central Asia-Caucasus Institute and Silk Road Studies Program. Washington, D.C.: Johns Hopkins University.

Fontana, Benedetto. 2006. "State and Society: The Concept of Hegemony in Gramsci." In *Hegemony and Power: Consensus and Coercion in Contemporary Politics,* edited by Mark Haugaard and Howard Lentner, 23–44. Lanham, Md.: Lexington Books.

Funabashi, Yoichi. 1993. "The Asianization of Asia." *Foreign Affairs* 72, no. 5: 75–85.

Hilgers, Irene. 2009. *Why Do Uzbeks Have to Be Muslims? Exploring Religiosity in the Ferghana Valley.* Berlin: LIT.

Human Rights Watch. 2005. *Bullets Were Falling Like Rain: The Andijan Massacre.* Human Rights Watch 17 (5D). Available at: http://www.hrw.org/sites/default/files/reports/uzbekistan0605.pdf (accessed March 1, 2010).

Jones, David. 1998. "Democratization, Civil Society, and Illiberal Middle Class Culture in Pacific Asia." *Comparative Politics* 30, no. 2: 147–169.

Jones Luong, Pauline, ed. 2004. *The Transformation of Central Asia: States and Societies from Soviet Rule to Independence.* Ithaca N.Y.: Cornell University Press.

Kandiyoti, Deniz. 2002. "How Far Do Analyses of Postsocialism Travel? The Case of Central Asia." In *Postsocialism: Ideals, Ideologies and Practices in Eurasia,* edited by Chris Hann, 238–257. London: Routledge.

———. 2003. "Pathways of Farm Restructuring in Uzbekistan: Pressures and Outcomes." In *Transition, Institutions, and the Rural Poor,* edited by Max Spoor, 143–162. Lanham, Md.: Lexington Books.

Karimov, Islom. 2009. *Jaxon moliyaviy iqtisodiy inqirozi, O'zbekiston sharoitida uni bartaraf etishning yo'llari va choralari.* Tashkent, Uzbekistan: O'zbekiston.

Kehl-Bodrogi, Krisztina. 2008. *"Religion is not so strong here": Muslim Religious Life in Khorezm after Socialism.* Berlin: LIT.

Khalid, Adeeb. 2007. *Islam after Communism: Religion and Politics in Central Asia.* Berkeley: University of California Press.

Koroteyeva, Victoria, and Ekaterina Makarova. 1998. "The Assertion of Uzbek National Identity: Nativization or State-Building Process?" In *Post-Soviet Central Asia,* edited by Touraj Atabaki and John O'Cane, 137–143. London: I. B. Tauris.

Kotkin, Stephen. 1995. *Magnetic Mountain: Stalinism as a Civilization,* Berkeley: University of California Press.

Lewis, David. 2008. *The Temptations of Tyranny in Central Asia.* London: Hurst.

Liu, Morgan. 2005. "Hierarchies of Place, Hierarchies of Empowerment: Geographies of Talk about Postsocialist Change in Uzbekistan." *Nationalities Papers* 33, no. 3: 423–438.

———. 2007. "A Central Asian Tale of Two Cities: Locating Lives and Aspirations in a Shifting Post-Soviet Cityscape." In *Everyday Life in Central Asia, Past and Present,* edited by Jeff Sahadeo and Russell Zanca, 66–84. Bloomington: Indiana University Press.

Louw, Maria Elisabeth. 2007. *Everyday Islam in Post-Soviet Central Asia.* London: Routledge.

Lubin, Nancy, and Barnett Rubin. 1999. *Calming the Ferghana Valley: Development and Dialogue in the Heart of Central Asia.* New York: Century Foundation Press.

March, Andrew. 2003a. "State Ideology and the Legitimation of Authoritarianism: The Case of Post-Soviet Uzbekistan." *Journal of Political Ideologies* 8, no. 2: 209–232.

———. 2003b. "From Leninism to Karimovism: Hegemony, Ideology, and Authoritarian Legitimation." *Post-Soviet Affairs* 19, no. 4: 307–336.

Massicard, Elise, and Tommaso Trevisani. 2003. "The Uzbek Mahalla: Between State and Society." In *Central Asia: Aspects of Transition*, edited by Tom Everett-Heath, 205–218. London: RoutledgeCurzon.

Matveeva, Anna. 2009. "Legitimising Central Asian Authoritarianism: Political Manipulation and Symbolic Power." *Europe-Asia Studies* 61, no. 7: 1095–1121.

McGlinchey, Eric. 2007. "Divided Faith: Trapped between State and Islam in Uzbekistan." In *Everyday Life in Central Asia, Past and Present*, edited by Jeff Sahadeo and Russell Zanca, 305–318. Bloomington: Indiana University Press.

Megoran, Nick. 2008. "Framing Andijon, Narrating the Nation: Islam Karimov's Account of the Events of 13 May 2005." *Central Asian Survey* 27, no. 1: 15–32.

Patico, Jennifer. 2008. *Consumption and Social Change in a Post-Soviet Middle Class.* Stanford, Calif.: Stanford University Press.

Rasanayagam, Johan. 2006. "'I Am Not a Wahhabi': State Power and Muslim Orthodoxy in Uzbekistan." In *The Postsocialist Religious Question: Faith and Power in Central Asia and East-Central Europe*, edited by Chris Hann and the "Civil Religion" Group, 99–124. Berlin: LIT.

———. 2011. *Islam in Post-Soviet Uzbekistan: The Morality of Experience*, Cambridge: Cambridge University Press.

Shlapentokh, Vladimir. 1999. "Social Inequality in Post-Communist Russia: The Attitudes of the Political Elite and the Masses (1991–1998)." *Europe-Asia Studies* 51, no. 7: 1167–1181.

Silverman, Bertram, and Murray Yanovitch. 2000. *New Rich, New Poor, New Russia: Winners and Losers on the Russian Road to Capitalism.* Armonk, N.Y.: M. E. Sharpe.

Starr, Frederick. 1999. "Civil Society in Central Asia." In *Civil Society in Central Asia*, edited by Holt Ruffin and Daniel Waugh, 27–33. Seattle: University of Washington Press.

Stronski, Paul. 2010. *Tashkent: Forging a Soviet City 1930–1966.* Pittsburgh: University of Pittsburgh Press.

Tang, Wenfang, and William Parish. 2000. *Chinese Urban Life under Reform: The Changing Social Contract.* Cambridge: Cambridge University Press.

Yurchak, Alexei. 2003. "Soviet Hegemony of Form: Everything Was Forever, Until It Was No More." *Comparative Studies in Society and History* 45, no. 3: 480–510.

11. Massacre through a Kaleidoscope

Fragmented Moral Imaginaries of the State in Central Asia

Morgan Liu

There is a curious link between state and sentiment. People today often have strong sentiments about how their governments should work effectively and fairly. Those thoughts and feelings, however, are partly shaped by the states themselves. Governments, especially more "authoritarian" ones, put out characterizations about the nation's purpose under the state's guidance. Many would call this propaganda, and every modern state to some extent, including democratic ones, attempts to coopt consent about its legitimacy by trying to manage how it is perceived.[1] These thoughts and feelings about a political community's distinctive purpose can have profound influence in organizing the experience of citizens, undergirding everyday moments (as in why one goes to work), to extraordinary ones (as in why one goes to war). Most take for granted their attitudes about society and politics and remain unaware of the influence that ideologies circulated by governmental apparatuses may be having on them.

Sentiments about the state get interesting, however, if something happens that utterly upsets assumptions about the state's nature and purpose. The contradictions revealed in an acute political crisis can produce a flurry of debates regarding the proper role of government in society. The fury of these arguments shows that there is much at stake politically and morally when a state or its leadership turns out to be quite different from what people were assuming. The question is how people make sense of the dissonance. Can a calamitous event alter basic understanding about the way their social and political world is put together? Living in interesting times often yields interesting mental coping, and an analyst can use these moments of crisis to uncover people's normally unconscious assumptions about how their own political community works.[2] Those taken-for-granted ideas (and the feelings associated with them) form what I will call a political imaginary. The concept of imaginaries will be explained later to make sense of a particular event that happened in the city of Andijan, Uzbekistan. At stake with this event is that curious link between state and sentiment, and how that link can be grotesquely disrupted. If we think of an imaginary as a lens people use to understand politics and society, and if that lens appears to offer a clear, focused picture of reality, then a crisis can shatter the lens. The results are kaleidoscopic.

Even though the crisis began in Andijan, this study focuses not on that city's residents, but on ethnic Uzbeks in Osh, a nearby city located in the neighboring republic of Kyrgyzstan. Why look at post-Soviet Uzbekistan's pivotal event from another country? Uzbeks living in Kyrgyzstan offer an insightful case study for us. Kyrgyzstani Uzbeks are connected to both republics, but in different ways. They have been citizens of Kyrgyzstan since the Central Asian Republics became independent in 1991, yet they felt more linked to Uzbekistan in terms of their ethnicity, culture, and aspirations during the 1990s. But both connections have been deeply troubled. Because ethnic Kyrgyz dominate Kyrgyzstan politically, Uzbeks there feel systematic discrimination, and the tense interethnic relations led to two major armed conflicts between them in 1990 and 2010.[3] The predicament of Osh Uzbeks occurs in the broader context of prolonged post-Soviet economic crisis experienced by all in Kyrgyzstan, a small, resource-poor, and land-locked republic. Sustained by foreign loans, aid, remittances, trade, and hydroelectric power, Kyrgyzstan has relatively few prospects to integrate advantageously into global economic networks.

At the same time, Kyrgyzstani Uzbeks are shut out from Uzbekistan because its president, Islam Karimov, has enforced strict border controls that restrict access even for them, ethnic Uzbeks just outside of Uzbekistan. Their shared ethnicity has translated into few benefits, and in fact increasing liability, for Kyrgyzstani Uzbeks with Karimov, who mostly disregarded them in the 1990s and then saw them as a potential threat in the 2000s because anti-Karimov Islamist movements appeared to take haven among Kyrgyzstani Uzbeks. Uzbeks in independent Kyrgyzstan are thus in a predicament of double exclusion: they face exclusion as minorities in one republic and as non-citizens in the other. Because they occupy a fraught, marginal political status within the entire post-Soviet nation-state system, they present a productive site from which to think critically about state and sentiment within the global order after the Cold War's end.[4]

I turn now to the so-called Andijan Events or "Massacre." But rather than try to give an objective account, I look at how Uzbeks in Osh, Kyrgyzstan made sense of what happened, and why this shattered the world as they once knew it.

Andijan through the Kaleidoscope

Consider the following two accounts of what took place in Andijan in May 2005.

> A group of twenty-three Islamic terrorists were on trial for several months for their attempt to overthrow the government of Uzbekistan and to establish an Islamic state. Supporters of these men were holding rallies at Andijan's central Babur Square outside the courthouse, and in the early hours of May 13, an armed group stormed the prison holding the accused men, freed them, and then occupied the provincial administration building. Meanwhile, a large angry crowd of people gathered on the city square to demand the resignation of Uzbekistan's president, Islam Karimov. Karimov himself flew to Andijan that morning, and personally instructed local authorities to ask the insurgents to surrender and the crowd to disperse. When the extremists, called "Akromia" or Akromists (after their leader, Akrom Yuldashev), refused to stand down, the Uzbekistani military was left with no choice but to put down the insurrection by armed force, killing 169 of the terrorists and their supporters.
>
> Not one innocent citizen was killed, although a number of policemen lost their lives in the line of duty. Many of the hooligans fled from Andijan across the border to nearby Kyrgyzstan, some still bearing arms. It was clear that the prison breakout and anti-government rally had been carefully planned and with help from foreign Islamic fundamentalists, including those based in southern Kyrgyzstan, whose ultimate goal was the overthrow of the government of Uzbekistan and the establishment of a Central Asian caliphate governed by shari'a. President Karimov did the exact right thing in suppressing the Akromi insurrection in the manner that he did, because the alternative would have been civil war, the disintegration of Uzbekistan (and, by spill-over effect, her neighboring states), and the establishment of Islamic law by extremists in power.

That was one account; here is another of the same events.

> Twenty-three Andijani businessmen were held in prison by Uzbekistani authorities. The businessmen ran very successful enterprises in the city, employing hundreds of people, and providing various social services and financial help to the community. The 23 represented the most wealthy members of a circle formed by many small Andijani businesses that pooled capital and circulated credit among themselves, given that state financial mechanisms did not function adequately. They formed a network of trust within a corruption-ridden society. The members were

religiously observant—they read *namaz* (the Muslim prayer) five times a day—because they believed that honesty in business was a key Muslim value, but their organization was neither religious, nor political, nor subversive.

The state of Uzbekistan, however, felt threatened by this group because it was fulfilling the social protection functions of the state—becoming a sort of mini-state in Andijan. And so the authorities responded by arresting these men. When the twenty-three were unjustly tried for months in early 2005, more and more sympathizers began to gather peacefully for their cause on the city square—family members, employees, and those who had benefited from the group's kindness. The rallies swelled in numbers and anti-government expression, fed by the deep general discontent and desperation of Andijanis with their harsh poverty since Uzbekistan's independence in 1991, where all political dissent was normally quashed. The frustration led to the armed takeover of government buildings on May 13, but the vast majority of protesters were unarmed ordinary people who finally had a venue to air their grievances, especially when it became known that President Karimov himself was coming to the city on that day.

But Karimov would permit no such expression, and ordered his troops to open fire on unarmed civilians, killing women, children, and the elderly. Machine guns mowed down fleeing and screaming crowds, some shouting "Don't shoot!" and the number of dead exceeded 500, maybe much more. Some escaped into Kyrgyzstan, all unarmed, all bearing testimony to what had really happened. It was a massacre of innocents. It was merciless and unnecessary.

The preceding passages exemplify two contrasting sets of interpretations about the Andijan Events that I heard from Osh Uzbeks in the fall of 2005, several months after they had occurred.[5] These particular versions are composite narratives assembled from my numerous conversations with Osh Uzbeks, but the actual accounts all followed the thrust of either one of these two basic scripts. The first version also captured the gist of, not surprisingly, the official narrative propagated by Uzbekistani television; and the second, that of other media sources and eyewitnesses.[6] In the actual accounts that I received, however, I found variation in every detail of the story, so that, like in Akira Kurosawa's often-referenced film *Rashomon,* I never heard the exactly same tale twice. Osh Uzbek accounts differed regarding the activities of the imprisoned men, the nature of their organization (even whether the name "Akromi" was applicable or merely a state invention for propaganda purposes), why the crowd gathered on the city square, who the people of the crowd were, what demands they made in public speeches, whether they had legitimate grievances, what Karimov did or said in response, whom the militia shot at, how many people were killed, who the refugees into Kyrgyzstan were, and whether the crackdown was justified.[7]

While most of my contacts held either a pro- or anti-Karimov stance, which influenced the alleged facts and interpretations they reported, there were also surprising "crossover" permutations in the details incorporated into the accounts, so that a pro-Karimov script could embed elements that undermined Karimov's own claims of facts or intentions. For example, many who gave a pro-Karimov version would admit, contrary to Uzbekistan's official account, that many hundreds were killed, including non-political innocents. These narrators would explain that the activists (variously called terrorists, Islamists, extremists, Akromis, Wahhabis, Hizb-ut-Tahrir, hooligans, criminals, etc.) had "agitated" among the ordinary people, deceiving them, or bribing them with money to gather on the square for the rally. When the government troops opened fire on them, they interposed these innocent people as live shields, and ran away like cowards. Others said the relatively small number of "Akromis" had simply gathered their relatives on the square (a crowd that somehow managed to number into the hundreds, but, they claimed, we are talking about famously large Uzbek families here!). No decent citizen was to be found in public when the troops fired, they claimed, only the "bad guys." Sherali, a retired Osh industrialist, commented that if Karimov had not fired on the demonstrators, his state would have fallen, just as Akaev fell a few months before in the largely bloodless "Tulip Revolution," when he refused to fire on the crowds at the gates of the White House in Bishkek. Sherali said that if freedom were to be given to Uzbekstanis, they would take the wealth away from the country and be seduced by Islamic extremism. Among those who felt Andijanis had no real grievance against the government, a few said that poverty was really not so bad in Uzbekistan, while others said that despite the hardships today, the people will get richer in time, "you'll see!" Some towing the Karimov line variously said that the Islamic extremists received aid from Saudi Arabia, Kuwait, or even the United States government and its proxies like George Soros, who were continuing their recent financing of democratic revolutions in the former Soviet sphere that started with Ukraine, Georgia, and Kyrgyzstan; this echoed such a claim made by Russian media at the time.

The great variation in accounting for almost every basic fact of the story was a function of the particular mass media environment in Osh, how they are trusted or distrusted by various groups of Osh Uzbeks, and the circulations of talk within circles of confidence in the Uzbek community. The state-controlled Uzbekistani media, which generally shows a stridently upbeat portrait of a prosperous, well-ordered republic, had to maintain a careful balance between talking up the direness of the threat in some moments (to justify the government's deadly response) and showing "business as usual" in others (to show its firm control).[8] During the few days after the incident, Uzbekistani TV maintained total news silence about it. At that time, an Osh Uzbek reporter working for Mezon, an independent Osh Uzbek language media company, went to the city of Fergana, Uzbekistan (about 80 km from Andijan), and found people there responding, "which events in Andijan?"[9] When the incident was covered, it was contextualized as being about religion, using a convenient script (given greater global resonance after 9/11 and the U.S. war next door in Afghanistan) that equates Islamic piety with extremism.[10] And months later, I watched the Uzbekistani news program "Davr" in September 2005, and the trial of the Andijan "terrorists" was covered only in a rather brief segment buried deep in the timeslot, after the international news segment late in the program, and before a casual story about a wildlife conference. The trial coverage only aired statements from the prosecutors saying, "How could you sell out your country?" The defendants sat silently in a metal cage looking quite inhuman, with shaven heads, prison clothes, and individual faces occluded by the bars. Ethnic Uzbeks in Osh tend to watch Uzbekistani TV, and in general, some articulate views con cerning Uzbekistan that closely parrot what they hear from state television.[11] On the other hand, Kyrgyzstan's Kyrgyz and Russian language media were highly critical of Uzbekistan in the wake of the crackdown, and gave accounts closer to the second version above. Some of Osh's local Uzbek language media, as typical of their delicate position of being ethnic Uzbek institutions in Kyrgyzstan, attempted to hew a measured middle path. OshTV, perhaps cowed by licensing problems with Kyrgyzstani authorities for being too independent and outspoken during the 1990s, offered only muted reports of the Andijan Events. According to one young Osh Uzbek man, OshTV's reportage amounted to saying: something horrible happened over there, but we must not rush to judgment for lack of reliable facts. However, another Osh Uzbek media outlet, MezonTV (or Halq TV), sent reporters to the Uzbekistani border to interview refugees, who gave harrowing reports of the incident and scathing invective against President Karimov. Many Osh Uzbeks received their information about the event from this channel (and its viewership skyrocketed), from a similarly frank radio station, Ozodlik, or from personal acquaintances who were present in Andijan.[12] For some younger Osh Uzbeks, the internet provided crucial news. The independent news service fergana.ru surged in hits, and its young Osh Uzbek journalist, Alisher Saipov, who had already distinguished himself with his uniquely bold writing on Uzbekistan, could be said to have made his name on his coverage here until his tragic assassination (some say by agents of the Uzbekistani government) outside his office in Osh on October 24, 2007.[13]

Interestingly, the main television stations of Russia, ORT and TRT, which are carried by Kyrgyzstani channels in the evening, reported the Andijan Events so openly that the information minister of Uzbekistan read a rebuttal of their coverage on Uzbekistan's Birinchi Kanal (Channel One), claiming that the Russian media was distorting the facts from their envy of Uzbekistan.[14] One of my Osh Uzbek interlocutors mentioned that "foreign media" were spreading lies about Andijan, so viewers like him discounted Russian and Western accounts of the incident.

These news sources fed into the communities of commentary and debate among Uzbeks in Osh. On neighborhood streets, at weddings, in teahouses, at workplaces, at regular social gatherings called *ziyofat,* there was great dispute during the summer of 2005 over what happened in Andijan and what it meant. The reputation of Uzbekistani television became fatally tarnished in the eyes of many Osh Uzbeks after an official claimed that the Andijan insurrection was supported by an Islamic terrorist training camp operating near Osh at an abandoned Kyrgyzstani military facility. The Kyrgyzstani defense minister went on TV to deny this vehemently, saying that the site was in active use by the Kyrgyzstani military. By the fall, I found that most Osh Uzbeks in their teens and 20s adhered to some anti-Karimov variant, most in their 40s and older adhered to a pro-Karimov variant, and those in their 30s went either way (perhaps more to the pro side), although there were definite exceptions in all these categories. Members in a single family could be divided in their allegiances, each side being dismissive of the other. The generational divide in attitude is partly explained by the segregated nature of Uzbek social life. Because Uzbek venues of social contact tended to be clearly distinguished by gender and age-set, information and interpretation were most circulated within socially homogenous circles of trust, with comparatively less discussion on this kind of topic between those circles.

Habibulla's family exemplified this split.[15] He was a son in his early 20s of an Osh family that I knew rather well in a *mahalla* (Uzbek-majority urban neighborhood) that I had frequented in the late 1990s, but he himself had studied and now worked in Andijan as a school gym teacher. When I spoke with him in late 2005, he was back in his father's house in Osh to get married and spend his honeymoon.[16] We were chatting casually on the street with a group of the mahalla's youth when I asked Habibulla what he knew about the Andijan Events, hoping to get an informed perspective. His expression immediately changed, and grabbing my arm, he announced, "Come on, let's go inside and talk," and we left his friends behind. Habibulla was an eyewitness to the incident, standing in the crowd in Babur Square on that day, and was nearly shot when a woman next to him was struck in the neck and collapsed onto him.

He strongly affirmed that the demonstration was peaceful and the people, unarmed.[17] I asked him, did he tell people what he saw after returning to Osh? To some, he answered, to those who asked, but not in general. He felt the matter to be too sensitive and painful to volunteer his account, he said, so that many in his mahalla probably did not hear about his experiences.

Given these sentiments, Habibulla's account was kept mostly among his peer group and less widely circulated. If other eyewitnesses coming to Osh had a similar reluctance to talk, this partially explains the lack of consensus in the Osh Uzbek community about the incident. But even if eyewitness accounts had been more widely circulated, they would have been subject to the spin, reframing, and dismissals of those who interpreted current events through the idea that President Karimov could do no wrong. Eyewitnesses or their transmitters could easily be discounted as lying, deluded, or seeing only an inaccurate, partial picture. The fact that many of the anti-Karimov interpreters were young probably did not help their credibility in the eyes of the older, pro-Karimov partisans. In fact, Habibulla's own father, with whom I spoke alone on another occasion, had a different view of the events. He saw the incident as having been instigated by the "Akromi Islamic sect" (*sekta,* Russian), who were "not true Muslims at all." He claimed that the Uzbekistani military had killed only the sect members and their relatives, not innocents. Nonetheless, he called Uzbekistan a "dictatorship like Pinochet" whose people were indeed living in great poverty. On yet another hand, he was sure that Uzbekistan had a bright distant future because of its resources, while Kyrgyzstan was hopeless. The father's mixed and cynical evaluation of the entire situation denied full credence to any vested viewpoint. In his very household, his son, an eyewitness nearly killed by the incident in question, sided bitterly against Karimov. As for Habibulla, he was still returning to his teaching post in Andijan with his new bride at the end of their honeymoon. A job was a job. But if there was a generational split in interpretation between Habibulla and his father, I also found families where the sons agreed strongly with their fathers regarding the Andijan incident and supported Karimov overall, although those did not include eyewitnesses.

The immediate aftermath of the incident impacted Osh and the rest of southern Kyrgyzstan in the flow of refugees fleeing Andijan and crossing the border, some on foot. Most of the refugees stayed in camps near the border and were eventually sent, after much wrangling during that summer, to Romania and other third countries; some were absorbed into Uzbek mahallas in cities like Osh. Many of those went with relatives, while others were quietly settled into volunteer host families by an Osh-based non-governmental organization (NGO), who offered them legal protection and anonymity.[18] The low profile these refugees kept probably contributed to the uneven circulation of first-hand accounts of the events in Osh.

What the Massacre Next Door Reveals

So what does the kaleidoscopic field of narratives about the Andijan Events reveal? For a start, they point to the tremendous stakes that Osh Uzbeks have in what goes on in neighboring Uzbekistan. These stakes are partly due to their sense of ethnic connection to the Uzbek-majority republic next door, which they feel unjustly cut off from because of Soviet-drawn boundaries that became international borders after independence.[19] Uzbeks in Kyrgyzstan are a discriminated minority in the Kyrgyz-dominated country of their citizenship, so that their aspirations for belonging were, during the 1990s at least, channeled toward the "land of the Uzbeks," the meaning of Uzbekistan. But the Andijan Events show that the connection Osh Uzbeks have to Uzbekistan is about more than ethnicity. Uzbekistan intrigued them because it appeared to them at the time as a model country with a prosperous and peaceful future. The most basic concern for them was not the promotion of Uzbek interests per se, but the question, what kind of postsocialist and postcolonial state should Central Asia have in a world without the Soviet Union?

The narratives reveal that the question was fraught with wrenching disagreement. They show how fragmented the interpretations and postures quickly became regarding the Uzbekistani state because of the crisis. Whereas Osh Uzbeks previously tended to voice strong, unequivocal approval about the way Uzbekistan was being governed, after the Andijan Events much more inchoate, fluid, and nuanced positions emerged. The diverse field of positions reflected differing responses to the collective trauma triggered when the Uzbekistani state acted so contrary to widespread expectations, expectations in which they had high stakes. I want now to make sense of how Osh Uzbek understandings of what makes a good state were affected by this event. To do that, I first need to grapple with the concept of imaginaries, and then see how using this illuminates how they saw first Uzbekistan's leadership and how that view was shattered.

An "imaginary" refers not to something fictitious or fanciful, but rather to people's tacitly held understandings and sentiments about the social-political world.[20] An imaginary is the grasp people have of the conventional actors, groups, actions, places, contexts, times, meanings, and interests involved in their collective life, encompassing not only explicit ideologies about society, but embodied social practice and the "fluid middle ground" between them.[21] It includes what philosophers call the background, that is, the "largely unstructured and inarticulate understanding of our whole situation within which particular features of our world show up for us in the sense they have."[22] It provides the frames of reference that give meaning to what people do, thus making social existence possible.

The notion of imaginary helps to uncover the everyday workings of the political by directing our attention beyond state ideologies toward the affective experience of everyday life under governmental power. This gets at that curious connection between state and sentiment that includes the subtle ways that the state is present in people's lives and the unintended social effects when institutions implement state ideologies.[23] Imaginaries of the state, because they span both discourse and practice, thus provide a unifying framework to consider models of a state's purpose, intentions, workings as articulated with ordinary life activity. They are about how the state is both conceptualized and lived under, and the connections between thinking, feeling, and enacting the state.

The totality of conceptions, sentiments, attitudes, and postures that Osh Uzbeks had concerning states and leadership constituted their political imaginary. During the first decade of Central Asia's independence in the 1990s, Uzbeks in Osh saw President Karimov of Uzbekistan as an ideal state leader. Their views about Karimov came up in many conversations that I had at the time with Osh Uzbeks, regarding all sorts of topics. So pervasive was the idea of Karimov's effective leadership that I realized their views formed an entire political imaginary that informed the way that they looked at everything political. The idea acted as the explanatory key to their entire post-Soviet condition. They were talking about Karimov as if he were a *khan figure,* a wise, virtuous, benevolent despot whose harsh ways are believed to work for the ultimate good of his republic. This "khan" imaginary was staunchly and widely held among Osh Uzbeks especially during the 1990s. The imaginary focused obsessively on Karimov's intelligence, selflessness, foresightedness, courage, and even paternal ruthlessness as the superior qualities of his moral constitution as leader. The policies that emanated from such a character would be, almost by definition, correct and beneficial to the people under his authority. Karimov-as-khan was a paragon of (masculinist) human action in the world that transcends ethnicity, situation, corruptibility, and even politics. He was an embodiment of the efficacious transformation that post-Soviet Uzbekistan needs to embrace for a bright future.

The khan imaginary exemplifies one answer to the most basic questions that Central Asians generally have faced since the collapse of the Soviet Union in 1991. Those questions are: "How to reform state and economy after communism?" (the postsocialist question), and "Who are we, and how do we fit into the world after Soviet rule and the Cold War?" (the postcolonial question). Osh Uzbeks' predicament of political geography, illuminated by the glare of the Andijan Events, becomes diagnostic of how this Central Asian community made sense of these questions in a precarious situation that would five years later be set ablaze with the June 2010 interethnic killings in Osh and Jalalabat. Living at the geographical cusp between the state paternalism of independent Uzbekistan and the relative liberalism of Kyrgyzstan, Osh Uzbeks were pre-

Figure 11.1. View of some Uzbek-majority neighborhoods in Osh. In the distance is the border with Uzbekistan, looking in the approximate direction toward Andijan (not visible).

sented in their everyday lives through experience and report with the effects of these contrasting postsocialist trajectories. They realized they possess "freedoms" to get rich that their relatives in Andijan did not have (and many have done so handsomely), yet they admired the apparent state-coordinated orderliness, purpose, and prospects in Uzbekistan. They pondered the relative merits of either side of the border on which they sit, debating about the proper role the state should play in the republic's economic development and connections with the world market after state socialism. Their concerns, however, extended beyond the mechanics of reform toward the question about what the stature of Central Asian or Uzbek distinctiveness is on the world stage and in global history, now that the grand narratives of the Soviet colonial project have been disavowed by Central Asian elites.[24] These postsocialist and postcolonial concerns converged on the urgent question, by what conceptual paradigm should post-Soviet Central Asian society be successfully transformed?

Osh Uzbeks loved Karimov not merely because he was Uzbek. This imaginary was not primarily about "ethnic sentiment," even though Osh Uzbeks faced discrimination within Kyrgyzstan and constraints on conventional political organizing.[25] Also, they loved Karimov not only because he was a "Soviet-style autocrat." The imaginary was animated by more than nostalgia for Soviet-era stability and state provision under the socialist paternalist contract.[26] The khan imaginary was compelling to so many Uzbeks in Osh because it presented a particularly Central Asian model of societal transformation under wise, harsh, paternalistic oversight on reforms and a tradition-rooted future worthy of world admiration. It was important for Osh Uzbeks that Karimov be this khan figure, who would exercise a kind of large-scale agency that creates the right conditions for peace and prosperity to be sustained across the republic. The imaginary was, however, paradoxical even before the Andijan Events. It was a unilateral expression of allegiance to Uzbekistan's president from *outside* of Uzbekistan that was not at all reciprocated: Karimov's policies showed utter disregard for and often hurt Uzbeks in Kyrgyzstan. Yet despite this, Osh Uzbeks still strongly idealized Karimov as harsh-but-wise leader. This reflex showed that the khan imaginary was not primarily about Uzbek ethnicity or even economic interests, but about effective authority.[27]

With this much riding on the rightness of the khan model for so many Osh Uzbeks, it is no wonder the Andijan Events represented for them a worldview-shattering bombshell. Yet the span of Osh Uzbek views and sentiments was already beginning to diversify before the Andijan Events. In my subsequent visits to Osh in the early 2000s, it became apparent that changes were afoot in the mix of socio-political imaginaries circulating among them. Osh Uzbeks, despite their continuing grievances with ethnic Kyrgyz rule and somewhat to their own surprise, found themselves becoming more comfortable with their status as Kyrgyzstani citizens as the second decade of independence advanced, at least until the harrowing violence of 2010 in Osh. It became increasingly clear that Kyrgyzstan's liberalizations were enabling some Uzbeks there to accumulate wealth, while most in Uzbekistan were suffering greater hardships.[28]

It took the Andijan Events of May 2005 to trigger a Copernican shift in the range of attitudes that Osh Uzbeks held regarding President Karimov, Uzbekistan, and themselves as citizens of Kyrgyzstan. Although not everyone changed their stances in response, as we saw, the vehemence with which many Osh Uzbeks talked about the incident months afterward revealed how hard they wrestled with its meaning communally, and certainly the overall field of positions shifted decisively. The Andijan Events were not the sole cause of the shift, but cleanly marked the culmination of economic, political, social, and intellectual trends already underway and increasingly apparent to Osh Uzbeks throughout the 2000s. Just in the year leading up to them, a long series of incidents throughout Uzbekistan revealed increasing frustration of Uzbekistanis with their difficult circumstances and inflexible government.[29] Though apparently unconnected with Andijan, these events accumulated Osh Uzbeks' sense of trouble in the state of Uzbekistan.

In the relatively short years after the apparent public consensus of the 1990s, the gradual *crescendo* of these trends, punctuated by the sudden *sforzando* of the Andijan Events sent reverberations through the Osh Uzbek community, hurling into radical question the certitude of the khan-led state as the preferred means for post-Soviet societal transformation. The high level of public unanimity holding Karimov in quasi-cult-like admiration became fragmented, producing a multi-vocal field of sentiments and positions that prompted both shifts in stance and entrenchments of former opinions. This revealed fissures in generation and background that, if they were present in muted form before, have become patently pronounced. For some, the events shattered the image of the benevolent khan with a jarring revelation that Karimov's rule was actually cruel and self-serving. For others, the events only confirmed that the khan's decisive, all-wise paternal iron fist saved the nation from "Islamic extremists" and probable civil war.

What actually happened in Andijan around May 13, 2005, as we saw in the narratives, was vehemently disputed among Osh Uzbeks in almost every aspect of the account. Fact and rumor, report and opinion, information and disinformation all lay strewn like a shattered mirror on the fragmented field of communal discourse after the incident. This was Andijan through the cracked looking glass. Now, a kaleidoscope serves as a poor instrument, if the goal were objective observation.[30] But my goal is to uncover ways of looking at the world.

The sharp contradictions and debates revealed a formerly united community scrambling to find their moral bearings when their reference point, Uzbekistan's President Karimov, suddenly proved false. Some Osh Uzbeks stubbornly kept believing this republic to be the "future great state," as the prevalent slogan goes, where Uzbekistan's harsh measures would be trusted as unfortunate, temporary, but necessary measures for the long-term common good.[31] Some rejected Karimov because he turned out not to be the wise benevolent despot they thought he was, but still held onto the model of the khan as the only paradigm for effective governance in Central Asia (so that another man needs to be found to fill the khan's shoes). Others forsook the khan idea altogether and turned toward Islamist-influenced visions of the pious, just society. Many abandoned, for the moment at least, any grand narrative of post-Soviet transformation and confined their energies toward building a viable existence under the Kyrgyzstani state, a stance put into uncertain crisis after the 2010 interethnic conflagration. These all were the shell-shocked postures revealed by the kaleidoscopic looking glass.

There is, I believe, another aspect of Osh Uzbek imaginaries that amplified the shock of the events. Andijan is in some ways an Uzbekistani counterpart to Osh, although the opposite should be said, as Andijan is the better-known city of the two.[32] The two cities are separated by only 40 km, are of comparable size (Osh with over a quarter million, Andijan, over three hundred thousand), are both coddled by the Fergana Valley, and are both provincial capitals. Historically they were closely connected long before the post-Soviet border separated them. Babur, the illustrious 16th century founder of the Mughal Empire in northern India, was born in Andijan and grew up in Osh. During the Soviet period, the pro forma republican border allowed extensive flows of people and goods between the cities, and Osh Uzbeks have more relatives in Andijan than any other city due to continual cross-city marriages (which Uzbekistan's tightened border regime has somewhat stemmed). Andijan can be said to occupy a special place in the aspirations of Osh Uzbeks after independence because that city offered to them a picture of what Osh might look like were it under Uzbekistani rule, the widely but quietly held desire among Osh Uzbeks during the 1990s. In that period, food and basic supplies were more available and cheaper in Andijan, because of state-supported prices, in contrast to the free market inflation in Kyrgyzstan. Osh Uzbeks were taking shopping excursions into Andijan, which prompted a comment by President Karimov that caused furious debate among Osh Uzbeks, charging that they were "taking away" Andijani bread.[33] Andijan's state university (as well as others in Uzbekistan) enrolled Osh Uzbek students, because until the establishment of private Uzbek-oriented universities in Osh (1997) and Jalalabat (1999), there were no opportunities for them to receive higher education in the Uzbek language within Kyrgyzstan. Andijan was also the envy of Osh Uzbeks because of its state-organized foreign-joint ventures, which boasted a sprawling automobile manufacturing plant set up by the South Korean company Daewoo near the Andijan airport.[34] Daewoo cars provided a lower cost, locally manufactured foreign alternative to the Mercedes, BMW, and Toyota cars coveted by Osh's newly rich families. Osh Uzbeks were clearly envious of Uz-Daewoo, and often referred to it in conversations with me in the late 1990s as a prime example of how Uzbekistan was deftly managing foreign investment, in contrast to Kyrgyzstan's mismanagement. "Andijan envy" was thus a proximate and palpable aspect of the imaginary that fixated on independent Uzbekistan as the reference standard for good post-Soviet statehood. The fact that the May 2005 events took place in Andijan made the subsequent shift in imaginaries all the more ironic and poignant for Osh Uzbeks.

Imaginaries of State after Andijan

Up until the Andijan Events, Osh Uzbeks tended to see a good state as not merely an instrument of political control but also a promoter of society's common good. Here, indeed, lies the core of the khan imaginary, because it envisions a state leader's virtuous character enabling beneficial reforms, security, and prosperity for the entire nation. When the apparently naked exercise of deadly power occurred in the admired city of Andijan next door, the moral authority of Karimov as benevolent khan was thus sent into radical question.

The question is where the Andijan Events has left the Uzbek community in Kyrgyzstan since then.

Even before the khan model was disrupted, many Kyrgyzstani Uzbeks, especially among the younger generation (those in their 20s during the 2000s), were also looking to Islam as a key to societal transformation. Certainly there has been a noticeable swell in Islamic dress and observance among Uzbeks in southern Kyrgyzstani cities, particularly since the mid-2000s.[35] Although the meanings of these signs of public piety are varied and complex, one idea that has broad appeal across Central Asia (and among Muslims worldwide) is Islam providing the basis of a just society. It is a society that is free of the endemic corruption of patronage inherent in every sphere of post-Soviet life, and where the state actually advances some version of the common good, rather than the narrow interests of a class or clan. An interesting question is how religious knowledge and practice are understood to effect societal transformation. Islamic imaginaries appear to give to Islam a similar kind of magical agency—magical in the anthropological sense of belief in efficacy by contiguity or association. This magical thinking also operates in the khan imaginary, where the khan figure is seen as having the power to shape the republic's socioeconomic conditions that eventuate in good outcomes for all.[36] The khan paradigm works top-down from the power of the paternal state, while the Islamic model works bottom-up from the influence of popular piety. But both imaginaries view moral influence as somehow dispersing into everyday social life. They both imagine efficacious renewal as somehow pervading society, making it right, in contrast to the futility and inequality of post-Soviet reform as experienced by most Central Asians. There is a particular spatial characteristic of these imaginaries, a spatiality of pervasive efficacy, that may contribute to the attractiveness of both imaginaries to Kyrgyzstani Uzbeks.[37]

At the same time, the Andijan Events drove Kyrgyzstani Uzbeks to intensify their attention to developing their local communities. Up until Kyrgyzstan's political crisis in 2010, Uzbek leaders in that republic were attempting to construct a viable space for Uzbeks to flourish economically and culturally within the framework of what they represented publicly as loyal Kyrgyzstani citizenship. Taking a pragmatic view in light of consistent discrimination by the Kyrgyz-dominated authorities and neglect by Uzbekistan, they sought to build institutions and enterprises serving the Uzbek communities of Kyrgyzstan's main southern cities, Osh and Jalalabat. The institutions were centered on two universities, Uzbek-language presses, television, cultural centers, and charities.[38] The Kyrgyzstani Uzbek leaders' move toward intense local initiatives appears to have intensified during the mid-2000s, the time of the Andijan Events. Local Uzbek patrons drove these initiatives, whose businesses and organizations acted as platforms for forming their power base and projecting their influence, first among Uzbeks (pitching themselves as admired patrons of the community) and then cautiously to the Kyrgyz-dominated authorities (as a dependable pro-government ethnic constituency). These institutions did more than provide education and media: they served as flexible multi-faceted centers meeting diverse needs of local communities. But in promoting these efforts, Kyrgyzstani Uzbek leaders were careful to avoid appearances of stoking "Uzbek nationalism." And so they partly framed their projects as serving the common good of all Kyrgyzstanis, particularly in their universities and television stations.

Kyrgyzstan's political crisis and interethnic killings in 2010 came at a bad moment for the republic's Uzbek communities. Granted, there is never a good time for upheaval, but there was particular irony in the timing. The crisis began for reasons unrelated to the republic's Uzbeks. Kyrgyzstani citizens of all ethnicities and political orientations recognized that patronage and power abuse worsened during the administration of Kurmanbek Bakiev, installed after the 2005 "Tulip Revolution" with promises of corruption reform. Kyrgyzstan's 2005 "color revolution" changed only the faces but not the ways of government.[39] Bakiev's tainted reelection as president in July 2009 only highlighted the unfair access to resources and opportunities that depended on ethnicity, clan, region, or personal connections, and he was finally ousted in 2010.[40]

The great misfortune of the 2010 crisis, the one that triggered the interethnic blood bath between Kyrgyz and Uzbeks in southern Kyrgyzstan, was that one prominent Uzbek leader, Kadirjan Batirov of Jalalabat, broke away from his habitual political caution and sided openly with the Provisional Government swept into power with President Bakiev's ouster in May 2010, leading to anti-Uzbek sentiment among the strong Kyrgyz pro-Bakiev element in Jalalabat, Bakiev's own power base. This appears to be at least one key factor precipitating the ethnicization of what had been until then a Kyrgyz-only political crisis. The irony here is that with one act, the Uzbek leader Batirov undermined over a decade of careful institution building and cultivation of good relations, albeit tense and limited, with the Kyrgyz-dominated state. That political project of peaceful co-existence seems to have come to a sudden and disastrous end, revealing its unfortunate fragility within the geopolitical predicament of double exclusion that Uzbeks in Kyrgyzstan live under. But for a short period at least, principally between the Andijan Events and the 2010 crisis, the Kyrgyzstani Uzbek leadership sought to move away from dependence on a beneficent state to secure their futures. Their constituents centered their aspirations on local patrons—scaled down khan figures, as it were.

Ironically, these were the sorts of figures that the Andijani businessmen, the "Akromis," at the focus of the May 2005 events probably were. They appear to be not a subversive Islamist sect, but a group of enterprising patrons who ran local initiatives to curry public favor, and were motivated by the notion of Islamic piety as foundational to successful business and prosperous society. If their endeavors were not a political conspiracy directed against the Uzbekistani state, their effects nonetheless helped undermine the state's legitimacy by threatening to "outperform" the state in providing social protection functions—employment, loans, assistance to the poor, and so forth—that the state inadequately delivers but is seen by post-Soviet citizens as having a moral obligation to provide. Returning to southern Kyrgyzstan, a similar move was being developed by Uzbek leaders there until 2010. That is, patron localism (with various degrees of Islamic foundation) may be emerging as a model for miniature quasi-states, as some service functions of the modern state are unbundled and taken up by local initiatives (see also the chapters by Ismailbekova and Reeves, this volume). What we would be left with is not a "weak" state, a term that assumes a canonical set of proper state characteristics, but rather a dispersed or unbundled regime of governance. It remains to be seen how this model may be grasped and lived out in people's imaginaries, and how those in turn scale down Soviet discourses of socialist paternalism and Islamic discourses of virtuous state.

It also opens up broader comparative questions. If post-Soviet Central Asia is moving toward emergent, modular quasi-state entities existing within official states, how would this illuminate understanding about the nature of state governance across the post–Cold War, post-9/11 world? There has been much "globalization" theorizing in the social science literature about the waning of the state and increasing influence of non-state entities such as transnational corporations, NGOs, and translocal grassroots movements. Could Central Asia contribute to the world record by offering for consideration a different, vernacular configuration of power that stands in particular relation with the nation-state, one animated by hybrid universalisms and intense localisms? The imaginaries considered in this essay, with their articulation around notions of common good, can perhaps be seen not as collective acts of desperation about the chronic inadequacy of states, but rather acts of hope. The imaginaries express hope that some socio-political arrangement exists to take the ideals that the state was always supposed to deliver and finally fulfill them.

Notes

1. According to theories of the modern state, media-based "propaganda" is just part of how the state tries to insert itself into the lives of citizens. More pervasive are the many places and moments where bureaucracies and other instruments structure everyday lives. What makes a modern state socially real to people are the various conjunctures of ideology and affect surrounding the state that frame social existence. Because experience of the state is "spread out" over different times and places, non-essentialist approaches present the state not as a unitary, agentive entity over society but rather as an emergent effect of modern institutionalized power exercised in various connected but

dispersed sites within society. The fact that the state appears as a monolithic causal entity is itself an effect of power (Ferguson and Gupta 2002; Mitchell 1990, 1991; Navaro-Yashin 2002). But it is difficult to talk about the state without using language that appears to assert its unity and agentive nature. Readers of this essay are to understand that references to what "the state does" refers to those as-if effects, and not to any ontological assertion of essentialism.

2. Specifically, those crisis moments can reveal the particular terms and associations with which people talk about the state, what has been called the vernacular "language of stateness" (Hansen and Stepputat 2001). Jarring instability and traumatic change tends in general to be productive of socio-political imaginaries that inform coping strategies for the new situations (Greenhouse, Mertz, and Warren 2002).

3. Kyrgyzstani Uzbeks report systemic exclusion from jobs in government, chances for university study, business loans at banks, help from police, and voting in Kyrgyzstan. Uzbeks have complained that their burden for proving their residency and registration at the polls is much more rigorous than for Kyrgyz voters. They claim to be cut off from positions of power in most administrative hierarchies, even in the urban cores in which they form the demographic majority (such as Osh, Jalalabat, and Uzgen).

4. In particular, Osh Uzbeks offer a unique vantage point from which to comparatively ponder the divergent postsocialist reform paths of these two republics (Liu 2012, 43–73). Being marginal or "liminal" to structures of power can allow one to reflect keenly on how those structures are constituted, as anthropologists have noted since Victor Turner (1967). This entire volume explores the diverse, often marginal sites in which the state comes to be imagined and enacted. This is necessary if the state is to be dereified and located squarely within a society's field of socio-political relations, answering the call to demystify the state (Ferguson and Gupta 2002; Mitchell 1991).

5. The fieldwork trips to Osh and Jalalabat for this article (1997–1998, 1999, 2003, 2005, 2009, 2011) were funded by the International Research and Exchanges Board (IREX), Fulbright-Hays, the University of Michigan, and the Harvard Society of Fellows.

6. Human Rights Watch (2005).

7. Several analyses of the Andijan Events have been published and too many more circulated on blogs and websites to be documented here. This incident has triggered as vehement a controversy with analysts as with Osh Uzbeks. Central Asian scholar Shirin Akiner produced a report affirming much of the Uzbekistani government's claims that the "Islamist Akromiya" intended a coup d'état in the manner of Kyrgyzstan a few months before (Akiner 2005). Akiner's report and her interview on the Uzbekistani TV program *Akhborot Plius* on May 29, 2005, generated furious reactions among scholars worldwide, mostly condemnation and dismissal. The majority weighed in closer to Eric McGlinchey, who argues that the circle of businessmen, as an independent source of wealth and quasi-regime of commercial regulation, posed a threat to Karimov's patronage system, where local officials were kept dependent on the center (McGlinchey 2011,121–123, 141–143). Indeed, Karimov sacked Andijan's governor, Qobiljon Obidov, a month before the twenty-three businessmen were jailed in 2004 because Obidov proved too responsive to local interests (McGlinchey 2005, 339). Despite well-known Islamic scholar Bakhtiyar Babadjanov's suspicions about Akrom Yuldashev, Alisher Ilkhamov similarly argues that Yuldashev's group constituted an Islamic "social democ-

racy" committed to enterprise, charity, and education with its circle of forty firms by 2005 (Ilkhamov 2006, 42–44). The Karimov administration, unable to distinguish between radical and moderate Islamic movements, saw them as a threat because they departed from the formalistic Islam of official sanction and operated independent of state control and patronage. The claim that Yuldashev's circle of businessmen constituted a "sect" is open to question and is probably an artifact of propagandists (Kendzior 2006). Adeeb Khalid likewise affirms that "the success of the Andijan businessmen was unacceptable to those who dominated the city's economy . . . their piety proved the best possible pretext to frame them" (Khalid 2007, 195). Nick Megoran identifies four themes in Karimov's discursive response to the events: criminality and terrorism, inauthentic Uzbekness and masculinity, constitutional illegitimacy, and subversion of the international order of states (Megoran 2008). Daniel Stevens uses these events to consider the deeper question of why potent social forces continue failing to institutionalize in Uzbekistan today (Stevens 2007).

8. Uzbekistan's carefully crafted self-representations have notably included history (Manz 2002), the nation (March 2002), morality (Kendzior, this volume), alphabet (Schlyter 1998), the cityscape (Trevisani, this volume), and public spectacle (Adams 2010).

9. According to Assamjon, interview on September 28, 2005. The rural population in Uzbekistan also has a low knowledge of Russian, much less English, and so had little access to outside media sources. Zairbek Ergeshov, a Kyrgyz historian, remarked to me that Karimov follows Stalin's technique premised on the assumption that, to the extent that the people are uneducated, they are easier to control.

10. Analogously, the government of the People's Republic of China, often supported by U.S. policy and Western media, interprets all Uyghur separatism as being rooted in Islam, whereas the socio-political reality is far more complex (Millward 2007, 322–352). See also Bellér-Hann, this volume.

11. Television programming from Uzbekistan had a profound, complex effect on Osh Uzbeks' view of the world (Liu 2012, 58–59, 167–170). Dissident poets in Uzbekistan, however, responded very differently to state media coverage of the Andijan Events (Kendzior 2007).

12. Ozodlik is the Uzbek service of Radio Free Europe/Radio Liberty (RFE/RL), which was subsequently expelled from operating in Uzbekistan in late 2005 and moved to Bishkek.

13. International Crisis Group (2008); Stern (2007). For Saipov's outspoken reportage in the context of Uzbekistan's repressive media environment, see Antelava (2007), McGlinchey (2011, 1).

14. Karimov quickly reconciled with Putin in the months after; however, the international community outside of Russia and China mounted pressure, demanding an independent investigation into the incident, which eventually led to the United States losing its military base in southern Uzbekistan for its operations in Afghanistan.

15. Personal first names used in this essay are pseudonyms to protect the anonymity of my interlocutors.

16. As an interesting linguistic aside, the Uzbek for honeymoon is *asal oy,* literally "honey month," a literal translation of the Russian *medovyi mesiats.* Uzbek marriages are arranged, and his bride was an Osh resident.

17. For one media report of eyewitness accounts, see Volosevich (2005).

18. The name of the NGO and its connections are withheld for security purposes. The lawyer from the organization, who turned out to be an acquaintance of mine from 1994, would not reveal to me where the refugees were settled or allow me to meet with them.

19. For the history of how the Soviet Central Asian republics were created and the borders drawn, see Hirsch (2005).

20. In Charles Taylor's formulation, the term refers to "the ways people imagine their social existence, how they fit together with others, how things go on between them and their fellows, the expectations that are normally met, and the deeper normative notions and images that underlie these expectations" (Taylor 2004, 23); see also Castoriadis (1998) and Cooper (2005); Taylor (2002). Humphrey (2002) applies the concept to the post-Soviet context.

21. Gaonkar (2002, 11).

22. Taylor (2004, 25).

23. Such a framework could work with but needs not assume a Foucauldian understanding of governmentality and its "capillary" penetrations into society and subjectivities. The imaginary as an analytical category leaves open for empirical investigation the extent that Foucault applies to a given case.

24. The question of how independent Uzbekistan stands with respect to the nation-states of the world is also a driving concern for cultural elites within Uzbekistan (Adams 2010).

25. The few Uzbek members of parliament, the Jogorku Kengesh, were pushing their limits on advancing demands concerning interests of Uzbeks in Kyrgyzstan, such as political representation, districting, career advancement of Uzbeks in government and other institutions, educational opportunities, municipal resources for Uzbek neighborhoods, Uzbek as one "official language" of Kyrgyzstan, and so forth. Not only did these efforts yield limited results but they also played a role in Kyrgyz perceptions of Uzbeks' lust for power in Kyrgyzstan, perceptions that fueled the 2010 conflicts and have prevented mutual understanding since.

26. Verdery (1996, 25).

27. The khan socio-political imaginary is argued for and analyzed in Liu (2012, 148–184).

28. The accumulating conditions leading to this tremendous shift in attitude are discussed in Liu (2012, 191–196).

29. Explosions in Tashkent (March–April 2004), an attempted mass protest calling for Karimov's resignation in Kashkardarya (June 2004), suicide attacks on the U.S. and Israeli embassies (July 2004), protest by bazaar sellers over controversial trade regulations in Kokand (November 2004), protests against the government bulldozing of houses to prepare for border changes with Kazakhstan (February 2005), demonstrations outside the U.S. embassy in Tashkent regarding a farm seized in Kashkardarya (May 2005). This year of mounting unrest, probably not directly related to each other, is summarized in Jane's Intelligence Review (2005, 14).

30. My interest here is not to reconstruct a definitive account of the events, but attempts toward that end exist (BBC News 2005; Human Rights Watch, Denber, and Levine 2005; International Crisis Group 2005). See the carefully researched and sensi-

tively presented documentary film by former Central Asia BBC correspondent Monica Whitlock (2010).

31. Even though Karimov's policies during the 1990s and 2000s directly hurt the interests of Osh Uzbeks, most vehemently defended those policies (Liu 2012, 45–49).

32. An Osh Uzbek man said to me that when he served in the Soviet army in the Caucasus during the 1950s, he used to tell others that he was from Andijan, since the average Soviet citizen would not have heard of Osh.

33. Uzbekistan's TV1 (*Birinchi Kanal*) broadcast Karimov's comments on February 19, 1999 (UzTV1 1999), but Osh Uzbek reactions to this comment were surprising: many refused to construe it as offensive against them (Liu 2012, 163–167).

34. After the Uz-Daewoo plant started operating in 1992, the car models Tico and Damas quickly became ubiquitous throughout the Fergana Valley, including in Osh.

35. Relevant research on Islam among Uzbeks includes Rasanayagam (2011) and McBrien (2006a, 2006b). For a review of anthropological studies on Islam in Central Asia, see Liu (2011, 120–123).

36. The state of the khan imaginary, described in Liu 2012 (178–184), is a particular case of Coronil's sense of state magicality, where the artifice of the narrative that the "state as a transcendent and unifying agent of the nation" is made convincing (Coronil 1997, 4).

37. These imaginaries can engage not only the visual faculties but also fuller sensorial apparatus of the body, because one experiences the alleged effects of moral influence in multiple aspects of everyday life (Liu 2012, 187–190). Csordas (1990) talks about "imagery" as not necessarily visual but corporeal.

38. This was the focus of fieldwork I conducted in Jalalabat and Osh in 2009 and 2011.

39. The political situation is made worse for Kyrgyzstan because of the relatively few faces available for rotation into power, compared with other Central Asian republics. For a keen comparative analysis of how post-Soviet Kyrgyzstan's political upheavals operated, see McGlinchey (2011). Beshimov, Shozimov, and Bakhadyrov (2011, 206–211) give an insightful account of Kyrgyzstani politics until 2008 that centers on the Fergana Valley.

40. Bakiev's 2009 electoral victory, assuming that he would have won without the irregularities reported by outside election observers such as the Organization for Security and Cooperation in Europe (OSCE), indicated only that he was preferable to the alternatives. Given the inevitable costs of payoffs in getting anything done, some Uzbeks in Osh said that they preferred to keep Bakiev in office so that they would not need to "feed another figure along with his people."

References

Adams, Laura L. 2010. *The Spectacular State: Culture and National Identity in Uzbekistan.* Durham, N.C.: Duke University Press.

Akiner, Shirin. 2005. "Violence in Andijan, 13 May 2005: An Independent Assessment." In *Silk Road Papers,* edited by Svante Cornell. Washington, D.C.: Central Asia-Caucasus Institute and Silk Road Studies Program.

Antelava, Natalia. 2007. "Uzbekistan's Silenced Society." *BBC News,* December 19.

BBC News. 2005. "How the Andijan Killings Unfolded." May 17.

Beshimov, Baktybek, Pulat D. Shozimov, and Murat Bakhadyrov. 2011. "A New Phase in the History of the Ferghana Valley, 1992–2008." In *Ferghana Valley: The Heart of Central Asia*, edited by S. Frederick Starr, Baktybek Beshimov, Inomjon I. Bobokulov, and Pulat D. Shozimov, 178–204. Armonk, N.Y.: M. E. Sharpe.

Castoriadis, Cornelius. 1998. *The Imaginary Institution of Society.* Cambridge, Mass.: MIT Press.

Cooper, Frederick. 2005. *Colonialism in Question: Theory, Knowledge, History.* Berkeley: University of California Press.

Coronil, Fernando. 1997. *The Magical State: Nature, Money, and Modernity in Venezuela.* Chicago: University of Chicago Press.

Csordas, Thomas J. 1990. "Embodiment as a Paradigm for Anthropology." *Ethos* 18: 5–47.

Ferguson, James, and Akhil Gupta. 2002. "Spatializing States." *American Ethnologist* 29: 981–1002.

Gaonkar, Dilip P. 2002. "Toward New Imaginaries: An Introduction." *Public Culture* 14: 1–19.

Greenhouse, Carol J., Elizabeth Mertz, and Kay B. Warren, eds. 2002. *Ethnography in Unstable Places: Everyday Lives in Contexts of Dramatic Political Change.* Durham, N.C.: Duke University Press.

Hansen, Thomas Blom, and Finn Stepputat. 2001. "Introduction: States of Imagination." In *States of Imagination: Ethnographic Explorations of the Postcolonial State*, edited by Thomas Blom Hansen and Finn Stepputat, 1–38. Durham, N.C.: Duke University Press.

Hirsch, Francine. 2005. *Empire of Nations: Ethnographic Knowledge & the Making of the Soviet Union.* Ithaca, N.Y.: Cornell University Press.

Human Rights Watch. 2005. "Burying the Truth: Uzbekistan Rewrites the Story of the Andijan Massacre." *Human Rights Watch/Helsinki Report* 17.

Human Rights Watch, Rachel Denber, and Iain Levine. 2005. "'Bullets Were Falling Like Rain': The Andijan Massacre, May 13, 2005." *Human Rights Watch/Helsinki Report* 17.

Humphrey, Caroline. 2002. "'Eurasia,' Ideology and the Political Imagination in Provincial Russia." In *Postsocialism: Ideals, Ideologies and Practices in Eurasia*, edited by Chris M. Hann, 258–276. London: Routledge.

Ilkhamov, Alisher. 2006. "The Phenomenology of 'Akromiya': Separating Facts from Fiction." *China and Eurasia Forum Quarterly* 4: 39–48.

International Crisis Group. 2005. "Uzbekistan: The Andijon Uprising." Bishkek, Kyrgyzstan: International Crisis Group. Available at: http://www.crisisgroup.org/~/media/Files/asia/central-asia/uzbekistan/b038_uzbekistan___the_andijon_uprising_.pdf.

———. 2008. "Political Murder in Central Asia: No Time to End Uzbekistan's Isolation." In *Asia Briefing.* Bishkek, Kyrgyzstan: International Crisis Group. Available at: http://www.crisisgroup.org/~/media/Files/asia/central-asia/uzbekistan/b76_political_murder_in_ca_no_time_to_end_uzbekistan_isolation.pdf.

Jane's Intelligence Review. 2005. "Uzbekistan Heads towards Violent Regime Change." *Jane's Intelligence Review* 12–19.

Kendzior, Sarah. 2006. "Inventing Akromiya: The Role of Uzbek Propagandists in the Andijon Massacre." *Demokratizatsiya: The Journal of Post-Soviet Democratization* 14: 545–562.

———. 2007. "Poetry of Witness: Uzbek Identity and the Response to Andijon." *Central Asian Survey* 26: 317–334.

Khalid, Adeeb. 2007. *Islam after Communism: Religion and Politics in Central Asia*. Berkeley: University of California Press.

Liu, Morgan Y. 2011. "Central Asia in the Post–Cold War World." *Annual Review of Anthropology* 40: 115–131.

———. 2012. *Under Solomon's Throne: Uzbek Visions of Renewal in Osh*. Pittsburgh: University of Pittsburgh Press.

Manz, Beatrice Forbes. 2002. "Tamerlane's Career and Its Uses." *Journal of World History* 13: 1–25.

March, Andrew F. 2002. "The Use and Abuse of History: 'National Ideology' as Transcendental Object in Islam Karimov's 'Ideology of National Independence.'" *Central Asian Survey* 21: 371–384.

McBrien, Julie. 2006a. "Extreme Conversations: Secularism, Religious Pluralism, and the Rhetoric of Islamic Extremism in Southern Kyrgyzstan." In *The Postsocialist Religious Question: Faith and Power in Central Asia and East-Central Europe*, edited by Chris M. Hann, 47–74. Berlin: LIT.

———. 2006b. "Listening to the Wedding Speaker: Discussing Religion and Culture in Southern Kyrgyzstan." *Central Asian Survey* 25: 341–357.

McGlinchey, Eric Max. 2005. "Islamists, Autocrats, and Democrats." *Current History* 104: 336–342.

———. 2011. *Chaos, Violence, and Dynasty: Politics and Islam in Central Asia*. Pittsburgh: University of Pittsburgh Press.

Megoran, Nick. 2008. "Framing Andijon, Narrating the Nation: Islam Karimov's Account of the Events of 13 May 2005." *Central Asian Survey* 27: 15–31.

Millward, James A. 2007. *Eurasian Crossroads: A History of Xinjiang*. New York: Columbia University Press.

Mitchell, Timothy. 1990. "Everyday Metaphors of Power." *Theory and Society* 19: 545–577.

———. 1991. "The Limits of the State: Beyond Statist Approaches and Their Critics." *American Political Science Review* 85: 77–96.

Navaro-Yashin, Yael. 2002. *Faces of the State: Secularism and Public Life in Turkey*. Princeton, N.J.: Princeton University Press.

Rasanayagam, Johan. 2011. *Islam in Post-Soviet Uzbekistan: The Morality of Experience*. Cambridge: Cambridge University Press.

Schlyter, Birgit. 1998. "New Language Laws in Uzbekistan." *Language Problems and Language Planning* 22: 143–181.

Stern, David L. 2007. "A Kyrgyz Reporter Is Killed, and Suspicions Fall on Uzbekistan's Government." *New York Times*, December 3.

Stevens, Daniel. 2007. "Political Society and Civil Society in Uzbekistan—Never the Twain Shall Meet?" *Central Asian Survey* 26: 49–64.

Taylor, Charles. 2002. "Modern Social Imaginaries." *Public Culture* 14: 91–124.

———. 2004. *Modern Social Imaginaries.* Durham, N.C.: Duke University Press.

Turner, Victor Witter. 1967. "Betwixt and Between: the Liminal Period in *Rites de Passage.*" In *The Forest of Symbols; Aspects of Ndembu Ritual,* edited by Victor Witter Turner, 93–111. Ithaca, N.Y.: Cornell University Press.

UzTV1. 1999. "Uzbek President on Real Economic Independence." *Uzland.info,* February 19.

Verdery, Katherine. 1996. *What Was Socialism, and What Comes Next?* Princeton, N.J.: Princeton University Press.

Volosevich, Aleksei. 2005. "Andizhanskie khroniki: Istorii iz goroda perezhivshego tragedeiiu 13 Maia" [Andjian Chronicles: Stories from a City Subjected to the Tragedy of 13 May]. *Vremia Novostei,* June 8.

Whitlock, Monica. 2010. *Through the Looking Glass: the Andijan Massacre.* Amsterdam: True Heroes Films, in association with FactionFilms.

12. Cold War Memories and Post–Cold War Realities

The Politics of Memory and Identity in the Everyday Life of Kazakhstan's Radiation Victims

Cynthia Werner and Kathleen Purvis-Roberts

Asan, an elderly Kazakh man, was nineteen years old when the first nuclear test exploded near his village on August 29, 1949.[1] Despite his young age, as a schoolteacher and a member of the Communist Party, he would have been viewed as a member of the village elite, or intelligentsia, at that time. When we interviewed him, Asan recalled how everybody in the village was completely taken by surprise during the first explosion. In his version of events, he was giving an exam at the local school, when one or two large explosions took place. From the windows of the classroom, he saw a very bright, mushroom-shaped cloud appear in the sky. He ordered the children, who were very afraid and hiding under their desks, to stand up and go outside. Asan explained how everybody in the village was confused about what was happening, and they were trying to come up with explanations to account for this very peculiar occurrence. Some people thought that it might be an unusual weather episode, and the strange noises and sights could be attributed to thunder and lightning. Soviet military personnel appeared in the village shortly after the explosion and started to ask villagers what they had seen. As he told us this story, he noted how he was eventually taken aside by "the soldiers" and told: "You are a Communist. You did not see anything and you do not know anything. That was the testing of the bomb that came from America. You will sign a document stating that you will not tell anybody." Asan's narrative is not unique. Similar to many of the other narratives that we collected, his account, filled with emotions of fear and anger, portrayed him as somebody who, despite his status within the village, was in a relatively powerless position compared to the formidable Soviet state, which he largely trusted at the time.

In other words, Asan's memories of nuclear testing in the present help assert his current identity as a victim of nuclear testing and a victim of the Soviet state.

This essay looks at the politics of memory and identity in post-independence Kazakhstan, We argue that the way that people remember and reimagine the past is shaped by nation-building projects and state politics in the present.[2] Memory allows people to connect the past with the present, yet memories of the past can be murky and the relationship between the past and the present is multifaceted. Pinter aptly notes: "The past is what you remember, imagine you remember, convince yourself you remember, or pretend to remember" (Pinter cited in Lowenthal 1985, 193). Connerton (1989, 2–3) notes that references to the past often serve to legitimate the present social order, but events in the present may also influence or distort how we remember the past. In contexts where acts of violence have been committed against groups or individuals, scholars such as Paul Antze and Michael Lambek (1996, vii) explore how memories, as "emblems of a victimized identity," provide much more than a mere record of the past.

In this chapter, we explore the following sets of questions: First, how do former Soviet citizens living in post-Soviet Kazakhstan remember events that were once unspeakable? How do their memories of the past, such as Asan's narrative above, help construct a collective identity of victimhood, a victimhood based on the acts of a cruel and immoral state that disregarded the health and welfare of some citizens in the name of national security? Second, how does the president of Kazakhstan's narrative of nuclear testing and the nuclear arsenal contribute to a larger project of developing Kazakh (and Kazakhstani) national identities? And, how does the president's public version of the past serve to distinguish an immoral state that inflicted this trauma on innocent citizens from a moral state that is concerned about its citizens' welfare? Finally, how do these distinct narratives of the past collide with the politics of distributing welfare benefits and assistance to those who have been defined as the victims of nuclear testing? In order to understand the politics of memory and identity in the present, it is necessary to start with a brief history of nuclear testing in Kazakhstan.

The Semipalatinsk Nuclear Test Site: The Historical Context

Throughout its seventy-year existence, the Soviet state was responsible for tremendous levels of personal suffering. In the 1930s and 1940s, the tragedies that resulted from the collectivization of agriculture, the repression of political opponents, and the deportation of ethnic minority groups helped cultivate a culture of fear and a political environment of limited freedom (Conquest 1987; Getty et al. 2010; Uehling 2004; Yurchak 2006). By the late 1940s, the emergence of the Cold War between the Soviet Union and the United States provided Stalin with further justification to maintain authoritarian rule over Soviet citizens. In this historical and political context, the Soviet government constructed a secret military site to test nuclear weapons on the steppes of the Kazakh Republic (Shkolnik 2002). Between 1949 and 1962, 116 above-ground tests were conducted at the Semipalatinsk Nuclear Test Site; an additional 340 underground tests were conducted between 1961 and 1989.

In both the United States and the Soviet Union, the state closely guarded information about nuclear testing, simultaneously reassuring local citizens that the tests were harmless while collecting medical data to the contrary (Barker 2004; Gusterson 1998; Masco 2006; Johnston 2007). The nuclear test site, popularly known as "the Polygon," was couched in secrecy from the very beginning. For nearly four decades, the state used a variety of techniques to preserve secrecy, maintain order, and limit public discussions about the tests. The test site, for example, was fenced off with barbed wire and heavily guarded with military personnel at twelve different outposts (Shkolnik 2002, 20). Similar to Gusterson's observations of the United States weapons program, Soviet state practices of secrecy not only reduced the likelihood that classified information would be leaked to foreign governments, they also served to create a social order that separated test site workers from ordinary citizens (Gusterson 1998, 68–100). In Kazakhstan, all residents who moved to the small town that served as the test site headquarters had to have security clearance. Like other secret cities in the Soviet Union's military-industrial complex, the city did not appear on maps until it was renamed Kurchatov in the 1990s in honor of the nuclear physicist Igor Kurchatov. The state also controlled all public information about the tests, and created an atmosphere of fear that limited public discourse about nuclear testing. National and local newspapers did not include any coverage of the nuclear tests.[3] The only information about the tests that local residents received came from public service warnings before each test. Village leaders were typically given short briefs about an upcoming test, and they were instructed to tell local villagers to take necessary precautions. This information was conveyed in an atmosphere of drama, as military personnel would arrive and depart in these remote villages by helicopter.

Justified by national security concerns, the state ensured that ordinary citizens living near the test site knew very little about the harmful health effects of radiation exposure. Although the site was selected in part because of its relatively low population density, over twenty thousand people lived in more than a dozen villages situated along the border of the 18,000 square km test site, and residents in several small settlements were relocated during the construction phase. Today, researchers estimate that over one million people living in nearby villages and cities may have received significant doses of radiation from nuclear testing at the Polygon.[4] Throughout the testing period, the Soviet state controlled the way that health statistics were collected so as to minimize the appearance of any health impacts related to nuclear testing. For example, a state procedure required doctors based in Almaty or Moscow to confirm all cancer diagnoses from the Semipalatinsk region. In an effort to learn as much as possible about the health impacts of radiation exposure, the state conducted highly classified research on local villagers without their knowledge or consent. Beginning in 1957, approximately twenty thousand individuals, including two thousand children, who lived near the test site were treated for minor ailments at a special clinic in Semipalatinsk. Unbeknownst to them, the "Anti-Brucellosis Dispensary Number Four" was actually a secret clinic whose primary mission was to conduct research on radiation-related illnesses. The Ministry of Health also collected medical data through a series of expeditions to several villages surrounding the test site (Shkolnik 2002, 100–114).

A dramatic shift away from secrecy and silence took place in the late 1980s when Mikhail Gorbachev introduced the policy of glasnost'. Within a few short years, the horrors and secrets associated with nuclear testing were discussed in the national media, and the people of Kazakhstan organized a series of effective protests calling for the closure of the test site (Schatz 1999). In early February 1989, the First Secretary of the Semipalatinsk Regional Committee of the Communist Party, Keshirim Boztaev, sent a telegram to the Central Committee of the Communist Party of the Soviet Union in Moscow requesting a temporary suspension of nuclear explosions due to public concerns. A few weeks later, the popular Kazakh poet Olzhas Suleimenov gave an emotional television address, calling for the end of nuclear testing in Kazakhstan and inviting people to a public rally. By the end of March, the newly formed Nevada-Semipalatinsk Anti-Nuclear Movement, headed by Suleimenov, had gathered over a million signatures of support. As the popular movement gained momentum, Kazakh politicians, including the Chairman of the Kazakh Republic's Central Committee Nursultan Nazarbayev, began to push harder for their demands. Meanwhile, the Nevada-Semipalatinsk movement continued to organize a series of public protests, criticizing the government's nuclear testing program. Rather than being punished for such disobedience, the anti-nuclear movement received several concessions (Nazarbayev 2001; Shkolnik 2002). In August 1991, the test site was officially closed and decades of secrecy ended, as the Soviet Union started to unravel. Almost immediately, the newly independent state of Kazakhstan took steps to construct a national past that highlighted the tragedy of nuclear testing.

Politics, Memory, and Identity: Theoretical and Methodological Underpinnings

This chapter bridges anthropological studies of the state that emphasize the lived experience of the state in everyday life with studies of memory that explore the political implications of remembering and interpreting the past. Lived experiences occur at multiple levels and in multiple locales, including in the "margins" of the nation-state that are best examined through an ethnographic approach. From this perspective, anthropologists argue that an understanding of the conceptual and territorial margins of the state can help us "rethink the state" by providing a more nuanced understanding of the political realm (Das and Poole 2004, 4–5). This chapter considers everyday encounters with the Soviet and post-Soviet state at the margins of Kazakhstan. We use the term "margins" in a conceptual sense in reference to the Semipalatinsk region of northeastern Kazakhstan where people who were already economically and politically marginalized were further victimized by the Soviet nuclear weapons testing program.

Lived experiences continue to have meaning in the present through memory. Cognitive psychologists and neuroscientists have studied how the brain works to process, store, and retrieve information. Meanwhile, scholars in the humanities have developed alternative theoretical approaches for understanding the interconnections between memory and individual experiences and the way collective memory plays a role in social identity construction (Connerton 1989; Halbwachs 1992; Lowenthal 1985; Olick 2007). When we speak of the ability to remember an event, we are implicitly acknowledging the potential to forget an event, or certain aspects of an event. Similar to Antze and Lambek (1996, xii), we accept Freud's notion that memories at best are distorted and mediated versions of reality, shaped by one's current preoccupations, yet we do not feel it is useful to think of the subject and the memory as metaphorically separate objects. Instead, borrowing from Antze and Lambek, we view memory as a practice, produced out of experience and linked to identity. The practice, or act, of remembering occurs when a person imagines an event that they have experienced and formulates their own version of the event into words (Antze 1996, 242). We distinguish between memories that are imagined by an individual and narratives that are communicated by language to other individuals. Narratives of the past thus essentially serve as semantic vehicles for memories (Antze 1996, 252; Ochs and Capps 1996).

We argue that individuals have considerable agency in how they choose to tell a story about the past. A person can choose to omit certain details of a story while emphasizing or even embellishing other details. By making choices, the narrating self actively shapes the identity of the narrated self (Antze and Lambek 1996: xviii). The narrated self, for example, may be characterized as a victim, a survivor, a perpetrator, or a hero. In the case of Kazakhstan's nuclear tests, individuals who live near the test site almost invariably present themselves as victims. While the narrators depict themselves as victims, they occasionally depict others as heroes and villains within their narratives.

Just as every person has his or her own memories of the past, so every country has its own history. At both the individual and the national level, the past is remembered and reconstructed in the present, and versions of the past may evolve and change over time as circumstances change. While individual memories of mundane events are unlikely to have much significance at the national level, we suggest that individual experiences of horrific events like nuclear testing often become an important part of the way the nation itself remembers its past. Antze and Lambek (1996) note that trauma plays an important role in the construction of a nation's collective memory and a nation's identity. In post-war Japan, for example, the national historiography emphasizes the victimization of innocent and peaceful Japanese in Hiroshima and Nagasaki, while obfuscating the colonial expansion and aggression of pre-war Japan (Yoneyama 1999). Similarly, Latvian memories of deportation and exile during the Soviet occupation serve as testimonies to the violent past that unite Latvians in the post-Soviet present (Skultans 1997). In the context of trauma and victimization, memories are never morally neutral. As several scholars have observed, "acts of remembering take on performative meaning within a charged field of contested moral and political claims" (Antze and Lambek 1996, vii). At the collective level, the act of remembering can involve a complex process of negotiation over what is remembered and what is forgotten (Sturken 1997).

Similar to other studies that rely on narratives of the past (Kamp 2001; Kendzior 2007; Megoran 2008; Skultans 1997), this study encountered a number of methodological challenges. Over the course of four summers, we conducted interviews with Kazakh and Russian villagers, medical doctors, research scientists, and non-governmental organization (NGO) employees. Our interviews took place in multiple sites, including the city of Semei (Semipalatinsk), the city of Kurchatov, and two villages near the Polygon (Kainar and Dolon). Kainar is a predominantly Kazakh village on the southeast side of the test site, while Dolon is an ethnically diverse village north of the test site. During our interviews with middle-aged and elderly residents of these two villages, we frequently asked them to describe their memories of nuclear testing and their experiences with the Soviet state in their everyday life. We were interested in how people articulated their narratives of the past in the post-Soviet present. We realized that our position as Western scholars may have influenced the way that they chose to present these narratives. For example, they may have perceived us to be individuals who had some power to improve their situation.

In addition to conducting interviews, we collected relevant newspaper articles in an attempt to understand how the individual narratives intersected with national discussions about the history of nuclear testing in Kazakhstan. Until the late Soviet years, residents of Kazakhstan were actively discouraged from talking about the tests or thinking about them from a critical perspective. The tests were not discussed in the media, and the visible, above-ground tests took place at a time when villagers did not have access to any technologies that would allow them to record and document the explosions. The tests took place in a society that was not geared toward consumer products, well before non-professional cameras and video cameras had saturated the market.

After decades of public "forgetting" or "not remembering," the emergence of the Nevada-Semipalatinsk Anti-Nuclear Movement in 1989 led to a deluge of media reports on nuclear testing. In reference to the waves of glasnost'-era publications that emerged throughout the Soviet Union in the late 1980s, Yurchak (2006, 2) notes that "discussing what one had read soon became a national obsession." Within Kazakhstan, multiple articles describe how the state used ordinary people as human guinea pigs to understand the impact of radiation on human health. People who lived in the surrounding area were forced to reinterpret their life experiences and to reimagine the Soviet state in a way that was previously unthinkable, and certainly unspeakable. People encountered a master narrative that emphasized their victimhood, and this master narrative is clearly reflected in their own personal narratives.

The moment in time when people living near the Polygon came to view themselves as victims coincided with the final years of perestroika, a time characterized by increased scarcity of consumer goods, a decline in public services, and a rise in bureaucratic corruption (Ries 1997). In her study of "Russian talk" during these years, Nancy Ries suggests that ordinary Russians regularly used a speech genre that she describes as a litany to express their misfortunes and tribulations. This genre was mostly reserved for those who were relatively powerless and thus suffering from the economic and political changes taking place at that time. Litanies provided a moral commentary on current events, which tended to distinguish fellow sufferers as morally superior to those who were in power and/or benefiting economically. Similarly, the production and circulation of individual narratives of nuclear testing helps connect victims to a larger society of sufferers, while articulating these moral distinctions between victims and villains. In the following section, we explore how Kazakh and Russian villagers construct an identity of victimhood in the narratives they tell about nuclear testing.

The Construction of Victimhood: Narratives of the Past

During our interviews with villagers who lived near the Polygon, we asked people to describe what they remember about the tests. We asked specific questions about what life was like on the days that the tests were conducted, what information they received before each test, and what health problems they have experienced due to radiation exposure. The elderly in our sample had lived experience with both above-ground and underground nuclear tests, while some of the middle-aged participants had limited memories of the atmospheric tests. Although our interlocutors are situated at the margins of the state, they all had relatively frequent encounters with the state in their everyday life. The significant presence and power of the state at such margins has become the focus of recent anthropological inquiry (Das and Poole 2004). In the narratives we collected, as well as the narratives that are presented in the media, the narrators, using a variety of linguistic mechanisms, consistently presented themselves as victims of the Soviet state. A victim is somebody who is harmed, killed or deceived by somebody or something. In this section, we explore how victimization is constructed through stories that limit the narrator's personal agency during the tests, stories that demonstrate how narrators were harmed by the tests, stories that describe how state actors deceived narrators, stories that portray the narrator's own naiveté, and stories that reveal enduring emotions of anger.

Victimhood entails a loss of personal agency. During our interviews, villagers repeatedly mentioned moments where they felt that the state controlled their actions and attempted to limit discussion about the nuclear tests. As Asan's narrative demonstrates, the villagers were very curious about the tests, yet the state discouraged people from talking about them. Another interlocutor, Ivan, an elderly Russian man, told us about his experience with one of the above-ground tests in 1954. As an active member of the Communist Union of Youth and a former military pilot, Ivan was working as the head of an agricultural brigade near Dolon when he saw the explosion. He recalled seeing birds fall out of the sky right before his eyes, and he remembered hearing loud crackling noises. Our interlocutors had varying responses when asked whether they knew at that time that the tests were harmful. Ivan's response was one of several that emphasized a lack of agency. He told us that he was not afraid of the explosions, but he was worried about what they would bring later. He emphasized that everything was secret at the time, and that "if you said something, they would convict you of being an 'American spy.'"

In some of the narratives, people recalled what happened when somebody broke the regime of silence. Several people told us the story of a local teacher in Kainar by the name of Bolat Zhakishev who tried to convince village leaders that the explosions were dangerous.[5] He was a physics teacher and repeatedly told people that these were nuclear tests that were exposing people to radiation. Although he was not arrested, he lost his job for being so vocal.

In addition to describing situations where the state restricted discussion about the tests, our interviewees described situations where the state forced people to do things that probably increased their exposure to radiation. For example, we interviewed a number of older men who remember herding collective farm livestock within the territory of the test site. For safety and security reasons, civilians were not supposed to be allowed into the test site. However, collective farm directors, under pressure to fulfill annual production quotas, apparently made agreements with military officials to allow herders to enter the Polygon in order to gather hay for the winter and to herd their animals. One elderly Kazakh man from Dolon recalled an occasion in which members of his herding brigade took their livestock to Ground Zero and to a small lake that had been created by a nuclear explosion. He remembers looking at the airplanes and automobiles that had been used in the tests. The security guards allowed them to go close to these radioactive objects but warned the herders not to touch them. In this way, the state lied to the villagers about the dangers of these military exercises, and encouraged activities that increased individual radiation exposure.

Other narratives emphasized the emotional trauma that people have experienced from witnessing horrific events and dealing with physical ailments. Several people, for example, have vivid memories of the 1953 explosion of the first thermonuclear device, the one time that the government evacuated people from the village of Kainar. According to one official publication, 2,250 villagers and 450,000 head of livestock were temporarily evacuated by military personnel to campsites that were 75 miles from Ground Zero (Shkolnik 2002). Most families left behind smaller animals, including cats, dogs, and poultry. For nearly two weeks, the villagers stayed at a temporary camp location. When the military allowed them to return home, they encountered unusual and frightening things: many of their chickens were dead, some of the baby chicks were deformed, their dogs and cats were losing their fur and some were covered with scabs. Several people described how their dogs and cats died before their eyes in the first few days after their return. Karlygash, a middle-aged woman from Kainar, was nine years old at the time and recalls the fear she experienced due to a physical reaction to this test: "after one day of our stay there, some kind of watery rash came out on my face. I still remember waking up and seeing the rash all over my face. I showed it to my mother. She looked at it, and told me to go back inside the tent. We were there for seven days. Then the rash disappeared."

Some of the most poignant descriptions of emotional damage came from women's experiences with childbirth. In an effort to conceal the impact of nuclear testing, doctors were not allowed to show parents their stillborn infants. One woman who gave birth to a stillborn child became very emotional as she told us: "I still don't know whether or not I gave birth to a monster child."

Not surprisingly, our narratives are filled with stories about the health effects of nuclear testing. With minimal prompting, our interlocutors told us countless stories of the ways that they themselves, their parents, spouses, and children have all been harmed physically by radiation exposure. Health problems include cancers and other diseases that affect the kidney, liver, heart, and thyroid. Many of the people we interviewed tend to blame all health problems on radiation. For example, after describing a wide-ranging list of health problems that she and her children have (intestinal ulcer, hemorrhages, kidney disease, varicose veins, and anemia), one woman declared that "these are all consequences of the Polygon."

Deception is a key aspect of victimization that frequently came up in our conversations. Typically, before each test, Soviet military personnel would communicate directly with the village leaders, who would then disseminate all necessary safety information to the village residents. Not wanting to alarm the public, the military always described the tests as "military exercises," rather than "nuclear tests" or "atomic bombs." Our interlocutors frame these warnings in a way that suggests that the state neither provided sufficient information nor enforced its own policies. Sabit, a middle-aged Kazakh man, for example, told us: "The soldiers used to come here to conduct some exercises. They flew here in a helicopter the day before the tests and brought some equipment. The next day, after the exercises, they would take those things back. The officers would always tell us that there was no harm . . ." In another account, Seitgaly, an older Kazakh man, recalled how he was serving as the chairman of the village council from 1977 to 1985. It was his job to serve as a host for the military personnel who would arrive by helicopter to measure the vibrations caused by the explosions. He explained how these officials would lie to the local people: "They measured the strength of the earthquake, which was around seven or eight. I was standing there watching them, and they lied to us saying that it was only two or three points on the scale. I told them not to lie to us." Through these stories, the narrators positioned themselves as victims of state actors that concealed the truth about the impacts of nuclear testing.

In addition to portraying state actors as deceitful villains, our interlocutors frequently described themselves as uninformed and naïve victims. Although the military provided people with safety information, many of the people we interviewed confessed that they rarely followed the instructions. Orazgul, an older Kazakh woman from Dolon, recalled how the soldiers took them to hollows in the ground and told them to lie down and to avoid looking in the direction of the explosion. She had young children at the time, and she explains that "we were curious, so we would look, and then we would lie down again." Another interlocutor, Oksana, an elderly Russian woman, regrets how her family did not understand the risks they took during the tests. She remembers one day they heard on the radio that there would be an explosion, but it seemed to be behind schedule. Frustrated by the delay, her mother, a milkmaid, came home from work and said: "Forget them with their blasts, let's go ahead and eat." Oksana remembers sitting at the table, when all of a sudden everything was covered with ash. Instead of throwing the food away, they blew the ashes off of the bread, and continued to eat their meal. Since radiation is invisible and tasteless, it was impossible for them to know that the ash contained a harmful substance.

Highlighting their own ignorance at the time of the tests, several of our interlocutors described the excitement of living near the Polygon. They knew that the tests were somehow significant, and as children, they were thrilled to live in a place where such important things were happening. Raushan, a middle-aged Kazakh woman, recalled: "When the helicopters came to the village, we were so dumb that we would run to be closer to the military guys. It was fun for us. They would put special devices on the ground to measure the size of the explosions. We would be running around laughing and having fun. We didn't know what was actually happening." Another interlocutor, Toregeldi, a middle-aged Kazakh man, also remembered the excitement of seeing the helicopters. He emphasized his own ignorance at the time by stating: "When the bombs exploded, we didn't understand what was going on. We thought that it was just something that the military had to do. We found out about radiation later." In such a way, his initial positive memory of nuclear testing has been recast in a new light.

Victimization is also represented through emotions of anger and betrayal, two persistent themes in the narratives we collected. While the villagers did not realize that these explosions were poisoning their bodies and endangering their health, they have little doubt that the government did realize the harmful effects of testing. One of our interlocutors, Dinmukhamed, shared his memories about the tests. Like others, he remembers his past self as somebody who enjoyed the excitement of the tests and somebody who disobeyed the orders to avoid looking at the explosion. But, then as his narrative turns to the present, he angrily remarks:

"Who would have known that it was so harmful and that things would be like they are today? Before the Polygon closed, it was not so obvious . . . When I was in school, many doctors would come and perform medical check-ups. We now know that they were conducting research on the effects of radiation on people. . . . At that time, we didn't know about that because they didn't say anything. We found out later when it was all revealed."

Taken together, these narrative accounts of everyday encounters with the Soviet state illustrate how villagers perceive themselves as victims of the state. In these stories, test site workers, soldiers, and supervisors embody the state. Through their narratives of the past, villagers construct victimhood by demonstrating that these state actors deceived them, and the tests harmed them physically and emotionally. The narrators also fashion victimhood by presenting their past selves as individuals who had limited agency and/or limited knowledge about the tests. And, finally, their present self is still angry about the events that transpired and the way that they were treated. These individual narratives are shaped by and feed into a "master narrative" about nuclear testing that emerged in the late 1980s, beginning with the formation of the Nevada-Semipalatinsk Anti-Nuclear Movement. The collective memory, or national memory, of nuclear testing includes narratives presented by politicians, journalists, medical researchers, and NGO actors. In the following section, we explore how the president's own personal narrative of nuclear testing has contributed to this collective, or national, memory of nuclear testing in Kazakhstan.

The Construction of a Nation: The Presidential Narrative of Nuclear Testing

Kazakhstan became a newly independent state in 1991 with the fall of the Soviet Union. In addition to building new state institutions, the leaders of the country had the responsibility of creating a new national identity. National identities are often framed and constructed around a shared ethnic identity, shared language, shared religion, and/or shared history. Several scholars have noted how the construction of a coherent national identity in post-Soviet Kazakhstan has been challenged by the country's demographic situation (Esenova 2002; Fierman 1998). In 1991, the Kazakhs at approximately 39.7 percent of the population did not represent a majority of the population, and approximately 40 percent of Kazakhs did not speak Kazakh as their first language (Fierman 2005, 405; Schatz 2000, 489). The Kazakhs were further divided into a few dozen clans, or lineages, which are manifested as sub-ethnic identities (Collins 2006; Esenova 2002; Schatz 2000). Meanwhile, the population of Kazakhstan included over 80 ethnic groups, including the Russians who made up approximately 33 percent of the entire population (Schatz 2000, 489). In the past two decades, the percentage of Russians in the republic has declined through out-migration and lower birth rates, and the percentage of Kazakh-speaking Kazakhs has increased as a result of new language policies. Within this context, the government has sought a balance between a national identity based on Kazakh ethnicity and a national identity based on the multi-ethnic realities of the country's population (Fierman 2005). As Schatz notes (2000, 491), the new government has developed a new form of "internationalism with a Kazakh face" in a way that "turn[s] Soviet-style internationalism on its head by offering a normatively appealing discourse to its non-titular population and a diffuse and ill-defined set of privileges to titular Kazakhs."

Noting that the construction of a Kazakh national identity was problematized by the fact that many Kazakhs do not speak the Kazakh language and few today identify with the Kazakh nomadic heritage, Esenova argues that Kazakhs instead turned to their history, especially the oral history of clan-based genealogies (*shezhyre*) (Eseneova 2002). These genealogies provided a way to unify Kazakhs based on a belief that they were all related by blood and shared common ancestry. We agree that the construction of Kazakh identity has been based on the notion of a shared history, but we would extend the argument to include a shared history of victimization under Soviet rule. In the post-Soviet period, two events in particular have been highlighted by Kazakhstani scholars and the Kazakhstani media: forced collectivization and nuclear testing. Numerous scholarly works on the tragedy of collectivization were produced in the 1990s, and the government organized a special commission that concluded that the famine that resulted from collectivization constituted a genocide that killed over two million people (Cameron 2010, 12). This point became been a rallying point for Kazakh nationalists because the disproportionate share of suffering experienced by Kazakhs shifted the demographic population of the republic to the point that the Kazakhs became a minority population. Cameron notes that several Kazakh scholars abruptly abandoned their research on collectivization around the turn of the century, and she questions whether this was due to a shift toward a more multi-ethnic national identity (Cameron 2010, 290).

Nationalist-minded Kazakhs have made similar observations about how Kazakhs have experienced a disproportionate level of suffering from nuclear testing. They point out that the region surrounding the nuclear test site has a greater population of Kazakhs, especially in the desert-steppe regions to the south, east and west of the test site. The region also has cultural significance as the birthplace of the famous Kazakh poet and scholar, Abai Kunanbaev. However, given that Kazakhs, Russians and members of other ethnic groups have also been affected negatively by radiation poisoning, the tragedy surrounding nuclear testing has simultaneously contributed to the creation of a supra-ethnic Kazakhstani identity (Schatz 1999, 2004).

The topic of nuclear testing has received attention in the scholarly and popular press. Beginning in the late 1980s, Kazakhstani newspapers have published dozens of articles covering individual experiences of nuclear testing, the health effects of nuclear testing, and the social injustices of nuclear testing. In addition, several scholarly and popular books have been published in Kazakhstan about the tragedy of nuclear testing (Balmukhanov et al. 2002; Boztaev

1997; Kuidin 1997; Qabdrakhmanov 2003; Yakubovskaya et al. 2000). Although it is beyond the scope of this chapter, it is worth noting that the story of nuclear testing in Kazakhstan has also been covered by the international media and documentary films produced by filmmaker Gerald Sperling. In addition to the villagers whose personal accounts of nuclear testing are occasionally presented in local newspapers, several other actors have contributed to the public discourse on nuclear testing. This includes narratives of nuclear testing articulated by Olzhas Suleimenov, a national poet and the founder of the Nevada-Semipalatinsk Anti-Nuclear Movement, Keshirim Boztaev, a former administrator and a leader of the Polygon–August 29 Social Fund, and Saim Balmukhanov, a leading medical researcher. Balmukhanov's narrative is particularly salient as his research findings regarding nuclear testing were frequently cited by our interlocutors and thus feed into the villagers' own narratives about the tests. In Balmukhanov's published narrative, he recalls how he collected data in the 1950s on the high level of radiation-related illnesses experienced by villagers living near the test site. He positions himself as an unsuccessful hero, who tried to warn Soviet leaders about the dangers of nuclear testing. He describes how he shared the results of his study with test site officials who urged him to remain silent. According to Balmukhanov's own account, he was harassed by the KGB and other institutions to such an extent that he practiced self-censorship for decades until the fall of the Soviet Union (Balmukhanov 2002).

In the remainder of this section, we limit our discussion to President Nursultan Nazarbayev's narrative accounts of nuclear testing. We focus on the president because he has taken an active role in the construction of a shared history of nuclear testing and because he uses his own narrative account of nuclear testing in Kazakhstan and Kazakhstan's nuclear arsenal to position himself (and his government) as a moral actor, relative to the immoral Soviet state. In the post-Soviet period, Central Asian presidents, such as Islam Karimov (the president of Uzbekistan), have published multiple books that serve to legitimate their rule, to present their version of historic events, and to promote their concept of a national identity (Megoran 2008 and Kendzior, this volume). President Nazarbayev is no different. His autobiography, *My Life, My Times, and the Future,* discusses his own personal experiences with nuclear testing, and another memoir, entitled *Epicenter of Peace,* focuses on his decision to close the Semipalatink nuclear test site and to relinquish Kazakhstan's nuclear weapons arsenal (Nazarbayev 1998; Nazarbayev 2001). Nazarbayev has also granted interviews to Western authors who have presented biographical information about him to a popular audience (Aitken 2009; Robbins 2008).

In all of these accounts, Nazarbayev portrays himself as a hero who closed the test site and transformed Kazakhstan into a nuclear-free country. He does deserve some credit for these milestones. Nazarbayev did in fact sign the agreement to close the test site in August 1991 before Kazakhstan achieved independence. Then, within the first few years of independence, he agreed to relinquish the 1,216 nuclear warheads that Kazakhstan possessed upon independence (Nazarbayev 2001, 9–16; Shkolnik 2002, 165–246).

In his published memoirs and biographies, Nazarbayev positions himself as somebody who was always troubled by the impacts of nuclear testing. He explains his decision to give up Kazakhstan's nuclear arsenal in moral terms, exploring his own memories of nuclear testing and its impacts in Kazakhstan. In one biographic account, one of his first memories of nuclear testing involves meeting some families who lived near the test site during a weekend vacation as a young adult. The families he met described the terrifying explosions and trembles that they had experienced, but they were afraid to talk about the reason behind these tests. Around the same time, Nazarbayev became close friends with a fellow metallurgy student who grew up near the test site in a family that had suffered enormously from radiation-related illnesses. He remembers his friend, Tuleutai Suleymenov (who later became the minister of foreign affairs) telling him about his father's death from brain cancer, one sister's death from leukemia, another sister's mentally handicapped status, and a third sister's chronic skin condition (Aitken 2009, 129–130). In another biographic account, Nazarbayev recalls meeting a man whose "sister went mad, one of his brothers suffered from anemia, and the other committed suicide," all due to nuclear testing (Robbins 2008, 201). He also recalls how his young daughters were frightened every time the ground would shake (Nazarbayev 2001, 41).

Nazarbayev's version of nuclear testing acknowledges that all people of Kazakhstan have suffered from nuclear testing, yet he places more emphasis on the misery experienced by the Kazakhs. He refers to Kazakh people's love of nature: "The most important place in our lives belongs to the land, the steppe that feeds us . . . Anything that violates that organic spiritual unity of man and land, violates our entire lifestyle" (Nazarbayev 2001, 41). He also makes an explicit connection between the Semipalatinsk region and the birthplace of the Kazakh poet Abai, referring to the "defilement of sites that are sacred to every Kazakh" (Nazarbayev 2001, 46). Yet, immediately after this paragraph, he mentions petitions signed by Karaganda miners (which would include Russians), admitting that "all of Kazakhstan, all its people, were caught up in a single goal—no to nuclear testing and no to atomic weapons" (Nazarbayev 2001, 46).

As Nazarbayev describes the high-level leadership positions he took on within the Kazakh republic, he describes himself as somebody who worked within the system to try to change things as new information became available. He claims that he was not told anything about the nuclear testing program when he first accepted the position of prime minister and only learned about the Semipalatinsk tragedy in the aftermath of the Chernobyl nuclear disaster (Aitken 2009). He expresses frustration that his appeals to get more information from high-ranking government officials and military personnel regarding the nuclear tests were dismissed (Nazarbayev 2001, 43). The subsequent revelations about the health impacts of nuclear testing disgusted him: "It was only then that I fully understood the extent of the crime that was committed against us" (Robbins 2008, 202). According to his biographic accounts, he received a directive shortly after this to expand the nuclear test site into the province of Taldykurgan. In response, he alleges that he secretly released military secrets and health statistics to leaders in this region in order to initiate a public protest. Nazarbayev also alleges that he gave clandestine support to the Nevada-Semipalatinsk Anti-Nuclear Movement that emerged the following year (Aitken 2009, 131–133; Robbins 2008, 202–203).

In reference to the events that led up to the closure of the test site, Nazarbayev positions himself as a nationalist hero who eventually followed his heart. He went public with his concerns about nuclear testing in May 1989, during an address to the Supreme Soviet in Moscow, calling for a "real, profound analysis of the effects of atomic explosions on the environment" (Aitken 2009, 135; Nazarbayev 2001, 43–44). Nazarbayev also claims responsibility for organizing an international conference and peace march in Almaty in May 1990 that included anti-nuclear protestors from Kazakhstan and abroad (Nazarbayev 2001: 45). And, finally, he takes full credit for issuing a presidential decree to close the test site on August 29, 1991, a week after the attempted coup that almost drove Gorbachev out of power.

Finally, as Nazarbayev remembers the moments that led up to the surrendering of Kazakhstan's nuclear arsenal, he positions himself as a moral actor. Kazakhstan's nuclear arsenal included intercontinental ballistic missiles, heavy bombers, and a significant amount of weapons-grade uranium (Shingleton 1997). While some Kazakhstani politicians were lobbying the president to keep the weapons so that Kazakhstan would be taken more seriously in the international realm of politics, several Western countries, including the United States, were offering international aid in exchange for giving up the weapons. In addition, Russia and China offered security guarantees (Aitken 2009; Xing 2001). By closing the test site and surrendering nuclear warheads, President Nazarbayev increased political legitimacy in both the domestic and international arenas. In his memoir, Nazarbayev states that his decision reflected the will of the Kazakh people who had already been so negatively affected by nuclear weapons. As he states, "we simply did not have the moral right to continue destroying our people and land with nuclear detonations" (Nazarbayev 2001, 23). By referring to people whose lives and lands have been destroyed, his narrative also contributes to the construction of victimhood.[6] Further, Nazarbayev's reference to morality suggests that the new state is a "moral" actor in comparison to the previous state that acted immorally in regards to the victims of nuclear testing.

Memory, Politics, and the Victims of Nuclear Testing in Kazakhstan

Scholars have demonstrated that social constructions of victimhood in the past are connected to political struggles for social justice in the present (Antze and Lambek 1996). Olick's work on the "politics of regret," for example, examines the proliferation of national and international political contexts in the second half of the twentieth century that are characterized by apology, reparations, and restitution (Olick 2007, 2009). He observes how modern states "demand reparations rather than sacking and plundering the defeated," building memorials rather than monuments, and how perpetrators are just as likely as victims to commemorate acts of wrongdoing (Olick 2009, 87). In this new political environment, memories told by ordinary citizens who have suffered from some tragic experience are used in courtrooms, legal testimonies, and other political discussions. Our interviews with villagers demonstrate how our interlocutors use a variety of linguistic mechanisms to construct an identity of victimhood. As evidenced by President Nazarbayev's narratives about the nuclear tests, there is also a broader collective memory of nuclear testing in Kazakhstan. In this section, we examine how memories of the past and identity of victimhood play out in the contemporary struggles for social justice in Kazakhstan.

In order to obtain justice, victims need perpetrators. For the radiation victims of Kazakhstan, there is no doubt that the Soviet state has been constructed as the perpetrator of human suffering. The Russian government has failed to accept responsibility for the sins of its predecessor. And, perhaps due to the authoritative nature of the Soviet state, there has not been an attempt to identify and try any individual state actors, such as military leaders or nuclear test designers, with any crimes against humanity. When the Soviet Union dissolved and ceased to exist, the newly independent state of Kazakhstan inherited the political fallout associated with nuclear testing. Interestingly enough, in his memoir and biography, Nazarbayev's narrative of nuclear testing ends with his decision to surrender the country's nuclear arsenal. Although he defines Kazakhstan as a "moral" state relative to the Soviet predecessor state, his biography and memoirs do not elaborate on how this translates into moral actions on behalf of the people whom he describes as the victims of nuclear testing. In other words, he describes himself as a hero for shedding light on the horrors of nuclear testing and for making the courageous decision to surrender the country's nuclear arsenal, but not for his efforts to alleviate the suffering of radiation victims.

In his memoir (Nazarbayev 2001, 34), Nazarbayev explicitly denies full responsibility for the victims of nuclear testing:

> The young independent state has been left alone to face the catastrophe, and all the people's complaints are addressed to the new state. But in the greater scheme of things, it is not the fault of Kazakhstan. To whom should they turn for compensation? To the military-industrial complex of a nonexistent country? To the world community? . . . As we acquired our independence, we immediately began government programs to rehabilitate the victims of nuclear testing and the population of regions contiguous with the Semipalatinsk Nuclear Test Site. But despite all measures we have adopted, it is not easy for Kazakhstan alone to correct what was done by the concerted efforts of the entire Soviet Union.

Later, in the same chapter of his memoir (2001, 39), he adds: "I have said on more than one occasion that the end of testing and the removal of nuclear weapons from Kazakhstan does not remove the collective responsibility of nuclear powers for the suffering and pain of the local inhabitants caused by above-ground, atmospheric, and underground explosions." These messages are clearly targeted toward an international audience. His statement suggests that other parties, ranging from the international community to other former Soviet republics, should play a significant role in helping the victims of nuclear testing. Nazarbayev's narrative account of nuclear testing thus simultaneously contributes to the construction of national identity, by emphasizing the shared suffering of all Kazakhstani citizens, and calls for international aid to alleviate that suffering, in the absence of a surviving perpetrator.

The only problem is that the international community, similarly to President Nazarbayev, placed a higher priority on the removal of Kazakhstan's nuclear arsenal than the health problems experienced by these victims of the Cold War. Although reparations, compensation and commemorative events can help victims make the transition to survivors, victims remain victims in the absence of these things. Forty years of nuclear testing has taken its toll on the health of people living near the test site. They have been affected by the radiation exposure they received after each test and from decades of chronic, low-dose radiation exposure from the environmental contamination of food, air, soil and water. Numerous studies indicate that people living near the test site have experienced higher rates of cancers (including leukemia), benign thyroid abnormalities, psychological problems, and physical deformities at birth (Teleuov 2003).

Initially, the international policy community appeared to regard the legacy of nuclear testing in Kazakhstan as a serious health issue. The United Nations, in particular, carried out an exhaustive needs assessment project and committed funding for humanitarian assistance and economic development. Approximately US$42 million was budgeted for a series of social programs that would be sponsored by the wealthier nations of the U.N. (In comparison, the United States spent approximately US$184 million to assist with the closing of the test site and the removal of the nuclear arsenal.) For the most part, bilateral aid has not been directed at nuclear test victims. In August 2001, President Nazarbayev admitted that the international community had only provided US$20 million dollars of funding, and declared that over a billion dollars was necessary to solve the health and environmental problems experienced by the region. Much of the funding for U.N.-sponsored programs has come from the Japanese government (Werner and Purvis-Roberts 2006).

In the absence of significant international aid, the government of Kazakhstan has taken some steps to help the victims of nuclear testing. In addition to appealing to the international community for assistance, the state has developed domestic programs for compensation and aid (Werner and Purvis-Roberts 2006).[7] The government of Kazakhstan first needed to come up with criteria for defining who counted as a "victim" and then come up with a system for providing compensation and assistance for those who qualified. As in similar cases of environmental disaster, experts discussed whether victims should be limited to those who have developed certain medical conditions associated with radiation exposure, or whether victims should be defined by permanent residence near the test site where exposure levels were significant. In an effort to bolster political support, the government of Kazakhstan took the latter option, and divided victims into four subcategories: minimal risk; above-minimal risk; maximal risk; and extraordinary risk. Through these distinctions, the state is creating what Petryna refers to as new categories of citizenship that link biology and identity, and a hierarchy of sufferers who compete in a "political economy of claims around radiation illness" (Petryna 2002, 18).

In 1992, a law on compensation was passed by the Supreme Soviet of Kazakhstan that enabled nearly two million citizens of Kazakhstan to receive "radiation passports" that list a person's dose category (International Labour Review 1993). Based on the law, all passport recipients are eligible for compensation. In practice, however, the government has only provided compensation to those who live in extraordinary risk zones and to elderly citizens living in Semipalatinsk (Semei). In 2005, the Ministry of Labor admitted that the outstanding debt on compensation payments was about US$95 million.[8] Even for those who received compensation, the amount was minimal. Extremely high rates of inflation in late 1992 ensured that the funds budgeted for compensation lost value before being transferred to radiation victims. As one recipient stated, the "compensation" she received "provided enough money to buy candy, and not much else" (Werner and Purvis-Roberts 2006).[9] This level of compensation has done little to ameliorate the suffering.

In addition to the compensation program, the government of Kazakhstan has modified Soviet bureaucratic structures in an attempt to privilege the victims of nuclear testing. In particular, the government has reduced the pension age for those living in regions surrounding the test site, added "ecological" supplements (*posobia*) to monthly paychecks, provided disability pensions for individuals who qualify, and provided medical benefits (Werner and Purvis-Roberts 2006). These efforts have also fallen short of making a significant impact in peoples' lives. For example, the ecological supplement program provides a supplement to the monthly salary of all eligible state employees, but the restructuring of the government and the dissolution of the state farm system severely reduced the number of rural residents who receive government salaries. As a result, the program tends to benefit households that already receive some income, but does not provide anything to the least fortunate households in rural areas (Werner and Purvis-Roberts 2006). Another example relates to disability benefits. We interviewed several needy individuals who were either found to be ineligible for disability benefits, or who did not bother to apply because of the bureaucratic obstacles entailed. One woman, for example, explained that she did not want her brother who suffers from mental problems to go through the stress of a week-long observation period in order to qualify for a relatively small benefit. In her opinion, it simply was not worth the time and hassle necessary to qualify for the disability status.

Efforts to provide medical care to the victims of nuclear testing have similarly been thwarted by efforts to reduce state subsidies for health care. In the Soviet past, the quality of health care had its shortcomings, but the cost of health care was low due to the socialist economy. In the post-Soviet period, health care costs have become increasingly expensive. According to local doctors, certain types of diagnoses and treatments are still free if supplies are available, but the more expensive medicines and more effective treatments are no longer free. For example, a patient might receive an x-ray for free, but she has to pay for x-ray film. In another example, a cancer patient we interviewed receives operations for free, but she has to pay for expensive medicine. According to doctors in Semipalatinsk, radiation victims may receive health care at reduced cost. However, several Polygon villagers explained why they feel that the health care system is inadequate for their needs. Many but not all of the villages have reduced the health care services provided at the village level. In Dolon and Sarzhal villages, for example, there are fewer medical workers in the village, no pharmacies, and limited medical facilities. Villagers find it expensive and time-consuming to travel to Semipalatinsk in order to be diagnosed and treated, though their hesitation to receive early medical care makes it more difficult to treat conditions such as cancer.

In assessing the programs developed by the post-Soviet state, it is important to acknowledge the ways in which the Semei region has been disempowered in the post-Soviet period. Here, we borrow Liu's (2005) argument about "hierarchies of place." Liu, for example, describes how there is a "hierarchy of place" among different regions in post-Soviet Uzbekistan based on unequal natural advantages and unequal access to markets and state resources. In the case of post-Soviet Kazakhstan, the region of Semei has been disadvantaged by the stigma of nuclear testing. Despite promises of foreign assistance to assist radiation victims, this region remains less developed than other regions of Kazakhstan that benefit from the extraction of natural gas, oil, and other mineral resources. Further, in the late 1990s, the state weakened the region by restructuring the administrative territories in a way that reduced the total number of oblasts. At this time, Semei and Ustkamen oblasts were combined to form East-Kazakhstan oblast', and Semei lost its status as oblast' capital. Although the city has retained its university and several hospitals, all oblast' administrative offices are located in Ustkamen, the center of East-Kazakhstan oblast'. Thus, officials who oversee programs that aid victims of nuclear testing live further away than they did before and are thus less likely to be committed to these programs. Equally important, this shift slows down economic development for the city of Semei and the villages surrounding the test site. Oblast' centers, similar to capitals, tend to receive more public and private financing for economic development. Related to this, it is important to note the huge amount of resources that the state has devoted to the construction of the new capital, Astana. In a sense, these potential resources have been diverted from the region where people are suffering from nuclear testing.

Conclusion

This chapter explores the links between politics, identity, and memory. For nearly forty years, people living in northeastern Kazakhstan were subjected to the explosions and earthquake-like tremors caused by the Soviet nuclear testing program. The Soviet state cultivated a culture of fear that limited public discussion, much less criticism, about the tests. During the late Soviet years, glasnost' policies allowed people to talk publicly about the health and ecological consequences of testing. Villagers who lived near the test site had little choice but to reinterpret their memories of the past and to reimagine the Soviet state in new ways. Through memory, lived experiences in the past continue to have meaning in the present.

In Kazakhstan, villagers who live near the test site tend to portray themselves and be portrayed by others as victims of the Soviet state. In this chapter, we demonstrate how they use a variety of linguistic mechanisms to position themselves as victims of the Soviet state. These mechanisms included stories that showed their limited agency during the tests, stories that demonstrate how they were physically and mentally damaged by the tests, stories that describe how the state deceived them, stories that establish their previous ignorance of the risks associated with nuclear testing, and stories that reveal enduring emotions of anger in the present.

These individual narratives of nuclear testing coexist with a broader social, and national, memory of nuclear testing that emerged in Kazakhstan in the late 1980s. Politicians, including President Nursultan Nazarbayev, have developed their own narrative accounts of nuclear testing. We argue that the president's narrative, presented in his memoirs and biographies, serves to legitimate his rule as a moral leader and serves to promote his own concept of Kazakh and Kazakhstani national identities. He positions himself as a hero who helped spread the news about the horrors of nuclear testing, closed the test site, and surrendered Kazakhstan's nuclear weapons cache.

Throughout this chapter, we argue that these narratives of the past are not morally neutral. As Jeffrey Olick (2007) notes, modern society is characterized by a new "politics of regret" in which ordinary citizens take on new roles as politically motivated interpreters of the past. Beginning with the Nuremberg trials, conflicting interpretations of the past emerge in political struggles regarding reparations, memorialization and conciliatory justice for acts of wrongdoing. In Kazakhstan, moral arguments are made by a variety of actors, including the victims of nuclear testing who believe the Soviet state intentionally exposed them to radiation, and the president who tries to distance himself from the actions of the Soviet state and appeals to the international community to assist radiation victims. Thus, in post-Soviet Kazakhstan, struggles for social justice are complicated by the fact that the perpetrator, the Soviet state, no longer exists, and neither Russia nor Kazakhstan is willing to accept full responsibility for the sins of the Soviet state. In this sense, the victims of nuclear testing are further victimized by contemporary politics.

Notes

1. Following anthropological standards, pseudonyms are used throughout this chapter to protect the identity of the people we interviewed.

2. We would like to thank Johan Rasanayagam, Madeleine Reeves, and Judith Beyer for their many helpful comments on this chapter.

3. Personal communication with Stan Brunn.

4. Lecture by Saim Balmukhanov, research scientist/professor, Kazakhstan Scientific Institute of Oncology and Radiology, Kazakhstan Academy of Sciences. Estimates vary because scientists use different methods to calculate dose, and they do not agree on what constitutes a significant dose.

5. Bolat Zhakishev died in a tragic car accident shortly after the test site was closed. We chose to use his real name rather than a pseudonym.

6. Johan Rasanayagam (2006) similarly demonstrates how statements made by the Uzbek president influence how people imagine what it means to be Muslim.

7. In a previous paper, the appeals to the international community are discussed in greater detail (Werner and Purvis-Roberts 2006).

8. Akim Bekenov, "Kazak Authorities 'Ignoring' Nuclear Victims," *Institute for War and Peace Reporting*, no. 395, part 2, July 11, 2005.

9. We learned a lot about compensation during two interviews in particular: interview with Nurlan Ibraev, Densaulyq State Agency for Health, East-Kazakhstan Oblast', June 12, 2001; and interview with Gulsim Kakhimzhanova, Iris—Union of Nuclear Test Victims, June 6, 2001.

References

Aitken, Jonathan. 2009. *Nazarbayev and the Making of Kazakhstan*. New York: Continuum Press.

Antze, Paul. 1996. "Telling Stories, Making Selves: Memory and Identity in Multiple Personality Disorder." In *Tense Past: Cultural Essays in Trauma and Memory*, edited by Paul Antze and Michael Lambek, 3–24. London: Routledge.

Antze, Paul, and Michael Lambek, eds. 1996. *Tense Past: Cultural Essays in Trauma and Memory*. London: Routledge.

Balmukhanov, Saim, G. Raissova, and Timor Balmukhanov. 2002. *Three Generations of the Semipalatinsk Affected to the Radiation*. Almaty, Kazakhstan: Sakshy Press.

Barker, Holly M. 2004. *Bravo for the Marshallese: Regaining Control in a Post-Nuclear, Post-Colonial World*. Belmont, Calif.: Thomson Wadsworth.

Boztaev, Keshirim.1997. *Semei poligony*. Almaty, Kazakhstan: Kazakhstan Publishers.

Cameron, Sarah. 2010. "The Hungry Steppe: Soviet Kazakhstan and the Kazakh Famine, 1921–1934." PhD diss., Yale University.

Collins, Kathleen. 2006. *Clan Politics and Regime Transition in Central Asia*. London: Routledge.

Connerton, Paul. 1989. *How Societies Remember*. Cambridge: Cambridge University Press.

Conquest, Robert. 1987. *The Harvest of Sorrow: Soviet Collectivization and the Terror-Famine*. Oxford: Oxford University Press.

Das, Veena, and Deborah Poole, eds. 2004. *Anthropology in the Margins of the State*. Santa Fe, N.M.: School of Advanced Research Press.

Esenova, Saulesh. 2002. "Soviet Nationality, Identity & Ethnicity in Central Asia: Historic Narratives & Kazakh Ethnic Identity." *Journal of Muslim Minority Affairs* 2, no. 1: 11–38.

Fierman, William. 1998. "Language and Identity in Kazakhstan: Formulations in Policy Documents 1987–1997." *Communist and Post-Communist Studies* 31, no. 2: 171–186.

———. 2005. "Kazakh Language and Prospects for Its Role in Kazakh 'Groupness.'" *Ab Imperio* 2: 393–423.

Getty, Arch, and Oleg V. Naumov. 2010. *The Road to Terror: Stalin and the Self-Destruction of the Bolsheviks, 1932–1939,* updated and abr. ed. New Haven, Conn.: Yale University Press.

Gusterson, Hugh. 1998. *Nuclear Rites: A Weapons Laboratory at the End of the Cold War.* Berkeley: University of California Press.

Halbwachs, Maurice. 1992. *On Collective Memory.* Chicago: University of Chicago Press.

International Labour Review. 1993. "Compensation for Nuclear Test Victims." *International Labour Review* 132, no. 3: 282.

Johnston, Barbara, ed. 2007. *Half-Lives and Half-Truths: Confronting the Radioactive Legacies of the Cold War.* Santa Fe, N.M.: School for Advanced Research Press.

Kamp, Marianne. 2001. "Three Lives of Saodat: Communist, Uzbek, Survivor." *Oral History Review* 28, no. 2: 21–58.

Kendzior, Sarah. 2007. "Poetry of Witness: Uzbek Identity in the Andijon Massacre." *Central Asian Survey* 26, no. 3: 317–334.

Kuidin, Yuri. 1997. *Qazaqstannyn yadrolyq qasireti* [Kazakstan Nuclear Tragedy]. Almaty, Kazakhstan: Social Anti-Nuclear Ecological Fund Phoenix.

Liu, Morgan. 2005. "Hierarchies of Place, Hierachies of Empowerment: Geographies of Talk about Postsocialist Change in Uzbekistan." *Nationalities Papers* 33, no. 3: 423–438.

Lowenthal, David. 1985. *The Past Is a Foreign Country.* Cambridge: Cambridge University Press.

Masco, Joseph. 2006. *The Nuclear Borderlands: The Manhattan Project in Post–Cold War New Mexico.* Princeton, N.J.: Princeton University Press.

Megoran, Nick. 2008. "Framing Andijon, Narrating the Nation: Islam Karimov's Account of the Events of 13 May 2005." *Central Asian Survey* 27, no. 1: 15–31.

Nazarbayev, Nursultan. 1998. *My Life, My Times, and the Future.* London: Pilkington.

———. 2001. *Epicenter of Peace.* Hollis, N.H.: Puritan Press.

Ochs, Elinor, and Lisa Capps. 1996. "Narrating the Self." *Annual Review of Anthropology* 25: 19–43.

Olick, Jeffrey. 2007. *The Politics of Regret: Collective Memory and Historical Responsibility in the Age of Atrocity.* London: Routledge.

———. 2009. "Time for Forgiveness: An Historical Perspective." In *Considering Forgiveness*, edited by Carin Kuoni and Alexandra Wagner, 84–92. New York: The Vera List Centre for Art and Politics.

Petryna, Adriana. 2002. *Life Exposed: Biological Citizens after Chernobyl.* Princeton, N.J.: Princeton University Press.

Qabdrakhmanov, Kanat. 2003. *Chelovecheskiye posledstviya ispytanii yadernogo oruzhiya v Kazakhstane.* Almaty, Kazakhstan: Olke Publishers.

Rasanayagam, Johan. 2006. "Healing with Spirits and the Formation of Muslim Selfhood in Post-Soviet Uzbekistan." *Journal of the Royal Anthropological Institute* 12: 377–393.

Ries, Nancy. 1997. *Russian Talk: Culture and Conversation during Perestroika*. Ithaca, N.Y.: Cornell University Press.

Robbins, Christopher. 2008. *Apples Are from Kazakhstan: The Land That Disappeared.* New York: Atlas & Company.

Schatz, Edward. 1999. "Notes on the Dog That Didn't Bark: Eco-Internationalism in Late Soviet Kazakhstan." *Ethnic and Racial Studies* 22, no. 1: 136–161.

———. 2000. "The Politics of Multiple Identities: Lineage and Ethnicity in Kazakhstan." *Europe-Asia Studies* 52, no. 3: 489–506.

———. 2004. *Modern Clan Politics: The Power of "Blood" in Kazakhstan and Beyond.* Seattle: University of Washington Press.

Shingleton, Bill. 1997. "Operation Sapphire and U.S. Proliferation Policy, Swords and Ploughshares." *Journal of International Affairs* 7, no. 2: 33–46.

Shkolnik, Vladimir, ed. 2002. "The Semipalatinsk Test Site: Creation, Operation, and Conversion." Washington, D.C.: U.S. Government Printing Office.

Skultans, Vieda. 1997. "Theorizing Latvian Lives: The Quest for Identity." *Journal of the Royal Anthropological Institute* 3, no. 4: 761–780.

Sturken, Marita. 1997. *Tangled Memories: The Vietnam War, the AIDS Epidemic, and the Politics of Remembering.* Berkeley: University of California Press.

Teleuv, Murat. 2003. "Fallout Exposure and Health Condition of the Population in the Semipalatinsk Region of Kazakhstan." *International Congress Series* 1258: 123–128.

Uehling, Greta. 2004. *Beyond Memory: The Crimean Tatars' Deportation and Return.* New York: Palgrave MacMillan.

Werner, Cynthia and Kathleen Purvis-Roberts. 2006. "After the Cold War: International Politics, Domestic Policy and the Nuclear Legacy in Kazakhstan." *Central Asian Survey* 25, no. 4: 461–480.

Xing, Guangcheng. 2001. "China and Central Asia." In *Central Asian Security: The New International Context,* edited by Roy Allison and Lena Jonson, 152–170. Washington, D.C.: Brookings Institution Press.

Yakubovskaya, E. L., V. I. Nagibin, and V. P. Suslin. 2000. *Semipalatinskii yadernyi poligon: vchera, segodnya, zavtra.* Novosibirsk, Russia: Sovetskaya Sibir.

Yoneyama, Lise. 1999. *Hiroshima Traces: Time, Space, and the Dialectics of Memory.* Berkeley: University of California Press.

Yurchak, Alexei. 2006. *Everything Was Forever, Until It Was No More: The Last Soviet Generation.* Princeton, N.J.: Princeton University Press.

Contributors

Ildikó Bellér-Hann is Associate Professor at the Department of Cross-Cultural and Regional Studies at the University of Copenhagen. She has carried out extensive empirical research in Turkey, China, and Kazakhstan. She is author of *Community Matters in Xinjiang 1880–1949: Towards a Historical Anthropology of the Uyghur.*

Judith Beyer is a Research Fellow at the Max Planck Institute for Social Anthropology in Halle, Germany. As a member of the project group Legal Pluralism at the Department of Law and Anthropology, she has carried out extensive local-language field research in Kyrgyzstan on legal pluralism, authority, the state, and constitutionalism. She is author of *Kyrgyzstan: A Photoethnography of Talas.*

Alima Bissenova is Assistant Professor at the Nazarbayev University School of Humanities and Social Sciences. From October 2011 to September 2012 she was a post-doctoral fellow with the Max Planck Institute for the Study of Societies in Cologne. She received her PhD in anthropology from Cornell University.

Eva-Marie Dubuisson is Assistant Professor of Anthropology in the Department of Sociology at Boğaziçi University, Istanbul. She earned her PhD from the University of Michigan in 2009 and held a Mellon Postdoctoral Fellowship at the University of California, Berkeley, before coming to Boğaziçi. Her work is published in the *Journal of Linguistic Anthropology* and in *Central Asia Survey* (with Anna Genina).

John Heathershaw is a Senior Lecturer in International Relations at the University of Exeter and Principal Investigator of the Economic and Social Research Council research project Rising Powers and Conflict Management in Central Asia. He is the author of *Post-Conflict Tajikistan: The Politics of Peacebuilding and the Emergence of Legitimate Order.*

Aksana Ismailbekova is a post-doctoral researcher at the Zentrum Moderner Orient in Berlin and a member of the competence network Crossroads Asia. She received her PhD in social anthropology from Martin Luther University Halle-Wittenberg. She has conducted research on patronage, kinship, and everyday politics in rural Kyrgyzstan.

Sarah Kendzior received her PhD in anthropology from the University of Washington–St. Louis. She studies digital media and politics in the former Soviet Union. She writes regularly for Registan, the *Atlantic,* and Al Jazeera, and her work has appeared in *American Ethnologist, Problems of Post-Communism,* and the *Journal of Communication.*

Mateusz Laszczkowski completed his PhD dissertation at the Max Planck Institute for Social Anthropology in 2012. He has carried out field research in Kazakhstan and Azerbaijan on topics including the politics of space, the state, and political identifications.

Morgan Liu is Associate Professor of Anthropology in the Department of Near Eastern Languages and Cultures, the Ohio State University. He studies Islamic revival, postsocialist states, and social justice movements in Central Asia. His 2012 book, *Under Solomon's Throne: Uzbek Visions of Renewal in Osh,* explores how ethnic Uzbeks in the ancient Silk Road city of Osh, Kyrgyzstan, think about political authority and post-Soviet transformations.

Kathleen Purvis-Roberts is Associate Professor of Chemistry at the W. M. Keck Science Department of Claremont McKenna, Pitzer, and Scripps Colleges in Claremont, California. Her research focuses on the chemical mechanisms behind particulate matter air pollution formation and the environmental impacts of nuclear testing near Semipalatinsk, Kazakhstan.

Johan Rasanayagam is a Senior Lecturer in Social Anthropology at the University of Aberdeen. He has conducted research in Uzbekistan, Central Asia, and his research interests include Islam, morality, and the state. He is author of *Islam in Post-Soviet Uzbekistan: The Morality of Experience* and guest editor of a special issue of *Central Asian Survey* entitled "Post-Soviet Islam: An Anthropological Perspective."

Madeleine Reeves is a Lecturer in Social Anthropology at the University of Manchester and a member of the ESRC Centre for Research on Socio-Cultural Change. Her research focuses on the anthropology of politics, place, and migration in rural Central Asia, with a particular interest in the Fergana Valley. She is editor of *Movement, Power and Place in Central Asia and Beyond: Contested Trajectories.*

Tommaso Trevisani is a Research Fellow at the Max Planck Institute for Social Anthropology, Halle. He earned his doctorate in social anthropology from the Free University in Berlin and has previously been a Junior Fellow at the Center for Development Research in Berlin. He is author of *Land and Power in Khorezm: Farmers, Communities and the State in Uzbekistan's Decollectivisation.*

Cynthia Werner is an Associate Professor and Head of the Department of Anthropology at Texas A&M University and President-Elect of the Central Eurasian Studies Society. Her current research projects focus on the legacy of nuclear testing in Kazakhstan and the transnational migration of Mongolia's Kazakh population.

Index